D1825934

LEARNING IN A CRUSADER CITY

Did the Crusades trigger significant intellectual activity? To what extent and in what ways did the Latin residents of the Crusader states acquire knowledge from Muslims and Eastern Christians? And how were the Crusader states influenced by the intellectual developments which characterized the West in the twelfth and thirteenth centuries? This book is the first to examine these questions systematically using the complete body of evidence from one major urban centre: Acre. It reveals that Acre contained a significant number of people who engaged in learned activities, as well as the existence of study centres housed within the city. This volume also seeks to reconstruct the discourse that flowed across four major fields of learning: language and translation, jurisprudence, the study of Islam and theological exchanges with Eastern Christians. The result is an unprecedentedly rich portrait of a hitherto neglected intellectual centre on the eastern shores of the medieval Mediterranean.

JONATHAN RUBIN teaches in the Department of Land of Israel Studies and Archaeology at Bar-Ilan University. His research focuses on the cultural and intellectual history of the Latin East.

Cambridge Studies in Medieval Life and Thought
Fourth Series

General Editor
ROSAMOND MCKITTERICK
Emeritus Professor of Medieval History, University of Cambridge, and Fellow of Sidney Sussex College

Advisory Editors
CHRISTOPHER BRIGGS
Lecturer in Medieval British Social and Economic History, University of Cambridge

CHRISTINE CARPENTER
Emeritus Professor of Medieval English History, University of Cambridge

ADAM J. KOSTO
Professor of History, Columbia University

ALICE RIO
Reader in Medieval European History, King's College London

MAGNUS RYAN
University Lecturer in History, University of Cambridge, and Fellow of Peterhouse

The series *Cambridge Studies in Medieval Life and Thought* was inaugurated by G. G. Coulton in 1921; Professor Rosamond McKitterick now acts as General Editor of the Fourth Series, with Dr Christopher Briggs, Professor Christine Carpenter, Professor Adam J. Kosto, Dr Alice Rio and Dr Magnus Ryan as Advisory Editors. The series brings together outstanding work by medieval scholars over a wide range of human endeavour extending from political economy to the history of ideas.

This is book 110 in the series, and a full list of titles in the series can be found at:
www.cambridge.org/medievallifeandthought

LEARNING IN A CRUSADER CITY

*Intellectual Activity and Intercultural Exchanges
in Acre, 1191–1291*

JONATHAN RUBIN

Bar-Ilan University

CAMBRIDGE
UNIVERSITY PRESS

CAMBRIDGE
UNIVERSITY PRESS

University Printing House, Cambridge CB2 8BS, United Kingdom

One Liberty Plaza, 20th Floor, New York, NY 10006, USA

477 Williamstown Road, Port Melbourne, VIC 3207, Australia

314–321, 3rd Floor, Plot 3, Splendor Forum, Jasola District Centre,
New Delhi – 110025, India

79 Anson Road, #06–04/06, Singapore 079906

Cambridge University Press is part of the University of Cambridge.

It furthers the University's mission by disseminating knowledge in the pursuit of
education, learning, and research at the highest international levels of excellence.

www.cambridge.org
Information on this title: www.cambridge.org/9781107187184
DOI: 10.1017/9781316941096

First published 2018

Printed and bound in Great Britain by Clays Ltd, Elcograf S.p.A.

A catalogue record for this publication is available from the British Library.

Library of Congress Cataloging-in-Publication Data
NAMES: Rubin, Jonathan, 1976– author.
TITLE: Intellectual activity and intercultural exchanges in Frankish Acre,
1191–1291 / Jonathan Rubin.
DESCRIPTION: Cambridge, United Kingdom ; New York, NY : Cambridge
University Press, 2018. | Series: Cambridge studies in medieval life and
thought | Includes bibliographical references and index.
IDENTIFIERS: LCCN 2018012049 | ISBN 9781107187184
SUBJECTS: LCSH: Acre (Israel) – Intellectual life. | Acre (Israel) – Civilization. |
Jerusalem – History – Latin Kingdom, 1099–1244.
CLASSIFICATION: LCC D195.A374 R83 2018 | DDC 956.94/5–dc23
LC record available at https://lccn.loc.gov/2018012049

ISBN 978-1-107-18718-4 Hardback

CONTENTS

ACKNOWLEDGEMENTS

The present book started out as a PhD dissertation submitted to the senate of the Hebrew University in the summer of 2012. As such, it represents my work and thoughts about Frankish Acre from a period of more than ten years, during which numerous teachers, friends and colleagues were kind enough to share with me their knowledge and ideas, or simply to support and encourage me along the winding road that led to the composition of the present book. It is likely that I will not remember them all, and I offer sincere apologies to those whom I might be forgetting.

My greatest professional debt goes, without question, to Benjamin Z. Kedar. It was at his first-year class on the Crusader Kingdom of Jerusalem that I became exposed to medieval history as a scholarly field, and had it not been for this course, it is improbable that I would have ever become a medievalist. But my debt to Kedar is much greater: it was in a discussion with him over the phone that the subject of this book was first sketched, and it was he who introduced me to many of its figures, such as John of Ancona, Benoit d'Alignan and William of Rubruck. As an advisor, Kedar closely accompanied the processes of research and writing, read all drafts and commented on an infinite number of issues. This book is thus, first of all, a fruit of the guidance of a great historian and an extraordinary teacher.

During the work, several other scholars were always there to advise and assist. Laura Minervini, with whom I was not personally acquainted at the time, kindly agreed to co-supervise the dissertation and greatly contributed to it, especially in the more literary and linguistic aspects. David Jacoby turned my attention to several important sources and shared with me some unpublished materials, and Cyril Aslanov supported the project, in particular with regard to Old French, but also, for example, when I needed to look at a few lines in Armenian. He also always offered new, exciting ways to look at Frankish Acre. I am greatly indebted to Charles

Burnett, who read my dissertation and commented on it in ways that proved very significant. Furthermore, as my host at the Warburg Institute during the postdoctoral year I spent there, he was extremely kind in sharing with me some of his vast knowledge on the transfer of information between the various cultures of the medieval Mediterranean. He also serves as a great example for me concerning both openness towards students and the ability to cooperate and generously share learning with colleagues. Iris Shagrir also read my dissertation and made important observations with regard to ways of improving it towards its publication. But she did much more: she always supported me and my work, particularly when I most needed such backing. I will always remain extremely grateful for that. I would also like to thank Ronnie Ellenblum for his belief in my work from its very early stages.

Comments made by listeners on various occasions when I presented parts of this project also contributed to the development of my thoughts on Acre's culture. Particularly worthy of note, Yvonne Friedman's remarks, made in a workshop at the Institute of Advanced Studies of the Hebrew University, proved fruitful with regard to questions concerning the movement of ideas between the West and the Latin East. I am also grateful to several scholars who sent me unpublished materials or published materials which are unavailable in Israel: Peter W. Edbury, Thomas E. Burman, Cornelia Linde, Fabio Zinelli, Martin Bertram, Katja Klement, Elisa Guadagnini, Cinzia Pignatelli and Adam M. Bishop.

It would have been impossible for me to complete this project without the support of a circle of friends. Among these, Pinchas Roth and Dotan Arad provided a source of encouragement as well as specific help with regard to Jewish medieval history; Naama Cohen-Hanegbi commented on some sections from this book and Matti Friedman read much of it, contributing to the improvement of my English style. Lastly, Hanan Harif was a permanent companion for long days in the library and numerous chats in which, among other things, we discussed ideas that found their way into this book.

During the years in which I worked on the dissertation that led to this book, as well as on this book itself, I was fortunate to benefit from the support of several generous grants. Among these, of particular importance were the Polonsky fellowship for PhD candidates in the humanities at the Hebrew University, a Yad Hanadiv postdoctoral fellowship, a Zvi Yavetz postdoctoral fellowship at the Tel Aviv University and an Alon fellowship.

Finally, the completion of this book provides an appropriate moment to thank my family for providing me with the environment that enabled and encouraged this kind of undertaking. To my parents, Edna Rubin

Acknowledgements

and Rehav (Buni) Rubin, I owe my attraction to history, language and texts but also to archaeology in general and to the Holy Land's Frankish monuments in particular. It was also at home, from a very early age, that I was trained to think critically of what I was taught, to raise questions and to strive to answer them in a manner as precise and complete as possible. These lessons are still with me today. Gali, my closest companion for the past twenty years, granted me the unconditional love and encouragement without which it would have been impossible to overcome points of difficulty along this long track. During the years which I devoted to this project our family knew both happiness and deep sorrow: We had three daughters born, Alma, Ahinoam and Hagar, bringing great joy and hope into our lives, but we also most tragically lost my brother, Yoav Rubin, a man of extraordinary wisdom and kindness, in whose short life inter-cultural dialogue played a central role. I had the pleasure of sharing some early thoughts regarding Acre's culture with him during the initial stages of this project, but he did not live long enough to see it advance. His absence accompanied my years of work on Acre, and this book is dedicated to his memory.

ABBREVIATIONS

Cartulaire	*Cartulaire général de l'ordre des Hospitaliers de S. Jean de Jérusalem*, ed. Joseph Delaville le Roulx, 4 vols., Paris, 1894–1906 [the references are to document numbers].
CCCM	Corpus Christianorum Continuatio Mediaevalis.
Cronaca	*Cronaca del Templare di Tiro (1243–1314): La caduta degli Stati Crociati nel racconto di un testimone oculare*, ed. and Italian trans. Laura Minervini, Napoli, 2000.
CSEL	Corpus Scriptorum Ecclesiasticorum Latinorum.
HO	Jacques de Vitry, *Histoire orientale*, ed. and trans. Jean Donnadieu, Turnhout, 2008.
Jacques de Vitry, *Lettres*	Jacques de Vitry, *Lettres*, ed. Robert B. C. Huygens, CCCM 171, Turnhout, 2000.
Joinville, *Vie*	Jean de Joinville, *Vie de Saint Louis*, ed. and trans. Jacques Monfrin, Paris, 1995.
MGH	Monumenta Germaniae Historica.
MP	Matthew Paris, *Chronica Majora*, ed. Henry R. Luard, RS 57, 7 vols., London, 1872–83.
Notitia	Wilhelm von Tripoli, *Notitia de Machometo; De Statu Sarracenorum*, ed. Peter Engels, CISC Series Latina 4, Würzburg, 1992.
PL	Patrologia Latina.
RHC, Lois	*Recueil des historiens des croisades, Lois*, ed. le comte Beugnot, 2 vols., Paris, 1841–3.

List of Abbreviations

RHGF	Recueil des historiens des Gaules et de la France.
RRH	Reinhold Röhricht, *Regesta Regni Hierosolymitani*, and *Additamentum*, Innsbruck, 1893–1904 [the references are to document numbers].
ZDPV	*Zeitschrift des Deutschen Palästina-Vereins*.

INTRODUCTION

On 18 May 1291 Frankish Acre was taken by the Mamluks and destroyed, marking, as Prawer has written, the end of the history of the Latin Kingdom of Jerusalem.[1] As is well known, during the preceding century Acre was a major urban centre which served as the capital of the Kingdom of Jerusalem and as a major commercial hub. But another important aspect of the thirteenth-century city remains unexplored: Acre housed a considerable number of learned men, some of whom possessed knowledge that was unique and rare. While in Acre, many of these scholars engaged in the accumulation, development and distribution of knowledge in a range of fields such as theology, jurisprudence and geography; some of them composed an impressive number of still-extant texts. These facts raise a variety of hitherto neglected questions. How can one characterize the intellectual and literary activities which took place in the city? Who participated in them? What degree of creativity and originality do they reflect? On what fields did they focus? To what extent were they shaped by intercultural exchanges that took place in and around the city? What was the relation between the intellectual activities undertaken in Acre and those which characterized the West at the time? These questions stand at the centre of the present study.

ACRE IN EARLIER PERIODS

Acre (Arabic: 'Akkā, Hebrew: Akko), located at the northern end of the bay of Haifa, is a settlement with a very long history. Mentioned in the Bible (Judges 1.31) as a city which was not taken by the tribe of Asher, Acre was later a Hellenistic city named Ptolemais, and, in the first century, a Roman colony where St. Paul is said to have spent a day on his way from Tyre to Jerusalem (Acts 21.7). Following the Muslim

---

[1] J. Prawer, *Histoire du royaume latin de Jérusalem*, 2 vols. (Paris, 1970), vol. II, p. 557.

I

conquest, the city served as an Ummayad, and later Abbasid, naval base and shipyard, with significant works in its port undertaken during the rule of Aḥmad Ibn-Ṭūlūn. In the century preceding the First Crusade, the city saw several dramatic events: it was damaged by a severe earthquake in 1063, taken by the Turcomans in 1074 and captured in 1089 by the Fatimid Munīr al-Dawla al-Juyūshī.[2]

Acre was not captured by the Franks during the First Crusade, but rather as part of their subsequent attempts to extend the young Kingdom of Jerusalem's territory. Having withstood a siege led by Baldwin I in April and May 1103, it was finally taken by the Franks in May 1104 with the aid of a Genoese and Pisan fleet. While some looting and killing followed the city's surrender, inhabitants willing to remain in the city were permitted to do so.[3] Thus the city became home to a varied population which during the twelfth century included Latins, Muslims, Jews and, in all likelihood, Oriental Christians as well.[4] It was a densely populated port city which served both as a gateway for pilgrims from the West and as a significant commercial centre.

THE THIRTEENTH-CENTURY CITY

Following the battle of Hattin, the city surrendered, on 9 July 1187, to the forces of Saladin. The whole Frankish population left Acre with whatever property they could carry, while Oriental Christians as well as Jews seem to have been permitted to remain.[5] But the Latins did not give up hope of regaining the city. During the summer of 1189 a Western army began to form around it,[6] gradually growing in the following months, until it was capable of imposing an effective siege. At the same time, however,

---

[2] M. Gil, *A History of Palestine*, trans. E. Broido (Cambridge, 1992), pp. 251–2, 410, 860; D. Pringle, *The Churches of the Crusader Kingdom of Jerusalem. A Corpus, IV. Acre and Tyre* (Cambridge, 2009), pp. 3–5.

[3] Prawer, *Histoire*, vol. I, pp. 269–70; H. E. Mayer, *The Crusades*, trans. J. Gillingham (Oxford, 1988), p. 69; Pringle, *The Churches IV*, p. 3.

[4] Ibn Jubayr mentions a small mosque which functioned in the city under the Franks. *The Travels of Ibn Jubayr*, trans. R. J. C. Broadhurst (London, 1952), p. 318. Muslims were also allowed to worship in a mosque built over the spring of the Oxen, a site Christians and Jews also venerated. Pringle, *The Churches IV*, pp. 165–6. Concerning Jews in twelfth-century Acre, see J. Prawer, *The History of the Jews in the Latin Kingdom of Jerusalem* (Oxford, 1988), pp. 61–2. The evidence for the existence of Oriental Christian communities in twelfth-century Acre is limited and mostly not unequivocal. Pringle, *The Churches IV*, p. 18; B. Z. Kedar, 'The Eastern Christians in the Frankish Kingdom of Jerusalem: An Overview', in M. Gálik and M. Slobodník (eds.), *Eastern Christianity, Judaism and Islam between the Death of Muhammad and Tamerlane (632–1405), Proceedings of the Humboldt-Kolleg, June 25–28, 2008, Dolná Krupá, Slovakia* (Bratislava, 2011), pp. 140–2.

[5] Concerning Oriental Christians, see Prawer, *Histoire*, vol. I, p. 658. With regard to the Jews, see Prawer, *The History of the Jews in the Latin Kingdom of Jerusalem* (Jerusalem, 2000), p. 257 [Hebrew].

[6] Prawer, *Histoire*, vol. II, pp. 41–2; Mayer, *The Crusades*, p. 142.

Saladin's forces reacted by besieging the besiegers and creating, as it were, a double siege. This epic conflict, which included numerous battles, lasted for almost two years until the Muslim city surrendered to the Western armies on 12 July 1191. Thus was formed the Second Kingdom of Jerusalem, which was to last until the spring of 1291 with Acre as its capital.

The intellectual arena with which this study is concerned grew out of the unique circumstances which characterized thirteenth-century Acre. Among these a central place should be given to the constitution of the city's permanent and transient populations. Thirteenth-century Acre's population consisted of numerous groups, the most dominant of which was comprised of people of Western origin.[7] This general category may be divided more carefully: among the city's residents were speakers of both French and Provençal, as well as different groups of Italian origin, concentrated mainly in the quarters of Genoa, Venice and Pisa. Speakers of German and English were also represented in the city.[8] The evidence for the residence of a significant Oriental Christian population in the city during this period is much more significant than that available for the twelfth century.[9] The city certainly hosted numerous Orthodox churches; the Armenians had a hospital in the city at least during 1190–2; Acre had a Jacobite bishop; there was a Nestorian community in the city; and the Maronites may have had a church there.[10] As is seen in what follows, Coptic presence in the city is also well documented. During the thirteenth century the presence of Oriental Christians increased because of the economic opportunities the city offered, as well as because of an inclination of Oriental Christians to leave territories which the Franks lost to the Muslims or which were threatened as a result of the Mongol advancement.[11]

The Jewish community which had already existed in the city during the twelfth century, and whose existence was probably not dramatically interrupted by the events of 1187–91, evolved into a very significant one during the next century.[12] This was at least partly the result of a growing inclination of Jews from the West, many of whom belonged to the most learned parts of Jewish society, to immigrate to the Holy Land. Because

---

[7] D. Jacoby, 'Society, Culture, and the Arts in Crusader Acre', in D. H. Weiss and L. Mahoney (eds.), *France and the Holy Land* (Baltimore, MD, 2004), p. 97.

[8] D. Jacoby, 'Aspects of Everyday Life in Frankish Acre', *Crusades* 4 (2005), p. 84.

[9] Much evidence regarding the presence of such groups in the city is presented in Chapter 6.

[10] Kedar, 'Eastern Christians', pp. 140–2. On Greek Orthodox institutions in Acre, see also Jacoby, 'Aspects', p. 87; D. Jacoby, 'Three Notes on Crusader Acre', *ZDPV* 109 (1993), pp. 83–8; J. Richard, 'La confrérie des Mosserins d'Acre et les marchands de Mossoul au XIIIe siècle', *L'Orient Syrien* 11 (1966), pp. 451–60.

[11] Jacoby, 'Aspects', pp. 84–5; Jacoby, 'Society', pp. 102–3.   [12] Prawer, *Jews*, pp. 62, 258.

settling or residing in Jerusalem at the time was difficult, these usually made Acre their home. Thus, many Jews, predominantly of northern French origin, ended up in Acre, contributing to the development of a major Jewish community. A recently discovered document provides extraordinary evidence for the relations between Jews and Franks in the city. While the document can only partially be read, it clearly shows that a Jew based in the city is lamenting a Frankish defeat, probably that of 1250, that he receives letters from Christians and that he is in some kind of contact with a 'provincial', which probably refers to an office holder in one of the mendicant orders.[13] This supports the general impression that thirteenth-century Acre provided a relatively convenient environment for Jews.[14]

An important issue remains the presence of Muslims in thirteenth-century Acre. While there is no evidence for an operating mosque in the thirteenth-century city or for a permanent Muslim community living there, some individuals of this faith must have resided in Acre. Among these one can count captives who served as slaves in the city as well as Muslims in the process of converting to Christianity.[15] Be that as it may, members of such social groups are unlikely to have had a direct impact on the city's intellectual environment and are thus of little relevance for the present study. Indeed, I did not come across any mention of a work attributed to a Muslim resident of thirteenth-century Acre.

While it is out of the scope of the present work to assess the size of the city's population, it is possible to say something about the relative weight of its two main components: the Latins on the one hand and the Oriental Christians on the other. Kedar has shown that while in Jerusalem non-Latin ecclesiastical buildings made up about 45 per cent of the total, in Acre they constituted only about a tenth.[16] It is thus highly probable that the Latin population was considerably larger than the Oriental Christian, and that thirteenth-century Acre was of a significantly more Western character than twelfth-century Jerusalem. This would have also been the result of the massive building activities the Franks undertook in the city,

---

[13] S. Glick (with Y. Schwartz, A. Levin and A. Grossman), *Seride Teshuvot of the Ottoman Empire Sages: From the Cairo Genizah in the Elkan Nathan Adler Collection of the Library of the Jewish Theological Seminary of America*, 2 vols. (Ramat Gan, 2016), vol. II, pp. 589–95 [Hebrew].

[14] There is, however, one piece of evidence for an incident of Christian persecution of Jews in the city. This comes from a recently discovered Halakhic notebook which, unfortunately, says only that 'it happened once in Acre that the gentiles wished to do evil to Israel'. S. Emanuel, 'Pages from the Halakhic Notebook of a Thirteenth-Century Pilgrim', *Ginzei Qedem* 7 (2011), p. 151. Nothing else is known about this occurrence.

[15] See pp. 53–4, 114.

[16] B. Z. Kedar, 'A Review of: Denys Pringle, The Churches of the Crusader Kingdom of Jerusalem, A Corpus, III', *Israel Exploration Journal* 60.1 (2010), p. 123.

particularly in sections of land which were annexed to it only during the thirteenth century.

In addition to these permanent groups, the city also attracted a great transient population which participated in two major fields of activity: commerce and pilgrimage. During the thirteenth century Acre's importance as a centre of trade grew to the extent that by the middle of the century the city rivalled Alexandria and Constantinople, becoming, according to Abulafia, 'the capital of a whole network of trade routes'.[17] It served as an outlet to the West for the overland trade from Asia, but at the same time was also a warehouse for goods in transit, fulfilling an important role in their concentration and distribution. Consequently, the income from the commercial activity in Acre, at least till the late 1250s, seems to have been huge.[18] As a major trade centre the city was frequented by numerous merchants and peasants from both Christian and Muslim regions. Among these were, for example, Oriental Christian and Muslim peasants who would bring daily basic victuals to the city, as well as Venetians returning from Damascus with high-quality silk textiles, or Tuscans leaving to Egypt with cloth.[19]

The second kind of population which spent short periods of time in the city was that of pilgrims. Before 1187, Acre was an important transit station for pilgrims on their way to the holy sites located mainly in and around Jerusalem. One can assume that it was in Acre that pilgrims made logistical preparations such as the hiring of guides or horses and donkeys. Following 1191, with Jerusalem remaining in Muslim hands (except for the brief interlude of 1229–44), Acre's importance for pilgrims increased, to the extent that it became itself a significant site with an institutionalized pilgrimage route established within its walls.[20] In other words, Acre now functioned not merely as a gateway into the Holy Land, but as a sacred space in its own right. Furthermore, it is noteworthy that in addition to pilgrims hailing from the West, the city was probably also visited by Oriental Christian pilgrims.[21]

Before moving on, it would be worthwhile to briefly mention one additional characteristic of the city which should be borne in mind when

[17] Pringle, *The Churches IV*, pp. 8–9; D. Abulafia, 'Trade and Crusade, 1050–1250', in M. Goodich, S. Menache and S. Schein (eds.), *Cross Cultural Convergences in the Crusader Period* (New York, NY, 1995), p. 19.

[18] Pringle, *The Churches IV*, p. 9; J. Riley-Smith, *The Feudal Nobility and the Kingdom of Jerusalem 1174–1277* (London, 1973), p. 64.

[19] Jacoby, 'Aspects', pp. 89–90; Abulafia, 'Trade and Crusade', p. 19.

[20] Jacoby, 'Society', p. 101. Regarding this see also Jacoby, 'Pèlerinage médiéval et sanctuaires de Terre Sainte: La perspective vénitienne', *Ateneo veneto*, Anno CLXXIII, 24 (1986), pp. 27–8.

[21] L. Minervini, 'Outremer', in P. Boitani, M. Mancini and A. Vàrvaro (eds.), *Lo spazio letterario del medioevo, 2. Il medioevo volgare, vol. 1, La produzione del testo* (Rome, 2001), pp. 637–8.

one explores its culture. As a capital of the kingdom, Acre housed numerous institutions. To mention just several of them, it accommodated the headquarters of the Hospitaller, Templar and Teutonic orders.[22] Additionally, throughout the thirteenth century the patriarchs of Jerusalem, who headed the church in the Kingdom of Jerusalem, resided in the city, and houses of the Franciscan and Dominican orders were established there. Acre also housed the kingdom's High Court as well as a Burgess Court, a Market Court and a so-called Court of the Chain.[23]

Acre's importance and affluence are reflected not only in written sources but also in the wealth of impressive physical remains which are continuously being revealed. During the past several decades archaeologists have been able to advance greatly in their work, exposing more and more vestiges of the Frankish city under the Ottoman one. Inter alia, they have brought to light significant remnants of the Hospitaller compound; streets and private houses in what is known as the Youth Hostel excavation; parts of a vaulted street possibly belonging to the city's Genoese quarter; the Church of Saint Andrew; and a public bathhouse. Furthermore, ceramics found in the city, and originating in a great variety of regions such as Iberia, Sicily, Greece and China, attest to its importance as a centre of commerce.[24] Notably, new archaeological finds studied along with written and visual source material also advance our understanding of the city's dimensions. Until 1187, the Franks seem to have used the outer walls as left by their Muslim predecessors. Due to various reasons, some already mentioned, the city's population grew significantly following 1191. This led to the building of new outer walls, which expanded the city towards the east and the north. The northern section that was thus annexed to the city was a suburb known as Montmusard.[25]

---

[22] Pringle, *The Churches IV*, pp. 19–20.

[23] For the various courts operating in the Kingdom of Jerusalem, see J. Prawer, *The Latin Kingdom of Jerusalem: European Colonialism in the Middle Ages* (London, 1972), pp. 114–21, 145–51, 153–6; for the Court of the Chain, see also D. Jacoby, 'Crusader Acre in the Thirteenth Century: Urban Layout and Topography', *Studi medievali*, 3rd series 20 (1979), p. 16.

[24] There is ample literature about Acre's archaeology. For a recent work that sums up earlier research but also includes much, often previously unpublished, information on recent excavations, see E. Stern, 'Acre during the Crusader Period and Its Maritime Aspects in the Light of Archaeological and Recent Historical Research', unpublished PhD thesis, University of Haifa (2015) [Hebrew with English abstract]. The aforementioned fourth volume of Pringle's *The Churches of the Crusader Kingdom of Jerusalem* is also most useful.

[25] The problem of Acre's outer walls received considerable scholarly attention. Especially significant are Stern, 'Acre during the Crusading Period', pp. 169–73; B. Z. Kedar, 'The Outer Walls of Frankish Acre', *Atiqot* 31 (1997), pp. 157–80; D. Jacoby, 'Montmusard, Suburb of Crusader Acre: The First Stage of its Development', in B. Z. Kedar, H. E. Mayer and R. C. Smail (eds.), *Outremer: Studies in the History of the Crusader Kingdom of Jerusalem Presented to Joshua Prawer* (Jerusalem 1982), pp. 205–17.

Acre was, then, a city of considerable size which housed a varied permanent population and attracted a substantial and diverse transient one, as well as immigrants of different religions and geographical origins. It was a rich centre of trade, as well as a significant location for pilgrims. But at the same time, thirteenth-century Acre was a city whose inhabitants often had good reasons to fear for their future. To mention just two examples, in April 1263 the Mamluks raided the city's suburbs, destroying the cemetery of St. Nicholas, and in May 1267 they killed a large number of people working in the fields outside the city, later destroying some mills and towers.[26]

The city's residents were certainly aware of their fragile position. This is reflected, firstly, in various attempts to improve Acre's defences.[27] Thus, for instance, the approach of the Mongols in 1260 drove the city's inhabitants to cut trees, demolish towers in nearby gardens and take tombstones from the cemetery of St. Nicholas for reuse in the city's defences.[28] The residents' understanding that they faced a serious threat can also be seen through evidence from outside the military field. The Hospitallers, for example, decided to transfer an important part of their archive, as well as a precious relic, to France sometime before 1283.[29] Various agreements which mention the possibility that Acre would fall to the hands of the Muslims reflect the same kind of sentiment,[30] as do these words, written by an anonymous author in 1273:[31]

However, it is known among the Christians, that there is no place which Baibars desires to subdue as much as the city of Acre ... some of us therefore assert that he pretends to be merciful toward the Christians so that the city of Acre would have a good opinion of him and would fully trust him, as if he were a friend, in order that, when the right time would be observed, he would be able to capture and hold it.

The city's population was thus very much aware of the imminent dangers. What is perhaps more surprising, or at least noteworthy, is that

---

[26] Pringle, *The Churches IV*, p. 11.   [27] Pringle, *The Churches IV*, p. 11.

[28] Pringle, *The Churches IV*, p. 10; R. Röhricht and G. Raynaud (eds.), 'Annales de Terre Sainte', *Archives de l'Orient Latin* 2 (1884), p. 449.

[29] Jacoby, 'Society', p. 98.

[30] See, for example, an agreement dated 1261 in E. Strehlke (ed.), *Tabulae ordinis Theutonici* (Berlin, 1869, reprinted Toronto, 1975), pp. 106–9, and, in particular, p. 108. For further evidence, see D. Jacoby, 'Refugees from Acre in Famagusta around 1300', in M. J. K. Walsh, T. Kiss and N. Coureas (eds.), *The Harbour of all This Sea and Realm: Crusader to Venetian Famagusta* (Budapest, 2014), pp. 57–8.

[31] *Notitia*, p. 328. 'Verumptamen apud christicolas notum est, quod nullum locum tantum desiderat [Baibars] subiugare sicut civitatem Acon ... unde nonnulli nostrorum autumant, quod ipse se fingit ad Christianos clementem, ut civitas Aconensis bonam de se habeat opinionem et plene tamquam de amico confidat, quatenus observato tempore possit eam postmodum capere et possidere.'

during the decades in which the threats to the city increased, people not only continued to live their lives in Acre, but – as we see later – intellectual activity in it flourished more than it ever did before.

Thus, this sizable and wealthy capital, home to the kingdom's most important institutions and to a heterogeneous population, was simultaneously a peripheral city, occasionally threatened and eventually captured and destroyed. Against this background, the present study aims to portray and analyse the intellectual activity that took place in Acre, while investigating the intercultural exchanges that it involved.

THE CONCEPT OF 'INTELLECTUAL ACTIVITY' IN MEDIEVAL HISTORIOGRAPHY AND IN THE HISTORY OF THE LATIN EAST: SOME INTRODUCTORY REMARKS

The object of this study is to provide a picture of what may be described as the web of concerns, knowledge, ideas and attitudes within which the authors of thirteenth-century Acre worked, and to which, in turn, they contributed. Obviously, the texts and the authors who composed them offer only a point of departure for the study of this cultural environment, in which numerous additional agents, belonging to a range of social and cultural groups, operated.

I have chosen to refer to the activities which stand at the focus of this study as 'intellectual' and to the web I have just described as an 'intellectual arena'. As the word 'intellectual' is a modern creation, this choice requires some justification and explanation. Despite its clearly non-medieval origins, the use of the term 'intellectual' by medievalists already has a respectable tradition behind it. Its most significant entry into medieval historiography is attributed to Jacques Le Goff, whose use of the term is highly suitable for the attempt presented here.[32] Le Goff defines the 'new intellectual work' that appears during the twelfth century as 'the joining together, in an urban and no longer monastic environment, of research and teaching'.[33] In his 1985 introduction he presents a wider understanding of this term, expressing a degree of self-criticism for not including in his original work the populizers, compilers and encyclopaedists, and for not discussing dissemination as a part of the activity of the intellectual milieu.[34] Le Goff hesitates to draw the line between academics in the strict sense and 'litterateurs', adding that 'all those who through their knowledge of writing, their expertise in law and

---

[32] J. Le Goff, *Intellectuals in the Middle Ages*, trans. T. L. Fagan (Cambridge, 1993). This edition includes, in addition to the original introduction, the introduction to the French 1985 edition in which Le Goff significantly updated his definition of the medieval intellectual.
[33] Le Goff, *Intellectuals*, p. xvii.   [34] Le Goff, *Intellectuals*, p. xvii.

particularly in Roman law, their teaching of the "liberal" arts and occasionally of the "mechanical" arts, enabled the town to assert itself and,
notably in Italy, enabled the commune to become a great social, political,
and cultural phenomenon, deserve to be seen as intellectuals of urban
growth'.[35] In other words, Le Goff offers an inclusive definition of an
intellectual, in the medieval context, as practically anyone who is
involved in the production and dissemination of knowledge, especially
such that is related, directly or indirectly, to written works. It is along
these lines that the word 'intellectual' is used in what follows.

Discussions of several other aspects of this term offer additional insights
relevant to the present study. One important issue is the relation between
intellectuals and institutions, particularly the university. Le Goff saw the
term 'intellectual' as enabling a shift of attention from institutions to
individuals.[36] In her elaborate discussion of the term 'intellectual', Rita
Copeland maintains, on the basis of Le Goff and de Libera's works, that
the 'formation of the intellectual figure or *habitus* needs the dynamic
interaction between the university and its non-professional cultural
environment'.[37] These comments bear particular relevance for the
study of Acre, which did not house a university (though, as we see in
what follows, it did accommodate some smaller study institutions), but
whose cultural arena was strongly influenced by individuals trained in
major Western study centres, and in which, consequently, interaction
between intellectual centres and periphery played an important role.

Another important issue is that of the 'detachment of the intellectual'.
Medieval intellectuals have sometimes been characterized as detached or
disinterested, but, as Copeland argues, such a notion is not a useful tool.[38]
And indeed, the figures studied later in this work surely had various
interests and were not motivated solely by a pure ideal of acquiring and
disseminating knowledge. Rather, related to institutions and milieus, they
were certainly influenced by a variety of 'earthly' motives. Consequently,
following Le Goff's tradition, the present study devotes attention to themes
such as the function and status of Acre's intellectuals.[39]

Little work has been dedicated specifically to the intellectual activity in
Acre. The only survey of such activities is found in Jaroslav Folda's book
on illustrated manuscripts from Acre, where in an introductory section

---

[35] Le Goff, *Intellectuals*, pp. xviii–xix.   [36] Le Goff, *Intellectuals*, p. xiii.

[37] R. Copeland, *Pedagogy, Intellectuals, and Dissent in the Later Middle Ages: Lollardy and Ideas of
Learning* (Cambridge, 2001), p. 39; A. de Libera, *Penser au moyen âge* (Paris, 1991).

[38] Copeland, *Pedagogy*, pp. 31–3.

[39] For the notion of function in the context of Le Goff's work on medieval intellectuals, see
A. Boureau, 'Intellectuals in the Middle Ages, 1957–95', in Miri Rubin (ed.), *The Work of
Jacques Le Goff and the Challenges of Medieval History* (Woodbridge, 1997), pp. 148, 152.

the city is presented as an intellectual centre and the texts produced there during the thirteenth century are listed.[40] Folda does not analyse the texts and does not try – as this is far from the aim of his book – to examine subjects such as the relations between the various texts or the characteristics of the cultural environment in which they were composed. Furthermore, since the publication of his book, the information available concerning works written in the city has increased considerably.

More generally, the intellectual activities undertaken in the Latin East, while not usually considered one of the central themes in the history of the Crusades and the Frankish Levant, are certainly a topic continuously touched upon by historians. Several of the best-known general histories of the Crusades and the Latin East include brief surveys of the intellectual activity in Outremer. As a rule, these evaluations are quite pessimistic with regard to the extent and value of such activities.[41] On the other hand, during the past decades these negative evaluations have been moderated by the careful work of historians such as Benjamin Z. Kedar, Peter Edbury, Laura Minervini, Charles Burnett and David Jacoby, whose research forms the foundation for the present study. To mention just several important examples, Kedar devoted two papers to the discussion of the relations – including exchanges in the sphere of learning – between Franks and Oriental Christians in the Frankish Levant,[42] and Minervini studied the production and circulation of manuscripts, the production of translations and other kinds of literary activities in Outremer.[43] In his work on the knightly culture of Outremer Jacoby touched on related issues,[44] and several studies have been devoted to the

---

[40] J. Folda, *Crusader Manuscript Illumination at Saint-Jean d'Acre 1275–1291* (Princeton, NJ, 1976), pp. 8–21. A quite similar survey appears in a more recent study of his *Crusader Art in the Holy Land, from the Third Crusade to the Fall of Acre, 1187–1291* (Cambridge, 2005), pp. 398–404.

[41] Mayer, *The Crusades*, pp. 191–5; J. Prawer, *The Latin Kingdom of Jerusalem*, pp. 527–30; S. Runciman, *A History of the Crusades*,3 vols. (Cambridge, 1951–4), vol. III, pp. 489–92.

[42] Kedar, 'Eastern Christians', pp. 137–47; B. Z. Kedar, 'Latins and Oriental Christians in the Frankish Levant, 1099–1291', in A. Kofsky and G. G. Stroumsa (eds.), *Sharing the Sacred: Religious Contacts and Conflicts in the Holy Land* (Jerusalem, 1998), pp. 209–22.

[43] L. Minervini, 'Produzione e circolazione di manoscritti negli Stati Crociati: biblioteche e scriptoria latini', in A. Pioletti and F. Rizzo-Nervo (eds.), *Medioevo Romanzo e Orientale. Il viaggio dei testi. III Colloquio Internazionale, Venezia, 10–13 ottobre 1996* (Soveria Mannelli, 1999), pp. 79–96; Minervini, 'Tradizioni linguistiche e culturali negli Stati Latini d'Oriente', in A. Pioletti and F. Rizzo-Nervo (eds.), *Medioevo Romanzo e Orientale. Oralità, scrittura, modelli narrativi* (Messina, 1995), pp. 155–72; Minervini, 'Outremer', pp. 611–48; Minervini, 'Modelli culturali e attività letteraria nell'Oriente latino', *Studi medievali* 43 (2002), pp. 337–48.

[44] D. Jacoby, 'Knightly Values and Class Consciousness in the Crusader States of the Eastern Mediterranean', *Mediterranean Historical Review* 1 (1986), pp. 158–86; D. Jacoby, 'La littérature française dans les états latins de la Méditerranée orientale à l'époque des croisades: diffusion et création', in *Essor et fortune de la chanson de geste dans l'Europe et l'Orient latin: Actes du XIe Congrès international de la Société Rencesvals pour l'étude des épopée romanes (Padua-Venice, 1982)* (Modena, 1984), pp. 617–46.

intellectual activities undertaken in specific cities in the Latin East, though on a scale smaller than that attempted here.[45]

And yet, the pessimistic view with regard to the intellectual activities in the Latin East has still not lost its dominance in scholarship. Thus, for example, Peter Lock's *Routledge Companion to the Crusades* hardly comments on the intellectual activity in the Latin East.[46] The same is true of the *Oxford History of the Crusades*, which wrongly states that 'no Arab books were translated into Latin or French in the Latin East'.[47] It seems that the minimalistic view concerning the intellectual activity in Outremer usually follows several general lines. Firstly, the question of the level of intellectual activity in Outremer is perceived as more or less identical with that of the absorption of Arabic/Muslim learning by the Latins in that region. As there is little evidence for such exchanges, especially when compared to what we know about Iberia or Sicily, the conclusion is that not much was going on, from the perspective of intellectual history, in the Latin East. Another recurrent argument is that Outremer lacked a university or, for that matter, any other study centre that would have enabled the preservation, circulation and development of texts. Consequently, it is argued, no significant intellectual developments could have taken place there. It is also often stated that the society of Outremer was isolated from the groundbreaking intellectual trends that characterized the West in the twelfth and thirteenth centuries, and that only a very limited number of learned men were active in it. The present study takes issue with such arguments by examining the surviving evidence from thirteenth-century Acre.

METHODOLOGY AND STRUCTURE OF THE PRESENT STUDY

The present book aims to make a significant advance in the study of the intellectual activity in Outremer by systematically exploring, for the first time, such pursuits in a major Frankish city during a considerable period of time. The term 'intellectual', used along the lines described earlier, enables us to look broadly at a wide range of activities centred on the production and dissemination of knowledge, and our focus on Acre makes it possible to view these activities within the context of the

---

[45] C. Burnett, 'Antioch as a Link between Arabic and Latin Culture', in I. Draelants, A. Tihon and B. van den Abeele (eds.), *Occident et Proche-Orient: Contacts scientifiques au temps des Croisades* (Turnhout, 2000), pp. 1–78; B. Z. Kedar, 'Intellectual Activities in a Holy City: Jerusalem in the Twelfth Century', in B. Z. Kedar and R. J. Z. Werblowsky (eds.), *Sacred Space: Shrine, City, Land, Studies in Memory of Joshua Prawer* (Jerusalem, 1998), pp. 127–39; R. Hiestand, 'Un centre intellectuel en Syrie du nord?' *Le Moyen Age* 100 (1994), pp. 7–36.

[46] P. Lock, *Routledge Companion to the Crusades* (New York, NY, 2006).

[47] J. Riley-Smith (ed.), *The Oxford History of the Crusades* (Oxford, 1999), pp. 233–4.

conditions and circumstances that characterized the city at the time. In other words, our intention is not to portray a sort of idealized, detached, intellectual arena, but rather to place it within the concrete realities of thirteenth-century Acre. Following this approach, we assess, on the basis of an unprecedented literary corpus, the quality and extent, as well as the limitations, of the intellectual activity undertaken in the Kingdom of Jerusalem's most significant cultural centre. The results of this survey enable us to place a 'new' noteworthy centre of intellectual activity on the shores of the Mediterranean and to characterize it.

The scope of the subject is defined by a location, the city of Acre, and a period of time, 1191–1291. Within these confines the activities of two main groups are studied: the Latins, i.e. Crusaders and other Christian immigrants from the West, as well as their descendants born in the Levant, and the Jews. The reason for this focus is straightforward: these are the groups which left behind written works composed in the city during the years in question. As noted, there is currently no evidence for Muslim texts written in thirteenth-century Acre. I have also found no evidence for original works written in the city by Oriental Christians, although we are aware of two Greek manuscripts taken as booty from the city in 1291.[48]

In addition to the usual dearth of source material which confronts all medievalists, any attempt to reconstruct the intellectual arena of thir-teenth-century Acre must contend with two particular difficulties. Firstly, much of what was written in Acre, and probably most of it, was destroyed in May 1291. Secondly, as medieval texts often lack reference to the circumstances in which they were composed, it is probable that various texts written in Acre have not yet been identified as such. Against this background, the present work uses two approaches. The first, which guides the first and second chapters, is structural, aiming to characterize the intellectual arena that existed in thirteenth-century Acre. Chapter 1 examines the role various social groups played in intellectual activities, asking questions such as what fields of knowledge stood at the centre of interest of each of the city's social groups, and what were their main contributions to the city's cultural arena. Chapter 2 systematically explores the study centres, both Christian and Jewish, which operated in the city.

The second approach reconstructs the intellectual activity undertaken in the city with regard to several major fields of knowledge. This is done in Chapters 3 to 6, each of which focuses on one of four themes (language

---

[48] J. Pahlitzsch, *Graeci und Suriani im Palästina der Kreuzfahrerzeit*, Berliner Historische Studien 33 (Berlin, 2001), pp. 228, n. 550, 330–1, 350–1.

and translation, jurisprudence, Islam and Oriental Christianity) which I found particularly significant among those discussed and studied in the city. Each of these chapters discusses, with regard to the field examined, questions such as: What knowledge circulated in the city? Where did it originate? In what ways was it developed by Acre's scholars? How innovative was their work in comparison with that of contemporaries of theirs working in the West? In what ways were developments in this field related to intercultural exchanges, and which cultural groups were involved in these exchanges?

A NOTE ON THE 'ACRE CORPUS'

The study of Acre's intellectual arena must obviously be based, first and foremost, on texts written in the city. But this requirement is not easy to fulfil: while some texts include an explicit statement as to the circumstances of their composition, many do not. In such cases a detailed analysis of the evidence is required in order to reach a conclusion as to where a certain text was produced. Furthermore, with regard to some texts no certain decisions can be reached, and one has to settle for the assessment that a text 'was probably written in Acre'. The appendix is intended to face this difficulty: it includes discussions of the evidence linking to Acre all extant texts which, according to my assessment, are likely to have been written there.[49] The texts examined in the appendix are divided into three categories according to the robustness of evidence connecting them to the city: those certainly written in the city, those almost certainly written in it and those probably written in it.[50] Texts thought to have been written in Acre but which are no longer extant are mentioned and commented upon in the body of the work, but are not included in the appendix. It should also be noted that, as a rule, letters, charters and notarial acts are excluded from this examination but are, of course, used in the body of the present work. Texts which may have been written in Acre, but regarding which we have no clear evidence that would connect them to the city, are obviously not included in the appendix. They are, however, occasionally used in the body of the study, accompanied by a note that discusses their relation to Acre.

In order to save the reader the trouble of constantly skipping to the appendix, the first mention of a text in each of the chapters is followed by

---

[49] As a rule, all texts discussed in the appendix are used in the present study. There are, however, several texts which I discuss in the appendix and are not used in this study. These are marked with an asterisk.

[50] Within each of the categories, the texts are presented, as far as possible, in chronological order.

two numbers appearing in brackets [**x:y**]. The first number indicates my assessment of its connection to Acre (**1**: certainly written in Acre; **2**: almost certainly written in Acre; **3**: probably written in Acre). The second digit refers to the place of the relevant discussion in the appendix.

Chapter 1

INTELLECTUAL ACTIVITY IN ACRE
Sociocultural Characteristics

Had we been able to land in Acre's port sometime in the thirteenth century, we would have certainly been impressed by the city's bustling markets, by the great variety of commodities traded in it and by the diversity of languages spoken by both residents and visitors. We would have also noted the city's opulence, exemplified by its monumental buildings. Noticing intellectual milieus operating in the city would have been much more difficult, as those belonging to them would not have been very numerous or, for the most part, very noticeable. But they were present in different quarters of the city, reading, writing, teaching and participating in networks that occasionally extended far beyond the city's walls. The aim of this chapter is to trace these milieus and system-atically explore their roles in the city's intellectual arena, or, in other words, their involvement in processes of production, dissemination and consumption of knowledge. Our exploration of Acre's intellectual domain first focuses on the city's Frankish society and then moves on to its Jewish community.

FRANKISH SOCIETY

The question of the extent to which the city's Frankish inhabitants were interested – and able – to participate in intellectual activity has not received a unanimous answer from scholars. It has been argued, on the one hand, that the society of Outremer consisted almost entirely of soldiers and merchants and that it therefore was not fit to 'create or maintain a high intellectual standard'.[1] On the other hand, it was claimed that:[2]

The relocation to Acre of the royal court, various ecclesiastical institutions, and numerous refugees from territories remaining under Muslim rule resulted in

---

[1] Runciman, *A History of the Crusades*, vol. III, p. 489.   [2] Jacoby, 'Society', p. 98.

a substantial concentration in the city of Latin nobility, clergy, and members of an educated elite consisting of notaries, lawyers, medical practitioners, and some teachers of the liberal arts and theology.

In the following paragraphs, an attempt to advance with regard to this question is made. We begin by looking at four social groups, clergy, mendicants, nobility and burgesses, asking questions such as: What texts did members of the group compose? What knowledge did they possess? What was their role in the patronage of intellectual projects in the city? This is followed by a survey of the involvement of four occupational groups in the city's intellectual arena: lawyers and jurists, scribes and notaries, physicians and envoys. Here we investigate who belonged to these groups and what their contribution was to the city's intellectual activity. Particular attention is paid in this subsection to the involvement of these groups in intercultural exchanges.

It is important to note that the borderlines between the different groups studied in what follows are not clear-cut, as demonstrated by careers such as Raoul de Mérencourt's, a notary of Henry II of Champagne, a *canonicus*, chancellor of the kingdom and, eventually, patriarch of Jerusalem,[3] or a certain Constantine's, who was a physician with a wide knowledge of law.[4] However, as different social and professional groups were generally linked to particular aspects of the city's culture, the categorization employed here is useful in order to portray the sociocultural setting for Acre's intellectual arena.

The Clergy

The clergy, and specifically the senior clergy, was probably the most influential group in Acre's intellectual arena. This group was unusually big in the city since it included not only clergymen whose responsibilities lay in Acre but also numerous ecclesiastics formally in charge of territories which, following 1187, were no longer in Frankish control. Thus, for example, the bishops of Bethlehem lived in Acre for at least much of the period, as did also those of Tiberias, Hebron and Lydda.[5]

---

[3] H. E. Mayer, *Die Kanzlei der lateinischen Könige von Jerusalem*, MGH Schriften, 40, 2 vols. (Hanover, 1996), vol. I, p. 317; vol. II, pp. 607–8.

[4] Regarding Constantine, see later in this chapter.

[5] Pringle, *The Churches IV*, pp. 18–19; B. Hamilton, *The Latin Church in the Crusader States* (London, 1980), p. 300. Note that even following the 1229 treaty which brought Jerusalem back to Frankish hands (1229–44) most of the Catholic clergy refused to leave Acre. B. Hamilton, 'The Latin Church in the Crusader States', in K. Ciggaar, A. Davids and H. Teule (eds.), *East and West in the Crusader States*, 3 vols. (Leuven, 1996), vol. I, pp. 18–19.

The dominance of this group in Acre's cultural life derived not only from the considerable number of churchmen who resided in the city, but also from the high level of learning that characterized many of them.[6] Thus, among the thirteenth-century bishops of Acre was John of Provins, earlier *decanus Parisiensis*, and among those of Bethlehem was Gaillard, previously a lector in the Dominican houses of Narbonne and Agen.[7] Albert of Vercelli, Patriarch of Jerusalem (1205–14), was trained as a youngster in the *artes liberales* and in civil law, and was also learned in theology and canon law.[8] Jacques Pantaleon, Patriarch of Jerusalem (1255–61) and later Pope Urban IV, was also a man of considerable learning. He attended the cathedral school of Troyes, and later the University of Paris, where he studied theology.[9] Furthermore, Jacques is possibly the author of two works: a geographical treatise on the Holy Land and a commentary on the *Miserere* Psalm.[10] His interest in intellectual activity is further attested by his connections, as a pope, with both Thomas Aquinas and the mathematician Campanus of Novara.[11] The Dominican Nicholas of Hanapes, the patriarch of Jerusalem at the time of the kingdom's fall, was also a figure of considerable intellectual ability. He spent several years in the Dominican convent at Paris, and, while still in the West, wrote the very popular *Liber de exemplis Sacre Scripture*.[12]

When one analyses the potential contribution of such men to the city's intellectual scene, another, rather practical, element should be taken into account: as the sees of much of the clergy residing in Acre were in Muslim hands, these men were relatively free of spiritual and material responsibilities.[13] While it is difficult to know what influence this had on them, it is quite possible that this enabled and even encouraged them

---

[6] Hamilton, *The Latin Church*, p. 280.

[7] P. Scheffer-Boichorst (ed.), *Chronica Albrici monachi Trium Fontium a monacho novi monasterii Hoiensis interpolata*, MGH SS 23 (Hanover, 1874, reprinted Stuttgart, 1963), p. 923; Hamilton, *The Latin Church*, p. 280.

[8] K.-P. Kirstein, *Die Lateinischen Patriarchen von Jerusalem* (Berlin, 2002), p. 412; J. A. Brundage, 'Latin Jurists in the Levant: The Legal Elite of the Crusader States', in M. Shatzmiller (ed.), *Crusaders and Muslims in Twelfth Century Syria* (Leiden, 1993), pp. 25–6; Hamilton, *The Latin Church*, pp. 249–50.

[9] H. K. Mann, The Lives of the Popes in the Middle Ages, *vol. 15:* Alexander IV to Gregory X (London, 1929), p. 136; *RRH* 1304.

[10] Adrichem lists a *Liber de Terra Sancta* composed by Pantaleon among the sources for his *Theatrum Terrae Sanctae*. C. van Adrichem, *Theatrum Terrae Sanctae* (Köln, 1682), p. 287. I have found no further information about this text. Regarding the commentary, see Mann, *Lives*, p. 141, n. 5; P. Daunou, 'Urbain IV, Pape', *Histoire littéraire de la France* 19 (1838), p. 64.

[11] Mann, *Lives*, pp. 144–6.

[12] V. LeClerc, 'Nicholas de Hanapes, Patriarche de Jérusalem', *Histoire Littéraire de la France* 20 (1842), pp. 64–6; J. T. Welter, *L'exemplum dans la littérature religieuse et didactique du Moyen Âge* (Geneva, 1973, reprint of Paris-Toulouse, 1927), pp. 230–3.

[13] Hamilton, *The Latin Church*, p. 281.

to devote considerable time to intellectual matters. This impression is supported by the explicit words of John of Ancona (probably not a churchman himself, however), who, enumerating the reasons that led him to write his canon law treatise [1:12], mentions his fear that being at leisure would damage his memory.[14]

In addition to resident clergy, visiting churchmen were present in the city. A clue to the frequency of such visits is provided by a decretal dating to 1207 and addressed by Pope Innocent III to Albert of Vercelli, Patriarch of Jerusalem:[15]

The prudence of your brotherhood asked to be instructed through the apostolic see whether you should permit these clergymen who come to the territories of Jerusalem without letters of recommendation to celebrate divine service.

Such a question would have made no sense if it were not a usual occurrence that members of the clergy from other parts of the Catholic world came to the East and wished to perform sacraments there. And indeed, there is considerable evidence for visits of Western churchmen in Acre. As examples, one may name Gautiers of Tournai, said to have been elected bishop while at Acre (ca. 1218);[16] Theobald Visconti, archdeacon of Liège, who was informed of his election as pope during his stay there; and Antony Bek, who had earlier spent several years in Oxford and accompanied Prince Edward on his crusade.[17]

Both resident and visiting churchmen played a significant role in the production of written works in the city. Surveying the clergy's contribution to the Acre corpus, it becomes clear that much of their energy was directed towards the support of Latin religious life in the Frankish East and specifically in Acre under the often challenging circumstances which characterized the kingdom at the time. Under this heading belong the original Carmelite Rule [3:35] probably written in the city by Albert of Vercelli, Patriarch of Jerusalem, as well as the *Pardouns d'Acre* [1:10],

---

[14] Regarding John's social status, see M. Bertram, 'Johannes de Ancona: Ein Jurist der 13 Jarhunderts in den Kreuzfahrerstaaten', *Bulletin of Medieval Canon Law* 7 (1977), pp. 52–3. The canon law text is discussed in detail in Chapter 4. For the relevant citation from John's work, see Bertram, 'Johannes de Ancona', p. 59.

[15] 'Tuae fraternitatis *discretio postulavit per sedem apostolicam edoceri*, utrum clericos illos, qui ad partes Hierosolymitanas sine litteris commendatitiis veniunt, permittere debeas celebrare divina.' PL 215.1083. This letter is cited in the *Liber extra* 1.22.3.

[16] Le Baron de Reiffenberg (ed.), *Chronique rimée de Philippe Mouskes, Évêque de Tournay au treizième siècle*, 2 vols. (Brussels, 1838), vol. II, p. 398, lines 22871–4.

[17] That Visconti was elected pope while in Acre is stated in the *Memoria* [3:43]. J. Paviot (ed.), *Projets de croisade* (Paris, 2008), p. 237. This is confirmed by Marco Polo's testimony: Marco Polo, *Le devisement du monde*, ed. P. Ménard, 6 vols. (Geneva, 2001), vol. I, p. 126. For Antony Bek, see C. M. Fraser, 'Bek, Antony (I) (*c*.1245–1311)', *Oxford Dictionary of National Biography* (Oxford, 2004), online edition, Jan. 2008 [www.oxforddnb.com/view/article/1970, accessed 4 Nov. 2009].

which describes a pilgrimage route within Acre's walls, and a set of statutes promulgated by Eudes de Châteauroux in the city [**1:9**].[18] The anonymous clergymen who phrased a prayer for the sick treated in the Hospitaller order's infirmary [**1:1**], as well as those who compiled a missal with a unique reference to the *dedicatio ecclesie Acconensis* were also working within this framework.[19] Within the same context, a breviary copied in thirteenth-century Acre reveals the ways in which Templar clergy sought to adapt the order's liturgy to the particular conditions of the Second Kingdom of Jerusalem – mainly, of course, the loss of Jerusalem.[20] To this category one should add sermons composed in order to be delivered in the city: there are reasons to believe that Jordan of Saxony, Eudes de Châteauroux [**3:38**] and Guillaume de Cordelle all preached in the city,[21] and a sermon presented by Theobald Visconti is mentioned in the *Memoria* [**3:43**].[22] Jacques de Vitry also preached in Acre, and two of his extant *Sermones vulgares* may have been presented in the city.[23] Unique evidence for clergymen's involvement in the production of texts in Acre is provided by a manuscript now in Barletta.[24]

[18] F. Romanini and B. Saletti, *The* Pelrinages communes, *the* Pardouns de Acre *and the Crisis in the Crusader Kingdom. History and Texts* (Padova, 2012); D. Jacoby, 'Pilgrimage in Crusader Acre: The Pardouns d'Acre', in Y. Hen (ed.), *De Sion exibit lex et verbum domini de Hierusalem: Essays on Medieval Law, Liturgy, and Literature in Honour of Amnon Linder*, Cultural Encounters in Late Antiquity and the Middle Ages 1 (Turnhout, 2001), pp. 105–17.

[19] L. Le Grand, 'La Prière des Malades dans les Hospitaux de l'Ordre de Saint-Jean de Jérusalem', *Bibliothèque de l'École des chartes* 57 (1896), pp. 325–38; J. Folda, *Crusader Art*, pp. 295–9; Hugo Buchthal, *Miniature Painting in the Latin Kingdom of Jerusalem* (Oxford, 1957. reprinted London, 1986), pp. 48–51 and appendix i. On this manuscript, see also S. E. Salvadó, 'The Liturgy of the Holy Sepulchre and the Templar Rite: Edition and Analysis of the Jerusalem Ordinal (Rome, Bib. Vat. Barb. Lat. 659) with a Comparative Study of the Acre Breviary (Paris, Bib. Nat., Ms. Latin 10478)', unpublished PhD thesis, Stanford University (2011), p. 56.

[20] Salvadó, 'The Liturgy', pp. 269–74, 288–90, 418, *et passim*. The breviary is found in MS Paris, Bibliothèque nationale de France, lat. 10478.

[21] For Jordan, see F.-M. Abel, 'Le Couvent des Frères Prêcheurs à Saint-Jean d'Acre', *Revue biblique* 43 (1934), p. 276; regarding Eudes, see P. Cole, D. L. d'Avray and J. Riley-Smith, 'Application of Theology to Current Affairs: Memorial Sermons for the Dead of Mansurah and on Innocent IV', *Historical Research* 63 (1990), pp. 230–31; for Guillaume, see B. Z. Kedar, *Crusade and Mission* (Princeton, NJ, 1984), pp. 139–40; A. Van den Wyngaert, 'Frère Guillaume de Cordelle, O.F.M.', *La France Franciscaine* 4 (1921), pp. 52–71.

[22] Paviot, *Projets*, pp. 237–8; B. Hamilton, 'Eleanor of Castile and the Crusading Movement', *Mediterranean Historical Review* 10 (1995), p. 99.

[23] In sermon 37, preached to the members of the Templar order, Jacques turns to an *exemplum* related to the fall of Ascalon, and then goes on to speak about a martyr pilgrim. Both of these anecdotes would have been much more relevant to Templars active in the Latin East than to those residing in the West. Sermon 38 also includes clues implying it was intended for an audience living in the Levant: it ends with a warning against putting trust in 'false Christians, Saracens or Bedouins', and includes an anecdote about a Templar riding from Tyre to Acre. J.-B. Pitra (ed.), *Analecta novissima Spicilegii Solesmensis, altera continuatio*, 2 vols. (Tusculum, 1888), vol. II, pp. 412–13, 420, 421; Kedar, *Crusade and Mission*, pp. 126–7.

[24] Barletta, Archivio della Chiesa del Santo Sepolcro, ms. s.n. According to Salvadó, this compilation was produced in Acre between 1202 and 1228.

According to Salvadó, who follows Kohler with regard to this matter, this manuscript, which includes among liturgical materials a short chronicle [3:34], was produced as a souvenir or historical record of the Holy Sepulchre rite,[25] suggesting that clergymen active in Acre were concerned with preserving the memory of the lost First Kingdom of Jerusalem.[26]

Resident clergymen also devoted considerable efforts to the writing of reports to the West regarding the conditions prevailing in Outremer. For example, following a request by Pope Innocent III, Raoul de Mérencourt, Patriarch of Jerusalem (1215–24), wrote, together with the masters of the Hospitaller and Templar orders, the *Relatio tripartita* [1:2], which focuses on the current political situation in the Ayyubid empire;[27] Gerold of Lausanne, Patriarch of Jerusalem (1225–39), wrote a report on Frederick II's treaty with the Muslims, which includes some of its paragraphs in French along with comments in Latin;[28] and Thomas Agni wrote to the leaders of the West concerning the deeds of the Mongols.[29] Also note in this context that attempts by Acre's clergy to gain knowledge concerning Oriental Christianity were often made with the intention of transmitting the newly acquired information to colleagues in the West. This is made clear by Jacques de Vitry's letter from Acre [1:3] and, to a lesser extent, also by Benoit d'Alignan's *Tractatus super erroribus quos citra et ultra mare invenimus* [2:24].[30] Working in a completely different direction but also aiming to describe the Latin East to Western readers, Freidank, who was probably a churchman, wrote a section of his didactic poem, known as *Bescheidenheit*, in the city [1:5].[31]

---

[25] Salvadó, 'The Liturgy', pp. 53–4. For Kohler's study of this manuscript, see C. Kohler, 'Un Rituel et un Bréviaire du Saint-Sépulcre de Jérusalem (XIIe–XIIIe siècle)', *Revue de l'Orient Latin* 9 (1900–1), pp. 383–500. The Chronicle is edited here on pp. 399–401. For an opposing view, according to which this volume was meant to be used in actual liturgical practice, see C. Dondi, *The Liturgy of the Canons Regular of the Holy Sepulchre of Jerusalem: A Study and a Catalogue of the Manuscript Sources*, Bibliotheca Victorina XVI (Turnhout, 2004), p. 78.

[26] It is interesting to note that another liturgical manuscript from the kingdom also includes a chronicle. Dondi, *The Liturgy*, pp. 181–8.

[27] J. Richard, 'Pouvoir royal et patriarcat au temps de la Cinquième Croisade, à propos du rapport du patriarche Raoul', *Crusades* 2 (2003), pp. 111–12.

[28] G. H. Pertz and K. Rodenberg (eds.), *Epistolae saeculi XIII e regestis Pontificum Romanorum*, MGH 1 (Berlin, 1883), pp. 296–8. Another letter by Gerold appears in the same volume on pp. 299–304.

[29] Ludwig Weiland (ed.), *Emonis et Mekonis Werumensium Chronica*, MGH SS t. 23 (Hanover, 1874), pp. 547–9.

[30] While Benoit was interested in circulating his work both in Outremer and in the West, its specific sections on Oriental Christianity would not have been very useful for people like Thomas Agni. J. Rubin., 'Benoit d'Alignan and Thomas Agni: Two Western Intellectuals and the Study of Oriental Christianity in the 13th-Century Kingdom of Jerusalem', *Viator* 44.1 (Spring 2013), pp. 189–99.

[31] Not much is known about Freidank, but evidence implies that he was a churchman. G. Eifler, 'Freidank', *Lexikon des Mittelalters* (München, 1989), vol. IV, pp. 894–5.

Beyond the composition of works, members of the clergy had a significant role in the initiation of intellectual undertakings in the city. John of Ancona was led to write his canonistic *summa* by William II of Agen, Patriarch of Jerusalem (1262–70), and by William of Lautario, an archdeacon:[32]

I attended to the composition of such a compilation according to the suggestion of the most holy father lord G., patriarch of Jerusalem and legate of the apostolic see, and according to the wise advice of the wise and prudent man, master William of Lautario, a man of the most acute nature, archdeacon of Acre, both of whom mainly led me to the composition of this work.

Furthermore, it was a comment by Henry of Marburg which encouraged Jean de Joinville to write a *Credo* [1:8] in Acre:[33]

Brother Henry the German, who was a very great cleric, said that no one could be saved if he does not know his *Credo*. And I, in order to arouse the people to believe that which they could not reject, first set out to compose this work in Acre.

Additionally, Theobald Visconti's curiosity resulted in the composition of William of Tripoli's *Notitia* [1:17]:[34]

As I understood that the devotion of your faith desires to know what the Saracens and their book think about Christian faith, I have applied myself, in the Lord, to be of service and present the desired material to your pious devotion.

Members of the Mendicant Orders

That members of the mendicant orders played a central role in the city's intellectual arena is hardly surprising given the very nature of these institutions.[35] Both the Dominicans and the Franciscans viewed learning

---

[32] '...compilationem huiusmodi ... facere procuravi secundum mandatum sanctissimi patris domini G. patriarche Ierusalemitani apostolice sedis legati et iuxta discretam suggestionem discreti et prudentis viri magistri Guillelmi de Lautario viri accutissimi ingenii archidiaconi Acconensis, qui ad texendum hoc opus me principiliter induxerunt.' MS Brugge, Stadtbibliotheek 377, fol. 342v; Bertram, 'Johannes de Ancona', p. 61.

[33] 'Freres Henris li Tyois, qui mout fu grans clers, dist que nus ne pooit estre saus se il ne savoit son Credo. Et je por esmouvoir les gens à croire ce de quoi il ne se pooient soffrir, fis-je premiers faire cest euvre en Acre.' Jean, Sire de Joinville, *Histoire de Saint Louis, Credo et Lettre à Louis X*, ed. and trans. N. de Wailly (Paris, 1874), p. 418, par. 777. Regarding Henry the German, see L. J. Friedman, *Text and Iconography for Joinville's Credo* (Cambridge, MA, 1958), p. 55.

[34] 'Quoniam intellexi fidei vestre devotionem cupere scire, quid gens Sarracenorum et liber eorum de fide sentiat christiana, vestre pie devotioni studui in Domino deservire et offerre cupita.' *Notitia*, p. 194.

[35] Obviously, the distinction between members of the clergy and members of the mendicant orders is not clear-cut. Several of the patriarchs of Jerusalem, for example, were mendicants. In order to face this difficulty, I discuss in this subsection only members of the orders who did not hold offices outside the order. Members who did hold such offices are included in the discussion of the clergy.

as a significant part of their activities and included highly learned members among their ranks. Additionally, both organizations viewed communication with non-Catholic groups and the accumulation of knowledge concerning them as central aspects of their activity. Furthermore, as both communities formed international networks, whatever knowledge they developed in Acre could have easily made its way to Western centres of knowledge and vice versa.

Both organizations ran convents in Acre between the 1220s and 1291.[36] These institutions would have been characterized by an element of continuity, enabling them to both preserve and develop knowledge. Additionally – and this is a point to which we return in greater detail – there is considerable evidence for the central role of the mendicants in the foundation of learning institutions in the city.[37] We are also aware of particularly learned friars who were active in Acre. To give just several examples, François Balme has shown that the Dominican Robertus Normannus, who was prior of the Acre convent in 1277, as well as his sub-prior, Berengarius Provincialis, were both either masters of theology or general preachers.[38] More surprising perhaps is that the Franciscan Elias of Cortona was known for his wide knowledge not only in Roman law but also in the natural sciences.[39] Indeed, although doubts have been raised about the authenticity of references to him in various texts on alchemy, there is strong evidence that he was very much engaged in this field, but unfortunately it remains unclear whether he devoted time to this branch of knowledge while serving in Outremer.[40] The Dominican Yves the Breton was known for his expertise in Arabic (and probably in additional languages as well) and was also responsible for introducing into the city pieces of information with regard to Islam. It is noteworthy that he was a prominent figure within the order, in all likelihood serving as the provincial prior of the Holy Land and, at least in one case, examining the details of a miracle taking place in Tripoli and putting them into writing.[41]

[36] The Dominican house was established in 1228–9; the Franciscan in 1217–21. For more about these institutions, see Chapter 2.

[37] See Chapter 2.

[38] F. Balme, 'La Province dominicaine de Terre-Sainte, de janvier 1277 à octobre 1280', *Revue de l'Orient Latin* 1 (1893), p. 530, n. 4.

[39] B. Roest, *A History of Franciscan Education* (Leiden, 2000), p. 3.

[40] This is most strongly confirmed by references to him in a text that should be attributed to Michael Scot. S.H. Thomson, 'The Texts of Michael Scot's *Ars Alchemie*', *Osiris* 5 (1938), pp. 523–59, and, in particular, pp. 557–8.

[41] For evidence that it was the same Yves who was later Provincial of the Dominicans in the Holy Land, see K. Ciggaar, 'An Illuminated Aristotelian Manuscript from the Crusader States. Some Preliminary Remarks', *Eastern Christian Art* 3 (2006), pp. 25–36; Gerardus de Fracheto, *Vitae*

Some of the most important works composed in the city were authored by members of the mendicant orders. Such are William of Tripoli's *Notitia de Machometo* and William of Rubruck's *Itinerarium* [2:23]. The Franciscan Fidenzio of Padua clearly collected in Acre information he later included in his text [3:44], while the Dominican David of Ashby possibly wrote his treatise about the Mongols there.[42] Another mendicant, the Franciscan Peter of Boreth, wrote in Acre texts which did not reach us:[43]

A certain brother, Peter of Boreth, of the Franciscan order, composed, while in Acre, some letters to the bishop of Bazas, where he says that Antichrist will be [coming] in March in ten years. The Holy Scriptures do not support this.

Another important Dominican author who in all likelihood contributed to intellectual life in the city is Burchard of Mount Sion, author of the *Descriptio terrae sanctae*, one of the most popular medieval descriptions of the Holy Land. Until recently, very little was known about the biography of this important author, mainly because his text, as edited by Laurent, provides hardly any information concerning him. Lately, work on manuscripts which Laurent did not utilize revealed much that was previously unknown about him. Most significant for the present discussion is evidence that Burchard's connection to the Holy Land, and specifically to Acre, was stronger than that of a pilgrim. Inter alia, he was personally acquainted with both the Latin and Greek patriarchs of Jerusalem, he uses terms typical of Frankish Outremer and he passed through Acre several times.[44] According to one manuscript he was actually a member of the Holy Land province of the Dominican order for a period of ten years:[45]

Truly, I brother Burchard of the Order of Preachers . . . wanting to satisfy their wish as far as I can, have both recorded and studiously described that land through which I have frequently passed on foot and which I have diligently

fratrum ordinis praedicatorum, ed. B. M. Reichert (Leuven, 1896), pp. 88–92. For more about Yves, see later in this chapter, as well as in Chapter 5.

[42] For more about William of Rubruck and David of Ashby, see the discussion of 'Envoys' later in this chapter.

[43] 'Quidam frater Petrus de Boreth de ordine Minorum, exsistens apud Acram, scripsit quasdam litteras episcopo Basacensi, ubi dicit, quod Antichristus erit in Martio decem annorum. Cui non consentiunt scripture.' Scheffer–Boichorst, *Chronica Albrici*, p. 920.

[44] J. Rubin, 'Burchard of Mount Sion's *Descriptio Terrae Sanctae*: A Newly Discovered Extended Version', *Crusades* 13 (2014), pp. 179, 181; J. Rubin, 'A Missing Link in European Travel Literature: Burchard of Mount Sion's Description of Egypt', *Mediterranea: International Journal on the Transfer of Knowledge* 3 (2018), pp. 55–90.

[45] 'Verum ego, frater Burcardus ordinis fratrum predicatorum . . . cupiens eorum desiderio satisfacere quantum possum, ipsam terram, quam pedibus meis pluries pertransivi et per x annos, quibus frater provincie illius fui, quantum potui consideravi diligenter, et notavi et studiose descripsi.' MS Zwickau, Ratsschulbibliothek, 1.12.5, fol. 113v.

inspected in so far as I have been able during the ten years in which I was a brother of that province.

The colophon of another manuscript of the *Descriptio* mentions Burchard as a Dominican and notes that he spent a long time in the Holy Land.[46] Whether or not these notes are taken to be authentic, it does seem likely that Burchard spent considerable periods of time in Acre, and if this was indeed the case, one may safely assume that he became involved in the city's intellectual arena, as he was not only a man of extremely wide horizons of knowledge and interest but also a person constantly seeking information from people he encountered along his journeys.[47]

The Nobility

Acre's nobility was also a major participant in the city's intellectual life. In particular, among its ranks were consumers of 'intellectual products', or literary works. As Jacoby argued, courtly literature played a role in preserving the nobility's unique culture and ethos as it reflected its values and way of life. Furthermore, the combination of the regular reading of such works with the constant contacts maintained between Outremer's nobility and that of the West contributed to the enduring cohesion of this class.[48] Three genres in particular seem to have been popular among Acre's nobility. Firstly, history probably made popular reading material in the city, as is attested by the number of extant manuscripts of both the French versions of William of Tyre's *Chronicon* and the *Histoire universelle*.[49] While it is hard to know who purchased them, members of the nobility must have bought at least some of them. Secondly, various French romances were also popular in the city. Indeed, such literature

---

[46] Florence, Biblioteca Medicea Laurenziana, MS Plut. 76.56, fol. 101v. For the Zwickau and Florence manuscripts, see E. Rotter, 'Windrose statt Landkarte. Die geografische Systematisierung des Heiligen Landes und ihre Visualisierung durch Burchardus de Monte Sion um 1285', *Deutsches Archiv für Erforschung des Mittelalters* 69 (2013), pp. 45–106; I. Baumgärtner, 'Burchard of Mount Sion and the Holy Land', *Peregrinations: Journal of Medieval Art and Architecture* 4.1 (Spring, 2013), pp. 5–41.

[47] His wide fields of interest are reflected, for example, in his description of the volcanic sites he explored on his way from Sicily to Italy, and in his portrayal of Rome. Rubin, 'Burchard', pp. 185–8. To this one may add that in the 1475 Lübeck edition Burchard describes himself as 'professorum sacre pagine minimus'. J. C. M. Laurent (ed.), *Peregrinatores medii aevi quatuor* (Leipzig, 1864), pp. 4, 11. For his communication with non-Latins, see, for example, the prologue to the *Descriptio*. Laurent, *Peregrinatores*, p. 20.

[48] Jacoby, 'Knightly Values', pp. 159–60, 164, 175 *et passim*.

[49] For a discussion of the various manuscripts attributed to Acre, see Folda, *Crusader Manuscript*, *passim* and, in particular, the catalogue, pp. 171–216; Buchthal, *Miniature Painting*, pp. 69–93. Criticism has been raised against some of these attributions. See, for example, Jacoby, 'Society', pp. 118–20.

was used as a basis for plays performed in Acre,[50] and Hospitaller regulations written there [1:18] mention brothers reading *romans* within the order's infirmary and others who owned such books at the time of their death.[51] Thirdly, chansons, mainly of political or satirical nature, were probably also popular among the city's nobles, as can be seen from the enthusiastic reception of one such work among the local audience.[52] The sojourn of men such as Freidank and Thibaut of Champagne in the city probably encouraged this cultural trend.[53]

The evidence for noble patronage of literary projects in Acre is rather scant. The only noble who certainly ordered the preparation of a text is William of Santo Stefano, a Hospitaller knight, probably of Italian origin, who around 1300 served as the order's commander of Cyprus.[54] William asked John of Antioch to prepare for him a translation of two classic Latin works on rhetoric: Cicero's *De inventione* and the anonymous *Rhetorica ad Herennium* [1:19]. William also initiated the collection and translation from Latin into French of certain documents found in the order's archive [2:30].[55] Another project undertaken under noble patronage almost certainly in Acre is the Anglo-Norman translation of Vegetius' *De re militari* [2:29], probably produced at the request of Eleanor of Castile as a present for her husband, Prince Edward. Furthermore, several hypotheses have been raised concerning additional cases of noble patronage. Plausibly, a Templar knight was the patron of Paris, Bibliothèque nationale de France, MS nouv. acq. fr. 1404, which includes a French translation of major sections of the Bible with original glosses,[56] and Paris,

[50] Jacoby, 'Knightly Values', p. 168.
[51] Minervini, 'Produzione', p. 94; *Cartulaire* 3039, articles 39, 42. Although the word *romans*, mentioned in these regulations, probably refers to fictional works, it can also stand for historic books, as in Eudes' inventory: A.-M. Chazaud, 'Inventaire et comptes de la succession d'Eudes, comte de Nevers (Acre, 1266)', *Mémoires de la société des antiquaires de France*, sér. 4, 2 (1871), p. 188 [1:11].
[52] Jacoby, 'La littérature française', pp. 625–6; Filippo da Novara, *Guerra di Federico II in Oriente*, ed. S. Melani (Naples, 1994), p. 116, par. 48. The fact that a *chançoner* was found in Eudes' property strengthens this argument. See Chazaud, 'Inventaire', p. 188.
[53] Regarding Freidank, see earlier in this chapter and Prawer, *The Latin Kingdom of Jerusalem*, p. 527. It is noteworthy in this context that Thibaut reached Acre accompanied by two other poets. S. Painter, 'The Crusade of Theobald of Champagne and Richard of Cornwall, 1239–1241', in K. M. Setton (ed.), *A History of the Crusades*, 6 vols. (Philadelphia, PA, 1955–89), vol. II, p. 474.
[54] A. Luttrell, 'The Hospitallers' Early Written Records', in J. France and W. G. Zajac (eds.), *The Crusades and Their Sources. Essays Presented to Bernard Hamilton* (Aldershot, 1998), p. 139.
[55] Luttrell, 'The Hospitallers', pp. 139–41; K. Klement, 'Alcune osservazioni sul Vat. Lat. 4852', *Studi Melitensi* 3 (1995), pp. 229–43.
[56] Folda, *Crusader Manuscript*, pp. 60, 66, 75–6. Nobel thinks that this suggestion is reasonable. P. Nobel (ed.), *La Bible d'Acre: Genèse et Exode* (Besançon, 2006), pp. xiv–xv. Nobel dated the *Bible d'Acre* to between 1170 and the early 1250s (p. xxxvi). Thus, while one can be certain that the glosses circulated in Acre, it is uncertain whether they were composed there. Interestingly, just like Nahmanides' *addenda* [1:13], these glosses include much geographical information.

Bibliothèque nationale de France, MS fr. 20125, which includes a unique version of the *Histoire universelle,* was produced under the patronage of Alice, countess of Blois.[57]

Several members of the Frankish nobility were more than mere readers or patrons of literary works, and themselves composed texts, either during their stays in Acre or later on. The most well known of these is, of course, Jean de Joinville, who wrote a *Credo* in the city, and who later authored the *Vie de Saint Louis,* which, to a considerable degree, is based on his experiences in the Levant in general and in Acre in particular.[58] Additionally, there is evidence for the engagement of nobles active in Acre in the composition of poetry. At least one member of the nobility wrote a poem during his stay in the city: this is Thibaut of Champagne who probably wrote a chanson in Acre in 1239 or 1240 [3:36].[59] Another poem [2:22], almost certainly composed in Acre, should perhaps also be attributed to a nobleman, and a poem authored by an anonymous Templar shortly following the fall of Arsur was possibly written in the city, and, in any case, within a very similar cultural context.[60] Further evidence for this cultural phenomenon is provided by the so-called Templar of Tyre, who inserted a poem he wrote into the well-known chronicle he composed following Acre's fall.[61] Although this poem, which discusses the fall of Acre, cannot, obviously, be considered part of the city's cultural products, the fact that a minor noble who had spent a long time there composed such a text is suggestive regarding the local atmosphere.

At least one Hospitaller knight was engaged, while in Acre, in what may be referred to as historical research. William of Santo Stefano, whose interest in history reached its apogee whilst he served in Cyprus,[62] was already operating within this field during his period in Acre. As was already mentioned, William had certain documents in the Hospital's archive copied and translated into French, and a compilation of texts

---

[57] Folda, *Crusader Manuscript,* pp. 95–102; A. Derbes and M. Sandona, 'Amazons and Crusaders: The *Histoire Universelle* in Flanders and the Holy Land', in D. H. Weiss and L. Mahoney (eds.), *France and the Holy Land* (Baltimore, MD, 2004), pp. 214–15.

[58] Joinville, *Vie.*

[59] Jacoby, 'Knightly Values', p. 164; J. Bédier and P. Aubry (eds.), *Les Chansons de Croisade* (Paris, 1909, reprinted New York, 1971), pp. 199–206.

[60] This work begins with the words 'Ir'e dolors s'es dins mon cor asseza'. The text is found, with an analysis, in A. de Bastard, 'La colère et la douleur d'un templier en Terre Sainte', *Revue des langues romanes* 81 (1974), pp. 356–7. Prawer suggested that the poem was composed in Acre. Prawer, *Histoire,* vol. II, p. 469.

[61] *Cronaca,* pp. 238–52. More about this author in what follows.

[62] During this period, following Acre's fall, William composed an account of the foundation of the Hospital in which he demonstrated a genuine historical and critical sensibility. J. Riley-Smith, *The Knights of St. John in Jerusalem and Cyprus c. 1050–1310* (London, 1967), pp. 33, 272–3.

relating to the order was prepared for him, almost certainly in the city, between 1278 and 1283.[63] Perhaps he was not the only nobleman in Acre to have engaged in such activities: it has been suggested that some of the continuations of William of Tyre's *Chronicon* [3:37] were authored by members of the city's nobility.[64]

To these should be added the nobility's involvement in the composition of reports to the West concerning the circumstances in Outremer. We have already seen that members of Acre's nobility participated, alongside prominent clergymen, in the preparation of such texts. Here it should be added that in some cases members of the nobility were the sole authors of such reports.[65] To this category one can perhaps add an account of a different sort, composed by Marsilio Zorzi, Venetian *bailo* in Acre, focusing on Venetian assets in the Kingdom of Jerusalem [1:7].[66]

Burgesses

The burgesses of Outremer were a relatively strong group which included some very rich members, especially among the Italians.[67] Acre's cultural atmosphere clearly reflected this phenomenon, and burgesses residing in the city played a significant role in several occupational groups studied later. At the same time, there is very little evidence for their involvement in other aspects of intellectual activity in Acre. And yet, the available source material does provide clues for several additional fields which seem to have attracted the attention of members of this group. As implied by the reference in the *Livre des assises de la cour des bourgeois* [2:21] to the *Livre dou conquest dou reaume de Jerusalem*, history was probably a field in which the city's burgesses were interested.[68] Entertainment seems to have attracted some young burgesses: in the *Livre des assises de la cour des bourgeois* one reads of a son or a daughter who 'despite his father or mother, practices with the jongleurs and becomes a jongleur'.[69] Additionally, merchants were obviously interested

---

[63] Luttrell, 'The Hospitallers', pp. 139–40; Klement, 'Alcune osservazioni', pp. 229–43.

[64] Jacoby suggests that the French chronicles from the Eastern Mediterranean were mostly, if not all, written by nobles. Jacoby, 'La littérature', pp. 644–5.

[65] See, for example, *RRH* 752, 787, 868, 1125.

[66] O. Berggötz (ed.), *Der Bericht des Marsilio Zorzi. Codex Querini-Stampalia IV3* (1064), Kieler Werkstücke, Reihe C: Beiträge zur europäischen Geschichte des frühen und hohen Mittelalters 2 (Frankfurt a/M, 1990). See also D. Jacoby, 'The Venetian Privileges in the Latin Kingdom of Jerusalem: Twelfth and Thirteenth-Century Interpretation and Implementation', in B. Z. Kedar, J. Riley-Smith and R. Hiestand (eds.), *Montjoie: Studies in Crusade History in Honour of Hans Eberhard Mayer* (Aldershot, 1997), pp. 155, 166–7.

[67] Jacoby, 'Knightly Values', p. 176.   [68] *RHC, Lois*, vol. II, p. 195.

[69] *RHC, Lois*, vol. II, p. 170. 'Maugré son pere ou de sa mere, use o jugleors et devient juglier.' It is noteworthy that in the *Lo Codi*, a text which exerted considerable influence on the *Livre*, the

in knowledge that would have facilitated their commercial activity, including information about sailing routes. This led them to use and, occasionally, even compile written texts. Thus, an anonymous Venetian merchant, probably residing in Acre, composed a manual of commercial practice to which was attached a nautical guide [2:41]. It is noteworthy that while working on this text the merchant not only collected oral information from tradesmen, seamen and notaries but also used written sources.[70] That merchants would have contributed to the accumulation of knowledge in Acre is also implied by evidence provided by none other than Marco Polo: he recounts how in 1269 his father and uncle arrived in the city and presented a message from the great khan to Patriarch William II of Agen.[71] It is hard to imagine that the two did not share with him, as well as with others in the city, some of the extraordinary knowledge they accumulated during their travels.

Having discussed the roles of four major social groups in the intellectual activities in Acre, it would now be worthwhile to examine several occupational groups which did not neatly fit into the usual categorization of medieval society, but which were characterized by particular fields of activity, knowledge and interest.

Lawyers and Jurists

As is widely known, law was an extremely popular subject among the Frankish inhabitants of Outremer.[72] Acre was no exception, and the number of persons from different social strata who lived in the city, or, at least, spent considerable periods of time in it, and who were interested and knowledgeable in law is considerable.

Some members of the clergy were both curious and informed about canon and civil law.[73] As was already mentioned, Patriarch Albert of Vercelli possessed considerable knowledge in jurisprudence.[74] Juridical knowledge was probably also found in the lower ranks of Acre's ecclesiastical hierarchy. Master Robert of Santonge, who was dean of Acre and

---

reference is to magicians rather than to jongleurs. H. Fitting (ed.), *Lo Codi in der lateinischen Übersetzung des Ricardus Pisanus* (Halle, 1906), 3.17, p. 49. The relation between the two texts is discussed in Chapter 4.

[70] D. Jacoby, 'A Venetian Manual of Commercial Practice from Crusader Acre', in G. Airaldi and B. Z. Kedar (eds.), *I comuni italiani nel regno crociato di Gerusalemme*, Collana storica di Fonti e Studi 48 (Genoa, 1986), pp. 418–23.

[71] Marco Polo, *Le devisement du monde*, vol. I, pp. 124–5. Notably, both the identity of the churchman with whom the Polos communicated, and the date of their arrival in the city, as provided by the text, are wrong. See the editor's note on page 181 of the same volume.

[72] An attempt to explore Acre's juridical arena is made in Chapter 4. The purpose of this section is only to examine the role members of different social groups played in that arena.

[73] Brundage, 'Latin Jurists', pp. 21–3.   [74] Brundage, 'Latin Jurists', p. 25.

official (*officialis*) of the papal legate, most probably had some formal legal credentials,[75] and this was likely also the case with Nicholas of Palermo, official of the patriarch of Jerusalem. Furthermore, cathedral chapters in the East seem to have sometimes functioned as virtual training academies for ecclesiastical administrators, so that at least some juridical knowledge was probably transferred in them.[76] The interest of members of the clergy in the development and circulation of jurisprudence can also be seen in the dedication by John of Ancona, which reveals that he composed his work on canon law following requests from two of the city's clergymen.

Outremer's nobility is specifically well known for its interest in jurisprudence. While the most prominent nobles associated with jurisprudence, such as John of Ibelin and Philip of Novara,[77] were not permanent residents of the city, existing evidence sheds light on city nobles strongly interested and engaged in legal matters. Nicholas Antiaume, a member of an important burgess family of Acre, who seems to have been knighted at some stage of his life, was highly respected for his legal expertise. In fact, he was described by Philip of Novara as a great pleader inside and outside court,[78] and by the author of the *Abregé du livre des assises* as very well acquainted with the kingdom's customs.[79] Furthermore, he was consulted by the great jurist John of Ibelin on behalf of the *bailli* of the kingdom of Armenia.[80] Stephan of Savegny and James Vidal are two additional nobles who were active in Acre and were well known for their legal expertise. James Vidal is mentioned in several documents as a knight and a legal expert, and was sent as an envoy to Lyon in 1273; Stephan of Savegny is mentioned as a syndic and agent of the Jerusalem seigniory.[81] A hitherto unutilized piece of evidence with regard to the two appears in John of Ancona's feudal *summa* [2:25]. Discussing kinds of feudal service, he writes:[82]

[75] Brundage, 'Latin Jurists', p. 22.
[76] Brundage, 'Latin Jurists', p. 30; Hamilton, *The Latin Church*, pp. 115–16.
[77] Regarding John of Ibelin, see P. W. Edbury, *John of Ibelin and the Kingdom of Jerusalem* (Woodbridge, 1997); for Philip of Novara, see Philip of Novara, *Le Livre de Forme de Plait*, ed. and trans. P. W. Edbury (Nicosia, 2009), pp. 14–19.
[78] Philip of Novara, *Le Livre*, p. 122.   [79] *RHC, Lois*, vol. II, p. 339.
[80] D. Pringle, 'Notes on Some Inscriptions from Crusader Acre', in I. Shagrir, R. Ellenblum and J. Riley-Smith (eds.), *In Laudem Hierosolymitani: Studies in Crusades and Medieval Culture in Honour of Benjamin Z. Kedar* (Aldershot, 2007), pp. 195–7.
[81] Concerning James, see *RRH* 1234, 1280, 1281, 1285, 1322, 1373, 1297a; *Cronaca*, p. 86; concerning Stephan, see *RRH* 1259. Regarding the status of the two, see also Riley-Smith, *Feudal Nobility*, p. 37.
[82] '...aut consistit [servitium] in faciendo puta ut consulat domino vel defe[n]dat iura sua quia est homo sapiens pre ceteris in consuetudinibus huius regni ut dominus Stephanus de Savegni vel dominus Iacobus Vitalis.' Nürnberg, Stadtbibliothek, MS Cent. II 90, fol. 263v.

[O]r the service consists of doing, for example, that the vassal would provide counsel to his lord or would defend his rights, because he is more knowledgeable than others in the customs of this kingdom, as are lord Stephan of Savegny or lord James Vidal.

Beyond providing additional evidence regarding these two men, this phrase also reflects a feature of court practice in the Latin East: the usage whereby a vassal aided a litigating party with *conseil*. As can be inferred from John's words, the *conseil* was a service like any other, and vassals were obligated to perform it.[83] This usage must have contributed to the development of juridical expertise within this social group. Additionally, the involvement of the nobility in litigation probably had wider implications for the city's intellectual environment as it seems to have brought members of this group to appreciate the importance of rhetoric and logic.[84]

The burgesses of the city were also involved in the field of jurisprudence. Philip of Baisdoin, a burgess of Acre, is mentioned by Philip of Novara in his juridical treatise, along with noble Nicholas Antiaume, as a great pleader in and out of court, and in his historical work as a wise man.[85] Raymond of Conches, mentioned in two documents signed in Acre, was considered by Philip of Novara a wise man who very often pleaded in the High Court.[86] The writing of the *Livre des assises de la cour des bourgeois* in Acre by a burgess resident of the city, or perhaps by several such individuals, bears further testimony to the interest of members of this group in jurisprudence.[87] Prawer has gone so far as to argue that the anonymous author of this text was a member of what we would call today a professional class 'of law practitioners or people connected with the functioning of the Court of Burgesses in the city', and raised the possibility that he was a *iuratus*.[88] The *iurati*, not to be confused with the *avantparliers*, served as jurors in the *Cour des Bourgeois* and the *Cour de la fonde*. They were the regular attendants of the court, chosen, probably by the viscount, for their reputation and elevated status in the community, though it is doubtful whether they were of professional standing.[89]

As Brundage pointed out, besides jurists who lived in the city permanently or at least for several years, one should also take into account

---

[83] Riley-Smith, *Feudal Nobility*, pp. 132–3.   [84] Chapter 4, pp. 86–7.

[85] *RRH* 1110b; Riley-Smith, *Feudal Nobility*, p. 123; *RRH* 1120, 1110b; Philip of Novara, *Le Livre*, p. 122; Filippo, *Guerra*, p. 230.

[86] Philip of Novara, *Le livre*, p. 107.

[87] For the suggestion that this work was composed by more than one author, see M. Nader, *Burgesses and Burgess Law in the Latin Kingdoms of Jerusalem and Cyprus 1099–1325* (Aldershot, 2006), pp. 51–2, and Chapter 4, pp. 91–2.

[88] J. Prawer, *Crusader Institutions* (New York, NY, 1980), p. 366.

[89] Nader, *Burgesses*, pp. 145–6, 152.

numerous legally trained men who spent only short periods there. Some of them were involved in commercial transactions, while others probably travelled to the Holy Land on pilgrimage. Many may have combined these two purposes.[90] To the jurists Brundage described in this context should be added judge Bartholomeus Bonellus who was sent to Acre by Charles of Anjou, along with two comrades. Unfortunately, we do not know what he was sent for or how long he stayed in the Levant.[91]

That several juridical manuscripts were produced in Acre provides further evidence for the interest in jurisprudence in the city.[92] It is noteworthy in this context that lack of juridical texts was not one of the considerations John of Ancona took into account when he decided to write his canon law treatise. On the contrary, he wanted to save his readers from the trouble of running from one text to another:[93]

And thus it happened that either judge or litigants in doubt were forced to leave cases undecided, or had to run through various books and notes, wasting lords a long time.

In other words, John's statement seems to attest that legal literature was quite common in Acre. This provides further support to the claim that jurisprudence was a popular subject among the city's Frankish inhabitants.

Scribes and Notaries

The numerous transactions signed in Acre attest to the great number of scribes and notaries who were active in the city. While some of them belonged to the clergy,[94] many of them were in all likelihood burgesses. Although we have no positive evidence for their participation in the city's intellectual arena, studies about the involvement of scribes and notaries in cultural life elsewhere make it very likely that they did play a significant role in it. Under Frederick II and Manfred, members of the imperial chancery were found in circles of learning and teaching, and between 1250 and 1350 notaries in Italy played a role in what has been described as

---

[90] See a discussion of this phenomenon in Brundage, 'Latin Jurists', p. 27.

[91] H. E. Mayer (ed.), *Die Urkunden der Lateinischen Könige von Jerusalem*, 4 vols. (Hanover, 2010), vol. III, p. 1282. Mayer raises the possibility that he is to be identified with a Bartholomaeus Bonellus who was in Barletta in 1297.

[92] John of Ibelin, *Le Livre des Assises*, ed. P. W. Edbury (Leiden, 2003), pp. 5–8; P. W. Edbury and J. Folda, 'Two Thirteenth-Century Manuscripts of Legal Texts from Saint-Jean d'Acre', *Journal of the Warburg and Courtauld Institutes* 57 (1994), pp. 243–54.

[93] 'Sicque contingebat quod vel iudex vel litigantes in dubio constituti casus cogebantur relinquere indecisos vel oportebat eos per libros diversos et notas discurrere longo tempore dominorum.' Bertram, 'Johannes de Ancona', p. 60.

[94] Mayer argues that in general the royal chancellors and notaries were churchmen. Mayer, *Die Kanzlei*, vol. II, pp. 803, 825.

an 'explosion of translation activity'.[95] I see no reason why Acre's notaries would not have functioned similarly, especially given the strong Italian and imperial presence there, in particular among notaries: Benencasa of Pisa is mentioned as Emperor Friedrich II's judge and notary,[96] and Aliottus Uguiccionis is referred to as judge, public notary and judge by imperial authority.[97] That the city's notaries played a role in its intellectual arena is further supported by Brundage's suggestion that Outremer's thirteenth-century notaries had substantial academic credentials.[98]

Such circles had a potential to serve as arenas of intercultural exchanges because they often included non-Frankish scribes capable of writing and reading Arabic, such as 'Nasser, the Arabic scribe', or 'Sayt the scribe'.[99] Further evidence for the role of non-Frankish clerks in the Latin administration is provided by the text of the 1283 treaty between the Kingdom of Jerusalem and the Mamluks. The extant version of this text includes, on the one hand, the Hijri date, and, on the other, the Seleucid-era dating. This implies that on the Frankish side the clerks phrasing the document were either Greek Orthodox or perhaps local Jews, who would have also used this dating system.[100] The deep acquaintance of such men with Arabic culture and their common work with Franks had the potential to create convenient circumstances for intercultural exchanges.

Furthermore, these professional groups also served as channels of intercultural exchanges since they included among their ranks some Frankish scribes who would have been able to read Arabic and were occupied, as a part of their activity, with Muslim documents. Working on such texts, they gained knowledge which they, at least occasionally, shared with wider Latin audiences. This was the case with the so-called Templar of Tyre: probably a member of the lower nobility of Outremer, he worked following ca. 1285 in the chancery of the Templar order at

[95] M. H. Schaller, 'Kanzlei und Kultur zur Zeit Friedrichs II und Manfreds', in M. H. Schaller, *Stauferzeit: Ausgewählte Aufsätze* (Hanover, 1993), pp. 528–9; A. Cornish, *Vernacular Translation in Dante's Italy* (Cambridge, 2011), pp. 2, 26–7. Obviously, in Acre the part of translation in the work of notaries was even greater.

[96] *RRH* 1157–62; Brundage, 'Latin Jurists', p. 40.

[97] *RRH* 1209, 1212, 1232, 1237, 1259, 1280–2, 1291. Concerning Aliottus, see also Mayer, *Urkunden*, vol. III, pp. 1179–80, 1401, 1409, and Chapter 4.

[98] Brundage, 'Latin Jurists', p. 24.

[99] *RHC, Lois*, vol. II, p. 220; *Cartulaire* 3213; Mayer, *Urkunden*, vol. III, p. 1360. Most of these were probably Oriental Christians rather than Muslims. B. Z. Kedar, 'The Subjected Muslims of the Frankish Levant', in J. M. Powell (ed.), *Muslims under Latin Rule, 1100–1300* (Princeton, NJ, 1990), pp. 157–8.

[100] P. M. Holt, *Early Mamluk Diplomacy (1260–1290). Treaties of Baybars and Qalāwūn with Christian Rulers* (Leiden, 1995), p. 74; P. M. Holt, 'Qalāwūn's Treaty with Acre in 1283', *English Historical Review* 91 (October 1976), p. 805.

Acre, where he functioned as a secretary, scribe and translator from Arabic.[101] As a part of his work he translated a letter by al-Malik al-Ashraf to the Master of the Templar order. Composing his chronicle, he included the French translation of this letter's opening, drawing his readers' attention to the salutation the sultan used.[102] In other words, the 'Templar of Tyre' presented his Latin audience with a piece of information concerning Muslim culture which he gained during his work in the Templar chancery.[103]

Physicians

Although the physicians who worked in the city formed an important professional group, the information we possess about them is rather scant. Usually all we know is that on a specified day a certain doctor witnessed a transaction of some kind. This, for example, is the case regarding *Magistri* Adjutus, Lambert and William.[104] About another trio of physicians, Bertrandus, Petrus and Maurinus, we can say that, rather than mere visitors, they were inhabitants of Outremer, since they are described as *testes transmarini*.[105] On the other hand, the available information concerning a certain 'master Philip, a physician from Florence', who witnessed an act signed in Acre in 1286, implies that he only visited the East.[106] More detailed information is found only regarding one Latin physician who spent a considerable time in thirteenth-century Acre. This is Constantine, John of Brienne's doctor, who was, notably, also learned in law.[107]

As a group, the city's physicians were probably routinely involved in professional discussions. This would have been a necessary consequence of the attempt to regulate the practice of the medical profession in

---

[101] *Cronaca*, p. 1 *et passim*.

[102] *Cronaca*, p. 204: 'Or vous vyaus mostrer la tenour de la dite letre, que lou soudan manda au dit maistre dou Temple, si porés savoir en quel guyze est devizee le salus que le soudan manda en ses letres, quy devizeent ensy.' For the English translation, see P. F. Crawford (trans.), *The 'Templar of Tyre'* (Farnham, 2003), p. 104. Regarding the text, see also B. Z. Kedar, 'Religion in Catholic–Muslim Correspondence and Treaties', in A. D. Beihammer, M. G. Parani and C. D. Schabel (eds.), *Diplomatics in the Eastern Mediterranean 1000–1500* (Leiden, 2008), p. 418.

[103] While the chronicle, as it now survives, was produced following the fall of Acre, there is no reason to assume that similar occurrences did not take place in the city before 1291. It is also possible that the so-called Templar of Tyre shared this short text with residents of the city before 1291.

[104] Brundage, 'Latin Jurists', p. 36; *RRH* 775, 824.   [105] *RRH* 959.

[106] Mayer, *Urkunden*, vol. III, p. 1299. No other mention of him is made in this collection. He is also not referred to in the *RRH*.

[107] Mayer, *Die Kanzlei*, vol. II, p. 322; H. E. Mayer, 'Einwanderer in der Kanzlei und am Hof der Kreuzfahrerkönige von Jerusalem', in H. E. Mayer (ed.), *Die Kreuzfahrerstaaten als multikulturelle Gesellschaft* (München, 1997), p. 39.

Outremer. According to the *Livre des assises de la cour des bourgeois*, when a person claiming to be a physician arrived in the city and wished to practise in it, he had to face a committee consisting of the best of the land's doctors and a bishop.[108] In the discussion that ensued he was probably asked to present his knowledge, which often would have been different from that of local practitioners. Thus, mutual learning, on the one hand, and debates, on the other, must have resulted from this regulation.[109]

The hypothesis that medicine in Acre involved a high degree of intercultural fertilization is supported by considerable evidence – albeit not specifically connected to the thirteenth-century city – that in Outremer non-Frankish physicians often treated Franks.[110] There is no reason to think that this was not the case in the city. Indeed, the career of Saliba Barjacobi Vagii, a Jacobite who was born in Edessa, studied medicine in Tripoli in the 1240s, and was nominated Jacobite bishop of Acre, seems to provide evidence for this phenomenon.[111]

Some evidence points to the exchange of knowledge concerning *materia medica* in the city: a considerable degree of similarity has been noted between the foods and spices mentioned in the list of commodities included in the *Livre des assises la cour des bourgeois* and those which appear in several Arabic drug lists.[112] Furthermore, an Arabic–French pharmaceutical glossary by a knight named Willame li Pulains and a pharmacist, converted to Christianity, named Jacques Sarasin may have been composed in Acre.[113] There is also one piece of evidence, possibly from the city, which reveals learned – rather than oral-practical – contact between Latin and Muslim medical traditions: an Arabic medical treatise titled *al-kutub al-mi'a fī al-ṣināa al-ṭibbiya* was probably studied and glossed in thirteenth-century Acre.[114]

Doctors, and especially those who received university training, could have contributed to intellectual life in Acre in fields other than

---

[108] *RHC, Lois,* vol. II, p. 169. 'Encement nul miege estranger, ce est qui veigne d'Outremer ou de Païnime, ne det meger d'orine nuluy jusques à ce que il soit esprovés par autres mieges, les meillors de la terre, en la presence dou vesque de la terre, devant qui se det estre fait.' For an English translation, see S. Edgington, 'Medicine and Surgery in the Livre des Assises de la Cour des Bourgeois de Jérusalem', *Al-Masāq* 17.1 (2005), p. 90.

[109] P. D. Mitchell, *Medicine in the Crusades* (Cambridge, 2004), p. 216.

[110] Edgington, 'Medicine and Surgery', p. 91; Mitchell, *Medicine,* pp. 31–40; F. Micheau, 'Médecins orientaux au service des princes latins', in I. Draelants, A. Tihon and B. van den Abeele (eds.), *Occident et Proche Orient: Contacts scientifiques au temps des Croisades* (2000), pp. 95–115.

[111] Mitchell writes that despite several religious appointments he was known to have continued to practise medicine. Mitchell, *Medicine,* p. 38.

[112] Edgington, 'Medicine and Surgery', p. 92.   [113] This document is studied in Chapter 3.

[114] E. Savage-Smith, 'New Evidence for the Frankish Study of Arabic Medical Texts in the Crusader Period', *Crusades* 5 (2006), pp. 99–112.

medicine.[115] A hint to that is provided by the involvement of doctors in matters relating to the composition of documents: a certain Magister Bertrandus is mentioned in a document signed at Acre in 1221 as a *notarius* as well as a *physicus*,[116] and Mayer raised the possibility that Constantine, who possessed considerable legal knowledge, was employed by King John not only as a physician but also in the chancery.[117]

Envoys

Another occupational group which played an important role in Acre's intellectual arena is that of envoys. These were men who, often as a result of their expertise in Eastern languages, engaged in contacts with prominent figures in foreign courts. This meant that they were able to serve as a channel through which information from alien societies could reach Acre. And in fact, there is evidence that at least some of them shared knowledge they accumulated during their missions with residents of the city.

Starting with emissaries sent from Acre to Muslim courts, Jean de Joinville refers to Yves the Breton, a Dominican friar who served as Louis IX's envoy and translator, and to John of Valenciennes, sent by Louis as an envoy to Egypt.[118] Further evidence with regard to Frankish envoys is found in an Arabic source, where we read about the activities of a certain Simon, scribe and envoy of the Hospitaller order, who in 1232 wrote down a treaty between the ruler of Aleppo and the Franks.[119] Additionally, Latin ambassadors to the Mamluk court are mentioned in a Muslim account of the 1283 negotiations.[120] Philip Mainbeuf, described by the Templar of Tyre as a knight from Acre who knew Arabic very well, also belongs here. He was sent as an envoy to Al-Malik al-Ashraf a few months before the fall of Acre. With him was a Templar knight from Cyprus named Barthelemé Pizan, as well as a Hospitaller whose name is not recorded and a scribe by the name of Jorge.[121]

---

[115] Mitchell, *Medicine*, p. 11.   [116] Mitchell, *Medicine*, p. 18.

[117] Mayer, *Die Kanzlei*, vol. I, pp. 324–5; Mayer, 'Einwanderer', p. 39.

[118] Regarding Yves, see Joinville, *Vie*, p. 218, pars. 444–5; pp. 224–8, pars. 456–63. Concerning John, see Joinville, *Vie*, pp. 228–30, pars. 464–7.

[119] That Simon was not an Oriental Christian but rather of Western descent can be seen by the Arabic spelling of his name (سيمون), which is different from that traditionally used by Arabs (سمعان). That he was a Latin official is also argued in H. M. Attiya, 'Knowledge of Arabic in the Crusader States in the Twelfth and Thirteenth Centuries', *Journal of Medieval History* 25.3 (1999), p. 206. We have no evidence that he resided in Acre, but his activity is probably indicative concerning other scribes of the order who did. Muhammad Ibn Abd al-Aziz al-Hamawi, *Al-Tarikh al-Mansuri*, ed. Abu al-Eid Dudu (Damascus, 1981), pp. 203, 261 [Arabic]. Unfortunately, no mention of this man is made in either the *RRH* or Mayer's *Urkunden*.

[120] Holt, *Early Mamluk Diplomacy*, pp. 72–3.   [121] *Cronaca*, p. 204.

There is also significant evidence for the presence in Acre of Westerners who visited Mongol courts. The best known of these is, of course, William of Rubruck. Having spent several years in the Levant, this Franciscan, who originally hailed from Flanders, probably left Acre on his way east during March 1253. While he was not a formal envoy, he did carry with him a letter of some sort from Louis IX to Sartaq, a Mongol prince and later khan of the Golden Horde. He was also asked by the French king to compose a report concerning what he saw during his journey.[122] Having spent a considerable time in Mongol territories, and having accumulated a great deal of unique knowledge, he reached Cyprus in June 1255. While his intention was to travel to Paris in order to personally report to Louis concerning his voyage, he was ordered by the Franciscan provincial minister to remain in Acre and teach there, and, as was already noted, it was there that he composed his *Itinerarium*.[123] Thus, a person possessing extraordinary knowledge found himself teaching in Acre in the mid-1250s.

Another important figure in this group is the Dominican David of Ashby, sent in 1260 by the regime at Acre to the Mongols, heading a group of Dominican envoys.[124] He then spent a very considerable period of time in Mongol territory. While we do not know how long he remained in the East, by 1274–5 David was recognized as belonging to Thomas Agni's milieu, and referred to as his *capellanus* and *familiaris*.[125] This probably means that by 1274 he had returned to Acre and had already spent a considerable period of time there. Furthermore, it was possibly during his stay in the city that David wrote a text about the Mongols titled *Des fais des Tatars*.[126]

---

[122] Guglielmo di Rubruk, *Viaggio in Mongolia*, ed. and Italian trans. P. Chiesa (Milan, 2011), p. 6; P. Jackson and D. Morgan (trans.), *The Mission of Friar William of Rubruck* (London, 1990), pp. 40–4.

[123] Guglielmo, *Viaggio*, p. 316.

[124] P. Jackson, *The Mongols and the West* (Harlow, 2005), p. 117; J. Richard, 'Le début des relations entre la papauté et les Mongols de Perse', *Journal Asiatique* 237 (1949), pp. 295–6. Jackson raised the possibility that Ashby was sent in late 1263. P. Jackson, 'The Crisis in the Holy Land in 1260', *The English Historical Review* 95 (July 1980), p. 505, n. 1.

[125] For Agni's career, see Chapter 6.

[126] P. Jackson, 'Ashby, David of (fl. 1260–1275)', *Oxford Dictionary of National Biography* (Oxford, 2008), online edition www.oxforddnb.com/view/article/92435, accessed 1 Oct. 2014. Ashby's work, which reached modern times in only one Turin manuscript, was, unfortunately, lost in a 1904 fire. Thanks to Auguste Scheler, who examined the manuscript before the fire, the beginning of the text along with its *tituli, explicit* and one chapter survive. These appear in C. Brunel, 'David d'Ashby, auteur méconnu des *Faits des Tartares*', *Romania* 79 (1958), pp. 39–46. The hypothesis that Ashby wrote his work on the Mongols in Acre is supported by the fact that all Mongol campaigns David chose to focus, in his *Faits*, on the Mongols' entry into Egypt and on their capture of Aleppo.

In the context of this study, the most significant question regarding such men is whether they shared 'new knowledge' they had accumulated during their missions with Acre's residents. In other words, did they serve as a channel through which new knowledge concerning Muslims and Mongols, as well as Muslim and Mongol territories, entered Acre? There seems to be no reason to doubt this. As his *Itinerarium* shows, during his journey William of Rubruck accumulated much knowledge which was rare, and sometimes non-existent, among Westerners at the time. Thus, for example, his *Itinerarium* includes the first European account of Buddhism, as well as the earliest Western description of Qaraqorum.[127] Further indication for the significance and novelty of the knowledge William possessed is provided by Roger Bacon's appreciation of both the work and its author.[128] It seems highly improbable that such a person, who indeed taught in the city, would not have shared his valuable knowledge with pupils and other interested groups. Similarly, although it remains uncertain where David wrote his text or for whom it was intended, it is very improbable that he too did not talk about his experiences with people around him. His connections with Thomas Agni, one of the city's most prominent figures, as well as his Dominican identity, make it all the more likely that he did share his unique knowledge with interested individuals and groups in Acre. Jean de Joinville's work provides explicit evidence for the manner in which Yves the Breton brought into the city unique knowledge concerning Islam. These pieces of information, as reflected in Joinville's *Vie de Saint Louis*, are far from being completely precise and trustworthy, but they certainly do provide evidence that envoys contributed to the acquaintance of Acre's Latin inhabitants with alien cultures.[129]

JEWISH SOCIETY

While the intellectual potential of Acre's Frankish population has received different evaluations, it is clear that Acre's Jewish community made an important intellectual centre. The lamentation dedicated to the fall of Acre by Joseph, son of Tanhoum of Jerusalem, reflects contemporary appreciation for the late thirteenth-century city as a centre of learning:[130]

---

[127] Jackson and Morgan, *The Mission*, pp. 49–50.

[128] Roger Bacon, *Opus Majus*, ed. J. H. Bridges, 3 vols. (London, 1897-1900), vol. I, p. 305; A. Power, *Roger Bacon and the Defence of Christendom* (Cambridge, 2013), pp. 28, 62, 214–15 and elsewhere.

[129] See Chapter 5, pp. 129–32.

[130] הה על גאונים שזרועם חשפו בקרב תעודות-אל כאיש בינים/ הה על חכמים שדבר פימו ברב חכמה כצוף ינעם') ('למלקוחים'). For the Hebrew text, see H. Shirman (ed.), 'Elegies on Persecutions in Eretz Israel, Africa, Spain, Germany and France', in *Kovetz 'al Yad*, new series, book iii (13.1) (Jerusalem, 1940), pp. 62–4 [Hebrew]. For the English translation, see J. J. M. S. Yeshaya, 'A Hebrew Elegy

Woe to scholars who with uncovered arms in the battle of God's Law resemble champions/Woe to sages whose mouth's speech in their great wisdom pleases the palate like honey.

The development of such learned circles in Acre resulted from the combination of two factors: the increase in the number of Jews, originating in the intellectual elite of Western Europe, who immigrated to the Holy Land, on the one hand, and, on the other, the growing difficulties of settling in Jerusalem, which led these newcomers to make Acre their home instead.[131]

These trends also contributed to the heterogeneity of Acre's Jewish community, which is readily revealed as one examines the intellectually prominent Jews active in the city at the time. Many of these came from the French tradition. Rabbi Samson of Sens, a prominent Tosafist[132] who died in Acre in 1214, spent some time there, presumably with colleagues and students, and is likely to have composed *responsa* there [2:20].[133] Samson was buried near Mount Carmel, as was usually the case with Acre's Jewish inhabitants, along with his son, Jacob. That the family settled in the city is supported by evidence that R. Solomon, Samson's grandson, was still in Acre around 1275.[134] Samson was an important representative of the northern French tradition, and, as Prawer has

---

by Yosef ben Tanḥum Yerushalmi on the Death of His Father and the Mamluk Conquest of Acre', *Frankfurt Jewish Studies Bulletin* 39 (2014), p. 42.

[131] E. Reiner, *'Pilgrims and Pilgrimage to Eretz Yisrael 1099–1517'*, unpublished PhD thesis, Hebrew University of Jerusalem (1988), p. 50 [Hebrew with English abstract]; Prawer, *Jews*, pp. 75–6, 264; B. Z. Kedar, 'The Jews of Jerusalem, 1187–1267, and the Role of Nahmanides in the Establishment of their Community', in B. Z. Kedar (ed.), *Jerusalem in the Middle Ages: Selected Papers* (Jerusalem, 1979), pp. 122–36 [Hebrew]. Note, however, that this wave of immigration was not confined to an intellectual elite and included a significant popular element. A. Cuffel, 'Call and Response: European Jewish Emigration to Egypt and Palestine in the Middle Ages', *The Jewish Quarterly Review*, N.S., 90.1/2 (Jul.–Oct. 1999), pp. 61–101.

[132] Tosafists are the compilers of the Tosafot [=Addenda], collections of comments on the Talmud arranged according to the order of the Talmudic tractates. For a basic discussion of this genre, see I. Ta-Shema, 'Tosafot', *Encyclopedia Judaica* (Jerusalem, 1971), vol. XV, pp. 1278–83.

[133] I. Ta-Shema, 'A New Chronography on the 13th Century Tosaphists', *Shalem* 3 (1981), pp. 320, 323; Reiner, 'Pilgrims', p. 60; Prawer, *Jews*, pp. 79, 266–7; Abraham Maimuni, *Wars of the Lord*, ed. R. M. Margalioth (Jerusalem, year not stated) [Hebrew], pp. 53–4. With regard to Samson, see also E. Kanarfogel, 'The *'Aliyah* of "Three Hundred Rabbis" in 1211: Tosafist Attitudes toward Settling in the Land of Israel', *Jewish Quarterly Review* 76 (1986), p. 192. To the evidence concerning his activity in the East one should add his use of the word *barde*, which originated from Arabic and was typical of the French of Outremer. L. Minervini, 'Les emprunts arabes et grecs dans le lexique français d'Orient (XIIIᵉ–XIVᵉ siècle)', *Revue de Linguistique Romane* 76 (2012), p. 109.

[134] 'Totz'ot Eretz Israel', in S. Assaf, *Sources and Studies in Jewish History* (Jerusalem, 1946), p. 77 [Hebrew]; A. E. Aharonov, 'Seder Ha-yahas Bi-shene Nusahim', *Ets Hayyim* 27 (2017), pp. 349–87 [Hebrew]; Abraham Zacuto, *The Book of Lineage*, ed. Z. Filippowski (London, 1857, reprinted Jerusalem, 1963), p. 222 [Hebrew]; Reiner, 'Pilgrims', p. 86.

written, the presence of such a scholar in Acre probably had a considerable influence on intellectual activities there.[135]

Some of the figures who signed a Halakhic decision in the city in 1235 [1:6] were also renowned French scholars.[136] Joseph b. Gershon, who organized this group, was a scholar of French (or possibly other Western) origin who had earlier served as a *dayyan* (judge) in Alexandria.[137] According to Eliezer b. Jacob Habavli, he was a man of extraordinary knowledge.[138] Signed on the document is also R. Jacob, son of Samson of Sens.[139]

Other sources provide further evidence for the presence of French scholars in the city. Sometime before 1235 a group of great French scholars seems to have travelled to the Holy Land, and, in all likelihood, specifically to Acre.[140] More evidence in this regard has to do with Yehiel of Paris. Although the view that this important scholar came to Acre and founded a great yeshiva there has been rejected,[141] the tradition he represented did have its continuance in Acre, since he embarked on his journey to the East with at least some of his students and was certainly accompanied by two scholars – one of whom was his son – who did make it to the city.[142] To the bearers of the French tradition who visited Acre one should now add the anonymous author of a Halakhic notebook. This man, who spent some time in France and whose world of knowledge is that of France and Ashkenaz, offers in his work several clues that he spent some time, during the second half of the thirteenth century, in the Holy Land, and specifically in Acre.[143]

---

[135] Prawer, *Jews*, p. 267.

[136] A. H. Freimann and S. D. Goitein (eds.), *Abraham Maimuni's Responsa* (Jerusalem, 1937), pp. 25–6 [Hebrew]. For the dating of this text, see Prawer, *Jews*, pp. 270–2. Reiner dates the document to February 1234. Reiner, 'Pilgrims', p. 75. More recently, Friedman dated it to shortly after April 1235. M. A. Friedman, 'The Nagid, the Nasi and the French Rabbis: A Threat to Abraham Maimonides' Leadership', *Zion: A Quarterly for Research in Jewish History* 82.2–3 (2017), pp. 252–3 [Hebrew].

[137] Reiner, 'Pilgrims', p. 75; J. Mann, *The Jews in Egypt and in Palestine under the Fatimid Caliphs*, 2 vols. (New York, NY, 1970), vol. II, pp. 370–1.

[138] S. Poznanski, *Babylonische Geonim im nachgaonäischen Zeitalter* (Berlin, 1924), p. 64.

[139] Reiner, 'Pilgrims', p. 75.   [140] Kanarfogel, 'The *'Aliyah*', p. 192.

[141] For the older view, see S. H. Kuk, 'R. Yehiel of Paris and the Land of Israel', *Me'assef Zion* 5 (1933), pp. 88–102 [Hebrew]. Joshua Prawer accepted the view that the yeshiva was in Acre: Prawer, *Jews*, p. 275, n. 67. It now seems that Yehiel did not make it to the Holy Land, but rather died in Paris, having returned there after becoming ill during his voyage to the East. S. Emanuel, 'R. Yehiel of Paris: His Biography and Affinity to Eretz-Yisrael', *Shalem* 8 (2008), pp. 91–4 [Hebrew].

[142] Reiner, 'Pilgrims', pp. 79–80; Ta-Shema, 'A New Chronography', p. 324 [Hebrew with English abstract]; 'Totz'ot', p. 77 refers to Yehiel's son as buried by Mount Carmel.

[143] Emanuel, 'Pages', pp. 145–65. It has recently been suggested, on the basis of similarity between arguments posed in their works, that this anonymous author and the R. Eliyahu mentioned later as sending Halakhic questions to Rashba were in fact the same person. Y. Friedman, 'Pages from a Halakhic Notebook of R. Eliyahu from Acre', *Emunat Itekha* 93 (Dec. 2011), pp. 8–23 [Hebrew].

The Spanish tradition was also well represented in the city. Indeed, the most prominent Jewish scholar who resided in thirteenth-century Acre is Nahmanides, who, having left Iberia as a result of the famous Barcelona debate, spent the last years of his life in the city (1268–70).[144] Despite the French ring of his name, Solomon Petit, another prominent intellectual working in Acre, also seems to have belonged to the Iberian tradition, since R. Solomon b. Adereth (mentioned later as Rashba and working in Barcelona) sent him several *responsa* referring to him as the head of Toledo's yeshiva.[145] A Kabbalist and an opponent of rational thinking, Petit led an attack in Acre on Maimonides' works, and travelled through the West in order to arouse opposition to them.[146] We also have first-hand evidence for his activity as a teacher in the city.[147] Further evidence concerns the visit of another Iberian scholar to Acre: Abraham Abul'afia, born in Aragon, arrived in the city around 1260, with the intention of travelling East towards the legendary Sambation River. He recounts in his book, however, that he was unable to do so because of the conflict between Muslims and Christians.[148]

Notwithstanding the fact that as the thirteenth century moved on, Western Jewry became more and more dominant within the city's elite,[149] Oriental Jewry was certainly also represented in Acre's learned circles. While some of the men signed on the 1235 document were French, others were probably of Oriental origin.[150] Maimonides' son, Abraham, is also known to have spent several years in Acre, and David, Maimonides' grandson, seems to have been present in the city during 1285–9/90.[151] It may also be assumed that at least some of Maimonides'

---

[144] Nahmanides reached the Holy Land in the summer of 1267. He then went on a pilgrimage to Jerusalem and Hebron in September of that year. Soon later, however, he settled in Acre. Reiner, 'Pilgrims', pp. 48–9, 80–1.

[145] Solomon ben Adereth [Rashba], *Responsa*, ed. A. Zeleznick, 5 vols. (Jerusalem, 1997–2005), vol. II, part 1, num. 253 [Hebrew]: 'א"י טוליטולא ישיבת בעל צרפתי שלמה רבי הגדול לחכם שהשבתי תשובות ועוד'. ('And more answers which I replied to the great sage R. Solomon Tzarfati, head of Toledo's yeshiva, God bless him.') A possibility has been raised that Petit was a name used by members of the Kimhi family from Narbonne. P. Roth, '*Later Provençal Sages – Jewish Law (Halakhah) and Rabbis in Southern France, 1215–1348*', unpublished PhD thesis, Hebrew University (2012), p. 159 [Hebrew]. For Solomon's activity before coming to Acre, see also Reiner, 'Pilgrims', p. 84; S. Z. Havlin (ed.), *Rashba's Responsa* (Rome, ca. 1470, reprinted Jerusalem, 1977), pp. 14–15, n. 20 [Hebrew].

[146] Reiner, 'Pilgrims', p. 84. For elaborate descriptions of the controversy, see Prawer, *Jews*, pp. 282–90; E. Ashtor, *The History of the Jews in Egypt and Syria under Mamluk Rule*, 3 vols. (Jerusalem, 1944–70), vol. I, pp. 131–41 [Hebrew].

[147] See Chapter 2, p. 59.

[148] Abraham Abul'afia, *Otzar Eden Ganuz*, ed. A. Gross (Jerusalem, 2000), p. 368 [Hebrew]; M. Idel, 'Eretz-Israel and Prophetic Kabbalah', *Shalem* 3 (1981), p. 119 [Hebrew].

[149] Prawer, *Jews*, pp. 273–4.   [150] Reiner, 'Pilgrims', p. 75.

[151] Regarding Abraham, see Prawer, *Jews*, p. 280. For David, see Ashtor, *History*, vol. I, pp. 130–40.

supporters in the city at the time of the controversy regarding the latter's philosophical works were of Oriental origin.[152]

The unique circumstances that characterized thirteenth-century Acre thus enabled complex exchanges between Jews coming from various traditions. Some of these must have been friendly, and one can assume that a considerable flow of knowledge took place between members of different groups.[153] Thus, for example, the only two explicit references to opinions of French scholars in Nahmanides' commentary occur in *addenda* he sent from Acre [1: 13].[154] On the other hand, there were certainly also some tensions. Elchanan Reiner discusses several cases of conflict between Oriental and Western Jews in the Holy Land. While these do not have to do specifically with Acre, we can assume that similar incidents took place in the city.[155] Indeed, Shalem Yahalom's analysis of Nahmanides' New Year sermon [2:26] reveals polemical elements aimed at the French Tosafists residing in the city.[156] Above all, it seems that such tensions contributed to the awakening of the third and final stage of the debate on Maimonides' philosophical works.[157]

The city enabled not only contacts between representatives of various faraway communities but also an encounter with written works, originating in diverse traditions. In other words, Jews visiting the city could have found works there which they had never before been able to consult. This is most noteworthy in Nahmanides' case. In his sermon, Nahmanides says that he found the 'long Tosafot' of R. Elhanan in 'this city', almost certainly referring to Acre,[158] and Reiner proposed that during his stay

---

[152] M. Ben-Sasson, 'Tradition and Change in the Patterns of Controversy of the Descendants of Maimonides', in J. Blau and D. Doron (eds.), *Heritage and Innovation in Judaeo-Arabic Culture* (Jerusalem, 2000), p. 85 [Hebrew]; A. Lichtenberg (ed.), *The Collection of Maimonides' Responsa and Letters* (Leipzig, 1859), 3rd part, p. 22 [Hebrew].

[153] See the description of the meeting of Abraham Maimuni with French scholars in Cairo: Abraham Maimuni, *Wars*, p. 53; Ben-Sasson, 'Tradition', p. 78. It seems that in general, Abraham was closely connected to French scholars active in Acre. Reiner, 'Pilgrims', pp. 77–8.

[154] Y. Ofer and J. Jacobs, *Nahmanides' Torah Commentary Addenda Written in the Land of Israel* (Jerusalem, 2013), pp. 367–72, 402–5; Moshe ben Nahman, *Exegesis on the Torah*, ed. C. B. Chavel, 2 vols. (Jerusalem, 1972), vol. II, pp. 74, 162 [Hebrew], and in English translation: Ramban, *Commentary on the Torah*, trans. C. B. Chavel, 5 vols. (New York, NY, 1971–6), vol. III, pp. 182, 406.

[155] Reiner, 'Pilgrims', pp. 62, 75–7. One such conflict was recently studied in detail, see R. Shweka, '"And every day they make quarrels": A Chapter from the History of the Jewish Community in Jerusalem in the 13th Century according to Letters of R. Yehiel the Frenchman', *Sefunot: Studies and Sources on the History of Jewish Communities in the East*, n.s. 10 (2017), pp. 13–55 [Hebrew].

[156] S. Yahalom, 'The Historical Background to Nahmanides' Sermon for Rosh-Ha-Shana in Acre', *Shalem* 8 (2008) pp. 100–25 [Hebrew]. For an English version of this paper, see S. Yahalom, 'Historical Background to Nahmanides' Acre *Sermon for Rosh ha-Shana*: The Strengthening of the Catalonian Center', *Sefarad* 68.2 (Jul.–Dec., 2008), pp. 315–42.

[157] Ben-Sasson, 'Tradition', pp. 75, 84; Prawer, *Jews*, pp. 282–3.

[158] Yahalom, 'The Historical Background', p. 105; J. Jacobs, 'Books Encountered by Ramban after He Arrived in the Land of Israel', *Jerusalem Studies, an Internet Journal* 11 (2012), p. 107 [Hebrew].

in the city Nahmanides became acquainted with additional materials from Elhanan's milieu.[159] Furthermore, Nahmanides' *addenda* to his exegesis on the Pentateuch reveal that he encountered in Acre, for the first time, several other texts, two of which originated in Kairouan.[160] Additionally, he found in the city a blessing included in a commentary on Sefer Yetzirah [**1:15**], and it was possibly also there that he became acquainted with the original Arabic version of Maimonides' commentary on the Mishna.[161]

Nahmanides was certainly not the only Jew who made use of his stay in Acre in order to consult written works which were new to him, or different versions of texts he was familiar with. The anonymous author of an itinerary known as 'Totz'ot Eretz Israel' writes that in the 'Land of Israel' (and thus possibly in Acre) he bought a copy of the Mishna in which he found a reading better than the one he previously knew.[162] Another suggestion concerning a text found in Acre has been raised: a colophon attests that it was in Acre that Samuel b. Abraham Secal found and copied Maimonides' commentary on the Talmudic Rosh Hashana tract.[163] However, it has been argued that the text was copied in Egypt and that the appearance of the word 'Acre' in the manuscript originated in a scribal error.[164]

As can be expected, practical Halakhic problems, and in particular such that were raised by the unique conditions characterizing the Holy Land, attracted the attention of Jewish scholars active in the city. Thus a certain R. Eliyahu sent Rashba a Halakhic question which concerns precepts that are only binding in the Land of Israel. Not being happy with the reply he received, Eliyahu repeated his question.[165] Remarkably, another learned Jew from the city, whose name has not reached us, heard about Rashba's responses to Eliyahu, and, having further queries concerning them, sent

---

[159] Reiner, 'Pilgrims', p. 81, n. 162.   [160] Jacobs, 'Books', pp. 105–18.

[161] D. Henshke, 'Two Maimonidean Comments', *Hama'ayan* 50.2 (2009), pp. 90–3 [Hebrew].

[162] 'Totz'ot', p. 79. Reiner argues convincingly against the hypothesis that this author was indeed Nahmanides' pupil. E. Reiner, '"Oral Versus Written": The Shaping of Traditions of Holy Places in the Middle Ages', in Y. Ben-Arieh and E. Reiner (eds.), *Studies in the History of Eretz Israel, Presented to Yehuda Ben Porat* (Jerusalem, 2003), pp. 341–2 [Hebrew].

[163] 'Copied overseas. It was copied by the lofty R. Samuel, son of R. Abraham Secal in Acre, from the writing of our rabbi R. Moses, light of the exile, blessed be his memory. And this he also found in the end of the book from the rabbi's writing and tongue.' (הועתק במדינת הים, העתיקו' הנעלה ר' שמואל ב"ר אברהם שקייל בעכו, מכתיבת הרב רבינו משה מאור הגולה ז"ל. וגם זה מצא בסוף הספר מכתיבת הרב ומלשונו.') For the Hebrew text, see I. Shailat (ed.), *The Letters and Essays of Moses Maimonides*, 2 vols. (Jerusalem, 1995), vol. I, pp. 224–7 [Hebrew].

[164] D. Henshke, 'Maimonides as His Own Commentator', *Sefunot* 23 (2003), p. 152, n. 135 [Hebrew]. This opinion is supported in Emanuel, 'Pages', p. 159.

[165] S. Emanuel, '"From Where the Sun Rises to Where It Sets": The Responsa by *Rashba* to the Sages of Acre', *Tarbiz – Quarterly for Jewish Studies* 83.3 (Sept. 2015), pp. 469–70 [Hebrew]; Rashba, *Responsa*, vol. III, part 5, pp. 31–5; vol. VI, pp. 92–4.

the famous rabbi three additional questions.[166] Additionally, there is evidence that scholars intending to immigrate to the Holy Land were in contact with Jews residing there concerning current Halakhic practices.[167] Note also in this context that Acre's Jewish community acquired a status of possessing a regional Halakhic authority. This is reflected in a question sent from Acre to Rashba in which we read that the sages of Jubayl (Byblos) had turned to Acre with a legal query which they were unable, or unwilling, to resolve by themselves. As Acre's learned Jews did not manage to reach a consensus concerning this issue, Joseph of Santis, a scholar residing in the city, decided to consult the prominent rabbi about the difficulty raised by Jubayl's Jews.[168]

Talmud was certainly studied in the city. Extraordinary evidence for this is provided by answers Rashba sent to Joseph of Santis. The famous rabbi sent Joseph more than seventy responsa, most of which are related to one Talmudic tractate. As Emanuel writes, this makes a rare case in which two Jews, living thousands of kilometres apart, studied a Talmudic text together. In several of the questions Joseph mentioned queries which other Jews, which he describes as neither his teachers or pupils, raised.[169]

What else can one say about the fields and activities which stood at the centre of attention of Acre's scholars? Clearly, learned Jews working in the city were interested in gaining information that would enable them to improve their understanding of the biblical text. This is particularly evident when one examines the *addenda* Nahmanides composed to his exegesis on the Pentateuch. Thus, for example, he studied an ancient inscribed coin, weighing it and making use of the neighbouring Samaritans' ability to read the inscription on it. He then utilized this new information in an attempt to solve a difficulty raised by Exodus 30.13.[170] Nahmanides' *addenda* also reveal that he made use of his stay in Acre, and more generally, in the Holy Land, in order to acquire geographical knowledge. One passage reveals, for example, that he learned from students coming from the territory known today as Iraq about the geographical location of Cuthah, and was thus able to solve an issue raised by Genesis 11.28.[171]

---

[166] Emanuel, "'From Where the Sun Rises'", pp. 471–2; Rashba, *Responsa*, vol. III, part 4, p. 40; vol. IV, pp. 94–6.

[167] Kanarfogel, 'The *'Aliyah*', p. 199.

[168] Emanuel, "'From Where the Sun Rises'", pp. 481–2. It has been suggested that 'Santis' should be identified with Saintes, a city some 120 kilometres north of Bordeaux. N. Aloni, 'Twelve Writers and Dozens of Books in the Middle Ages', *Aresheth: An Annual of Hebrew Folklore* 6 (1980), pp. 36–9 [Hebrew].

[169] Emanuel, "'From Where the Sun Rises'", pp. 472–81.

[170] Ofer and Jacobs, *Nahmanides' Torah*, pp. 337–42.

[171] Ofer and Jacobs, *Nahmanides' Torah*, pp. 121–30. This passage is cited in Chapter 2.

Interest in geography was probably not limited to the requirements of biblical comprehension. In all likelihood, one could have found in Acre various Hebrew texts related to local pilgrimage traditions. Such texts, or lists, were sometimes taken with Western travellers back to the West, as happened with a certain R. Jacob, an envoy from R. Yehiel's Paris yeshiva, who brought back with him to France a list he found in the Holy Land. In other cases, such lists were used as a basis for more elaborate compositions.[172] Furthermore, some itineraries, such as R. Samuel b. Samson's, may have been composed in the city.[173]

Kabbalah seems to have also been a popular subject in the Holy Land during the thirteenth century, and one may assume that some of the activity in this field took place in Acre. Moshe Idel has written that there probably existed in the Holy Land a mystical tendency inspired by Sufi ideas, and that it is likely that the ideas of R. Abraham Abul'afia were also studied there.[174] It would thus seem that, at least potentially, this field was not only an important element in the spiritual lives of Jews residing in Acre but also one which was characterized by intensive intercultural exchanges. While, at the current state of research, it is difficult to tie evidence regarding these matters to Acre, the fact that Abraham, Maimonides' son, and David, his own son, both strongly identified with Sufi influence on Jewish spirituality, spent some years in the city suggests that this trend was present in thirteenth-century Acre.[175]

The question that arises in this context is whether Jewish scholars dealt with fields not directly related to religion, such as medicine and science. The documentation for such activities is scant. A rare piece of evidence in this regard is provided by R. Shem-Tov b. Isaac of Tortosa, who writes that while in Acre he encountered a rabbi studying geometry.[176] We also have evidence regarding a Jewish resident of Acre who served as an oculist's aide. This was the brother of Abu Zichri b. Eliyahu, himself an oculist serving under al-Malik al-'Azīz, and the son of Eliyahu B. Zecharia, known to us as a judge.[177] Taking into consideration the

---

[172] Reiner, 'Oral Versus Written', pp. 320, 328–39.   [173] Prawer, *Jews*, pp. 77, 215–21.

[174] Idel, 'Eretz-Israel', pp. 121–3.

[175] For Abraham, see E. R. Russ-Fishbane, *'Between Politics and Piety: Abraham Maimonides and His Times'*, unpublished PhD thesis, Harvard University (2009), p. iii. For David, see E. P. Fishbane, *As Light before Dawn: The Inner World of a Medieval Kabbalist* (Stanford, CA, 2009), p. 29.

[176] Prawer, *Jews*, p. 265; S. Montner, 'R. Shem Tov Ben Isaac of Tortosa about the Life of the European Jewish Physician and His Ethics', in Y. L. Hacohen-Maimon (ed.), *Sinai: A Jubilee Volume* (Jerusalem, 1958), p. 330 [Hebrew]. Prawer wrote that the rabbi in question studied mathematics, but the word used in the text, תשבורת, means geometry. Furthermore, Shem Tov's use of the word in additional places in the cited text makes clear that in using this term he was referring to this specific field rather than to mathematics.

[177] S. D. Goitein, *Palestinian Jewry in Early Islamic and Crusader Times* (Jerusalem, 1980), pp. 260–3, 268–75, 323 [Hebrew].

status of his family, this man was certainly more than a mere servant, perhaps an apprentice studying ocular medicine. In any case, it is probable that knowledge regarding this profession circulated among the city's Jews. Another possible piece of evidence regarding scientific, or medical, information circulating among the city's Jewish community comes from Nahmanides' commentary on the Torah. In one of his *addenda* he wrote, on the basis of what he saw in a few 'books of experiments', that a baby drinking pig milk will become a leper. This book has not been identified yet, but given that this is its only mention in Nahmanides' exegesis, it is likely that he found it in Acre.[178]

An intriguing question remains whether an intellectual give and take existed between Jews and Latins in thirteenth-century Acre. Unfortunately, there is no explicit evidence for such exchanges. On the other hand, there are several clues that such communication did occur here and there. We study in detail in what follows evidence from the *Notitia* which suggests that its author, William of Tripoli, benefitted from the guidance of an anonymous Jew with regard to Islam.[179] The lamentation composed by Joseph, son of Tanhoum of Jerusalem, may be seen as evidence for a different kind of communication between the groups. Joseph refers to some learned Jews in Acre as such 'who with uncovered arms in the battle of God's Law resemble champions'. The expression translated here 'battle of God's law', or, more literally 'battle of God's documents', should in all likelihood be understood as referring to disputes concerning matters of religion, and may imply that inter-religious debates took place in the city.[180] To these pieces of evidence may perhaps be connected a recently published Halakhic question from Acre which reveals a Jew in Acre who receives letters from Christians and is in some kind of contact with an office holder in one of the mendicant orders.[181]

CONCLUSION

A. Frankish Society: We have seen that numerous individuals, belonging to different social groups, were involved, in various manners, in intellectual pursuits in Acre. The survey presented in this chapter also reveals that the range of fields in which residents engaged was

---

[178] Ofer and Jacobs, *Nahmanides' Torah*, p. 362.   [179] See Chapter 4, pp. 135–7.

[180] For this expression, see Alharizi's use of 'battle of documents', which the editors take for scientific debate. Judah Alharizi, *Taḥkemoni or the Tales of Heman the Ezraḥite*, eds. J. Yahalom and N. Katsumata (Jerusalem, 2010), p. 289 [Hebrew].

[181] Glick, *Seride Teshuvot of the Ottoman Empire Sages*, vol. II, pp. 589–95. The document's poor state of preservation makes it impossible to say anything else about the content of these exchanges.

extremely wide, and included theology, jurisprudence, history, poetry and geography. Additionally, Acre's intellectuals paid much attention to the accumulation, development and dissemination of knowledge concerning Oriental Christianity and the Muslim and Mongol worlds. As many of the involved agents were prominent figures, one must conclude that the impact of these intellectual pursuits was considerable. Thus, Acre should be seen as a significant intellectual centre on the eastern shores of the Mediterranean.

Additional conclusions have to do with the contact between Acre and other cultural centres. We have seen in various contexts that Acre's intellectual community included permanent residents as well as numerous visitors – both short- and long-term – who were connected, in one way or another, to important cultural centres in the West. Consequently, new ideas coming from the West continually entered the city through its port.[182] It can safely be assumed, then, that rather than being an isolated intellectual or cultural island, Acre's learned community was constantly updated regarding new ideas developing in the West. At the same time, a significant flow of knowledge existed also in the opposite direction, so that information collected and developed in Acre made its way to Western intellectual centres. This was the case not only with reports and letters put together in order to be sent to Western leaders but also with works such as Jacques de Vitry's second letter, a personal document sent by Acre's bishop to friends in Paris which, at the same time, is also an account of various religious groups he had encountered in the city.[183]

The strong ties between Acre and various Western cultural centres resulted in a situation where the city's intellectuals were working with at least three audiences in mind: some of their projects were of a clearly local nature and were intended to contribute to the Frankish culture of Outremer. Such were, for example, John of Ancona's canon law treatise and the sermons composed in the city. Other works, such as the aforementioned reports or William of Rubruck's *Itinerarium*, were written with a Western audience in mind. A third category was aimed, at least partly, to serve Western visitors to the Holy Land. Among these texts was the *Pardouns d'Acre*, as well as William of Tripoli's *Notitia de Machometo*.

Note that in some cases intellectual activities in Acre brought together members of different social groups. Thus we have seen, for example, that the same description of juridical expertise was employed concerning a burgess and a nobleman. Similarly, we later explore a discussion with

---

[182] Cf. Kedar's comments in 'A Symposium', in B. Z. Kedar (ed.), *The Horns of Hattin* (Jerusalem, 1992), p. 352; Jacoby, 'Society', p. 97.

[183] The flow of information from the West to the city and from it to the West of course plays a significant role in the next chapters.

an Armenian ambassador, led by Thomas Agni, and attended by Frankish nobles and jurists.[184] This crossing of social boundaries also took place in the context of preparation of reports to the West concerning developments in Outremer. This was certainly the case with texts, such as the *Relatio tripartita*, which were signed by members of more than one social group. But even when signed only by members of one group, such reports must have often been dependent on information transmitted by individuals belonging to other circles and organizations.[185] In other words, communities of learning developed in the city which occasionally transcended social and institutional boundaries.[186]

A last conclusion has to do with the initiation of intellectual projects: as can be inferred from the discussion presented earlier, evidence for patronage of intellectual pursuits is limited, and we have found no person, or even milieu, which systematically encouraged such activities.[187] In other words, the considerable intellectual activity that stands in the centre of this study took place despite the lack of organized support by individuals or institutions. When one wishes to compare, in this respect, Acre to Toledo, or to Frederick II's court, this trait must be taken into account.

B. **Jewish Society**: Housing some prominent Jewish scholars, the most important of whom was Nahmanides, Acre became a significant Jewish centre of learning, which, as we see later, attracted scholars to come and study in it. The main fields of Acre's Jewish intellectual activity were all directly linked to religious life and included biblical scholarship, Halakha, holy geography and probably Kabbalah as well. The circumstances within which the city operated enabled contacts between members of communities which were usually unable to meet, and offered visitors texts not readily available elsewhere. Such contacts probably also contributed to the awakening of tensions and conflicts, most notably in the case of the controversy on Maimonides' philosophical work. On the other hand, while Acre's Jewish society certainly shared many aspects of its life with the neighbouring Frankish one, the evidence for intellectual exchanges between the city's Jewish and Latin populations is limited and indirect.

---

[184] See Chapter 6, pp. 155–6.

[185] Thus, for example, it is hard to imagine how Thomas Agni would have been able to compose his letter without being informed by military men.

[186] For the term 'communities of learning', see C. J. Mews and J. N. Crossley (eds.), *Communities of Learning: Networks and the Shaping of Intellectual Identity in Europe, 1100–1500* (Turnhout, 2011), pp. 1–7.

[187] This reaffirms Laura Minervini's comment regarding the lack, in Outremer, of a person such as Raymond of Toulouse. Minervini, 'Tradizioni', p. 172.

Chapter 2

ACRE'S CHRISTIAN AND JEWISH CENTRES OF TEACHING AND LEARNING

The question of teaching activities in the Frankish Levant and, in particular, in the Kingdom of Jerusalem has often been raised, and yet very little has been done to systematically engage with it.[1] A careful examination of the evidence, both direct and indirect, with regard to such institutions in Acre can thus make a significant contribution to the scholarly discourse concerning intellectual life in Outremer. Our attempt is to draw as complete a sketch as possible of the teaching institutions in thirteenth-century Acre and of the training they provided. While in other sections of this book we discuss a range of mechanisms by which knowledge was developed, accumulated and distributed, here we focus on establishments which engaged with the more formal manners of instruction.

CHRISTIAN CENTRES OF LEARNING IN ACRE

It is expedient to begin our attempt to present a picture of the Latin teaching activities in thirteenth-century Acre by looking at the mendicant orders. That is so since we know that both the Franciscans and the Dominicans were strongly represented in the city, and since, relatively speaking, considerable evidence regarding their activities in Acre survives. But looking at them is convenient also from another point of view: much has been written about learning in both of these organizations using data from provinces which left more traces than the Holy Land. Since these were well-organized institutions, and since some of their most prominent members were active in the Latin East, it is reasonable to assume that such findings can be of use in reconstructing the Franciscan and Dominican centres of learning in thirteenth-century Acre.

---

[1] Some important comments on education in Outremer as a whole appear in Riley-Smith, *Feudal Nobility*, pp. 129–30. For a preliminary step in this context with regard to Acre, see Folda, *Crusader Art*, p. 400; Folda, *Crusader Manuscript*, pp. 18–19.

Christian Centres of Learning in Acre

The Dominican Convent

Acre's Dominican convent, arguably the largest in the Latin East, was founded during 1228–9.[2] We are fortunate enough to know approximately where it was located, as Riccoldo of Monte Croce says about the friars slaughtered in the city in May 1291 that they could have escaped since the Dominican convent was located by the sea. This claim is confirmed by Paolino Veneto's map, which places it on the shore just north of the Genoese quarter.[3] Extant sources shed some light on the Dominican teachers who taught in Acre. As we have seen, Robertus Normannus, prior of the convent in 1277, and his sub-prior, Berengarius Provincialis, were both either masters of theology or general preachers,[4] and are thus likely to have taken part in the training of younger friars in the city. There is also evidence that two Dominicans who were active teachers in the West spent time in Acre: Henry the German (known also as Henry of Marburg), who served as a master of theology in the monastery of Cologne before he became prior of the Holy Land, and who escorted Louis IX on his crusade;[5] and Gaillard, titular bishop of Bethlehem (around 1277), who had been a lector in the Dominican houses of Narbonne and Agen before travelling to the East.[6] It seems quite improbable that such men, and similar ones who have left no traces in our sources, would have refrained from taking part in teaching activities in Acre. It has also been suggested that Yves the Breton, an Arab-speaking Dominican who played a significant role in the contacts between the Franks of the city and various Muslim courts, lectured in the city's convent.[7]

There is no direct evidence with regard to the curriculum followed in Acre's Dominican convent, except a reference, in a letter from Philip, the Dominican prior of the Holy Land, which reveals that by 1237 Oriental languages were taught in all Dominican convents of that province and thus clearly also in Acre.[8] Under these circumstances, the only way to advance in our enquiry is to assume that Acre's was not entirely different

---

[2] Kedar, *Crusade and Mission*, p. 145; Balme, 'La Province', p. 528.

[3] R. Röhricht, 'Lettres de Ricoldo de Monte-Croce', *Archives de l'Orient latin* 2 (1884), p. 289. The location of the convent has been thoroughly discussed in Abel, 'Le Couvent', pp. 266–72.

[4] Balme, 'La Province', p. 530.   [5] Friedman, *Text and Iconography for Joinville's Credo*, p. 55.

[6] Hamilton, *The Latin Church*, p. 280.

[7] Folda, *Crusader Manuscript*, p. 14. For Yves, see also Chapter 1, pp. 22, 35.

[8] MP, vol. III, pp. 396–9. On this issue, see Chapter 3, pp. 63–4. It is noteworthy that Lull does not mention, in his discussion of the importance of linguistic instruction, language teaching centres which existed before he wrote his treatise. *Raimundi Lulli opera Latina*, ed. A. Madre, CCCM 35 (Turnhout, 1981), pp. 252–5.

from other Dominican convents, and, accordingly, to apply the conclusions of studies on the Dominican educational system to the city.

According to Barone, there was not, or should not have been, a convent without a school of theology, and every Dominican house had a *lector*, meaning a professor of theology.[9] It seems safe to assume that these elements existed in Acre, in which an important convent existed and in which leading members of the order spent some time. Michèle Mulchahey has further demonstrated that by the end of the thirteenth century the convent school course included two daily lectures (one on the Bible and the other on Peter Lombard's *Sententiae*), a daily repetition over these, a weekly disputation and a weekly *repetitio generalis* in which all of the material studied that week was reviewed.[10] Again, it is likely that such a course existed, at least partially, in Acre during the latter part of the century. In this system, lectures and disputations were open to the public, so one may safely assume that their impact would transcend mendicant circles and the ideas expressed in them would resonate beyond the convent's walls.[11]

In 1259 the Dominican general chapter issued an order according to which 'some *studium artium* or more than one should be arranged in the provinces lacking in this respect where the young would be taught'.[12] The question of what exactly was taught in these *studia* is open to debate. While some historians argue that this decision marked the Dominican acceptance of the 'largely Aristotelian syllabus' published by the Parisian Arts Faculty in 1255, Mulchahey claims that these *studia* were logic schools.[13] Be that as it may, such a *studium artium* probably operated in the city during the latter part of our period, and an Aristotelian manuscript, likely circulating among the Dominicans of Acre, was perhaps related to it.[14]

---

[9] G. Barone, 'Les couvents des mendiants, des collèges déguisés?', in O. Weijers (ed.), *Vocabulaire des collèges universitaires (XIIIe–XVIe siècles)* (Turnhout, 1993), p. 150.

[10] M. Mulchahey, *'First the Bow is Bent in Study . . .' Dominican Education before 1350* (Toronto, 1997), p. 134.

[11] Mulchahey, *'First the Bow is Bent in Study . . .'*, p. 168.

[12] 'Item, quod ordinetur in provinciis, que indiguerint, aliquod studium artium vel aliqua, ubi juvenes instruantur.' H. Denifle and A. Chatelain (eds.), *Chartularium Universitatis Parisiensis*, 4 vols. (Paris, 1899, reprinted Brussels, 1964), vol. I, p. 385, num. 335; M. Mulchahey, 'Dominican Educational Vocabulary and the Order's Conceptualization of Studies before 1300. Borrowed Terminology, New Connotations', in M. C. Pacheco (ed.), *Le vocabulaire des écoles des Mendiants au moyen âge* (Turnhout, 1999), pp. 89–118.

[13] Mulchahey, *'First the Bow is Bent in Study . . .'*, pp. 222–5.

[14] Ciggaar, 'An Illuminated Aristotelian Manuscript', pp. 25–36.

The Franciscan Convent

Acre's Franciscan convent was founded between 1217 and 1221, during Elias of Cortona's office as *minister provincialis*.[15] We are fortunate to have evidence with regard to one teacher who taught there. This is William of Rubruck who writes, in the epilogue to his *Itinerarium* [**2:23**], as follows.[16]

> The Minister determined that I was to teach in Acre and would not let me join you, ordering me to send in writing, by the bearer, what I wished to say. I did not dare to oppose him, which would be contrary to [the vow of] obedience, and have done it to the best of my ability and skill.

The precise duration of William's teaching activity in the city is unclear. He must have started lecturing there in the fall of 1255, but it is difficult to say when he returned to the West, the only indication for this being his meeting with Roger Bacon, which, unfortunately, cannot be dated with any precision though it must have occurred after 1256.[17] Nothing further is known with regard to William's activity in Acre, and it is impossible to state with any certainty what he was supposed to contribute to the convent's curriculum or why the minister insisted on his staying in Outremer. It is extremely unlikely, however, that he did not share some of the unique knowledge he had accumulated during his journeys in the East with Acre's Franciscan friars or with wider Frankish audiences. Of particular significance within a Franciscan context would have been his experience in preaching to and disputing with non-Latin audiences, as well as his knowledge of Eastern languages, customs of various groups he encountered and geography. Perhaps one may learn about the enthusiasm with which Rubruck would have been received by fellow Franciscans from extant evidence concerning Giovanni da Pian del Carpine. Salimbene says that while he stayed in the convent of Sens, Giovanni passed through it with his newly written text on the Mongols. The friars, Salimbene goes on to recount, read from the book in the author's presence, while Giovanni expounded and explained things that seemed obscure and difficult to believe.[18] William of Rubruck's arrival

---

[15] S. Vecchio, 'Elia d'Assisi', *Dizionario biografico degli italiani* (Rome, 1993), vol. XLII, p. 450. It is noteworthy in this context that Elias seems to have had a very significant role in the development of Franciscan education. B. Roest, *Franciscan Learning, Preaching and Mission, c. 1220–1650* (Leiden, 2015), pp. 18, 24, 49.

[16] 'Et diffinivit minister quod legerem Acon, non permittens me venire ad vos, precipiens ut scriberem vobis ea que vellem per latorem presentium. Ego autem, non audens reniti contra obedientiam, feci prout potui et scivi.' For the English text, see Jackson and Morgan, *The Mission*, p. 276. For the original Latin, see Guglielmo, *Viaggio*, pp. 316–18.

[17] Guglielmo, *Viaggio*, pp. xli–xlii; J. Charpentier, 'William of Rubruck and Roger Bacon', *Geografisca Annaler* 17, Supplement: Hyllningsskrift Tillagnad Sven Hedin (1935), pp. 256–7.

[18] Salimbene de Adam, *Cronica*, ed. G. Scalia, CCCM 125–125A, 2 vols. (Turnhout, 1998), vol. I, p. 321.

at Acre's Franciscan convent must have aroused similar interest. Furthermore, as William did not have a ready-made book based on his travels when he arrived in the city, but rather produced it during his stay there, it is likely that the composition of the work was influenced by his discussions with fellow friars or other Franks residing in Outremer. A reference William makes in his description of Mongolia to the Syrian taxation system supports this hypothesis.[19]

No additional direct evidence regarding Franciscans who taught in the Acre convent has come down to us. It is, however, likely that Benoit d'Alignan taught in it: Benoit is known to have been a Franciscan,[20] and it seems that by 1230, i.e. before his first visit to Outremer, he had already joined the order, since during that year he signed a letter as a friar.[21] There is no reason to assume that such a man would not have contributed from his knowledge to the order to which he had attached himself. Robert of Turnham, a Franciscan teacher and preacher who escorted Edward on his crusade, may have also taught in that convent during his stay in the city.[22]

What about the curriculum of the Acre convent? As in the Dominican case, given the absence of direct evidence, the only way in which one can attempt to answer this question is by using conclusions from research on other provinces. But before one can use these findings, the question of the status of the Franciscan house in the city must be answered. Fortunately, extant documents shed light on this issue, revealing that in 1256 Acre was taken to be a custodial centre and that Gelebertus, who was *custos* in 1286, resided there.[23]

Bert Roest's examination of the Franciscan schools enables us to present the kinds of training likely available in such a centre. Firstly, the convent would have provided young friars with some training in Latin and logic.[24] Theological studies including mainly lectures on the Bible and the *Sententiae* would have also taken place there, and it is plausible that some training in canon and Roman law was also available.[25] Finally, activities such as recitation, collation, disputation and sermons also likely took place in the convent and the friars would have been provided with a range of reading materials.[26]

---

[19] Guglielmo, *Viaggio*, p. 32.   [20] Salimbene, *Cronica* 2.834.

[21] 'Nos frater Benedictus'. For a discussion of the question of when Benoit joined the order, see G. Golubovich, *Biblioteca Bio-Bibliografica della Terra Santa e dell'Oriente francescano*, 5 vols. (Florence, 1913), vol. I, p. 238. Villads Jensen adopts Golubovich's position on this matter: K. Villads Jensen, 'War against Muslims according to Benedict of Alignano OFM', *Archivum Franciscanum Historicum* 89 (1996), p. 182.

[22] Golubovich, *Biblioteca*, vol. I, p. 281.

[23] *Codice diplomatico del sacro militare ordine Gerosolimitano*, ed. S. Pauli, 2 vols. (Lucca, 1733–7), vol. I, pp. 151–3; R. Röhricht, 'Syria Sacra', *ZDPV* 10 (1887), p. 22.

[24] Roest, *A History*, pp. 137–9.   [25] Roest, *A History*, pp. 123–33, 146–8.

[26] Roest, *A History*, pp. 133–7.

The Teaching of Muslim Converts and Oriental Christians

Relatively extensive evidence is available regarding teaching aimed at Muslim converts. Describing Frankish raids conducted in the Galilee in 1217, Oliver the Scholastic writes that 'the bishop of Acre baptized the children which he was able to obtain by money or by request and, distributing them among religious women, arranged for them to study the letters'.[27] Although Oliver does not say where these converts were instructed, we can safely assume that this educational activity took place in Acre, which was by far the most important Frankish centre in the region, and the city in which the bishop who initiated the project exerted the greatest influence. Several sources provide evidence for similar teaching activities undertaken in the city more than three decades later. In the *Vie de Saint Louis par le confesseur de la reine Marguerite* we read that:[28]

[W]hen the blessed king was delivered from the Saracen prison [May 1250] and remained in Outremer, many Saracens . . . came to him. He had them baptized and instructed in the faith by the Friars Preachers and by others whom the blessed king had prepared accordingly.

Geoffroi de Beaulieu provides evidence pointing at the same direction, writing that 'during his [Louis IX's] sojourn many Saracens approached him in order to take up Christianity. These he happily received, and had baptized and diligently instructed in Christ's faith.'[29] The *Chronique de Primat*[30] similarly says that some Muslim emirs 'had been first taught by

---

[27] 'Episcopus autem Acconensis parvulos, quos precio vel prece obtinere potuit, baptizavit et distribuens inter religiosas feminas litteris applicare disposuit.' Oliverus Scholasticus, *Historia Damiatina*, ed. H. Hoogeweg, Bibliothek des Litterarischen Vereins CCII (Tübingen, 1894), p. 167. Almost identical phrases appear in Oliver's *Relatio de expeditione Jherosolimitana*, printed in the same volume, p. 289, and in Jacques de Vitry, 'Historia Hierosolymitana', in *Gesta Dei per Francos*, ed. J. Bongars (Hanau, 1611), p. 1130 (this reference is to a phrase from the third book of the *Historia* which is not included in Donnadieu's edition).

[28] '. . .comme li benoiez rois fut delivrez de la chartre des Sarrazins et demorast encore es parties doutremer, mout de Sarrazins . . . vindrent a lui, lesquex il fist baptizier, et les fesoit enseigner en la foi par freres preecheeurs et par autres que li benoiez rois avoit a ce ordenez.' P.-C.-F. Daunou and J. Naudet (eds.), *Vie de Saint Louis par le confesseur de la reine Marguerite*, RHGF 20 (Paris, 1840), p. 66.

[29] 'Insuper, in morae illius spatio Sarraceni multi ad ipsum pro christianitate suscipienda venerunt, quos gaudenter recipiebat, et baptizari faciebat, et in fide Christi instrui diligenter.' Gaufridus de Belloloco, *Vita Sancti Ludovici*, eds. P. Daunou and J. Naudet, RHGF 20 (Paris, 1840), p. 16.

[30] Primat, a monk at the abbey of St. Denis, authored a Latin account of the reigns of Louis IX and Philip III. The Latin version is now lost, but most of the text survives in Jean de Vignay's French translation of the late 1320s or the 1330s. Primat seems to have passed away in the last decade of the thirteenth century. Regarding Primat, see the introduction to the edition cited later, as well as L. Brun, 'Primat', in G. Dunphy (general editor), *Encyclopedia of the Medieval Chronicle*, 2 vols. (Leiden, 2010), vol. II, p. 1235.

the Friars Preachers and the Friars Minor, and given instruction in the faith'.[31]

Clearly, these teaching activities focused, first and foremost, on religious matters, but as is implied in Oliver's general reference to the study of letters, it can safely be assumed that Muslim converts received at least a degree of linguistic instruction, since otherwise they would have been incapable of either comprehending basic religious texts or communicating with their Western instructors. The much earlier case of Nāṣir al-Dīn, captured by the Templars in the 1150s, is instructive regarding the connection between conversion and the acquisition of linguistic skills, since, if we are to trust William of Tyre, the Muslim captive learned the *litteras Romanas*.[32]

A unique document provides probable evidence that not only Muslim converts to Christianity but also Arabic-speaking Copts were taught by Franks in Acre. Appended to a Coptic lexicographic treatise, extant in a sixteenth-century manuscript – Paris, Bibliothèque nationale de France, MS Copte 43 – is (in two versions) an Old French–Arabic glossary, in which the French is transmitted by Coptic letters.[33] While the precise circumstances in which this text was produced have been the subject of some debate, it does seem very likely that it was intended to be used by Copts travelling to the Kingdom of Jerusalem and, probably, specifically to Acre, which is the only toponym which appears in the glossary.[34] Of specific relevance for our discussion is the inclusion, in the phrasebook, of a considerable number of words related to study activities, such as 'teacher', 'pen', 'inkstand', 'writing-board', 'read' and 'book' (which, very interestingly, is used to translate the French 'Psauter'), and phrases meaning 'read well' and 'he does not read well'. The appearance of such words and phrases in the glossary makes it likely that it echoes the instruction of Copts by Franks residing in Outremer and, plausibly, specifically in Acre.

---

[31] '... [pluseurs admiraus] avoient esté premièrement entroduis des frères Preescheurs et des frères Meneurs, et entroduis en l'ensaignement de la foy'. N. de Wailly, L. Delisle and C.-M.G. Jourdain (eds.), *Chronique de Primat*, RHGF 23 (Paris, 1894), p. 14.

[32] Willelmus Tyrensis, *Chronicon*, ed. R. B. C. Huygens, 2 vols. (Turnhout, 1986), vol. II, p. 823.

[33] This text was first published in G. Maspero, 'Le vocabulaire français d'un Copte du XIIIe siècle', *Romania* 17 (1888), pp. 481–512. It was re-edited and thoroughly analysed in C. Aslanov, *Evidence of Francophony in Mediaeval Levant* (Jerusalem, 2006).

[34] For the main views with regard to this text, see L. Minervini, 'La français dans l'orient Latin (XIIIe–XIVe siècles). Éléments pour la caractérisation d'une *scripta* du Levant', *Revue de Linguistique Romane* 74 (2010), p. 136; Aslanov, *Evidence*, pp. 6–7; Maspero, 'Le vocabulaire français', pp. 179–80. My interpretation is closest to Minervini's.

Other Christian Centres of Learning

Having discussed the evidence regarding the Dominican and Franciscan convents, as well as that which concerns the instruction of converts and Oriental Christians in the city, we can now turn to the examination of several sources which shed light on additional teaching activities in Acre.[35] One of the articles in an agreement, dating to 1175, between the bishop of Acre and the Master of the Hospitaller order says that 'the lord bishop of Acre will not prevent young men wishing to be taught in the house of the Hospital [from doing so]'.[36] As Jonathan Riley-Smith wrote, this means that the Hospitallers had a school in Acre from as early as 1175.[37] There is no reason to think that such an institution did not continue to operate in the city after 1191, when, as a result of Jerusalem's loss, the order's presence in Acre must have actually become more pronounced. This is confirmed by a statute dating to 1193, in which we read about sons of nobles brought up in the house of the order ('in domo Hospitalis nutriti').[38]

But the 1175 text also implies that there was in the city at the time also a cathedral school, since that would best explain why the bishop felt he was competing with the Hospitallers for potential students. Again, if such an institution existed in the city in 1175, it would be hard to imagine that after 1191, when the city's importance greatly increased, it would cease to operate. Two other pieces of evidence may be associated with the existence of such an institution. The first comes from one of Jacques de Vitry's letters, dated to 1218,[39] where, while mentioning people who died in the preceding year, he asks his addressees to pray for 'master Leonius who taught theology in the city of Acre'.[40] While we do not know where Leonius taught, it is possible that his activity was connected to a cathedral school.[41] Another theologian, magister Thomas, who died

---

[35] Of some importance for our discussion is Hamilton's argument that a very considerable number of the bishops in the patriarchate of Jerusalem who held office between 1192 and 1291 were trained in Syria. Hamilton, *The Latin Church*, p. 280. Hamilton does not, however, provide evidence for his argument. Furthermore, it is possible that at least some of the clergymen he counts as having been instructed in the East in fact spent certain periods of learning in the West. Mayer claims that the education required for serving as a bishop was unavailable in the Holy Land. Mayer, *Die Kanzlei*, vol. I, p. 279.

[36] '...pueros, in domo Hospitalis doceri cupientes, dominus Acconensis episcopus non prohibebit.' *Cartulaire* 471.

[37] J. Riley-Smith, 'The Death and Burial of Latin Christian Pilgrims to Jerusalem and Acre, 1099–1291', *Crusades* 7 (2008), pp. 178–9, n. 89.

[38] *Cartulaire* 1193.   [39] Jacques de Vitry, *Lettres*, p. 535.

[40] 'Orate etiam pro ... magistro Leonio, qui legebat de theologia in civitate Acconensi.' Jacques de Vitry, *Lettres*, p. 594.

[41] It is noteworthy in this context that the Jerusalem Church of the Holy Sepulcher had a *magister scholasticus* as early as 1103 (*RRH* 40). This has led scholars to believe that there was a cathedral school attached to this church, and that it was perhaps in this institution that William of Tyre

in *Castrum peregrinorum* [mod. 'Atlit], may have also been active in such an institution.[42]

Beyond teaching activities associated with institutions operating in Acre, a considerable amount of instruction was probably done in the city by private tutors. While there is no direct evidence for this kind of teaching in the city, Philip of Novara, an important spokesman of Outremer's nobility, recommended this manner of education:[43]

Prominent men and those who have power and who have much to do and cannot take care and nourish their children, should provide them with the best master they can.

Further evidence for teaching in Acre comes from the *Livre des assises de la cour de la bourgeois* [2:21]. In chapter 218 we read:[44]

If it happens that the son of some man who is in his power and by his will went to school to study some science, reason judges and commands that his father or mother are held to pay whatever he borrowed for his living or for paying his teacher.

The attempt to reveal what this comment can tell us with regard to teaching activities in Acre raises some difficulties. Firstly, the *Livre* is heavily influenced by a Provençal treatise of Roman law, so that, theoretically at least, the cited text may be no more than a paragraph copied from a text which bears no relevance to the realities of life in Outremer.[45] Looking at the parallel Provençal text, however, it becomes clear that this is not the case, since the reference to learning is far less elaborate in that text, mentioning study as only one possible reason for the son's travels and not referring to specific kinds of expenditure.[46] Consequently, it is expedient to follow the line of thinking presented by Joshua Prawer, who discovered the relation between the *Livre* and the *Lo Codi*, and who wrote that the numerous differences between these two texts necessarily mean that the author of the *Livre* intended 'to adapt the treatise which served him as a model for the redaction of the usages of the Latin

---

received his basic education. P. W. Edbury and J. G. Rowe, *William of Tyre* (Cambridge, 1988), pp. 13–14.

[42] Jacques de Vitry, 'Historia Hierosolymitana', p. 1131 (this citation is taken from the third book of the *Historia* which is not included in Donnadieu's edition).

[43] 'Li haut home et cil qui ont pooir et qui ont assez a faire, et ne pueent entendre a lor anfanz garder et norrir, lor doivent porchacier maistre le meillor qu'il porront.' Philippe de Navarre, *Les quatre ages de l'homme*, ed. M. de Fréville (Paris, 1888), p. 12; Riley-Smith, *Feudal Nobility*, p. 130.

[44] 'C'il avient que le fis d'aucun home et qui est en son poier, et par sa volenté est en escole alés por aprendre aucune science, la raison juge et coumande que le pere ou la mere de celuy sont tenus de paier ce que il a enprunté por son vivre ou por son maistre paier.' *RHC, Lois*, vol. II, p. 149.

[45] For more on the relation between the *Livre* and the *Lo Codi*, see Chapter 4, pp. 91–2.

[46] Fitting, *Lo Codi*, p. 109, par. 4.47.

Kingdom'.[47] In other words, it is likely that in this case the text of the *Livre* reflects the actual customs of Outremer and responds to circumstances which characterized this region.

Analysed in this light, the law under discussion seems to echo cases in which young Franks who travelled to acquire education or professional training exhausted the resources which they had brought with them and borrowed money from local creditors. It is unlikely that this law is meant to respond to Franks travelling from the West to study in Outremer, since it is improbable that the Latin East attracted potential students. It is also unlikely that the law concerns inhabitants of the crusading states travelling to study in the West, because in such cases one imagines that the loan would have been made across the sea and the creditors would not appeal to a court placed in the East.[48] Consequently, my suggestion is that the law under discussion refers to cases in which students travelled between cities or regions within the Latin East and, more specifically, to Acre.[49] This would explain why the *Livre* does not refer, as the *Lo Codi* does, to schools in *aliena terra*. Some support for this hypothesis is provided by a document, dated to 1286, which describes a settlement concerning the debt of a certain Bertoccius to Petrus de Brundusio, a law professor residing in Tripoli.[50] Interestingly, according to the agreement, Bertoccius' father, Latinus Valensanus, a resident of Acre, will help his son to resolve a debt he is currently unable to pay by himself. The document does not say how Bertoccius got into debt, but given that the creditor was a professor of law, and that he resided in Tripoli while Bertoccius' father lived in Acre, we possibly have before us a situation similar to that envisaged by the jurists who phrased the previously cited law from the *Livre*.

JEWISH TEACHING ACTIVITIES IN ACRE

The sources surviving from thirteenth-century Acre provide us with an opportunity to explore, within the same urban context, both Latin and Jewish teaching activities. Having presented the evidence for the former, we can now move on to the latter. At the elementary education level, one

---

[47] Prawer, *Crusader Institutions*, p. 377.

[48] For students from the Latin East going to study in the West, see É. Berger (ed.), *Les registres d'Innocent IV*, 4 vols. (Paris, 1884–1921), vol. III, p. 515, num. 8059.

[49] Note, that both the editor of the text, Count Beugnot, and Prutz did not hesitate to see this phrase as an indication for the existence of lay schools in thirteenth-century Acre. See the footnote below the text in the *Livre* (see above, n. 44) and H. Prutz, *Kulturgeschichte der Kreuzzüge* (Berlin, 1883), p. 557.

[50] G. Müller (ed.), *Documenti sulle relazioni delle città toscane coll'Oriente cristiano e coi Turchi* (Florence, 1879, reprinted Rome, 1966), pp. 105–6.

would expect to find in Acre some teachers paid by parents, or, in the case of poor children, by wealthy parents of other children (as was customary in the West) or by the community (as was customary in the East).[51] In Eastern communities, these teachers would be expected to provide young children with the basic abilities required for participation in synagogue activities, mainly, reading the Torah. In the West, children would normally be taught biblical reading, translation and basic interpretation and, perhaps, some rudiments of Talmudic studies.[52] Unfortunately, only one, indirect, piece of evidence survives with regard to elementary education from thirteenth-century Acre: in a letter that has to do with the death of his brother in Acre, one of al-Malik al-'Azīz's physicians, a Jew, writes that the deceased's cloth is being kept by Jacob 'who used to teach the children of Abū'l-Waḥsh Al-Sabbāgh'.[53] We thus have here a clear indication that a private teacher, working, in all likelihood, within the Eastern tradition, lived in Acre.

The evidence concerning teaching activities in the city can be supported by the information presented earlier concerning the activities of Jewish scholars in Acre. In other words, it is likely, for example, that at least some of the persons who signed the 1234 rabbinical decision [**1:6**] engaged in teaching.[54] Similarly, while, it is now agreed that R. Yehiel of Paris did not reach Acre, and that the yeshiva he headed was located in Paris rather than in the East, the tradition he was a part of surely had its continuance in Acre, which is likely to have resulted in teaching activities there.[55] Furthermore, we have seen that Joseph of Santis' questions to Rashba shed light on the study of Talmud in the city by Joseph as well as by others. At the same time, however, the fact that Joseph studied a Talmudic tract with Rashba, living thousands of kilometres away, may attest that at

[51] S. D. Goitein, *Jewish Education in Muslim Countries* (Jerusalem, 1962), p. 36 [Hebrew]; E. Kanarfogel, *Jewish Education and Society in the High Middle Ages* (Detroit, MI, 1992), pp. 19–21.

[52] Goitein, *Jewish Education in Muslim Countries*, p. 36; Kanarfogel, *Jewish Education and Society*, p. 31. For Jewish education in medieval Egypt, see also J. Olszowy-Schlanger, 'Learning to Read and Write in Medieval Egypt: Children's Exercise Books from the Cairo Geniza', *Journal of Semitic Studies* 48.1 (Spring 2003), pp. 47–69.

[53] The latter part of the name could also mean painter. For the letter, see Goitein, *Palestinian Jewry*, pp. 260–3, 268–75 [Hebrew]. See also Chapter 1, pp. 44–5.

[54] Prawer went a bit further to argue that 'those who signed the statutes do not appear as members of a court, but rather as members of an Academy or perhaps even different schools which taught in the city.' Prawer, *Jews*, p. 272. See Chapter 1, pp. 39–40.

[55] Reiner, 'Pilgrims', p. 78. Prawer, who wrote that Yehiel died on the voyage, still thought that the yeshiva was in Acre. Prawer, *Jews*, p. 275, n. 67. In a later Hebrew version of the same book he is more careful with regard to this matter. See Prawer, *Jews*, p. 227, n. 122 [Hebrew edition]. See Chapter 1, p. 39.

the time when Joseph sent his questions (1270–91), the level of learning available in the city would not have been very high.[56]

More direct evidence regarding the existence of Jewish study centres in Acre comes from Isaac of Acre, an important Kabbalah scholar who received his education in the city. In a book Isaac composed years later, introducing a tale concerning Aristotle and Alexander the Great's wife, he says:[57]

And I, Isaac, son of R. Samuel, may the Lord save him, of Acre, may it be rebuilt, take heaven, land and their creator as my witnesses, that one day, in Acre, may it be rebuilt, we students sat and learned in the presence of my teacher, R. Shlomo Tzarfati [=the French] Hakatan [=small, petit], blessed be his memory, and incidentally we got to speaking in his presence about Aristotle and the mighty wisdom he attained that he was a divine man.

From this we can learn that Isaac, along with other pupils, studied at Acre with Solomon Petit, a prominent scholar.[58] The story recounted following the introduction shows that Solomon meant to deride Aristotle, which is hardly surprising given his anti-rationalist view also expressed in his strong opposition to Maimonides' philosophical works.[59]

In another work of his, titled *Otzar Ha-Hayim* (*The Treasure of Life*), Isaac provides yet more evidence regarding his experiences as a pupil. He describes a discussion which refers to a section of R. Abraham Abul'afia's 'Life in the Afterworld':[60]

And I heard from my teacher, may he rest in heaven, who said that 'lad' is an appellation, because he [Moses] is the oldest of all created and should have been called 'old' and not 'lad', and he said this is nothing but an appellation because in Arabic old is 'shekh' and the secret [meaning the arithmetic value according to the system of Gematria] of 'lad' [na'ar] is [equivalent to that of] shekh. One of the pupils said: But in Arabic no one says 'shekh', without 'i' but rather 'sheikh', with

---

[56] Emanuel, "'From Where the Sun Rises'", pp. 477–80.

[57] ואני יה"ב שנ"ר דעת"ו [יצחק הצעיר ברבי שמואל ברבי רחמנא נטרי תיבנה ותכונן] מעיד עלי שמים וארץ ואת בוראם כי בעכו ת"ו היינו יום אחד אנחנו התלמידים יושבים ושונים לפני מורי הרב ר' שלמה צרפתי הקטן ז"ל ואגב גררא הגענו לדבר לפניו על אריסטוטליס בעוצם חכמתו אשר השיג שהיה איש אלהי... Isaac of Acre, 'Meirat Einayim', ed. A. Goldreich, unpublished PhD thesis, Hebrew University (1981), part 2, p. 56 [Hebrew]. This tale was recently discussed within the context of its Christian versions: A. Melamed, 'The Hebrew Versions of the Story on Aristotle and Alexander's Wife', *Daat: A Journal of Jewish Philosophy and Kabbalah* 74/75 (2013), pp. 325–56 [Hebrew]. For Isaac, see also Fishbane, *As Light before Dawn*.

[58] See Chapter 1, p. 40.   [59] See Chapter 1, pp. 40–41.

[60] ושמעתי מפי מורי נ"ע שאמר נ"ע כי נער הוא כינוי כי הוא [משה] הזקן שבכל הנבראים והיה ראוי ליקרא זקן ולא נער' ואמר כי אין זה אלא כינוי שכן בלשון ערבי אומרין לזקן שך ועור סודו שך אמר לו אחד מהתלמידים והלא בערבי אין אומרין שך בלא יוד רק כזה שיך ומה נעשה בעשרה אלה היתרים ולא ענהו כלום ונשאר הדבר בספק 'This work has not yet been edited. I cite here from the following manuscript: Moscow, Ginzburg, MS 775, fol. 131b. This story is cited and commented on in Idel, 'Eretz-Israel', pp. 122–3 [Hebrew].

'i', and what do we do with these extra ten? And he did not reply and this remained doubtful.

Here we witness a classroom scene, in which Arabic is used for Gematria (the system of assigning numerical values to words), and a student argues with a teacher over the spelling of a word in that language. Presumably, the teacher knew no Arabic and simply followed Abul'afia's argument, while the pupil who was well versed in Arabic corrected him. While Isaac provides no evidence as to where this incident took place, it is likely that, as Idel argued, it occurred in the Holy Land.[61]

The study centres which operated in Acre seem to have attracted scholars from distant regions. An interesting piece of evidence for Western Jews travelling to the city for scholarly reasons comes from a colophon which recounts how a father and son, travelling to Venice in order to embark on a ship to Acre, stopped at Ferrara, where their host became interested in buying a book they had with them, and, as the father refused to sell it, decided to copy it. The father, described in the colophon as a 'pupil' (תלמיד), was probably connected to some kind of study centre, and it is likely that he intended to join another at Acre.[62]

It is probable that some students came to the city to benefit from the opportunity of learning with Nahmanides. In the *addenda* to his Torah exegesis [1:13], composed in Acre, he writes:[63]

Furthermore, we have investigated and know it from the word of many students who lived in that country that Cuthah is a large city between Haran and Assyria, far from the country of Babylon. The distance between it and Haran is about that of a six-day journey. It is, however, included in the term, 'beyond the river', because it lies between Mesopotamia and the river Euphrates – which is the border of the land of Israel – and the Tigris which goeth towards the east of Assyria.

---

[61] Idel writes that, theoretically, Isaac may have learned Abul'afia's ideas in Spain, or in Italy, while he was on his way to Spain. In his opinion, however, that is improbable, since no evidence connects Abul'afia's students to Iberia, or attests to the activity of Abul'afia's pupils in Sicily – Abul'afia's stronghold – after 1291, the year in which Isaac left the Holy Land. Idel provides several additional citations that also have to do with Isaac's experiences as a pupil. None of these, however, includes indications as to their geographical context. Idel, 'Eretz-Israel', pp. 122–3.

[62] I. M. Ta-Shema, *Studies in Medieval Rabbinic Literature* 4 (Jerusalem, 2010), pp. 264–5 [Hebrew]; Reiner, 'Pilgrims', p. 83; I. S. J. Wolfson, 'The Parma Colophon of Abraham ben Ephraim's Book of Precepts', *Journal of Jewish Studies* 21 (1970), pp. 39–47, and Chapter 5, p. 136.

[63] 'ועוד חקרנו וידענו על פי תלמידים רבים שהיו יושבי הארץ ההיא, כי כותא עיר גדולה בין חרן ובין אשור רחוקה ממדינת בבל, ובינה ובין חרן כמו ששה ימים, אבל היא נכללת בעבר הנהר בעבור היותה בין ארם נהרים ובין נהר פרת גבול ארץ ישראל, ובין חדקל ההולך קדמת אשור'. Moshe ben Nahman, *Exegesis*, vol. I, p. 72 [Hebrew]. For the English translation, see Ramban, *Commentary*, vol. I, pp. 157–8.

While this is not stated explicitly here, it is likely that at least some of the numerous pupils whom Nahmanides describes as flocking to the city from the East were specifically interested in studying with him and that this was their main reason for travelling to Acre. That scholars indeed travelled to Acre to study with Nahmanides is further supported by evidence concerning R. Sheshet who is said to have travelled to the city with the specific purpose of consulting Nahmanides regarding Kabbalistic matters.[64]

CONCLUSION

Despite the fragmentary nature of the available evidence, the material presented in this chapter does enable us to say that considerable and varied teaching activities were taking place in thirteenth-century Acre. As far as Frankish society is concerned, the Dominican and Franciscan convents played a central role in such activities, probably along other institutions such as the Hospitaller house and the city's cathedral. Among the teachers operating in the city – or those present in the city and likely to have taught in it – one finds persons who brought with them from the West advanced learning, as well as others who accumulated extraordinary knowledge in the East. Frankish teaching in the city may have been attractive enough to draw to Acre students from other cities and regions of the Latin East. To this should be added that some of the teaching activities taking place in Acre were unusual, and in part unique, when compared to those known at the time in the West. Under this category belong the instruction of non-Latins, that is Muslim converts and Eastern Christians, as well as the teaching of Eastern languages in the Dominican convent.

We have also presented the available evidence for instruction within Acre's Jewish communities, showing that during the thirteenth century teaching activities related to several traditions were taking place. While the very limited body of extant source material makes it hard to assess the level of learning which was possible to attain in Acre, we did provide evidence showing that some Jews came to the city from faraway regions specifically in order to study in it. In that sense, one can argue that, at least during some of the period under discussion, Acre's intellectual appeal within Jewish society was quite high and, notably, stronger than that within Christian society.

---

[64] 'And my teacher told me that in the last part the Rabbi's life, R. Sheshet went to him in Acre and asked him the secret.' ['... . ואמ' לי מורי כי באחרית ימי הרב הלך ר' ששת אליו לעכו ושאל ממנו הסוד'] Isaac of Acre, 'Meirat Einayim', p. 37. G. Scholem, 'On the Study of "Torat Ha-Gilgul" in 13th-Century Kabbalah', *Tarbiz* 16 (1945), p. 140 [Hebrew].

Chapter 3

LANGUAGE AND TRANSLATION

Had we been given the chance to walk through the bustling markets and streets of thirteenth-century Acre, we would have been struck by the great variety of languages used. Other than French, which was the dominant language spoken in the city, these would have included Provençal, various Italian and German dialects, English, Arabic and Greek.[1] According to Laura Minervini, the composite character of the Latin East's population and its mosaic-like structure resulted in a plurilingual situation in which different linguistic communities shared a given territory with only a small number of people serving as intermediaries.[2] It is the aim of this chapter to explore the implications of the presence of a variety of languages and linguistic systems in and around the city for the intellectual life that developed in it, while also asking whether the different linguistic communities active in this cultural environment were as isolated as Minervini's definition implies.

ACRE AS A CENTRE OF EASTERN LANGUAGES EXPERTISE

Latin Christendom in the thirteenth century was a cultural world in which the knowledge of Eastern languages was rare. This is well exemplified by the testimony of Roger Bacon, who recounts how on one occasion the king of France was unable to find anywhere in his kingdom a person who could translate a letter he received from a Muslim leader.[3] Against this background, Acre was to acquire the reputation of a centre of linguistic expertise, as is reflected in the words of Giovanni Villani, who wrote that translators of all of the world's languages could be found in the city.[4] While he clearly exaggerates, it is noteworthy that years after the fall

---

[1] Minervini, 'La français', pp. 119–98; Jacoby, 'Aspects', p. 99.   [2] Minervini, 'La français', p. 129.
[3] Roger Bacon, *Opus Majus*, vol. III, p. 120.
[4] '…e turcimanni v'avea di tutte le lingue del mondo, sì ch'ella era quasi com'uno alimento al mondo.' *Cronica di Giovanni Villani* [ed. not mentioned], 7 vols. (Florence, 1823), vol. II, p. 356.

of the city a Western author perceived the presence of interpreters skilled in a great variety of languages as one of Acre's main traits. In the following pages we explore the existing evidence with regard to processes of accumulation and employment of knowledge of Eastern languages in the city.

One kind of activity which contributed to the accumulation of such knowledge in Acre was the organized teaching of languages. Unfortunately, the evidence for such activities is very scarce. However, one explicit, and very significant, piece of evidence regarding this issue does survive. It appears in a letter addressed by Philip, prior of the Dominicans in the Holy Land, to Pope Gregory IX and dated 1237. In this letter, as provided by Matthew Paris, we read the following:[5]

> Therefore seeing the door so wide open that the truth of the Christian message could be spread, we dedicated ourselves to learning the languages of the gentiles; and we set up a language *studium* in each convent, adding new labour to old. And through the grace of the Lord they [the brethren] already speak and preach in new languages, and especially in Arabic, which is the more common among the gentiles.

In other words, before 1237 the Dominicans already had several *studia* in the Holy Land province devoted to the instruction of Oriental languages, and, in particular, of Arabic. This is very significant not only because at the time such activities were rare but also because this is the earliest piece of evidence for a Dominican programme for the study of foreign languages.[6] By initiating this programme, the Dominicans of the Holy Land followed a decision made in the 1236 general chapter of the order.[7] Their motivation for such activities is made clear by Philip's letter: they were intended to enable friars to preach to Muslims. Notably, however, this was done very rarely, and the knowledge of Arabic, as well as that of additional Eastern languages, was actually employed more often in three

---

[5] 'Unde videntes ostium tantum apertum, ut veritas evangelii dilatetur, dedimus nosmetipsos ad linguas gentium addiscendas; et studium linguarum in singulis conventibus statuimus, laborem novum veteri apponentes. Et jam per Dei gratiam linguis loquuntur novis et praedicant, et maxime in Arabica, quae communior est inter gentes.' MP, vol. III, p. 398. Another version of this letter appears in Scheffer-Boichorst, *Chronica Albrici*, pp. 941–2. The two versions have no substantial differences between them.

[6] J. Rubin, 'The Beginnings of the Study of Foreign Languages in the Dominican Order: Regulation, Implementation and Impact', in C. Linde (ed.), *Making and Breaking the Rules. Discussion, Implementation, and Consequences of Dominican Legislation* [forthcoming].

[7] In the 1236 general chapter of the order it was stated that: 'Monemus quod in omnibus provinciis et conventibus fratres linguas addiscant illorum quibus sunt propinqui.' B. M. Reichert (ed.), *Acta capitulorum generalium* (Rome, 1898), vol. I, p. 9 ('We instruct that in all provinces and convents friars should learn the languages of those to whom they are near.')

other fields of action: communication with Oriental Christians, the composition of polemical texts and diplomatic missions.[8]

No further evidence exists for the organized study of Eastern languages by Acre's Frankish inhabitants. However, it is likely that friars belonging to the order of the Trinity also benefitted from some form of linguistic instruction in Arabic, without which they would not have been capable of accomplishing their main task – the liberation of Christian captives held by Muslims. Furthermore, there is evidence that in Toledo brothers of the Trinity learned Arabic to facilitate their activities.[9] Additional evidence for the learning of Arabic by Franks in Acre comes from a manuscript dating to 1196, which includes an Arabic medical text with Latin marginalia, which were probably added in the city during the thirteenth century. As certain characteristics of the manuscript suggest that it was intended for someone whose first language was not Arabic, it is likely that its owner was a Latin who was active in Acre and had learned Arabic there.[10]

The linguistic knowledge circulating in the city was also enriched by people who learned Eastern languages, or gained information about such languages, elsewhere. Such were probably some of the Dominican friars whom Philip says he sent to Armenia in order to learn Armenian.[11] Another case of accumulation of linguistic expertise in foreign territories, which was later brought into Acre, is that of William of Rubruck, who during his travels clearly reached some, although certainly not very high, level of knowledge in several Eastern languages. Writing in his *Itinerarium* [**2:23**] about his inability to preach through an insufficiently skilled interpreter, he comments: 'Later, when I acquired some little knowledge of the language, I noticed that when I said one thing he [the interpreter] would say something totally different, depending on what came into his head.'[12] Later in his journal he says that Qutai, one of Mangu's wives, 'also began to teach me the language, making fun of me because my lack of an interpreter rendered me dumb'.[13] But, perhaps more significant is the fact that in his work, most probably composed in Acre, William

---

[8] Regarding the beginnings of the study of foreign languages and the employment of such knowledge among the Dominicans, see Rubin, 'The Beginnings'.

[9] C. Burnett, 'The Coherence of the Arabic-Latin Translation Program in Toledo in the Twelfth Century', in C. Burnett, *Arabic into Latin: The Translators and Their Intellectual and Social Context*, Variorum Collected Studies (Farnham, 2009), num. vii, p. 253.

[10] Savage-Smith, 'New Evidence', pp. 99–112.

[11] 'Et nos iam festinamus mittere quatuor fratres in Armeniam, ad linguam addiscendam.' MP, vol. III, pp. 397–8 ('And we are just now hastening to send four friars to Armenia to learn that language.')

[12] Jackson and Morgan, *The Mission*, p. 108. For the Latin text, see Guglielmo, *Viaggio*, p. 64.

[13] Jackson and Morgan, *The Mission*, p. 198; cf. Guglielmo, *Viaggio*, p. 192.

included some original linguistic observations, admired by modern scholars.[14] For example, he is considered the first to have noticed the connection between the languages of the Russians, the Poles, the Bohemians, the Slavonians and the Vandals.[15] He was also well informed concerning the script of various Eastern peoples, and was the first Western author to comment on the Chinese written characters.[16]

While there is evidence that William taught in Acre's Franciscan convent, we do not know whether his fields of instruction included Eastern languages.[17] However, given the emphasis on the study of such languages in the mendicant orders, it is likely that he shared at least some of his knowledge with friars active in Acre. Furthermore, linguistic information brought by William into the city would have also been relevant to Franks based there and involved in activities such as long-distance trade or diplomatic missions. The Dominican David of Ashby presents a similar case. Starting from 1260 he spent a long period in Mongol territory, at times accompanying the Mongol army. Then, sometime before 1274, he returned to Acre. David, who also accompanied a Mongol embassy on its way to Lyon, must have had some knowledge of Oriental languages, which he possibly shared with some of the city's residents.[18]

The concentration of linguistic expertise in the city is also attested to by the recurrent use of translators from Acre by the city's leaders, by Westerners staying in the city and by those travelling through it. Several Franks from Acre, who knew Arabic well and functioned as envoys, have already been mentioned.[19] Additionally, in 1255 William of Rubruck met at Ani four Dominicans sent by the French province to whom was attached a fifth friar in Syria, perhaps in order to serve as a translator into Arabic.[20] A group of Dominican envoys headed by David of Ashby, and capable of speaking Mongol or, at least, Persian, was sent in 1260 by Thomas Agni and the Kingdom of Jerusalem's regent to the

---

[14] A. Borst, *Der Turmbau von Babel*, 4 vols. (Stuttgart, 1957–63), vol. II, p. 773; B. Bischoff, 'The Study of Foreign Languages in the Middle Ages', *Speculum* 36.2 (1961), p. 214. It is noteworthy that Bischoff refers to William's observations as 'quite amazing'. Peter Jackson and David Morgan also admire his achievements with regard to linguistics. Jackson and Morgan, *The Mission*, pp. 50–1.

[15] Jackson and Morgan, *The Mission*, p. 139 and note 5 there; Guglielmo, *Viaggio*, p. 104 and note on p. 410.

[16] Jackson and Morgan, *The Mission*, pp. 50, 203–4, n. 1; Guglielmo, *Viaggio*, p. 200.

[17] Concerning William's teaching in Acre, see Chapter 2, pp. 51–2.

[18] Regarding David of Ashby, see Chapter 1, pp. 23, 36.   [19] See Chapter 1, p. 35.

[20] Guglielmo, *Viaggio*, p. 310; J. Richard, *La papauté et les missions d'Orient au moyen âge* (Rome, 1977), p. 78; P. Pelliot, 'Les Mongols et la papauté II', *Revue de l'Orient Chrétien* 28 (1931–2), p. 78. Note that William says that the five 'non habebant nisi unum garcionem infirmum qui sciebat Turkum et parum de Gallico.'

Mongols.[21] In 1271 (or perhaps in 1272), while Nicolo and Maffeo Polo visited Acre, they were provided with two Dominican friars who were supposed to escort them on their way to the East.[22] These too must have had some knowledge of languages spoken in Central Asia. In 1278 Charles of Anjou asked Roger of Saint Severinus, his representative in the Kingdom of Jerusalem, to provide a translator for a group of messengers heading to the Mongol khan.[23] As it is clear that at the time Roger was expected to be in Acre, this document attests that Charles thought that it was possible to get a translator in the city who would be useful for an expedition to the khan.[24] Note that Acre's translators were also used for the preparation of letters taken on such expeditions: William of Rubruck took with him on his voyage letters by Louis IX with translations into Arabic and Syriac which were produced in the city.[25]

The growing acquaintance of Westerners in Acre with Eastern languages, and the presence of translators in the city, created favourable conditions for the undertaking of various projects involving translation. Jacques de Vitry used translators for the preparation of letters written in Arabic, in which, as he recounts, he presented to Muslims 'their errors and the truth of our law', and which were sent to Muslim territories. While these texts did not reach us, they must have been elaborate polemic tracts rather than plain letters, the preparation of which required a significant effort, not only by Jacques but also by the translators working with him.[26]

Another project which demanded linguistic skills, and which may have been undertaken in Acre, is the production of an Arabic–French pharmaceutical glossary in which both languages are represented by Latin characters. This document, which has received little scholarly attention, begins with a title in which its two authors are described: the first is Willame, described as a 'poulain', that is a person of Frankish origin who was born in the East, and as a 'chevalier'. The other is Jacques, described as a 'new Christian' and as an apothecary. While there is no positive evidence with regard to the circumstances in which this text was written, its linguistic characteristics suggest that it was composed in the Latin East

---

[21] Richard, 'Le début des relations', pp. 295–6.
[22] This matter is discussed in detail by Engels, in his introduction to William of Tripoli's *Notitia*; see *Notitia*, pp. 28–32.
[23] Mayer, *Urkunden*, vol. III, pp. 1284–5. The letter dates to 28 August 1278.
[24] Mayer, *Urkunden*, vol. III, pp. 1282–3.
[25] Describing his visit to Sartach's court, William writes: '. . .optuli ei litteras vestras cum transcriptis in Arabico et Siriano: feceram enim eas transferri in Acon in utraque lingua et littera. . . ' Guglielmo, *Viaggio*, p. 76.
[26] Jacques de Vitry, *Lettres*, p. 577.

around 1300.[27] More specifically, Acre, a port city in which *materia medica* was intensively traded, and a place in which an Outremer-born knight and a Muslim convert could have easily met, seems to be the most likely setting for such a project.

The result of this case of intercultural exchange was a sizable glossary consisting of 565 entries, including the names of plants, minerals and animals, which must have been intended to provide apothecaries or merchants with some basic, practical understanding of Arabic pharmacological terminology. Very often all that is included is an Arabic term and its French equivalent with or without the word 'dicitur' ('is called') connecting them. Thus, for example, we find this entry: '*anzarut* dicitur *cercaculle*' ('anzarut means cercaculle').[28] In such cases, one must assume that the substance under discussion was known to the glossary's intended audience, that is, most likely, Western merchants or apothecaries, and so all that was required was to provide them with the equivalent French term. In other cases, however, the phrasing of the entry reveals that a French parallel did not exist or, at least was unknown to the glossary's authors or intended audience: '*Asnen* dicitur une purre que on lave le mains utre mer' ('asnen [ushnan] means a powder [with] which people wash their hands in Outremer').[29] Another phrase sheds further light on the cultural context in which the glossary was compiled: 'Baurach, che e[st] une man[er]e de sel' ('Baurach [=bawraq], which is a kind of salt').[30] Interestingly, in this case an equivalent Latin term, 'borax', was already known in learned circles in the West, but was not used by the authors, implying that the glossary was both composed by and intended for people who would not have been familiar with Latin pharmacological terminology, and thus represents a separate discourse from that focused on Latin pharmacological texts.

Several additional projects involving the crossing of language barriers are related to the Dominican friars, who, as we have seen, were pioneers in the study of Eastern languages. Firstly, the Maronites sent books of theirs to the Dominicans of the Holy Land, so that the latter would correct them. What books these were is unknown, but it is quite clear that they consisted of sacred texts. If we are to trust Humbert of Romans, the master general of the order (1254–63), the friars took this task very seriously.[31] An additional project in which the city's Dominicans seem to

---

[27] G. Ineichen, 'Il glossario arabo-francese di messer Guglielmo e maestro Giacomo', *Atti dell'Instituto Veneto di Scienze, Lettere ed Arti*, 130 (1971–2), pp. 353–407; Laura Minervini considers this text as indicative of the French of Outremer. Minervini, 'Les emprunts', pp. 99–197, *et passim*.

[28] Ineichen, 'Il glossario arabo-francese', p. 364; Minervini, 'Les emprunts', p. 108.

[29] Ineichen, 'Il glossario arabo-francese', p. 365.

[30] Ineichen, 'Il glossario arabo-francese', p. 368; Minervini, 'Les emprunts', p. 113.

[31] See Chapter 6.

have participated is the translation of a collection of Marian legends from Latin or French into Arabic [**3:42**].[32] This was a significant enterprise which included the translation of at least seventy-four stories and brought about their adoption by the Coptic and later Ethiopian churches.[33] Interestingly, even the earliest Arabic manuscripts of this collection reveal that the stories included were, to use Baraz's term, 'Copticized'. According to his analysis, in comparison to the Western source, the Arabic versions present a milder portrayal of both sinners and their actions, and an emphasis on the sinners' acts of penitence. Additionally, the Arabic versions are characterized by the omission of didactic and moralizing sentences, as well as by a more elaborate literary character. Finally, the Arabic translations omit various elements which were irrelevant outside the Latin world such as names of specific churches and holy days from the Catholic calendar.[34] These differences between the original Western legends and the Arabic versions suggest that the friars did not produce this collection by themselves but rather cooperated closely with members of the Coptic Church.

Another major project undertaken in the milieu of Acre's Dominicans is the composition of William of Tripoli's *Notitia de Machometo* [**1:17**]. In more than one way this work, dated to 1271, attests to the linguistic skills and sensibilities found among some learned Franks active in Acre. Firstly, William acknowledges the Qur'an as extraordinary in its sweetness and exquisite eloquence.[35] Secondly, he expresses a wish that his readers would be provided with actual Qur'anic texts in translation rather than with descriptions of the holy book's content.[36] For that reason, William tells us, he translated various Qur'anic sections which he thought were particularly relevant for his audience.[37] While the question of William's command of the Arabic language – and therefore of his ability

---

[32] That this collection was produced within a Dominican context is made clear by the considerable number of stories included which are associated with the order. D. Baraz, 'Bartolomeo da Trento's Book of Marian Miracles', *Orientalia Christiana Periodica* 60 (1994), pp. 75–6.

[33] D. Baraz, 'Coptic-Arabic Collections of Western Marian Legends: The Reception of a Western Text in the East – A Case of Intercultural Relations in the Late Middle Ages', *Acts of the Fifth International Congress of Coptic Studies* II (Rome, 1993), p. 23.

[34] Baraz, 'Bartolomeo da Trento', p. 83; Baraz, 'Coptic-Arabic', pp. 23–32.

[35] 'Compilaverunt itaque librum multa diligentia et profunditate obscura; et dulcedine mirabilis et exquisite facundie. . . ' *Notitia*, p. 212. For more concerning the *Notitia*, see Chapter 5.

[36] '. . .nolui per aliena verba narrare nec mutare sensum nec verba, et pietate vera et fide sincera transtuli de arabico in latinum. . . ' *Notitia*, p. 222.

[37] These translated sections are not discussed in T. Burman, *Reading the Qur'an in Latin Christendom 1140–1560* (Philadelphia, PA, 2007). The translated sections appear in the *Notitia* in: p. 212, lines 25–7; p. 216, lines 34–8 (not mentioned explicitly as a translation); p. 218, lines 2–5, 8–11; p. 226, lines 3–9, 10–13, 14–16, 17–21, 22–34; p. 228, lines 35–45, 46–53; p. 230, lines 54–62, 63–6, 67–9, 70–6; p. 232, lines 77–81, 82–6, 87–93, 94–100, 101–7; p. 234, lines 111–18, 119–25, 126–36; p. 242, lines 47–8, 50–4; p. 258, lines 51–3; p. 260, lines 72–3.

to have actually produced such translations himself – is open to debate,[38] it remains a fact that a Frankish scholar working in Acre was able to include in his work impressive (from the point of view of their overall accuracy) translations from the Qur'an.[39] As these translated sections are not attested to elsewhere, they are likely to have either been produced specifically for William's work (by him or by someone else) or to have been prepared in his cultural environment and employed by him.[40] They thus provide evidence for the high degree of linguistic competence that characterized some learned Latins active in Acre. Furthermore, they reveal that at least some of the city's scholars thought it was important to provide their readers with exact translations from Arabic in order to inform them about Muslim culture. This attitude is also evident in the work of the so-called Templar of Tyre. As mentioned earlier, in his chronicle he provides a French translation of the opening of al-Malik al-Ashraf's letter to the master of the Templar order, drawing the readers' attention to the precise phrasing of the salutation.[41]

The sociolinguistic conditions prevalent in the city also enabled learned men staying in Acre to widen their knowledge of Eastern languages. This phenomenon left traces in the works of two of the most prominent scholars who spent time in the city: Moses Nahmanides and Jacques de Vitry. In one of his *addenda* to the Torah exegesis [1:13], we see that during his stay in Acre, Nahmanides learned a Greek word which he found useful for his discussion of Genesis 43.20. This word is probably βία, and its pronunciation as described by him – beginning with the sound 'v' rather than 'b' – suggests that he learned it from a contemporary Greek speaker.[42] Nahmanides' discussion of the old coin he saw in Acre also reveals a case in which Jews residing in the city acquired linguistic knowledge through their contact with members of other cultural groups: in this case, Samaritans deciphered the paleo-Hebrew script on the coin, thus helping Nahmanides in the solution of a difficulty raised by the biblical text. Another *addendum* provides possible evidence for Nahmanides' growing sensitivity to different manners of translation.[43]

---

[38] *Notitia*, p. 88; see Chapter 5, pp. 124-6.

[39] As seen later (Chapter 5, pp. 124-6), the translations included in chapters 7 and 9 of the *Notitia* – and which make the great majority of translated sections in this work – are quite exact. Those which appear in other parts of the work are of lower quality.

[40] I compared sections from the *Notitia* with parallel sections from both of the Latin translations of the Qur'an which existed at the time – Mark of Toledo's and Robert of Ketton's – as these appear in M.-T. d'Alverny, 'Deux traductions latines du Coran au moyen âge', *Archives d'histoire doctrinale et littéraire du moyen âge* 22–3 (1946–8), pp. 69–113. As far as can be inferred from this partial comparison, there is no dependence between these works.

[41] See Chapter 1, p. 33.   [42] Ofer and Jacobs, *Nahmanides' Torah*, pp. 268–9.

[43] Ofer and Jacobs, *Nahmanides' Torah*, pp. 260–1. See also Chapter 1, p. 43.

Jacques de Vitry's interest in foreign languages is revealed through his description of various religious groups he encountered in the Latin East. These include comments on the languages employed by their members in different spheres of life. Thus, in his *Historia orientalis* [**1:4**], Jacques writes that the *Suriani* use Arabic in their everyday conversation, and employ Arabic writing in contracts and transactions, as well as in all other activities except in spiritual matters, in which they use Greek. He also notes that for this reason, their laymen, who speak no language other than Arabic, do not understand their clergy as these recite the divine office, while the *Graeci*, who employ Greek both in everyday communication and in writing, can follow their priests.[44] Similar discussions appear in the *Historia orientalis* also with regard to the Jacobites, the Nestorians, the Maronites, the Armenians and the Georgians,[45] revealing how intriguing the variety and complexity of the linguistic systems found in Acre were for a person such as Jacques. Notably, his comments are based on an earlier text, the *Tractatus de locis et statu sancte terre* [**3:32**], but, not content with copying the comments found in his written source, Jacques elaborated them. Thus, for example, while in the *Tractatus* we read only that the Armenians have their own script, Jacques writes that they have their own language and letters, and that they pronounce the divine scripture in their everyday language, so that the clergy is understood by the laymen just as in the case of the Greeks.[46] One can conclude, then, that the complexity and the variety of ways in which different Eastern groups used their languages attracted, at least occasionally, Frankish attention.

OLD FRENCH IN FRANKISH ACRE

More surprising, perhaps, than the fact that Acre became an arena in which unique knowledge concerning Eastern languages circulated and developed, is the city's importance in the history of French and its literature. The city housed significant translation projects from Latin into French, and, perhaps more important, novel ideas concerning the status of the vernacular circulated there.

Before moving into the field of translation and perceptions of the vernacular, it is important to ask, as with regard to Eastern languages, whether French was taught in the city. The answer to this question is probably yes. A French–Arabic glossary preserves evidence suggesting that Copts were taught by Franks in Acre, and thus must have also

---

[44] *HO*, p. 298.   [45] *HO*, pp. 310, 314, 318, 322.

[46] Cf. B. Z. Kedar, 'The *Tractatus de locis et statu sancte terre ierosolimitane*', in J. France and W. G. Zajac (eds.), *The Crusades and Their Sources: Essays Presented to Bernard Hamilton* (Aldershot, 1998), p. 124, and *HO*, p. 318.

acquired some knowledge of French.[47] The fact that Muslim converts were instructed by Franks in the city points in the same direction, as such converts must have been taught at least some Latin and French.[48] It is noteworthy that the evidence concerning the teaching of both Copts and Muslim converts is strongly related to the Dominicans. Given the findings presented earlier with regard to the activities of the order, this is hardly surprising. Rather, this provides additional support to the notion that Acre's Dominican convent was a significant centre of linguistic instruction and expertise.

Acre's corpus provides evidence concerning the production of several translations from Latin into French in the city. Firstly, an Anglo-Norman translation of Vegetius' *De re militari* – the earliest known translation of this work into French – was almost certainly produced in Acre [**2:29**], shedding considerable light on intellectual life in the city. As seen earlier, it was probably prepared at the request of Eleanor of Castile as a present for her husband, Prince Edward,[49] thus providing a rare example for noble patronage in the city. Furthermore, it has been persuasively argued that this translation was produced in a cultural context in which an older, now lost, French translation of the *De re militari* was circulating. This is supported by errors in the translation which can only be explained as copyist errors, as well as by the translation's title, which reads 'Vegetii philosofi de re militari de Latino in Gallicum *de novo* translatus'.[50] Additionally, the manuscript which provides this translation, Add. Ms. 1 of the Marlay Collection of the Fitzwilliam Museum, includes a Latin text of Vegetius' work which is strongly related to the French text but could not have been its direct source. This seems to mean that both the Latin and French texts included in the Fitzwilliam volume are based on an earlier Latin manuscript.[51] Furthermore, it has been suggested that the Fitzwilliam translation is in part dependent on another Latin witness of the *De re militari*.[52] From this primarily philological evidence one may safely conclude that several codices including the *De re militari*, in Latin and in French, circulated in the city. But that is not all. A recent study provides strong evidence for the production of another French translation of Vegetius' work in the Latin East and perhaps specifically in Acre. This anonymous translation is extant in two manuscripts which include

---

[47] See Chapter 2, p. 54.   [48] See Chapter 2, pp. 53-4.   [49] See Chapter 1, p. 25.

[50] L. K. Carely, 'The Anglo-Norman Vegetius: A Thirteenth Century Translation of the *De re militari*', unpublished Ph.D. thesis, University of Nottingham (1962), pp. 51–3, although note that 'de novo' may also mean 'recently'.

[51] Carely, 'The Anglo-Norman', pp. 59–60.

[52] E. De la Cruz Vergari, 'Édition critique d'une traduction française anonyme en prose du XIII_e siècle de l'*Epitoma rei militaris de Végèce*', unpublished PhD thesis, University of Barcelona (2016), pp. 51–2.

illuminations which seem to connect them to the city, and present *scripta* characteristic of the French of Outremer.[53] In other words, Vegetius' work was very popular in Acre, partly among groups unable to fluently read Latin. The appeal of the *De re militari* for such circles in a city in which war played a central role is not surprising given that this work was often seen, in the eyes of medieval authors, as providing relevant practical advice.[54]

At least two additional translations are associated with the city. William of Santo Stefano, a prominent Hospitaller knight probably from Lombardy, had certain documents in the order's archive, including the order's rule, translated from Latin into French, perhaps by John of Antioch [2:30]. These were included in a compilation edited between 1278 and 1283.[55] Around the same time, William commissioned John of Antioch to translate from Latin into French two Latin treatises on rhetoric [1:19]. John almost certainly also translated the *Otia imperialia* into French, but whether this was also done in Acre remains unknown.[56]

Of Acre's French into Latin translations, that of the works on rhetoric is the most significant, enabling us to peek into Acre's intellectual arena and, in particular, to explore the encounter between norms and notions prevalent in the West at the time and the culture that emerged in Outremer. This text, dated to 1282, reached us in a single manuscript now in Chantilly, which is probably the original codex presented by John to his patron, William of Santo Stefano. This volume includes four

---

[53] De la Cruz Vergari, 'Édition critique', *passim*.

[54] C. Allmand, The *De re militari of Vegetius: The Reception, Transmission and Legacy of a Roman Text in the Middle Ages* (Cambridge, 2012), p. 67. That the *De re militari* was often perceived by medieval authors as providing relevant practical advice can be seen through the use of extant manuscripts of the work. Allmand, The De re militari, p. 347.

[55] Luttrell, 'The Hospitallers', pp. 139–41.

[56] Paris, Bibliothèque nationale de France, MS fr. 9113 includes a French translation of Gervais of Tilbury's *Otia imperialia* to which are added five original chapters, probably written by the translator. It is most likely that the translator of this work, mentioned in the manuscript as 'maystre Harent d'Antioche', is John of Antioch, since in the aforementioned manuscript including the translations of the works on rhetoric, he is referred to as 'Johan d'Antioche, que l'en apele de Harens'. This was the opinion of both Léopold Delisle and Gaston Paris. Although it was later rejected by Raphael Levy, there seems to be no reason to doubt this identification. More recently, in an introduction to an edition of a considerable part of this translation, it was again maintained that John was the *Otia*'s translator. C. Pignatelli and D. Gerner, *Les traductions françaises des Otia Imperialia de Gervais de Tilbury par Jean d'Antioche et Jean de Vignay, edition de la troisième partie* (Geneva, 2006), pp. 25–9, 51–4, 431–8; C. Pignatelli, 'Un traducteur qui affiche ses croyances: l'ajout d'exempla au corpus des *Otia imperialia* de Gervais de Tilbury dans la traduction attribuée à Jean d'Antioche', in M. Colombo Timelli and C. Galderisi (eds.), *'Pour acquerir honneur et pris'. Mélanges de moyen français offerts à Giuseppe Di Stefano* (Montréal, 2004), pp. 47–58; R. Levy, *Chronologie approximative de la littérature française du moyen âge, Beihefte zur Zeitschrift für Romanische Philologie* 98 (1957), pp. 22–4; L. Delisle, 'Maître Jean d'Antioche, traducteur et Frère Guillaume de Saint-Ettienne, hospitalier', *Histoire Littéraire de la France* 33 (Paris, 1906), pp. 18–19; G. Paris, *La Littérature française au moyen âge (XIe–XIVe siècle)* (Paris, n.d.), p. 153.

elements: an original introduction by John based on well-known Western traditions;[57] French translations of Cicero's *De inventione* and the anonymous *Rhetorica ad Herennium* (referred to, by John, as one work titled *Rectorique de Marc Tulles Cyceron*); an original epilogue discussing the work of translators; and a short treatise on logic.

On the one hand, this project, which reveals a high degree of interest in classical works on rhetoric, should be seen as a part of a wider cultural trend which resulted in texts such as Brunetto Latini's *Rettorica* or Bono Giamboni's *Fiore di rettorica*. In that sense, the translation reveals the impact of intellectual fashions in the West on leading figures in the Latin East, such as William of Santo Stefano. On the other hand, however, as John was producing a proper French translation rather than an adaptation, his undertaking makes a highly novel and original project within the context of late thirteenth-century Western culture.[58] Jacques Monfrin mentions John's translation of the texts on rhetoric as one of the two, or perhaps three, earliest works which, on the one hand, are 'real translations' into French rather than adaptations, and, on the other, include texts that are not of a strictly technical character.[59] Robert Lucas' survey of French translations of Latin classics to 1500 provides a similar picture: of the numerous translations that he mentions, only ten are dated to any time before the end of the thirteenth century.[60] Additionally, according to Minervini, John was the first to translate a rhetorical work into French.[61]

The novelty of John's project is also evident by the inclusion of the treatise on logic in the codex he prepared.[62] This short treatise, made with the explicit intention of introducing this field to those who cannot learn it properly, consists mostly of excerpts from the two first books of Boethius' *De topicis differentiis*, translated into French and having undergone various editorial emendations.[63] The degree of John's involvement in the

[57] E. Guadagnini, 'Cicéron et Boèce en Orient: quelques réflexions sur la *Rectorique* de Jean d'Antioche', in A. Petrina (ed.), *The Medieval Translator* 15 (Turnhout, 2013), pp. 40–5.

[58] E. Guadagnini (ed.), *La Rectorique de Cyceron tradotta da Jean d'Antioche, Edizione e glossario* (Pisa, 2009), p. 11; V. Cox, 'Ciceronian Rhetoric in Italy, 1260–1350', *Rhetorica: A Journal of the History of Rhetoric* 17.3 (Summer 1999), pp. 239–41.

[59] J. Monfrin, 'Humanisme et traductions au moyen âge', *Journal des savants* (Jan.–Mar. 1963), p. 168. See also J. Monfrin, 'Humanisme et traductions au moyen âge', in A. Fourrier (ed.), *L'humanisme médiéval dans les littératures romanes du XIIe au XIVe siècle* (Paris, 1964), p. 224.

[60] R. H. Lucas, 'Mediaeval French Translations of the Latin Classics to 1500', *Speculum* 45 (1970), pp. 225–53.

[61] That is, with the exception of some sections included in Brunetto Latini's *Trésor*. Minervini, 'Tradizioni', p. 167.

[62] For the relation of this part of the manuscript to Acre, see Appendix [1:19].

[63] For the form of Boethius' work's title, see E. Stump, *Boethius's De topicis differentiis* (London, 1978), p. 14. The discovery regarding the relation between John's treatise and Boethius' work was made by Elisa Guadagnini. See Guadagnini, 'Cicéron et Boèce', pp. 37–8.

development of this treatise is, at this stage, unclear, and he may have merely copied French excerpts he happened to find somewhere into the volume he was preparing. But Guadagnini makes a strong case for the argument that John found Boethius' text, perhaps already in the form of excerpts, in the Latin manuscript from which he translated the *Rectorique*, and then translated it into French.[64] Another possibility is that he translated excerpts from a Latin codex devoted to Boethius.[65] As Guadagnini writes, if John indeed translated these sections, then we owe him one of the first vernacular texts in logic. The innovativeness of engaging with logic using the vernacular is revealed by the words of Roger Bacon:[66]

[A] logician would not be able to express his logic if he had taught using his maternal language's vocabulary. He would have needed to invent a new vocabulary, and therefore would not have been understood by anyone save himself.

In other words, less than two decades before John presented his *Rectorique* to William, one of Europe's greatest thinkers perceived vernacular treatment of logic impossible. And indeed, in order to treat logic in the vernacular, John undertook to create new French terms. Thus, for example, his work includes the word *entimeme* (*enthymème*), which seems not to be attested elsewhere in medieval French.[67]

One can thus conclude that John was of the opinion that French could convey, in a precise manner, complex ideas in fields such as rhetoric and logic, which, at the time, were still normally reserved for Latin. John was certainly not the only one in Acre to hold this view. We can be certain that William shared John's attitude towards the vernacular, not only because John's translations of the *Rectorique* were produced at William's request, but also as, some years later, William himself composed works in history and jurisprudence using French.[68] It is also probable that others in their cultural circles held similar views on this issue: after all, a fancy codex such as the Chantilly manuscript was certainly meant to be shown.[69] These findings support the general assessment of Outremer as characterized by an inclination to use the

---

[64] Guadagnini, 'Cicéron et Boèce', pp. 39–40.

[65] It is noteworthy that a booklist which seems to be a twelfth-century book catalogue of a religious house in Nazareth includes both a volume described as consisting of '*Commenta Boetii*' and another listed as '*iii Boetii cum glosulis*'. For the catalogue, see J. S. Beddie, 'Some Notices of Books in the East in the Period of the Crusades', *Speculum* 8.2 (Apr. 1933), pp. 240–2.

[66] '. . .logicus non poterit exprimere suam logicam si monstrasset per vocabula linguae maternae; sed oporteret ipsum nova fingere, et ideo non intelligeretur nisi a seipso.' Fratris Rogeri Bacon, *Opera quaedam hactenus inedita*, ed. J. S. Brewer (London, 1859), p. 90. The *Opus tertium* is dated to 1267.

[67] Guadagnini, 'Cicéron et Boèce', pp. 39–40.   [68] Luttrell, 'The Hospitallers', pp. 146–7.

[69] Unfortunately, nothing can be said about the later use of this text.

vernacular in fields which, at the time, were usually preserved for Latin, such as historiography, prose and law.[70]

A closer examination of John's work can advance us towards a more complete understanding of his ideas concerning translation and the vernacular, and thus also of the notions that circulated in Acre and in Outremer with regard to these subjects. A particularly significant piece of evidence in this context is provided by John's methodological epilogue. Explaining why a translator should follow the author's treatment of the subject under discussion, but not his manner of speaking, he writes:[71]

[B]ecause the manner of speaking in Latin is not generally the same as that of French. Neither the properties of words nor the methods of arranging arguments and words in Latin are the same as those of French. And that is [so] generally in every language. Because every language has its own properties and its manner of speaking [*maniere de parler*]. And for that [reason] no translator or interpreter could ever translate well from one language to another if he does not instruct himself in the manner and properties of that language to which he translates. For that reason it was useful for the translator of this science to translate sometimes word for word, and sometimes and more frequently sentence for sentence, and sometimes because of the great obscurity of a sentence to add to it and lengthen it. Likewise, in a certain place in the *elocucion* he had to change and modify examples because of the discordance of letters and syllables that he found between the two languages.

Clearly, John's discussion belongs to a very long Latin tradition of contrasting *ad verbum* translations with *ad sensum* translations,[72] and he is likely to have been exposed to it, as well as to a preference among various authorities to non-literal translation, through works such as Horace's *Ars Poetica*, or Jerome's letter to Pammachius.[73] In this sense, John of Antioch

---

[70] Minervini, 'Tradizioni', p. 157.

[71] ' . . . car la maniere dou parler au latin n'est pas semblable generaument a cele dou françois, ne les proprietez des paroles, ne les raisons d'ordener les araisonemenz et les diz dou latin ne sont pas semblables a celes dou françois. Et ce est comunaument en toute lengue, quar chascune lengue a ses proprietez et sa maniere de parler, et por ce nul translateour et interpreteor ne porroit jamais bien translater d'une lengue a autre s'il ne s'enformast a la maniere et as proprietez de cele lengue en qui il translate: por la quel chose il covint au translateor de ceste science de translater aucune fois parole por parole et au(cu)ne fois et plus sovent sentence por sentence et au(cu)ne fois por la grant oscurté de la sentence li (con)vint il sozjoindre et acreistre. Autresi li (con)vint en aucun leu en l'elocucion de changier et müer exemples por la discordance de letres et de sillabes qu'il trova entre les ii lengues.' Guadagnini, *La Rectorique*, p. 350. Note that *elocucion* is the subject of the sixth book of the *Rectorique*.

[72] Guadagnini, 'Cicéron et Boèce', pp. 45–6.

[73] Horace, *Epistles Book II and Epistle to the Pisones* ('Ars Poetica'), ed. N. Rudd (Cambridge, 1989), p. 62: ' . . . nec verbo verbum curabis reddere fidus interpres . . . '; Hieronymus, *Epistularum pars I*, ed. I. Hilberg, CSEL 54 (Vienna, 1996), ep. 57, pp. 508–10: 'ego enim non solum fateor, sed libera voce profiteor me in interpretatione Graecorum absque scripturis sanctis, ubi et verborum ordo mysterium est, non verbum e verbo, sed sensum exprimere de sensu.' It is noteworthy that the booklist from a religious house in Nazareth includes both a volume described as consisting of

shows himself to be well acquainted with a well-known Western tradition. And yet it is possible that in developing his views concerning translation John was also influenced by works closer to him in terms of time and cultural environment, such as Philip of Tripoli's translation of the *Secretum secretorum*. This translation was produced in the Latin East around 1230 by a man who served as a canon in Tripoli from 1227, and who used an Arabic manuscript found in Antioch.[74] In the prologue to this work Philip writes the following:[75]

In turn, desiring humbly to obey your mandate and your will . . . I have translated with great labor and clear prose from the Arabic language into Latin – . . .sometimes literally, and sometimes according to the sense, since there is one way of speaking [*loquendi modus*] among the Arabs and another among the Latins – this book which the Latins were lacking because it is found very rarely among the Arabs.

It is possible that John, a native of Antioch, knew this work and acquired some of his views on translation from it. Support for this hypothesis is provided by the similarity between Philip's *modus loquendi* employed in the cited passage and John's *maniere de parler* which appears in his epilogue on the work of translators. It is worthwhile to add at this point that while the expression *modus loquendi* is found in medieval Latin texts, its use in the context of differences between languages seems to have been quite unusual.[76] Furthermore, as Antioch witnessed several translation projects in the Frankish period, one should bear in mind the possibility that John was related to some local tradition.[77]

'*ii Oracii cum glosulis*' and another consisting of '*Epistule Ieronimi et Augustini*'. Beddie, 'Some Notices', pp. 240–2. For this tradition, see, for example: R. Copeland, *Rhetoric, Hermeneutics and Translation in the Middle Ages* (Cambridge, 1991), pp. 37–55.

[74] S. J. Williams, 'Philip of Tripoli's Translation of the Pseudo-Aristotelian *Secretum secretorum* Viewed within the Context of Intellectual Activity in the Crusader Levant', in I. Draelants, A. Tihon and B. van den Abeele (eds.), *Occident et Proche-Orient: Contacts scientifiques au temps des Croisades* (Turnhout, 2000), pp. 80–5.

[75] 'Porro vestro mandato cupiens humiliter obedire et voluntati vestre . . . hunc librum, quo carebant latini eo quod apud paucissimos arabes invenitur, transtuli cum magno labore et lucido sermone de Arabico ydiomate in Latinum . . . eliciens quandoque litteram ex littera et quandoque sensum ex sensu, cum alius loquendi modus sit apud Arabes, alius apud Latinos.' For both the Latin text and the translation (slightly emended here), see S. J. Williams, *The Secret of Secrets: The Scholarly Career of a Pseudo-Aristotelian Text in the Latin Middle Ages* (Ann Arbor, MI, 2003), pp. 361, 364.

[76] A search in the 'Library of Latin Texts – Series A' database reveals that the term appears quite rarely in the same context as the words *linguae* or *idiomata*.

[77] For Antioch as a centre of intellectual activities, see S. Edgington, 'Antioch, Medieval City of Culture', in K. Ciggaar and M. Metcalf (eds.), *East and West in the Medieval Eastern Mediterranean*, vol. 1, Orientalia Lovaniensa Analecta 147 (2006), pp. 247–59; Burnett, 'Antioch as a Link between Arabic and Latin Culture', pp. 1–69.

Another text which may have influenced John in this regard is Aquinas' discussion of translation in his *Contra errores Graecorum*:[78]

It therefore belongs to the task of the good translator, when translating matters of the Catholic faith, to preserve the meaning, while changing the manner of speaking [*modus loquendi*] according to the special character of the language into which he is translating ... when these which are said in one language are translated to another in such a manner that a word is taken for a word, it is no wonder if some doubt would remain.

Clearly, this text presents views which are very similar to John's: in order to preserve the sense of the text, the translator must change the 'manner of speech'; this must be done in conformity with the characteristics of the target language; a literal translation is not a good one. But besides the similarity in the ideas presented, note that, like Philip, Aquinas uses the term *modus loquendi*, the equivalent of John's *maniere de parler*. Furthermore, it is quite likely that the *Contra errores* circulated in cities such as Acre and Antioch since it was highly relevant for places in which contacts between Westerners and Greeks were intensive.

So far, we have examined an element from John's epilogue which should be seen as a part of a long Western tradition. But the epilogue also includes one notion which was rather unusual at the time. In the passage cited earlier John stresses the difference, in terms of structure and vocabulary, between Latin and French, but he does so while arguing that the same kinds of differences exist between any two languages. In other words, the disparity between Latin and French is not a result of any deficiency on the part of the French language. Rather, all languages are unique and any two given languages differ from one another. As Serge Lusignan writes, this line of thinking leads to a conception, rare during the Middle Ages, that tends to view French and Latin as equal.[79] Indeed, medieval thinkers often described the vernacular as incapable of transmitting complex ideas.[80] Thus John reveals his belief in the capacity of the vernacular both in his practice as a translator, and through his explicit – and unusual – discussion of the interrelation between Latin and the vernacular in the epilogue to his *Rectorique*.

---

[78] 'Unde ad officium boni translatoris pertinet, ut ea quae sunt catholicae fidei transferens, servet sententiam, mutet autem modum loquendi secundum proprietatem linguae in quam transfert ... quando ea quae in una lingua dicuntur, transferuntur in aliam, ita quod verbum sumatur ex verbo, non est mirum si aliqua dubietas relinquatur.' Thomas Aquinas, *Opuscula omnia*, ed. R. P. P. Mandonnet, 5 vols. (Paris, 1927), vol. III, p. 279.

[79] S. Lusignan, *Parler vulgairement: Les intellectuels et la langue française aux XIIIe et XIVe siècles* (Paris, 1987), p. 144.

[80] Lusignan, *Parler*, pp. 43, 73.

The *Rectorique* provides evidence for an additional aspect of John's perception of the vernacular: his notion of French grammar. Serge Lusignan argued that the word *gramaire* was rare in the texts he surveyed, and that where it was found, it signified Latin.[81] Furthermore, while during the thirteenth century some paradigms from Latin grammar were applied to French, it was only in the fourteenth century that French became the subject of grammatical reflection.[82] Seen against this background, John's views regarding vernacular grammar, as they are revealed in the *Rectorique*, are indeed unusual.[83] In its prologue, discussing the different parts of philosophy, John says that *gramaire* teaches us to speak properly and rightly.[84] Being aimed at a non-Latin reading audience it seems very unlikely that these words were to be understood as relating to Latin.[85] Another occurrence of the word *gramaire* in the *Rectorique* is even more instructive. In order to comprehend John's use of the term here and to understand what views of Old French it exposes, it is necessary to compare the original Latin text with the French translation. The Latin text reads:[86]

Barbarism is when by words something is wrongly expressed.

John's translation includes a much more elaborate text:[87]

Barbarism is when some word is found defective in itself in pronunciation or in writing; in pronunciation, as when someone would say 'hospital' protracting the 'pi'; in writing as when someone would write or pronounce in the said word 'b' for 'p.'

The comparison between these phrases both provides evidence concerning John's intellectual background and reveals the way in which he drew the Latin concept of *barbarismus* into his own cultural environment. Firstly,

---

[81] Lusignan, *Parler*, pp. 167, 170–1.

[82] T. Städtler, *Zu den Anfängen der französischen Grammatiksprache*, Beihefte zur Zeitschrift für romanische Philologie 223 (Tübingen, 1988), p. 10 *et passim*.

[83] John's notion of a vernacular grammar may have been related in some manner to Peter Helias' argument that there are Hebrew and Chaldean grammars and that French grammar could also be discussed. Lusignan, *Parler*, pp. 21, 190.

[84] ' ... gramaire nos enseigne convenablement et droitement parler'. Guadagnini, *La Rectorique*, p. 75.

[85] Note that the *Image du monde*, which was probably copied in Acre, explicitly says about grammar: 'Ce est celé qui ensaingne a fourmer parole, soit en latin ou en roumanz ou en touz autres langages parlans.' For the text, see O. H. Prior (ed.), *L'image du monde de maître Gossouin. Rédaction. en prose: Texte du manuscrit de la Bibliothèque nationale fonds français no. 574, avec corrections d'après d'autres mss., notes et introduction* (Lausanne, 1913), p. 81. For the work's connection to Acre, see Minervini, 'Produzione', pp. 92–3.

[86] 'Barbarismus est, cum verbis aliquid vitiose efferatur.' F. Marx (ed.), *Ad C. Herennium de ratione dicendi* (Leipzig, 1964), p. 123.

[87] 'Barbarism si est quant aucune parole est trovee vicieuse en soi meisme au prononcier ou en l'escrit: au prononcier si come qui diroit "hospital" proloignant le "pi", en l'escrit si come qui escriveroit ou prononcieroit au devant dit mot "b" por "p".' Guadagnini, *La Rectorique*, p. 303.

John's statement that the concept of barbarism is relevant to pronunciation and to writing is in all likelihood based on Donatus' definition of this term in his *Ars maior*, revealing that he was well acquainted with this advanced grammar.[88] It is perhaps also from Donatus' work that John took the idea of providing examples at this point. Remarkably, in order to explain to his readers what this term means he chose a word which was particularly significant for him and for the patron of the project, William of Santo Stefano. The connection of this discussion to John's intended audience is further enhanced by the mention of an error which may well reflect the influence of Arabic pronunciation on the vernacular: the pronunciation or writing of 'hosbital' instead of 'hospital'. John's next phrase, which, notably, is not an exact rendering of the Latin text, goes on to create a clear association between the practice of the vernacular in Outremer and the field of *gramaire*: 'By what method we can avoid these two defects, the art of *gramaire* teaches us very clearly.'[89] Thus, John produces a text which presents *gramaire* as a field of knowledge that can help French users, including – and perhaps first and foremost – those who live in the Latin East, to speak and write properly.

The novelty of John's views of vernacular grammar is also reflected in another phenomenon in his work: the use of French grammatical terms. Generally speaking, such terms appeared during the twelfth and thirteenth centuries and were mostly used in vernacular discussions of Latin grammar.[90] Against this background, John's use of such terms places him, again, in a rather uncommon position. This can be demonstrated by his employment of the word *preterit*. The earliest evidence for the use of this term is in a late twelfth-century gloss to Aelfric's Latin grammar.[91] Its next appearance is in Henri d'Andeli's *Bataille de vii ars* (ca. 1245), again referring to Latin grammar. The word also appears in a few French translations of Latin grammars dated after 1250.[92] In other words, at the time John was preparing his translation, this term did not yet have a long tradition behind it, and its employment was in all likelihood associated mainly with vernacular discussions of Latin. And yet, in his *Rectorique*,

[88] Cf.: 'barbarismus fit duobus modis, pronuntiatione et scripto'. H. Keil (ed.), *Grammatici Latini*, 8 vols. (Leipzig, 1855–80, reprinted Hildesheim, 1961), vol. IV, p. 392. For Donatus' *Artes*, see R. Copeland and I. Sluiter (eds.), *Medieval Grammar and Rhetoric: Language Arts and Literary Theory, AD 300–1475* (Oxford, 2009), pp. 82–5. I am grateful to Rita Copeland for identifying this connection between John's work and Donatus'.
[89] 'Par quel raison nos puissons ces ii vices eschiver, l'art de gramaire nos enseigne bien clerement.' Guadagnini, *La Rectorique*, p. 303. The parallel Latin text is: 'Haec qua ratione vitare possumus, in arte grammatica dilucide dicemus.' ('By what method we can avoid these [errors], we will clearly state in the "Grammatical Art".') For the Latin text, see Marx, *Ad C. Herennium*, p. 123.
[90] T. Städler, 'Témoins précoces de la terminologie grammaticale française', *Travaux de linguistique et de philologie* 37 (1999), pp. 123–9.
[91] Städler, 'Témoins', p. 124.   [92] Städler, *Zu den Anfängen*, p. 268.

John inserted this term three times into places where the Latin original does not have the equivalent *praeteritum*.[93] The third of these seems to be the most instructive. It follows a more or less exact translation of a general's speech, whose purpose is to present dilemmas he faced in a certain situation. Following the general's comments, John adds:[94]

One can also turn a *subiectio* thus made entirely into *preterit* or into *futur*.

What can we make of this insertion? Firstly, that not only John, who would have become acquainted with the *praeteritum* during his training in Latin, but also his audience were acquainted with the term *preterit*. This conclusion can be supported by the two other aforementioned occurrences in which this term, along with two other terms denoting tenses, were added by John to the text he translated in order to facilitate its reading.[95] But, more significantly, John's employment of the term here is clearly intended to suggest to his readers a certain manner of expression in French. This phrase thus reveals that John was capable of thinking about *preterit* in the context of French rhetoric and independently of Latin grammar, and that he expected his audience to be able to implement his comment in the vernacular. This is clearly different from the situation described earlier where French terms were used to describe Latin grammar. It thus seems that in Acre, at least in some quarters, an advanced attitude existed towards French grammar.

We have seen that John of Antioch, a native of the Latin East, who, as far as one can tell from the existing evidence, never attended any major study centre, reveals in his *Rectorique* unusual perceptions concerning the capacity and status of the vernacular as well as the significance of vernacular grammar. We have also noted that at least to some extent these views must have been found among the audience to which he was writing, that is, the Kingdom of Jerusalem's nobility. While at first glance this may seem surprising, an examination of different aspects of the thirteenth-century Kingdom of Jerusalem's linguistic environment can do much to explain why such perceptions appeared in Acre. One possible

---

[93] Cf. Guadagnini, *La Rectorique*, p. 88, and Cicero, *Rhetorici libri duo qui vocantur de inventione*, ed. E. Stroebel (Stuttgart, 1965), p. 10; Guadagnini, *La Rectorique*, p. 109 and Cicero, *De inventione*, p. 33; Guadagnini, *La Rectorique*, p. 316 and Marx, *Ad C. Herennium*, p. 143. Of course, it cannot be completely ruled out that John used a Latin manuscript that did have the word *praeteritum* in these places. However, this term does not appear in the critical texts I used (neither in the presented text nor in the apparatus). In a fourth case, the word appears in a place where the Latin text does include the Latin *praeteritum*. Guadagnini, *La Rectorique*, p. 238; Marx, *Ad C. Herennium*, p. 30.

[94] 'Si faite subgection peut on torner autresi dou tout au preterit ou au futur.' Guadagnini, *La Rectorique*, p. 316. Cf.: Marx, *Ad C. Herennium*, p. 143.

[95] Cf. respectively: Guadagnini, *La Rectorique*, p. 88, and Cicero, *De inventione*, p. 10; Guadagnini, *La Rectorique*, p. 109, and Cicero, *De inventione*, p. 33.

explanation would be that in Outremer knowledge of Latin was not as common as it was in Western centres. This would have led to the composition in French of works belonging to genres that in the West were reserved for Latin, and, in turn, to a growing belief in the capacity of the vernacular to function in new fields. The rising inclination to employ the vernacular in new genres was possibly also facilitated by the lack of a dominant academic elite committed to the exclusivity of the Latin language. In other words, the limited presence and standing in Acre of learned persons holding views similar to that of Roger Bacon may have eased the introduction of French into new fields of knowledge.

Such hypotheses may be connected to another possible explanation for the appearance of novel ideas regarding the vernacular in Acre: in Outremer the *langue d'oïl* became the language of the elite.[96] Thus its prestige increased and it became easier to envisage its use in fields which in the West were usually still kept for Latin.[97] Furthermore, the combination of the vernacular's prestige with its frequent employment – often, very partial and limited to the use of some important terms – by non-native speakers is likely to have created a degree of sensitivity, among some French speakers with regard to its use. If our analysis of the comment concerning the word 'hospital' is correct, it reflects such sensitivity on the part of native French speakers. Such criticism towards errors in pronunciation and writing, necessarily based on some criteria concerning the proper employment of the language, probably contributed to the inclination to reflect on the vernacular. The teaching of French in Acre, evidence for which was presented earlier, probably further encouraged the perception of the vernacular as a legitimate subject for grammatical reflection. Indeed, there is clear evidence that, in the case of England, the fact that French was taught as a second language led to engagement with the vernacular in very similar ways to those used much earlier for the instruction of Latin.[98] Such developments can partly explain John's unusual views concerning vernacular grammar as well as his employment of grammatical terms.

Another possible explanation for the development of novel ideas regarding language in Acre has to do with the impact of contact with various foreign linguistic systems on the ideas of Westerners concerning

[96] C. Aslanov, 'L'ancien français, sociolecte d'une caste au pouvoir: Royaume de Jérusalem, Morée, Chypre', in B. Fagard, S. Prévost, B. Combettes and O. Bertrand (eds.), *Évolutions en français. Études de linguistique diachronique* (Berne, 2008), pp. 3–4; Minervini, 'Outremer', p. 617.

[97] It is noteworthy that twelfth-century England also saw pioneering employment of French in a variety of genres. M. Townend, 'Contacts and Conflicts: Latin, Norse and French', in L. Mugglestone (ed.), *The Oxford History of English, Updated Version* (Oxford, 2006), p. 83.

[98] Lusignan, *Parler*, p. 93.

their own languages. Aslanov raised the possibility that the encounter of the Franks with a different linguistic environment led them to reinterpret or modify their own system.[99] Specifically, he argues that the Frankish encounter, in the context of the Fourth Crusade, with Greek culture, where prose histories were a well-established genre, resulted in the appearance of the first French prose histories by Geoffrey de Villehardouin and Robert de Clari. It seems likely that similar processes took place in thirteenth-century Acre, where Latins not only encountered a variety of linguistic systems but also, as we have seen, were attentive towards them. Latins may have been specifically impressed, and perhaps even influenced, by the encounter with languages which were used for both everyday matters and literary purposes, as was the case with both Arabic and Greek.[100] Such an encounter may have encouraged some Franks to view the vernacular as useful for fields which were up to that time strictly preserved for Latin, thus contributing to the appearance of works such as John of Antioch's *Rectorique* and perhaps also to the inclination to discuss, and learn, French grammar.

CONCLUSION

For contemporaries, the variety of languages used in and around Acre was certainly among the city's most evident characteristics. In this chapter, we traced the consequences of this cultural phenomenon for the city's intellectual scene. We have observed that in this field, Acre was far from being a backwater of Western culture. Rather, its position as a predominantly Western city located within a generally Eastern cultural environment created in it favourable conditions for the accumulation and development of unique linguistic knowledge and thought. Thus an unusual level of expertise developed in the city concerning Eastern languages, and some of its intellectuals participated in pioneering undertakings, such as the study of Arabic in the city's Dominican convent or the translation into that language of Western Marian legends. Beyond unusual activities related to Eastern languages, thirteenth-century Acre also saw considerable original work with regard to French, the Frankish vernacular. We have seen that several translations from Latin into French were produced in the city and that within some circles in Acre unusual ideas existed with regard to the capacity of the vernacular to convey complex ideas, for example in logic, as well as concerning the

---

[99] Aslanov, 'L'ancien français', pp. 13–17.
[100] According to Aslanov, the Franks perceived both the Greek and Arabic systems as monolingual diglossias. Aslanov, 'L'ancien français', p. 14.

existence of an independent vernacular grammar. While exploring the engagement with language in Frankish Acre, we have also been able to shed considerable light on intercultural exchanges taking place in the city. These included, for example, discussions in which Jacques de Vitry attempted to acquire knowledge concerning various linguistic systems, or Dominicans correcting books sent to them by the Maronites.

At this point it is worthwhile to return to Minervini's definition of Outremer's linguistic system as characterized by plurilinguism. The use of this term is clearly intended to describe a situation distinct from that of multilingualism, which relates to people capable of using more than one language, and is often studied in relation to the employment of French in the Middle Ages.[101] Clearly, this is an important distinction, but perhaps, at least in the case of Acre, it should not be overstated. Firstly, multi-lingualism did exist within Frankish society not only among those relatively few Latins who acquired command of Arabic but also, for example, in the case of Italians fluent in French.[102] Indeed, having become the language of the elite, it is likely that Westerners who were not native French speakers would have made an effort to acquire at least some ability to communicate using it. Furthermore, the concept of multilingualism, or perhaps 'partial multilingualism', is also useful for exploring the study, in various levels, of French or Latin by native speakers of Eastern languages, as well as that of Arabic by Westerners. Secondly, the relatively restricted number of Westerners who attained proficiency in Eastern languages should not downplay the linguistic and cultural significance of exchanges between speakers of Eastern and Western languages in and around Acre. The originality of thinking about languages in the city was probably related to different kinds of exchanges, such as the daily communication with non-native French speakers, or the teaching of native Arabic speakers. In other words, the contacts between speakers of different languages, so characteristic of Acre and its environs, are likely to have contributed to the development, in some Frankish circles, of original notions about the vernacular, and to the production of pioneering translations in the city. In that sense, it may be misleading to overstress the isolation of the different linguistic systems operating in the city.

---

[101] As was already seen, the British case offers some insights on the situation in Outremer. In this context, see E. M. Tyler (ed.), *Conceptualizing Multilingualism in England, c. 800–c. 1250* (Turnhout, 2011); J. Wogan-Browne (ed.), *Language and Culture in Medieval Britain: The French of England c. 1100–c. 1500* (Woodbridge, 2009); Townend, 'Contacts', 75–105.

[102] Jacoby, 'Society', p. 118.

Chapter 4

ACRE AS A MEETING POINT OF JURIDICAL TRADITIONS

Among the different fields of intellectual activity, none is as strongly connected in modern historiography to the Latin Kingdom as jurisprudence.[1] Indeed, among the authors identified with the Latin East hardly any are as well known as John of Ibelin or Philip of Novara.[2] Furthermore, various aspects of the kingdom's legal history have received considerable attention.[3] And yet, very little systematic work has been done in order to characterize the intellectual activities undertaken in this field in the Latin East. In other words, questions focusing on the accumulation, development and circulation of juridical knowledge have hardly been asked. Furthermore, the study of the Kingdom of Jerusalem's juridical history has been dominated by several treatises,[4] all belonging to what may be referred to as the customary – as opposed to learned – legal tradition.[5] The aim of the present chapter is to characterize, in as detailed a manner as the extant sources can support, the

---

[1] Some of the materials presented here are included in a paper of mine: 'John of Ancona's *Summae*: A Neglected Source for the Juridical History of the Latin Kingdom of Jerusalem', *Bulletin of Medieval Canon Law*, 29 (2012), pp. 183–218. See Brundage, 'Latin Jurists', p. 18 *et passim*. Riley-Smith, *Feudal Nobility*, p. 128.

[2] Regarding John and Philip, see, respectively, Edbury, *John of Ibelin*; Philip of Novara, *Le Livre*, pp. 14–19.

[3] See, for example: B. Z. Kedar, 'On the Origins of the Earliest Laws of Frankish Jerusalem: The Canons of the Council of Nablus, 1120', *Speculum* 74.2 (Apr. 1999), pp. 310–35; J. A. Brundage, 'Marriage Law in the Kingdom of Jerusalem', in B. Z. Kedar, H. E. Mayer and R. C. Smail (eds.), Outremer: Studies in the History of the Crusader Kingdom of Jerusalem Presented to Joshua Prawer (Jerusalem, 1982), pp. 258–71; Riley-Smith, *Feudal Nobility*; Prawer, *Crusader Institutions*.

[4] These texts are: *Le livre au roi* [**3:33**], dated to between 1197 and 1205, and probably written in Acre by a member of the king of Jerusalem's entourage; *Le livre des assises de la cour des bourgeois* [**2:21**], written by an anonymous middle-class burgess (or more than one) between 1229 and 1244; Philip of Novara's *Le livre de Forme de Plait*, the main body of which was written in the early 1250s, although it also includes later chapters; *Le livre des assises*, written by John of Ibelin, one of the most prominent nobles of the kingdom, and completed between 1264 and 1266. For the two latter works, see, respectively: Philip of Novara, *Le Livre*; John of Ibelin, *Le livre des assises*.

[5] By 'learned law', I mean law based on knowledge obtained in the rising universities of the West, and practised by professionals. This distinction is further developed in what follows.

intellectual activities of the jurists working in thirteenth-century Acre, taking into account the various legal traditions present in the city, and providing a portrayal of the encounter and exchange between them.

CUSTOMARY LAW IN ACRE: TRADITION BEARERS AND MECHANISMS OF DISSEMINATION AND DEVELOPMENT

The dominant legal tradition within the Kingdom of Jerusalem seems to have been a customary legal tradition carried first and foremost orally and represented in its clearest form in texts such as John of Ibelin's or Philip of Novara's juridical treatises. We have seen (Chapter 1) that in addition to such well-known figures who, while not permanently residing in the city, played a role in juridical discussions in and around its courts, a considerable number of lesser-known nobles operated within this tradition, as did also some of the city's burgesses. Among these nobles were, for example, Stephan of Savegny and James Vidal, while Philip of Baisdoin and Raymond of Conches were burgesses distinguished by their legal expertise. We have also seen that a legal custom practised in the kingdom – namely the usage whereby vassals aided litigating parties with *conseil* – encouraged knights to become knowledgeable concerning legal matters.

Extant sources enable us to shed additional light on the framework within which such figures operated. Firstly, they offer glimpses of the processes of transmission of this legal tradition in Outremer. The most elaborate description of the training of knight-jurists in the Latin East – the basic characteristics of which seem to be applicable to Acre – comes from a passage in which Philip of Novara tells his readers how he started to acquire legal knowledge:[6]

It happened that I was at the first siege of Damietta with my lord Peter Chappe, and one day my lord Ralph of Tiberias ate with him. ... My lord Ralph slept little and badly, and when I had read as much as he wished, he himself told me many things about the kingdom of Jerusalem and of the usages and assises. ...

---

[6] 'Il avint que je fui au premier siege de Damiete o messire Piere Chape, et messire Rau de Tabarie menga un jor o lui...Messire Rau dormet poi et malvaisement, et quant je avoie leu tant com il voleit, il meismes me conteit moult de chozes dou royaume de Jerusalem et des us et des assises...Aprés usai entour mon seignor de Baruth le viell jusqu'a sa mort, qui moult de chozes m'aprist la soie merci a ma requeste... Aprés fui moult acointé de mon seignor de Saeste a Baruth et a Acre et en Chypre, et moult de chozes m'aprist la soie merci volentiers. Et Aprés tous ces grans seignors et sages usai moult en cort entor messire Guillaume Vesconte et messire Harneis de Giblet et messire Guillaume de Rivet le joune, qui moult estoient grans plaideors. Et au reaume de Jerusalem fui je moult acointé de messire Nicole Anteaume et de sire Phelippe de Baudoin, qui estoient grans plaideors en cort et hors court.' Philip of Novara, *Le livre*, pp. 122 (French), 261 (English translation).

Later I spent time around my lord of Beirut the elder until his death; he taught me many things at my request for which I am grateful. ... Later I was much acquainted with my lord of Sidon at Beirut and at Acre and in Cyprus, and many things he taught me freely of his own volition. After all these great and wise lords I spent much time in court around my lord William Viscount, and my lord Arneis of Gibelet and my lord William of Rivet the younger, who were very great pleaders. In the Kingdom of Jerusalem I was well acquainted with my lord Nicholas Antiaume and sire Philip de Bauduin, who were great pleaders in the court and elsewhere.

Thus, we see a process whereby the older knight-lawyers informally transmitted their knowledge and experience to younger members of their milieu. Occasionally, it should be noted, nobles specifically instructed their sons.[7] In addition to non-formal instruction outside court, transmission of legal knowledge also took place in the kingdom's courts as young knights would accompany experienced jurists. Like Philip, John of Ibelin mentions as his sources for legal knowledge those who were the most knowledgeable of his time. Furthermore, John's comments, like Philip's, reveal that his informal training also included seeing older experts litigate. Interestingly, he speaks in this context about what he heard, learned and remembered, which supports the view that books and writing were not a part of the learning process of such jurists.[8] Beyond the instruction of young men with regard to legal practice, the sources also provide evidence for the discussion of juridical matters among older knights who were already accomplished legal experts. Such conversations occasionally took place even when these issues were not, at that specific moment, debated in court.[9]

There is very little evidence with regard to the training such knight-jurists acquired in fields other than law. The closest extant evidence seems to come from Philip of Novara's comments concerning the training that nobles in general and jurists in particular should go through:[10]

The art which underpins knowledge is logic, for logic teaches to speak skillfully of the things of this world. One can learn much of human activity from the books of the authorities. Those who do not have the capacity or the will to learn or the leisure to remain long in school should at least learn how to read and write. That way their secrets ought to be better kept.

---

[7] *RHC, Lois*, vol. II, p. 339.   [8] John of Ibelin, *Le livre des assises*, p. 56.

[9] Philip of Novara, *Le livre*, pp. 161–2 (French), 291–2 (English translation).

[10] 'Et l'art qui affiert a science si est logique, car logique enseigne a parler soutilment des fais terriens. Et es livres des actors meismes peut l'on moult aprendre des fais dou siècle. Et ceaus qui n'ont poeir ou volenté ou loisir de demourer longement en escole deivent aprendre au mains tant que il sachent lire et escrire. Car lor segré en devra estre meaus celé.' Philip of Novara, *Le livre*, pp. 170 (French), 298–9 (English translation).

In other words, logic, or, rather, rhetoric, seems to be of central importance as is also the ability to read and write. The latter, however, is deemed useful mainly for secret keeping. Speaking of the 'books of the authorities' Philip had in mind a category of texts which he perceived as useful, but unfortunately he leaves no clue as to the body of literature to which he is referring. In terms of the knowledge expected from knight-jurists in Acre, one can conclude that at least ideally they would be literate, and would have some training in rhetoric and perhaps also in logic. Interestingly, this calls to mind John of Antioch's project which includes texts on rhetoric and a basic treatise in logic [**1:19**]. Placed together, Philip's comments and John's project suggest that among the nobles of Outremer a belief existed in the significance of these fields.

But the juridical arena of thirteenth-century Acre cannot be understood solely by looking at these milieus of knight-jurists. Indeed, even their own activities cannot be explained when one focuses merely on them in isolation from the bearers of other legal traditions present in the city. In order to gain a full understanding of Acre's juridical arena one needs to explore the role played in it by, firstly, Western customary legal traditions and, secondly, the learned, Latin, juridical tradition, associated with the rising universities and the Roman law.

LATIN SYRIA'S LOCAL LEGAL TRADITION AND WESTERN CUSTOMS

While the Kingdom of Jerusalem certainly developed a legal tradition of its own, it is very likely that customs prevalent in various Western regions continued to influence Outremer's legal development and juridical discourse throughout the Frankish period. In fact, John of Ibelin went so far as to write that Godfrey of Bouillon, as well as the kings and lords who followed him, saw to it that in each period of *passage*, that is, of arrivals to the city's port, wise men from various regions would be asked about the *usages* of their lands. Their answers would be written down and, in cases where it was thought fruitful, used, in order to improve the *assises* and *usages* of the kingdom.[11] Although this is probably not a completely accurate description,[12] there is no reason to doubt that it does have a grain of truth in it. In fact, there was at least one case in the twelfth century in which the opinion of a visitor from the West brought about a change in law (or, at the very least, thus thought thirteenth-century jurists). Count Stephen of Blois, who was in the East in 1171, was

---

[11] John of Ibelin, *Le Livre*, pp. 53–4. This is discussed in Riley-Smith, *Feudal Nobility*, p. 195.

[12] Joshua Prawer wrote that in this description, John was following a literary tradition, perhaps that of Livy, about the redaction of the first laws of Rome. Prawer, *Crusader Institutions*, p. 430.

remembered as having brought to the Kingdom of Jerusalem the custom whereby co-heiresses were to divide their inheritance in the absence of a male heir.[13] Furthermore, Philip wrote that the count, through the king and his men, emended very many of the *usages* and *assises* of the kingdom.[14]

It has also been shown that in two of the major legal disputes that took place in thirteenth-century Acre, reference was made to French custom. As Edbury showed, in the bailliage disputes of the mid 1260s [2:28], Hugh of Brienne argued that since those who had established the usages of the kingdom were French, the customs of the Kingdom of Jerusalem should conform to those of France.[15] The debate, presented before Prince Edward while he was in Acre [1:16], on whether the liegemen of Cyprus owed their king service outside the island, provides further evidence in the same direction. Firstly, the mere fact that the case was brought before Edward implies that foreign custom and opinions were, at least in particular cases, thought to be useful in order to solve local disputes. Additionally, the perception that Western custom was relevant in attempts to solve juridical conflicts in the kingdom of Jerusalem was made explicit in the discussion by James of Ibelin, who argued that since the founders of the Kingdom of Jerusalem originated in the crown of France as well as in other provinces found 'over the mountains', it is unlikely that they established different laws in their new territory. Rather, in his opinion it was most probable that they brought with them the usages of their country or of neighbouring territories. This led him to rhetorically ask:[16]

Now, consider whether there is any province across the mountains where men owe their lord this kind of service [i.e. service outside the kingdom in which they reside]. Certainly we believe not.

Clearly, then, Westerners visiting Acre were at least occasionally asked regarding the customs prevalent in their lands of origin or for their opinion with regard to specific issues, and occasionally such information had an impact on local legal decisions and practices. To this one should

---

[13] Philip of Novara, *Le Livre*, pp. 141 (French), 273 (English translation) and n. 219. See also John of Ibelin, *Le Livre des assises*, pp. 763, 766.

[14] Philip of Novara, *Le livre*, pp. 141, 273.

[15] P. Edbury, 'Law and Custom in the Latin East: Les Letres dou Sepulcre', in B. Arbel (ed.), *Intercultural Contacts in the Medieval Mediterranean: Studies in Honour of David Jacoby* (London, 1996), p. 78; For the text of the dispute, see P. Edbury, 'The Disputed Regency of the Kingdom of Jerusalem, 1264/6 and 1268', Camden Miscellany 27, *Camden 4th series*, vol. 22 (1979), pp. 28, 34 *et passim*.

[16] 'Or esgardés c'il y a nulle province d'outre les mons où les homes deivent à leur seignor tel maniere de servise: certes nos creons non.' *RHC, Lois*, vol. II, p. 431.

also add that among Acre's literate population there was certainly interest in legal questions arising in the West. Thus one of the so-called continuations of William of Tyre's *Chronicon* includes a discussion of a change in the custom relating to the succession to the Duchy of Burgundy.[17] While it is hard to tell how influential the discourse on foreign legal practices was in Acre, it has been suggested that the challenge posed by Western legal practices may have played a role in the decision of jurists such as Philip of Novara to put in writing what was in essence an oral legal tradition.[18]

Extant evidence demonstrates that the conflict between varying local customs characterized also Acre's ecclesiastical institutions. Evidence for this is provided in John of Ancona's canonistic *Summa* [**1:12**] to which we soon return. John raises the question of 'what if different customs would be held by different neighboring churches?'[19] He then offers several solutions. One possibility suggested by John is following the custom of the metropolitan church. The second possibility is choosing the custom which can be followed without damaging the holders of other customs. The third option seems, at a first glance, rather obscure. Looking at the cited law from the *Digest*, however, it becomes clear that John is referring here to an opinion of other jurists according to which the selected custom should be the one which is less costly.

THE LEARNED LEGAL TRADITION IN ACRE

As we have seen, knight-jurists were developing their juridical tradition in the Latin East, discussing problems and transmitting their knowledge, based on both precedents and opinions of leading figures of past generations, to younger members of their milieu. We have also seen that local laws and customs were influenced by parallel traditions originating in various parts of the West and, mainly, in France. But, at the same time, a completely different juridical tradition was gaining currency in Western legal centres. Universities were training professional lawyers on the basis of a corpus of authoritative Latin texts, that is, the Roman law corpus. A legal system developed which competed, eventually very successfully, with the regional, vernacular, oral, non-professional tradition.[20]

---

[17] Riley-Smith, *Feudal Nobility*, p. 128; *RHC, Lois*, vol. II, p. 463.

[18] Philip of Novara, *Le livre*, pp. 22–6.

[19] 'Quid autem si diverse fuerint consuetudines in diversis proximis ecclesiis?' Brugge, fol. 13v. For the Latin text of the complete discussion, see Rubin, 'John of Ancona's *Summae*', p. 192.

[20] Note that in this period canon law should be seen as a part of the learned tradition being Latin, text-centred, studied in universities and strongly related to the Roman law.

Not surprisingly, the learned tradition was not slow to reach Acre and influence its juridical arena.[21] This took place mainly through the arrival in the city of legal experts trained within the new academic tradition. James Brundage's work suggests that a significant number of men with substantial legal training acquired in Western law faculties were working in the Latin states during the thirteenth century,[22] and we have presented evidence for expertise in canon and civil law among prominent figures in Acre.[23] The arrival of merchants from the Italian city states who would have also been exposed to the learned legal tradition probably provided further support to this trend.[24]

The impact of the 'new' learned tradition on Acre's legal discourse is difficult to establish, but an indication that it was significant is provided by the appearance of Roman legal terms in charters signed in the city. One legal expert working in Acre is particularly noteworthy in this context. This is Aliottus Uguiccionis, a judge and notary, who worked for both the *Cour des Bourgeois* and the Hospitallers in Acre.[25] In two documents produced in the city, one in 1255 and the other in 1260, Aliottus included specific references to the *Senatusconsultum Velleianum*,[26] a rule appearing in the *Code* as well as in the *Digest*.[27] Aliottus also introduced into documents he edited another Roman law term: *possessio corporalis*.[28]

It is significant, from a cultural point of view, that such new terms did not remain confined to the realm of Latin texts. A case in point is a charter regulating the relations between the Kingdom of Jerusalem and the merchants of Ancona.[29] Within this text, written mostly in French, one finds several appearances of the term *syndiques*, clearly based on the Roman law term *syndicus*.[30] According to the *Trésor de la langue Française* this is the first time in which this word occurs in the French language. It would thus seem that in some cases learned jurists not only brought with them to Acre learned Latin vocabulary but also enriched the vernacular with such terms, and in fact produced new French words. Thus, while the arrival in Acre of the learned tradition should be seen

---

[21] Some clues for the impact of the renewed emergence of Roman law on the Kingdom of Jerusalem's legal arena have been discussed in Prawer, *Crusader Institutions*, pp. 430–68.

[22] Brundage, 'Latin Jurists', pp. 18–41.   [23] See Chapter 1, pp. 17, 28–9.

[24] Prawer, *Crusader Institutions*, pp. 386–7.   [25] Mayer, *Die Kanzlei*, vol. II, p. 260.

[26] Brundage, 'Latin Jurists', p. 29; Joseph Delaville le Roulx, *Les archives, la bibliothèque et le trésor de l'ordre de Saint-Jean de Jérusalem a Malte* (Paris, 1883), pp. 186–7; *Cartulaire* 2949.

[27] *Cod.* 4.29.23; *Dig.* 16.1.

[28] *Dig.* 41.2.25.2, S. Pauli (ed.), *Codice diplomatico del sacro militare ordine Gerosolimitano*, 2 vols. (Lucca, 1733–7), vol. I, pp. 294, 295, 297.

[29] Mayer, *Urkunden*, vol. III, pp. 1407–9.

[30] *Dig.* 3.4. *Syndicus* means an agent or representative charged with the handling of the matters of a group.

mainly as a juridical phenomenon, it also had wider cultural and linguistic consequences.

Considerable evidence for the presence of the learned juridical tradition in thirteenth-century Acre comes from the *Livre des assises de la cour des bourgeois* [2:21]. The authorship of this text, as well as the purpose for which it was written, is unclear and often debated. Prawer thought that this work was written by a member of what we would call today a professional class of law practitioners or people connected with the functioning of Acre's Court of Burgesses. More recently, it has been suggested that this work is actually the result of the activity of more than one author.[31] This seems probable since, as Nader has shown, the book includes contradicting statements which are very unlikely to have been included in a text composed by one person.[32] Be that as it may, at a first glance there is much in the *Livre* that ties it to the local, vernacular, juridical tradition. It is written, for the most part, in French, and has a distinctly local nature, expressed inter alia by expressions such as 'par l'assise dou reaume de Jerusalem', which, in its various variations, is very common in the work. The inclusion in the *Livre* of a list of duties collected at the royal *fonde* of Acre further exemplifies the local nature of this compilation. The connection of this work to the local customary juridical tradition is also demonstrated by the repetitive use in it, as in the *Livre au roi* and in Philip of Novara's *Livre de forme de plait*, of expressions such as 'ici orrés' ('here you will hear') and 's'il avient' ('if it happens') in the *tituli* and opening lines of chapters and discussions. The similarity in the presentation of materials in these texts suggests that they should be understood as echoing related kinds of discourse.

At the same time, however, the *Livre des assises de la cour des bourgeois* provides much evidence for the presence of the academic legal tradition in Acre around the mid-thirteenth century. Its basic structure seems to follow that of the Roman law,[33] and it includes *tituli*, phrases and complete chapters in Latin.[34] Additionally, as Joshua Prawer has shown, it is heavily influenced by the *Lo Codi*, a Provençal treatise of Roman law which was constantly being used by theoreticians of law.[35] Furthermore, a recent study shows that the *Livre des assises de la cour des bourgeois* also

---

[31] See Chapter 1, p. 30.   [32] Nader, *Burgesses*, pp. 51–2.

[33] Prawer, *Crusader Institutions*, p. 369; M. Grandclaude, *Étude critique sur les Livres des assises de Jérusalem* (Paris, 1923), pp. 63–4.

[34] Grandclaude, *Étude*, pp. 57–61.

[35] Prawer, *Crusader Institutions*, p. 362. Nader is much more careful with regard to the influence of the *Lo Codi* on the *Livre*. However, he agrees that there are similarities between the two books and that these suggest that a copy of the Provençal work was available in the Latin East. Nader, *Burgesses*, pp. 56–7.

includes sections which borrow directly from the Roman legal corpus rather than through the intermediation of the *Lo Codi*.[36]

Thus, at least one of the authors who participated in the complex process that resulted in the production of the *Livre des assises de la cour des bourgeois* as we now know it was a jurist learned in Roman law. Given the variety of manners in which elements from the Roman law were incorporated into the *Livre des assises de la cour des bourgeois*, it seems very likely that, indeed, more than one author, or compiler, was involved in this process. The insertion of materials from the Roman law into the *Livre des assises de la cour des bourgeois* was certainly meant to meet the particular circumstances characteristic of the thirteenth-century Kingdom of Jerusalem,[37] but it would have also added to the compilation's prestige and authority.

But, returning to the question of the work's aims and audience, it is perhaps possible to go even one step further. Looking carefully at the *Livre des assises de la cour des bourgeois* one can see that in several places there appear, within French chapters, phrases in Latin which are immediately translated, or paraphrased, into French.[38] In chapter 41, for example, we read the following: ' ... because no one is allowed to act against his own agreements [Latin], that is, all men are obligated to do whatever they have in agreement considering that the agreement is not against the law or the *assise* [French]'.[39] What we have here is a quote from *Institutes* 2.3.29 with a French paraphrase which also explains and interprets the original Latin. Such an occurrence suggests that the *Livre des assises de la cour des bourgeois* was intended for jurists whose knowledge not only in Roman law, but also in Latin, was very limited.[40] At the same time it also reveals that such practitioners were supposed to receive from the *Livre*, inter alia, a taste of the Roman legal tradition.[41]

Clearer evidence for the emergence of learned law in Acre is related to one – until recently very much obscure – jurist: John of Ancona. Most of what we know about him comes from a canon law *summa* [1:12] provided

---

[36] A. Bishop, 'Adaptations of the Roman *Lex Aquilia* in the Burgess Assizes of Jerusalem', in *Proceedings of the Third International Symposium on Crusade Studies* [forthcoming].

[37] Bishop, 'Adaptations'.

[38] Note that in many places Latin phrases appear following French chapters. Such are probably readers' comments inserted into the text by scribes and thus of a limited value for understanding the earlier stages of the *Livre*'s textual tradition. See Grandclaude, *Étude*, pp. 57–8.

[39] '... quia nemini licet contra sua pacta venire. Ce est, tos homes sont destreins de faire se qu'il li ot en covent puis que le covent n'est contre lei ne contre l'asize.' E. H. Kausler (ed.), *Livre des assises de Jérusalem* (Stuttgart, 1839), p. 74.

[40] For a similar occurrence, see Kausler, *Livre*, p. 46.

[41] That the *Livre* was 'in many ways' a handbook of instruction for anyone interested in the finer points of law was argued by Nader, *Burgesses*, p. 54.

by one manuscript: Brugge, Stadtbibliotheek 377. From the text provided by this manuscript we learn that the *summa* was written by a certain 'Johannes domini Guidonis de Ancona', and that the author was induced to write his *summa* by William, Patriarch of Jerusalem and papal legate, and by William of Lautario, archdeacon of Acre.[42] We also learn from the text that at the time he began working on the *summa*, John was in charge of Templar juridical matters ('patronus in causis') and that from time to time he also took care of such matters for virtually all prelates and nobles of this kingdom ('alias causas quasi omnium prelatorum et nobilium regni huius per diversa tempora procurarem').[43] John also authored, while in the Kingdom of Jerusalem, a *Summa super usibus feudorum* [**2:25**], but it is unknown who initiated its writing or for whom it was intended. On the basis of information provided by the texts, it seems that the former was composed between 1265 and 1268 and the second between 1258 and 1266.[44] John is also mentioned, along with a certain Bienvenu de Vidal, in the aforementioned document describing the rights of the merchants of Ancona in Acre, as a *syndic, procureor, actor et special message dou comun d'Ancone*.[45]

The prologue to the canonistic *summa* is instructive not only for understanding John's purpose in composing it but also for the evidence it provides concerning Acre's juridical arena. Explaining what made him daring enough to undertake such a project, he includes among the reasons the following:[46]

[B]ecause, as in the carrying out of ecclesiastical legal proceedings, judges and lawyers, for the settlement of many cases and of particularly useful questions, frequently had recourse to the *summa* of the venerable man lord Goffredus [=Goffredo da Trani's *Summa super titulis decretalium*],[47] they could not find there what they looked for because of the brevity of the text. And thus it

---

[42] See Chapter 1, p. 21.   [43] Bertram, 'Johannes de Ancona', p. 59; Brugge, fol. 1r.

[44] Rubin, 'John of Ancona's *Summae*', pp. 185–8 and the references there.

[45] Mayer, *Urkunden*, vol. III, pp. 1407–9. It is noteworthy that this document also attests that John of Ancona probably knew Aliottus. One may hypothesize that the two belonged to, and perhaps stood at the centre of, a milieu of learned jurists active in Acre.

[46] '...quia cum in exercicio iudiciorum ecclesiasticorum frequenter ad decisionem multorum casuum et plurimum utilium questionum ad summam reverendi viri domini Goffredi haberent iudices et advocati recursum, ibi propter brevitatem tractatus quod querebant non poterant invenire. Sicque contingebat quod vel iudex vel litigantes in dubio constituti casus cogebantur relinquere indecisos vel oportebat eos per libros diversos et notas discurrere longo tempore dominorum. ... Ideoque ego Johannes de Ancona ... non ad detractionem summe tanti viri, sed ad utilitatem propriam et commodum eorum, qui hoc opusculum assumere voluerint ... notavi et excerpsi non sine magno labore ex corpore iuris canonici et ex notis diversimodis specialiter probabilium doctorum quecumque ad proprietatem cuiuslibet tractatus credidi pertinere, adnectens in singulis titulis de facto plurimas questiones, per quas multa que prius erant dubia declarantur.' Bertram, 'Johannes de Ancona', p. 60.

[47] Gottofredo da Trani, *Summa super titulis decretalium* (Lyon, 1519, reprinted Darmstadt, 1992).

happened that either the judge or litigants remaining in doubt were forced to either leave cases undecided or to run through various books and notes wasting [their] lords a long time. ... Therefore I, John of Ancona ... not in order to disparage the *summa* of such a man but for its own utility and to the convenience of those who should wish to take up this little work ... noted and extracted, not without great labor, out of the *corpus iuris canonici* and out of various notes, specifically those of acceptable doctors, whatever I believed pertains to the property of any tractate, attaching to each of the *tituli* very many questions concerning the matter through which many things which were earlier doubtful are made clear.

As John not only composed this text in Acre, but was led to write it by two prominent members of its ecclesiastical milieu, this text should be read as indicative with regard to the city's juridical arena. We see here that legal experts in the city were operating within the learned tradition before John arrived in the city, and that Goffredo's *summa* was a very popular canon law text in Acre, but certainly not the only one circulating and being consulted there. The fact that two members of the church encouraged John to write his own canon law *summa* implies that there was some thirst in the city for works composed within the academic juridical tradition which would take account of the unique problems that rose in the Kingdom of Jerusalem. As we see later, an examination of the actual content of the *summa* supports these conclusions, as John elaborates in it on various points which do not appear in Goffredo's original text and which can be shown to have been particularly relevant for the kingdom.

In contrast to his canonistic *summa*, John's *Summa super usibus feudorum*, as it reached us, includes no comments as to the circumstances which led to its composition. Nonetheless, it too can clearly be seen as a local adaptation of a well-known Western work, being directly or indirectly inspired, like all thirteenth-century feudal *summae*, by Pillius' *Summa feudorum*.[48] At the same time, however, while the work's format places it within the learned juridical tradition, it includes references to specific customs and circumstances which characterized the Kingdom of Jerusalem as well as to well-known figures who were active there.[49]

---

[48] G. Giordanengo, 'Les Feudistes', in *El Dret Comú i Catalunya: Actes del II Simposi Internacional* (Barcelona, 1992), pp. 74–5, 97–9, 103–4, 113–15 *et passim*.

[49] Some of this text's references to the Kingdom of Jerusalem are studied later. For a complete list of the individuals mentioned in the *summa* and known to have been active in the kingdom, see Rubin, 'John of Ancona's *Summae*', pp. 188–9, notes 24–5.

CUSTOMARY AND LEARNED LEGAL TRADITIONS IN ACRE: COMPETITION, MUTUAL APPRECIATION AND EXCHANGE

Bearers of the learned tradition obviously could not support the way in which local knight-jurists were trained, and had other ideas with regard to the question of who should teach law. John of Ancona writes:[50]

According to the laws, no one should be accepted to teach laws unless he is examined and approved by a college [of examiners],[51] and this is also observed in practice in Bologna when an assembly is taken up so that [a candidate], first examined if he was worthy, would be approved and would receive a permission to teach. Thus is also in Paris in theology and justly so because the untaught cannot teach others and cannot introduce learning which they do not have.

Considering the fact that Goffredo's parallel chapter includes no similar discussion,[52] and the importance of informal instruction for the local elite of Outremer, it is likely that we have here a piece of evidence for a conflict between two approaches to legal training.

Not surprisingly, the customary law experts were trying to defend their tradition in the face of such attacks. Peter Edbury suggested that it became more and more difficult for practitioners working in the kingdom's courts to justify their procedures against the challenge of learned lawyers, and that the treatises by John of Ibelin and Philip of Novara were intended to provide support for the traditional system against the more rational and streamlined alternative.[53] One phrase in particular in John of Ibelin's work seems to provide direct evidence for the conflict between the customs of the kingdom and the Latin juridical texts originating in the West. Having explained that *assises* are confirmed as such either by their usage through a long period of time or by the fact that they were thought to be used as *assises*, John goes on to say that 'this is the manner of proof and thus it should be and is held in the Kingdom of Jerusalem and of Cyprus more than laws, *decreta* or *decretales*'.[54] The reference in this phrase to two major corpora of learned law suggests that for John there was

---

[50] 'Secundum leges nemo debet recipi ad docendum leges nisi sit examinatus et approbatus a cetu, C de magistris qui in urbe constantinopolitana l. i [*Cod.* 12.15.1], et sic et observatur de facto Bononie [MS: banonie] quando assumitur conventus ut examinatus prius si dignus fuerit approbetur et detur ei licentia docendi. Sic etiam Parisius in theologia et merito quia indocti alios docere nequeunt nec doctrinam insinuare quam non habent.' Brugge, fol. 286r.

[51] *Cod.* 12.15.1.   [52] Gottofredo, *Summa*, pp. 409–11.

[53] John of Ibelin, *Le livre des assises*, p. 43.

[54] 'Et ce est maniere de la preuve et doit estre et est tenue ou reiaume de Jerusalem et de Chipre meaus que loys ne decres ne decretales.' John of Ibelin, *Le Livre des assises*, p. 258. See also Edbury's comments on this phrase on p. 38. This sentence seems to be based on a similar one which appears in Philip of Novara, *Le livre*, pp. 119 (French text), 260 (translation).

a conflict, or a competition, between such bodies of law and the *assises* and customs to which he wished to adhere.

At the same time, it would be completely wrong to conclude that two isolated traditions operated in Acre with little or no contact and exchange between them. There is much evidence to show that legal experts working in Acre appreciated the academic juridical tradition and even acquired some knowledge from jurists trained within it. A case in point is the *Livre des assises de la cour des bourgeois*, which combines elements from both the local, vernacular, oral tradition and the academic, Latin, written one. If we accept Nader's suggestion that the *Livre des assises de la cour des bourgeois* was well known in the city, that would imply a considerable demand for such a work, including its engagement with the Roman law.[55]

Evidence for communication between knight-jurists and legal experts trained within the academic tradition can also be found in the works of Philip of Novara and John of Ibelin. Discussing forfeiture as a penalty for treason, Philip of Novara wrote: 'and that there is written law in which it is stated that the relatives of him who is condemned for treason are disinherited to several degrees'.[56] This phrase seems to echo the *Lex Julia* as presented in the *Code* (9.8.5), thus revealing that Philip acquired some vague knowledge of what the Roman law has to say on penalties for treason. Thus, one should probably assume that Philip spoke to a legal expert with at least some knowledge of the Roman law corpus. On the other hand, Philip clearly did not consult the actual text to which he is referring here.

Interestingly, some years later, John of Ibelin wrote that:[57]

[T]he Code of Emperor Justinian, which is one of the best legal books of the emperors which they produced in ancient times and in a fixed manner, because they wanted them to be held by the world, and because that book was modified and made from other legal collections by great sense and by great study, states and declares that the heirs of traitors should suffer a punishment much graver than to

---

[55] Nader, *Burgesses*, p. 54.

[56] '...et qu'il y a loy escrite en laqueil il contient que les apartenanz de celui qui est forjugiés de traison sont desserités en pluisours degrés.' Philip of Novara, *Le livre*, pp. 74 (French text), 233 (translation).

[57] '...el coude de l'enperere Justignien, qui est i des meillors livres de lais des enpereors qu'il firent ancienement et establisement que il vostrent qu'il fucent tenus par le monde, et que cel livre fu des autres livres des leys concuillis et amendés et fait par grant sen et par grant estuide, estuidit et devise que les heirs des traytors doivent molt plus grief peine soufrir que estre desherités del fié del traytor et forjugé. Et se que l'enperere Achades en dist trova l'on qui quere le voudroit el noveime livre dou code en la loy qui est apelee la loy Julie. Et je cuit qu'il dist en celle loy que le traytor devroit morir de mort hontouse et que tous les biens doivent venir a l'enpereor.' John of Ibelin, *Le livre des assises*, p. 437.

be disinherited and deprived of the traitor's fief. And whoever would like to search it would find that which the emperor Achades said about this in the ninth book of the Code in the law which is called Julia's law. And I think that he said in this law that the traitor should die a shameful death and that all of his property should go to the emperor.

Evidently, John was able to get some more specific information concerning the *Lex Julia* than that which he had found in Philip's work.[58] Otherwise he would not have been able to refer to book nine of the *Code*, to know that this was a part of the *Lex Julia* and to mention Achades, a corrupted form of Arcadius, who is in fact mentioned in the *Code* as one of this chapter's authors.[59] On the other hand, as Edbury wrote, the words 'I think' show that John too did not consult the actual text. One can thus conclude that two of the most famous customary law experts of the Latin East discussed this issue with people who possessed at least some knowledge of the Roman law. While we do not know where these contacts took place, there is no reason to assume that such exchanges did not take place in Acre. These two discussions also show that while it is very likely that, as Edbury suggested, people like John and Philip felt that their own legal tradition was being threatened by the arrival of the learned law to the Latin East, they also appreciated its power and authority and, in any case, were not completely indifferent or hostile towards it. On the other hand, as this is the only reference to the Roman law in both works, their inclination to actually employ this corpus was certainly very limited. This, again, can be explained by the fact that its intensive use would have weakened the tradition with which they identified themselves.

That the learned and customary legal cultures in Acre were not isolated from one another can also be seen when one examines additional aspects of John of Ancona's work. Firstly, as was already mentioned, John referred to James Vidal and Stephan of Savegny as 'more knowledgeable than others in the customs of this kingdom'.[60] John's comment clearly indicates, therefore, that he did not decry the knowledge that men such as James and Stephan held but rather respected their expertise. To this one should add that John was, in all likelihood, personally acquainted with a considerable number of local legal experts. This would have been a necessary consequence of his activities as a practitioner. Furthermore, as was already mentioned, John appears in a document concerning the commercial privileges of merchants from Ancona in Acre, and it is most likely that during the negotiations leading to the signing of this

---

[58] For the argument that Philip's work influenced John's, see John of Ibelin, *Le livre des assises*, p. 13.
[59] *Cod.* 9.8.5.   [60] See Chapter 1, p. 29.

document, John would have become personally acquainted with legal experts such as Stephan of Savegny who also took part in these contacts. The personal familiarity of jurists arriving from the West with local practitioners is not specific to John, of course. A glance at the *RRH* reveals various instances in which Aliottus Uguiccionis also cooperated with local jurists. Thus, for example, in both 1254 and 1255 Aliottus documented transactions in which James Vidal served as witness.[61]

John's respect towards local practitioners is also revealed through the discussion of local customs in his texts. These imply that he communicated with lawyers and members of clergy active in Acre and learned from them about both prevalent customs and difficulties they raise. Thus, for example, John learned about a certain local custom related to the selling of fiefs in situations of financial distress, and in another case he speaks of local customs relating to the obligations of members of clergy in funerals.[62] It is noteworthy in this context that during his stay in Acre John acquired knowledge not only concerning the local customs and conditions of the Kingdom of Jerusalem but also regarding those of other regions such as France and Cyprus.[63] This means that John made use of his stay in Acre to learn not only from the bearers of the local Syrian tradition but also from people acquainted with the legal conditions in other regions.

AN ATTEMPTED RECONSTRUCTION OF THE JURIDICAL DISCOURSE IN ACRE: THREE EXAMPLES

We have seen that several legal traditions were present in Acre, and also that among their bearers existed a complex web of relations including elements of competition, appreciation and exchange. The rest of this chapter is devoted to the examination of the discourse in the city with regard to three legal questions. Such a procedure is made possible, first and foremost, by John of Ancona's *summae* which, in contrast to most of the other legal sources extant from the thirteenth-century kingdom, can be securely placed and dated in a very precise manner. As already seen, these texts belong to the late 1250s and to the 1260s, and were both composed in Acre. We also have some information concerning their author's cultural background and legal activity. With regard to one of them, the canonistic *summa*, we

---

[61] *RRH* 1212, 1234.   [62] Brugge, fol. 209r.
[63] Bertram, 'Johannes de Ancona', pp. 62–4. That he acquired these pieces of knowledge in Acre and not in the West is made most likely by the fact that no such references appear in his earlier work, the feudal *summa*, but several of them do appear in the later canonistic work.

even know why, and for whom, the text was composed. But here a seeming difficulty arises: as these texts were authored within the learned tradition, much of their content is not directly related to the circumstances which characterized the thirteenth-century Kingdom of Jerusalem. It has even been argued that readers who expect to find in the feudal *summa* many precise details will quickly be disappointed. In Meijer's opinion, 'l'auteur était un jurisconsulte beaucoup trop savante pour entrer dans ces détails'.[64] A very similar argument was made regarding the *Summa iuris canonici*.[65] And yet both texts should be considered as local variants of major juridical texts, and as such must be seen as useful for the understanding of Acre's juridical arena. Furthermore, we analyze below discussions from both *summae* which specifically address the legal conditions prevalent in the thirteenth-century Kingdom of Jerusalem. Note that John's texts include additional sections which, implicitly or explicitly, relate to the realities of the Latin East. Thus, for example, he discusses the question of whether churches can be fortified, speaking explicitly of Acre's Saint Michael's Church,[66] and engages with problems related to the death of pilgrims having no testament.[67]

Given the exact information we have concerning the composition of John's works, such cases, in which the *summae* do treat issues specifically relevant to the kingdom, can easily be placed within the context of late thirteenth-century Acre's juridical arena. Furthermore, once such a discussion is identified, it is also possible to examine references to the same legal issues in other local sources, be they treatises or charters. As Philip of Novara and John of Ibelin were strongly attached to the city's juridical milieus, and as the charters of the period would have been mostly phrased by jurists working in Acre, the result of such a procedure is a reconstruction of fragments of Acre's juridical discourse which reveals, for example, disagreements between John of Ancona and the local Frankish jurists, but also local customs with which John became acquainted while in Outremer, and even changes in legal practice over time.

---

[64] Meijers did, however, provide his readers with one example for a custom of the kingdom mentioned in the treatise: he cited a small part of the discussion presented later concerning the sale of a fief by a vassal burdened by debts. E. M. Meijers, *Études d'histoire du droit*, eds. R. Feenstra and H. F. W. D. Fischer, 3 vols. (Leiden, 1959), vol. III, p. 105.

[65] Bertram, 'Johannes de Ancona', p. 62.

[66] Bertram, 'Johannes de Ancona', p. 64; Brugge, fol. 243r. For this church, see Pringle, *The Churches IV*, pp. 149–50.

[67] Brugge, fol. 206r. For several additional examples, see Bertram, 'Johannes de Ancona', pp. 62–4.

1   The Controversy Concerning Ecclesiastical Jurisdiction

In his feudal *summa*, John discusses a situation in which there is a judicial dispute over a fief between a vassal and a foreigner who is not a vassal.[68] According to John, the judge in such a case should be the *ordinarius* of the possessor, rather than the lord of the fief.[69] That is so, says John, since no one should be allowed to judge in his own matter when the foreign party objects to it. What John must have had in mind is that in such a situation the lord would obviously be interested in having his vassal hold the fief. Consequently, he may be unable to judge impartially and so his authority must be limited.[70] John then describes what he sees as a mistake on the part of local advocates: they refuse to appear in ecclesiastical courts, arguing that their clients hold fiefs from the king and that, therefore, they are prepared to appear before him, but not before an ecclesiastical court. On the basis of his previous argument, John sees this claim as self-contradictory: if indeed these men hold fiefs from the king, having him judge in a case they have against someone who is not a vassal of his would obviously be problematic, and the 'non-vassal' party would be able to refuse his judgment.[71] As, according to John, in the kingdom there is no secular judge who is independent of the king, cases such as the afore-mentioned must be tried in ecclesiastical courts. John also says that, accordingly, rulings were made against knights, because of lack of knowl-edge on the part of their lawyers, since they should have referred to ecclesiastical courts.[72] John completes this discussion by advising the

---

[68]   In the discussion of this issue, as well as in the other two, John of Ancona's texts appear in the notes with the references to Roman and canon law literature in a modernized form. For the complete Latin texts of these sections, see Rubin, 'John of Ancona's *Summae*', pp. 193–213. The text presented in the following notes is basically that of MS Nürnberg, fol. 271r, though in some cases I adopted readings from Paris, BnF, lat. 16008, fols. 78v–79r and from Bamberg, Staatsbibl. Can. 48, fol. 185v. For the complete apparatus, see Rubin, 'John of Ancona's *Summae*', pp. 193–4.

[69]   In Roman law, an *ordinarius* is a judge who exercises his office by right rather than by delegation. I. S. Robinson, 'Reform and the Church, 1073–1122', in D. Luscombe and J. Riley-Smith (eds.), *The New Cambridge Medieval History IV, c. 1024–1198, Part I* (Cambridge, 2004), p.386. In Goffredo da Trani's *Summa*, which, as we have seen, formed the basis for John's canonistic work, we read that an *ordinarius* is a judge elected by a college and confirmed by a superior. Gottofredo, *Summa*, pp. 108–9 [modern pagination].

[70]   'Cum autem inter extraneum qui non est vasallus et vasallum lis oritur de feudo tunc sive extraneus possideat sive agat erit iudex ordinarius possessoris [C. 11 q. 1 c. 15; X 2.2.8], non dominus feudi quia non potest esse iudex in re sua litigatore extraneo recusante [*Cod.* 3.5; X 2.1.13].'

[71]   'Et ideo puto errare advocatos cismarinos qui ad declinandum forum ecclesie allegant milites possessores esse feudatarios et rem habere in feudum a rege coram quo paratos offerunt se respondere, si quidem propter hoc non tenetur actor agere coram domino feudi ratione predicta quia in sua causa non debet esse iudex. Verisimile est enim quod dominus feudi iudicaret pocius esse suam rem quam actoris iure proprii dominii vendicantis [*Cod.* 3.5.1; *Dig.* 2.1.10]. Item merito ut suspectus poterit recusari quia dominus est adversarii [X 1.29.17; X 1.29.25].'

[72]   'Item per hanc exceptionem non declinant iudicium ecclesie sed pocius se submittunt i. astringunt iuridictioni ecclesie apertissima ratione, videlicet quia in regno Ierusalem non est alius iudex

holders of land to say that they are prepared to appear before an *ordinarius*, adding that – as was already stated at the beginning of the section – such a case would have to be presented before the possessor's judge.[73]

In his canon law *summa* which was written several years later, John included similar comments.[74] Here the emphasis is on litigation between clerics and lay landholders. John confronts a claim made by advocates that, as the contested matter is feudal, it should be presented before a feudal lord, rather than before an ecclesiastic. He argues that ecclesiastics who are not vassals do not have to agree to be tried before a feudal lord. As in the Kingdom of Jerusalem there is no *ordinarius* except the king, who is in fact a feudal lord, such cases should be presented before an ecclesiastic. John supports his arguments by actual juridical decisions: he writes that the aforementioned claim was rejected in the kingdom and that such was also the decision of the papal legates.[75]

What can one learn from these texts about the juridical discourse in Acre? Firstly, we can see that although it had been agreed, since as early as 1120, that the church had jurisdiction in various kinds of cases,[76] the limits of ecclesiastical jurisdiction, in particular with regard to feudal matters, were still contested at the time John was writing his feudal *summa*.[77] Some landholders, supported by local advocates, were inclined

---

secularis nisi rex vel eius officiales, qui cum non possint esse iudices <ut> in causa sua, ut dictum est, iam necessario deficiente iudice seculari ecclesia erit iudex, et ita fuit actenus iuste contra milites iudicatum propter imperitiam advocati s. quod debeant coram iudice ecclesiastico respondere, [X 2.2.10], ibi "ad iudicem secularem recurrere nequeant", [X 2.2.11], ibi "dummodo per iudicem secularem", et cetera.'

73 'Consultius ergo facient possessores si conventi simpliciter se asserant possidere <quo casu actor quicumque> asserantque se paratos coram ordinario suo iudice respondere. Quo casu actor quicumque sit clericus vel laicus debet reum possessorem coram suo, scilicet rei, iudice convenire secundum notam regulam: actor sequitur forum rei [*Cod.* 3.19.2; *Dig.* 5.1.19; *Auth.* 6.11.1 (*Nov.* 83.1)].'

74 Brugge, fol. 93va. This section was published in: Bertram, 'Johannes de Ancona', p. 63. Just preceding this discussion John makes an argument very similar to the one with which he opened the section from his feudal treatise presented earlier: in a case between a vassal and a non-vassal on land which the former claims to hold as a fief, the judge should not be the lord of that fief, but rather the *ordinarius loci*.

75 'Et ideo puto minus provide avocatos antiquos cismarinos opposuisse coram iudice ecclesie exceptionem de foro contra prelatos, vendicantes rem esse feudalem et se paratos esse coram feudi domino respondere. Nam actor clericus vel ecclesia, qui non est vassallus, non debet coram domino feudi agere tali casu et merito hoc in contrarium opponentis secutum in regno Ierusalem, quia si non invenitur alius ordinarius in regno quam rex, qui [est] dominus feudi et coram ipso non debet actor, ut dictum est, experiri, tunc in defectu iudicis secularis oportet quod iudex ecclesiasticus sit iudex et coram eo questio ventiletur [X 2.2.10], et sic est actenus per legatos Romane curie iudicatum.'

76 Kedar, 'On the Origins', pp. 331–4. For later evidence on ecclesiastical jurisdiction, see Kausler, *Livre*, pp. 53–4.

77 This piece of evidence makes it hard to accept Marwan Nader's opinion that 'the king, his lords, the church and the courts were agreed as to the parameters of ecclesiastical jurisdiction'. Nader,

to evade ecclesiastical courts, while John, on the other hand, was attempting to widen the jurisdiction of such courts.

That this debate was not theoretical is demonstrated by two documents, dated 1254.[78] In them we read about a case, presented in Rome, between the Teutonic brothers of Acre and Aimery Barlays, concerning the contested ownership of two lower Galilea villages, Sakhnīn and ʿArrāba. A major part of the discussion focused on the question of jurisdiction. Rejecting the Teutonic claim that, being *persone religiose*, they had to be tried by an ecclesiastic, Aimery's representative argued that since the villages in question had been fiefs of the kingdom, the Teutonic brothers could have been summoned to appear ('conveniri poterant') before the king so as before a feudal lord. He added that as Aimery began the case as a feudal one, the Teutonic knights were obligated to obey their summons at least so that it would be decided whether the case belonged to the king's jurisdiction. The Teutonic procurator, on the other hand, claimed, inter alia, in a manner reminiscent of John's argument, that the rule that feudal matters should be tried before the fief's lord applies only in cases between two parties which acknowledge holding a fief from the same lord. Otherwise, it may seem that the landlord judges in his own case.[79] The papal curia's decision was in favour of the Teutonic order.[80] This case shows that John's discussion was not detached from the juridical reality of the kingdom. In fact, arguments similar to the ones he mentioned were used in litigation.

Furthermore, a comparison between John's discussions of this controversy implies both that the discourse regarding this issue was not static, and that John was closely following developments in the practice of legal experts working in Outremer. As we have seen, in the feudal treatise, dated to 1258–66, John says that he thinks that 'lawyers on this side of the sea are mistaken when they argue'. But in the canon law *summa*, John phrased his words differently, saying that he thinks that 'the lawyers of old

---

Burgesses, p. 182. Regarding the church courts in the kingdom, see also J. L. La Monte, *Feudal Monarchy in the Latin Kingdom of Jerusalem, 1100–1291* (Cambridge, MA, 1932), pp. 109–10. Nader's opinion is perhaps based on La Monte's; see *ibid.*, 215–16. For an older account of the kingdom's ecclesiastical courts, see G. Dodu, *Histoire des institutions monarchiques dans la Royaume latin de Jérusalem 1099–1291* (Paris, 1894), pp. 325–8.

[78] Strehlke, *Tabulae*, pp. 85–8.

[79] 'Quod autem dicitur questionem feudalem coram domino feodi esse tractandam, tunc demum locum habere dicebat, cum vertitur inter duos, qui feodum ab eodem domino recognoscunt, ne alias videatur in causa propria iudicare.' Strehlke, *Tabulae*, p. 86.

[80] The connection between this case and John's discussion was first suggested by Jonathan Riley-Smith as Benjamin Z. Kedar presented the feudal *summa* in a workshop held at the Institute of Advanced Studies of the Hebrew University in 1999 (I thank Benjamin Z. Kedar for this comment). Regarding this case, cf. Riley-Smith, *Feudal Nobility*, pp. 188–9.

times in this side of the sea had opposed unwisely'.[81] The difference between the two texts reveals that while John was writing the canonical *summa* (1265–8), circumstances had changed, and lawyers were no longer arguing against ecclesiastical jurisdiction by claiming that the matter at hand was feudal, and that they were therefore prepared to appear before their feudal lord, but not before an ecclesiastical court.

Another issue raised by the two presented passages deserves particular attention. As was mentioned, the feudal *summa* clearly states that in the Kingdom of Jerusalem there were no secular judges other than the king and his officials. The same is said, in a somewhat more implicit manner, in the canon law *summa* as well. These comments are somewhat difficult to understand, since some lords obviously had the right of judgment.[82] John of Ancona's statements may be explained, in part, by the *Assise sur la ligece*, which made all knights 'peers' of their lords and their fellow knights, with regard to the king.[83] Consequently, the *Assise* weakened the local noble courts and strengthened the power of the *Haute Cour*.[84] Additionally, some of the lordships which originally had courts no longer existed at the time John of Ancona was writing his works, either because they had been occupied by the Muslims, or because they had been transferred to the military orders.[85] Both of these processes probably contributed to the weakening of secular jurisdiction.[86]

But one may also understand John's comment as a polemical statement rather than a descriptive one: perhaps he was trying, in his discussion of this matter, to weaken the power of the baronial courts, while supporting the *Haute cour*. This may be connected to John's view of the king's status which echoes in the formula of feudal oath with which he provided his readers: 'Also, I will aid and defend the lord himself . . . against all persons of this world except the emperor . . . or the king or another lord to which he is subject.'[87] John, in other words, thought that a vassal was not supposed to aid his lord against the king. But there was no consensus

---

[81] Cf. 'puto errare advocatos cismarinos qui... allegant' (feudal *summa*); 'puto minus provide avocatos antiquos cismarinos opposuisse' (canonistic *summa*).

[82] John of Ibelin, *Le Livre des assises*, pp. 603–6; Edbury, *John of Ibelin*, pp. 155–6. Obviously, John of Ibelin's list includes lordships which, while John of Ancona was writing, were no longer in Frankish hands. However, some seigneurial courts must have still been operating in the thirteenth century as well.

[83] Prawer, *Crusader Institutions*, p. 41.   [84] Riley-Smith, *Feudal Nobility*, p. 35.

[85] Edbury, *John of Ibelin*, p. 167.

[86] Peter Edbury wrote, concerning lordships taken over by the military orders, that 'the military orders could well have dispensed with having to convene the seigneurial courts ... they [the military orders] might have deliberately sought ways of getting rid of any existing vassals'. Edbury, *John of Ibelin*, p. 161.

[87] 'Item iuvabo et defendam ipsum dominum ... contra omnes homines huius mundi excepta persona imperatoris ... vel regis vel alterius domini cui subset.' Bamberg, fol. 176v.

with regard to this matter in the kingdom, and the local, customary, juridical tradition seems to have given the king a much weaker position. John of Ibelin was significantly less decisive about this question, putting much more stress on the commitment to the *premier seignor* than to that towards the chief lord.[88] It is thus likely that in John of Ancona's discussion of the limits of ecclesiastical jurisdiction we encounter an issue related to a wider juridical controversy which characterized thirteenth-century Acre, that which concerned the commitment due to the king versus that due to one's immediate lord.

2   The Selling of Fiefs in Cases of Financial Distress

Another issue which stood in the centre of juridical discourse in Acre is the selling of fiefs in order to repay debts. Obviously, the selling of a fief was problematic in any feudal system, as it threatened to weaken the military powers of the overlord. This problem certainly existed in Outremer and was discussed by various jurists. In general, it was prohibited to sell fiefs, but an exception had been made with regard to cases in which the vassal was burdened by a grave debt.[89] The earliest juridical work from the Latin East, the *Livre au roi*, dated to around 1200 [**3:33**], says that when a vassal holding a fief is burdened by a debt which he has no means to pay back, and which would prevent him from exercising his feudal obligations unless he sold his fief, he has to present this state of affairs to his lord, supporting it with an oath. The lord is then to approve the sale, which the vassal would then declare in three towns. The author of the *Livre au roi* adds here various conditions with regard to the time and place of the sale, giving precedence, in purchasing the property, to the vassal's lord or relatives. The section ends with the enumeration of the kinds of people who are not permitted to buy fiefs.[90]

There is some evidence that these regulations were practised. In September 1231 a certain Nicholas sold the Hospitaller order his fief. In the document describing this transaction we read the following:[91]

[S]ince Nicholaus . . . put out . . . his fief for sale in the royal court for his benefit and need, and according to the custom of the Kingdom of Jerusalem had the sale

---

[88] John of Ibelin, *Le Livre des assises*, pp. 439, 443, 467. John does, however, say that in case of a conflict between the immediate lord and the *chief seignor*, a vassal should, under specific circumstances, leave the former: John of Ibelin, *Le Livre des assises*, pp. 443–6.

[89] P. Edbury, 'Feudal Obligations in the Latin East', *Byzantion* 47 (1977), p. 343.

[90] M. Greilsammer (ed.), *Le livre au roi* (Paris, 1995), pp. 269–72. The text in the earlier edition of the *Livre* is not significantly different. *RHC, Lois*, vol. I, pp. 639–40.

[91] '. . .cum Nicholaus . . . feodum suum . . . pro utilitate et necessitate sua in curia regia exposuisset ad vendendum, ac juxta consuetudinem regni Jerosolimitani apud Accon, Tyrum et Cesaream venditionem feodi clamare fecisset . . . domui Hospitalis Jerusalem . . . dictum feodum. . . vendidit.' *Cartulaire* 1996.

of the fief announced in Acre, Tyre and Caesarea . . . he sold the said fief . . . to the Hospitallers.

Although not all of the elements mentioned in the *Livre* appear here, this document does support some of the information provided by the treatise, particularly the need to declare the sale in three towns.[92]

Around 1260–5, Philip of Novara discussed the same issue. His description of the *assise* is, in general, similar to that of the *Livre au roi*, including, for example, the mention of the local custom of declaring the sale in three towns.[93] What seems to be the most substantial difference is that here the lord, rather than the vassal, is in charge of the selling process. As did the author of the *Livre au roi*, Philip also gives precedence, in the buying of the fiefs, to family relatives of the vassal. He then says that the buyer must be a person who can provide the services related to the fief, adding several limitations concerning the buyer's family and background. John of Ibelin also discussed the *Assise de vente* in his famous treatise. While John's discussion is much more elaborate, referring to many issues not mentioned by Philip or by the author of the *Livre au roi*, it is generally similar to Philip's, including, among other elements, the need to declare the sale in three cities.[94]

At about the same time, but coming from a different tradition, John of Ancona treated the same issue in his feudal treatise.[95] The discussion appears within the context of the question of whether a vassal is allowed to alienate fiefs. John starts this passage by referring to feudal contracts that concede the vassal's right to do so. In such cases, says John, he would be able to do that without his lord's consent ('sine domini voluntate'). He continues by asking whether in cases in which the right of alienation was not conceded in the feudal contract, a vassal would, in any case, be able to alienate his fief without the will of his lord. It seems, John writes, that this could be done. He continues referring to the custom we encountered in the aforementioned sources: 'if a vassal has debts that he cannot pay back

---

[92] Related to this issue is also a document in which we read about the sale of Johannes Tortus' house in Acre. According to the document, Johannes asked the curia for permission to sell a house he owned in Acre, in order to be able to pay off his debts. At first, this request was rejected. Later, however, Johannes said that, because of his debts, he had no choice but to sell either his fief or his house. The *bailli* of the kingdom took counsel regarding this issue, and decided to permit the sale of the house, in order to enable Johannes to keep his fief. This provides evidence for the need to get permissions even for the sale of non-feudal property and for the importance attributed to the preservation of fiefs. This document also bears testimony to the connection between debts and sale permissions. Strehlke, *Tabulae*, p. 33.

[93] *RHC, Lois*, vol. I, pp. 500–1.   [94] John of Ibelin, *Le Livre des assises*, p. 409.

[95] The text presented in the next notes is basically that of MS Nürnberg, fol. 265v. In some cases, I preferred the readings of Bamberg, fol. 179v. For the text with a complete apparatus, see Rubin, 'John of Ancona's *Summae*', pp. 202–3. The abbreviation LF refers to K. Lehmann (ed.), *Consuetudines Feudorum* (Göttingen, 1896).

landlord, with questions arising such as whether the military orders were to be perceived as vassals of the crown. Were they expected to do *homagium* to the king? Were they to be members in the *Haute cour*?

It is therefore not surprising that John of Ancona included in his feudal *summa* an elaborate discussion of the question of whether vassals can grant fiefs to the military orders.[106] The context in which he raises this question is that of grants, made by vassals, to the church. John says that such transactions are legal if done with the consent of the lord. But what if the grant is to be done without such consent? John argues that in such cases the answer seems to be negative, because the church cannot fulfil the military duties tied to the fief. He then turns to the particular case of the military orders, asking whether this prohibition holds also when the church's men are fit to serve the lord with arms, as are the Hospitallers, Templars and Teutonic knights. In other words, within the context of the argument that grants should not be made to ecclesiastical institutions without the consent of the lord, John turns to the military orders, which not only do perform military services, but actually do it better than secular men. In this case, he argues, the logic of the prohibition does not seem to be valid.[107]

John then turns to facing another, less obvious, difficulty with grants to the church: while a lord who granted a fief to a secular vassal had a chance of regaining it, for example, when the noble family holding it died out, the granting of a fief to the church meant that no such opportunity would arise, because, as John writes a few lines before the beginning of this discussion, 'the church never dies without an heir'.[108] This difference is not to be taken lightly, since we know that such occurrences provided landlords with a major tool for reshaping their fiefs, thus affecting their future military and economic potential.[109] The solution John provides to this issue is based on an analogy between a fief given to a church and usufruct held by a city. The *Digest* asks whether usufruct could be granted to a municipality. In such a case, just as in a grant to the church, a danger of it becoming perpetual arises. This difficulty is faced, in Roman law, by

---

[106] The text provided here is generally that of MS Nürnberg, fol. 266r. In some cases, I preferred the readings of Bamberg, fol. 180r. For this text with a complete apparatus, see Rubin, 'John of Ancona's *Summae*', pp. 206–8.

[107] 'Quid autem si habiles sunt homines ecclesie ad serviendum domino cum armis sicut sunt hospitalarii vel templari vel teotonici, qui prae aliis secularibus possunt iuvare dominum contra hostes, maxime in regno Ierusalem, ubi sunt ad offendendum ostes et ad defensionem terre christianorum potentialiter constituti? Videtur predicta ratio prohibitionis cessare.'

[108] '...ecclesia sine herede non decedit et sic semper rem haberet quod esset grave ut dominus re<s> sua omni tempore privaretur.' Nürnberg, fol. 266r.

[109] S. Tibble, *Monarchy and Lordships in the Latin Kingdom of Jerusalem, 1099–1291* (Oxford, 1989), pp. 6–7.

limiting the usufruct given to a municipality to 100 years – a term of time equivalent to the maximum life expectancy of a man.[110] John suggests, in the same manner, that fiefs will be granted to the church for a period of 100 years, citing the *Code* (1.2.23) to argue that in such matters cities and ecclesiastical institutions are equivalent.[111] The next argument John uses is that of custom or precedence: he writes that grants to the church are no novelty, and that therefore, no lord will be able to convict his vassal for such a transaction, adding that the development of this custom may have been tolerable in the kingdom because of its security needs.[112]

John then makes a statement which, at a first glance, is somewhat peculiar: the military orders' strength should not stand in their way in obtaining benefices.[113] This argument is difficult to understand, since, as we saw earlier, the main problem that was naturally associated with granting fiefs to the church was that it was not sufficiently strong, rather than that it was too strong. How, then, are we to interpret this comment? A look at the citation John provides holds the key to the solution of this problem. What the *Code* says in the cited paragraph is that when a party claims that it signed a contract as a result of fear, the argument that the other party was a senator will not suffice.[114] In other words, the power of a dignitary involved in a contract does not a priori weaken its legitimacy. How is this relevant to our discussion? John seems to be confronting here a claim that property is, at least occasionally, given to the orders illegitimately as a result of their extraordinary power.[115] Plausibly, this bears testimony that such an argument was in fact used in Frankish juridical discourse.

The discussion then turns to the interest that the king has in having strong and even rich subjects. This provides further support for granting

---

[110] *Dig.* 7.1.56(63).

[111] 'Sed instabis: non cessat infinitas illa quia ecclesiasti[ci] sunt homines qui non possunt mori sine herede ut dictum est supra. Sed ad hanc posset probabiliter responderi ut sicut quando constituitur ususf[ructus] civitati tenet quamvis civitas semper duret ut tamen usque in c. an[nos], quibus finitis ad dominum reddeat huius ususf[ructus], sic dicatur durare feudum ecclesie usque ad c. annos, quibus finitis, ad dominum revertetur [*Dig.* 7.1.56(63)]. Par enim est ecclesia et civitas quo ad ista [*Cod.* 1.2(5).23(20); *Dig.* 7.1.56(63); *Dig.* 33.2.8].'

[112] 'Preterea non est novum nec insolitum concedi feudum ecclesiis vel prelatis [LF 2.40.3]. Unde si infeudavit ecclesiis predictis non poterit dominus redarguere vasallum sic ecclesie infeudantem cum ipse dominus consueverit similiter ecclesiis infeudare [*Dig.* 13.7.12; *Dig.* 22.1.13.1]. Hoc forsitan posset tollerari in regno Ierusalem, propter favorem defensionis faciende ab eis contra Saracenos invadentes cottidie iura regni.'

[113] 'Et quamvis ipsi nimium sint potentes, tamen hoc non obstat eis ad beneficium capescendum [*Cod.* 2.19(20).6].'

[114] *Cod.* 2.19.6.

[115] It is at least possible that the military orders were able to pressure individuals into selling property to them. Obviously, this is most probable in cases in which the other party was not noble (e.g. RRH 1209, 1236).

the military orders fiefs that would further enrich them. In John's opinion this argument is relevant, however, only when fiefs granted by the king are concerned.[116] In this context, John also emphasizes that such grants will be valid only as long as the orders will fulfil their obligations.[117] If, on the contrary, the church neglects to fulfil its obligations, it shall lose its fief. For John, this result is problematic, but can be justified using the argument that by neglecting to fulfil his obligations, a member of the clergy can actually cause damage to the church.

Finally, John examines a situation in which a fief is alienated by a vassal of a 'dominus singularis'. Although it is hard to be certain what exactly is meant by this term, it is clear that John refers to a landlord other than the king.[118] Such a lord, according to John, would be in a more difficult situation – that is, in comparison to the king – should a vassal of his alienate his fief to a military order. The reference to the *Digest* reveals that what John had in mind are difficulties in litigation vis-à-vis a person of greater influence. How is this related to this discussion? As we have seen, John thought that if one of the king's vassals alienated his fief to a military order, this would actually strengthen the king. He thus would have no real reason to stop this from taking place. Evidently, John now turned to a situation in which a secular lord, other than the king, loses control of a fief in the same manner. If a vassal of such a lord alienates his fief to one of the military orders, the latter's position may be significantly weakened, since he may, for example, have trouble enforcing jurisdiction rights in his lands. Furthermore, as the selling vassal may lose his place in the Crown's council as the result of the transaction,[119] the seigneur's political powers will also be weakened.[120]

How should one view John of Ancona's discussion of this issue against the background of the kingdom's jurisprudence? John of Ancona's opinion seems to be a reaction to that held by John of Ibelin who wrote that if someone alienated his fief putting it 'en main d'yglise ou de relegion' without the consent of the lord, the latter would have the right of

---

[116] 'Et interest regis habere subditos potentes et etiam locupletes [*Auth.* 2.2 (*Nov.* 8.1)]. Hanc autem si velis tenere opinionem poteris eam servare quando rex erat dominus feudi, quo nemo potentior est in regno, cuius interest precipue habere milites sic armatos ad defensionem faciendam contra persecutionem rebelium paganorum.'

[117] '...et durabit hoc ius apud ipsos donec servitium debitum exibebunt [*Cod.* 11.62(61).1?; LF 1.5.6]. Si autem negligenter serviat [MSS: servire], cadet ecclesia a iure feudi ipso iure [LF 2.24.6], nam et hoc est alias [*Cod.* 1.2(5).10]. Solutio: quod negligendo vel ommittendo potest prelatus facere conditionem ecclesie deteriorem [X 2.26.1; C.16 q.3 c.15; X 3.24.2].'

[118] There is a consensus among the manuscripts with regard to the word 'singularis'.

[119] Prawer, *The Latin Kingdom of Jerusalem*, p. 268.

[120] 'Si autem feudum esset alicuius domini singularis tunc grave esset domino si vasallus alienaret alicui de predictis quibus dominus principalis par esse non posset et ideo eius durior esset causa [*Dig.* 4.7.3].'

confiscating it.[121] As we have seen, the *summa* explicitly says that if done with the consent of the lord, alienation to the church poses absolutely no problem. Having said that, John makes an attempt to show why, even without the consent of the lord, the granting of fiefs to the military orders is permitted. He thus seems to be reacting to the general – and rather strict – principle presented by John of Ibelin, first and foremost by turning the attention of his readers to the activity of the orders within the special circumstances of the Latin kingdom, thus addressing the fear that grants to ecclesiastical institutions may weaken the lord's military strength.

John of Ancona's discussion of this issue was clearly meant to confront actual cases which troubled landlords in the kingdom. A case in point is provided by evidence concerning Julian of Sidon. During the 1250s Julian had been selling off estates to the military orders, probably because he could not finance their defence, and in 1260 he alienated what remained from his lordship of Sidon and Beaufort to the Templars. At the time, it was impossible for anyone in the kingdom to prevent Julian from doing this, but later, when Hugh III became king of Jerusalem (1269), or perhaps earlier when he became regent of the kingdom (1264), he decided to regularize Julian's act. While he could not undo what had been done, he did reach an agreement with Julian under which the latter was obligated to serve the king out of his income from the order.[122] Interestingly, Philip of Novara seems to have written a piece of advice to the Templars regarding this matter, in which he says that the king cannot demand anything from the order 'for you [that is, the Templars] are not his vassals, and so he cannot say that you have done him any wrong'.[123]

The concern of the kings of Jerusalem, or their representatives, with regard to the loss of fighting power as a result of concessions to the military orders, also left its marks in charters from the kingdom. Thus, a document dated to 1255 which describes the granting of lands in the vicinity of Acre to the Hospitallers, mentions the possibility that the king or the court will nullify the transaction.[124] The motivation of the king to oppose such transactions is very likely to have been related to the concern

---

[121] John of Ibelin, *Le Livre des assises*, p. 311. It is noteworthy in this context that in contrast to the lords of Arsuf and Sidon, John did not sell his fiefs to the military orders (although at an early stage in his career he did sell minor properties to them). Edbury, *John of Ibelin*, pp. 66, 99.

[122] Edbury, 'Feudal Obligations', p. 343; Philip of Novara, *Le Livre*, pp. 321–2, n. 324.

[123] '. . .quar vos n'estes mie ses homes, qu'il puisse dire que vos li aiez rienz mesfait.' Philip of Novara, *Le Livre*, pp. 197 (French), 322 (English translation).

[124] '. . .se il aveneit que nous ne le peussions faire, c'est assavoir que le seignor del reaume de Jerusalem ne soffrist en quelque maniere que ce fust que vos eussiez les devant dites pieces de terre, que je vos ai donées en aumosne, si com il est desus devisé, ou que vos, par droit de cort, les

that they will lessen his military power. In a later document which is dated to 1261 and which describes the renting of the seigneurie of Arsur by Balian of Ibelin to the Hospitallers, Hugues Revel, grand master of the order, obligates himself, as well as the order, to serve Hugh II, king of Jerusalem and Cyprus, according to what the seigneurie of Arsur owed in terms of knights.[125] Clearly, this document was phrased in order to, inter alia, ensure that the king will not lose such services as a result of this transaction.

Under such circumstances, it is quite possible that John was trying to influence the way jurists perceived feudal grants to the military orders, while also providing litigators in such cases with useful arguments in support of such transactions. In this context, it is important to note that, as was already stated, during his stay in Acre John worked for the Templars, and also, as he put it, took care of cases of practically all of the kingdom's prelates and nobles, which may include some of the other military orders as well. It is likely, then, that in developing such arguments he was also trying to specifically assist groups to which he was related. In other words, in this case John was, on the one hand, trying to justify a common practice using learned law, and on the other, confronting rival jurists holding different opinions.

CONCLUSION

As we have seen, jurisprudence, one of Outremer's central fields of intellectual pursuit, was studied, taught and debated in Acre. Prima facie, the main group engaged in these activities was that of noble jurists, who developed and transmitted a customary, vernacular and mostly oral legal tradition within their ranks. But this is only a part of the picture. Distant from the great study centres of the West, but, at the same time, a very popular port of call and great centre of commerce, Acre became a meeting point of several legal traditions. In addition to the bearers of the local, customary legal tradition, the city saw the arrival of both foreigners bringing with them regional customs from various Western territories, and legal experts trained within the rising academic juridical tradition of the time.

The encounters between bearers of such different traditions certainly resulted in a degree of competition, and even conflict, but, at the same

perdeissiez, je … promet et sui tenu de rendre et paier … les devant diz deus mile bezans Sarracins.' *Cartulaire* 2753.
[125] 'Et devens nos et nostre maison faire faire [*sic*] le servize au tres haut et puissant monsegnor Hugue … roy dou royaume de Jerusalem et de Chypre … tel com la seignorie d'Arsur le doit de chevaliers, sauf le servize que la meisme seignorie d'Arsur doit de cors.' Note that the phrase ends in a restriction, the nature of which is unclear, since its continuation is lacking in the text published by Delaville le Roulx. Delaville le Roulx, *Les archives*, p. 195. For the date, see *RRH* 1313.

time, also in fruitful discussions and mutual learning. The various results of these encounters are evident in John of Ancona's feudal and canonistic *summae* to which we devoted much of this chapter. These reveal that while John must have been highly critical towards the local legal tradition, he also appreciated the expertise of at least some of its practitioners. He was also interested in local customs and, rather than being a detached theoretician, devoted considerable attention to actual legal developments and difficulties typical to Outremer. Examining specific issues which were discussed by him but also touched upon by customary law experts and engaged with in charters, it is possible to reconstruct sections of the juridical discourse that developed in the city, in a manner that takes into account the various legal traditions represented in thirteenth-century Acre.

Chapter 5

THE STUDY OF ISLAM

For thirteenth-century Acre's Latin residents, Islam had a very real, though not equally clear, presence. While no significant Muslim community seems to have permanently lived in the city during this period, Acre's Franks would have often had opportunities to encounter bearers of this faith. Muslims entered the city in order to sell goods;[1] a considerable Muslim population lived in the villages adjacent to the city;[2] Muslim captives were held by the Franks as slaves and carried out various tasks in and around Acre;[3] Muslims in the process of converting to Christianity also resided in the city.[4] But perhaps more importantly, Acre's Christians, living in what eventually became a tiny Latin enclave within a great, often turbulent, Muslim world, constantly felt the presence, and repeatedly also the threat, of Muslim political and military powers. Against this background, it is not surprising that within the corpus of writings which reached us from the thirteenth-century city, references to Islam are very common. The aim of this chapter is to explore the discourse in Acre with regard to Islam, asking questions such as what was known about Islam in the city; which milieus engaged in such a discourse; and what were the sources of knowledge concerning Islam available to Latins curious about the rival religion.

WRITING ABOUT ISLAM IN FRANKISH ACRE: TEXTS AND GENRES

Much was written, within different genres and contexts, about Islam in thirteenth-century Acre. Reports to the West composed in the city often

---

[1] *Cronaca*, p. 200.

[2] Fidentius de Padua, 'Liber recuperationis terre sancte', in Golubovich, *Biblioteca*, vol. II, p. 54 [**3:44**].

[3] *Cronaca*, p. 90. Although the Templar does not mention their location, one must assume that at least a part of the slaves to which he refers were held in the city.

[4] See Chapter 2, pp. 53–4; J. Guiraud (ed.), *Registres d'Urbain IV*, 4 vols. (Paris, 1892–1958), vol. II, num. 874. See also Urban IV's letter, edited in Kedar, *Crusade and Mission*, p. 215.

dealt with some aspects of the neighbouring religion. Thus comments concerning Islam can be found in the *Relatio tripartita* [**1:2**], written by Raoul de Mérencourt, Patriarch of Jerusalem, with the aid of the masters of the Templar and Hospitaller orders. Similarly, a letter in which much space is devoted to Islam was brought from the East to St. Albans by the master of the Church of St. Thomas, later to be paraphrased in Matthew Paris' *Chronica majora.*[5] Chroniclers writing in the city, or describing events taking place in and around it, also included in their works comments concerning Islam. Such comments can thus be found in the chronicle written by the so-called Templar of Tyre as well as in Joinville's *Vie de Saint Louis.*[6] Clergymen working in Acre were similarly often curious about the rival religion and several of them discussed Islam in their works. Jacques de Vitry, for example, devoted much of the first chapters of his *Historia orientalis* [**1:4**] to Islam,[7] and Benoit d'Alignan included in his *Tractatus super erroribus* [**2:24**] comments concerning it,[8] as did Fidenzio of Padua, who surely obtained much of the material for his *Liber recuperationis terre sancte* [**3:44**] in Acre. Indeed, it is with a Dominican friar from Acre, William of Tripoli, that Frankish writing concerning Islam reached its peak: William's *Notitia de Machometo* [**1:17**] is an elaborate and generally accurate text devoted in its entirety to Islam, composed following a request by Theobald Visconti, later Pope Gregory X. Finally, the references to Islam found in Thietmar's itinerary reveal that pilgrims passing through the city also participated in discussing Islam and accumulating knowledge concerning it.[9] Thus, in terms of quantity, it is possible to conclude that Acre's Franks were interested in Islam and devoted to it considerable attention. Furthermore, the fact that all of the texts mentioned reached the West, and that some of them became quite popular, suggests that Acre played a significant role in the transmission of information, and sometimes disinformation, on Islam to Europe.

THE QUALITY OF INFORMATION ON ISLAM IN TEXTS COMPOSED IN ACRE

The intensiveness with which Islam was commented upon in the city cannot be taken as meaning that the texts composed in Acre uniformly provide precise knowledge concerning this religion. While in some works

---

[5] MP, vol. VI, pp. 348–9.

[6] *Cronaca*, pp. 82, 286; Joinville, *Vie*, pp. 176–8, pars. 360–1; pp. 218–20, pars. 446–8.

[7] *HO*, pp. 106–46.   [8] Paris, BnF, lat. 4224. See, for example, fols. 228v, 229r.

[9] J. C. M. Laurent (ed.), *Magistri Thietmari Peregrinatio* (Hamburg, 1857), pp. 11–12, 49–50. Thietmar's pilgrimage, which took place in 1217, began and ended, as was common, in Acre. Possibly, he wrote at least parts of his text in the city.

we find accurate information on the neighbouring religion, other texts include comments which have little to do with reality. This can be demonstrated by an examination of various discussions, produced in the city, concerning basic issues such as Muhammad's and Christ's status in Islam. The *Relatio tripartita*, written by men in a position to study Islam, says, in one extant version, that Muhammad is worshiped by Muslims just like the pope is by Christians,[10] and in another that he is worshiped by Muslims just like Christ is by Christians.[11] Jacques de Vitry wrote that in every period in which the Muslims possess the Temple Mount, they place a statue of Muhammad in the *Templum Domini*,[12] and the master of the Church of Saint Thomas in Acre described a statue of Muhammad at Mecca destroyed by lightning.[13] The so-called Templar of Tyre, who was not only a native of the Latin East but also had a good command of Arabic, wrote that Muslims venerated Muhammad in their mosques.[14] Joinville, who did not write his *Vie de Saint Louis* in the city, but who did spend a long time in it, and who was in touch with people very knowledgeable concerning Islam, occasionally referred to Muslims as pagans.[15]

At the same time, most of the texts written in the city reveal a reasonable level of acquaintance with Islam. Several texts written in Acre show, first of all, that their authors were familiar with the basic tenets of Islam. Jacques de Vitry wrote that the Muslims believe in one omnipotent creator God, but reject the Trinity.[16] William of Rubruck [2:23] recognized that Islam was monotheistic,[17] and even Benoit d'Alignan, whose work reveals no great effort to learn about Islam, was aware of Islam's basic position towards Christ and Mary. Implicitly, he also acknowledged the Muslim belief in one God:[18]

---

[10] Jacques de Vitry, 'Historia Hierosolymitana', p. 1125.
[11] Ryccardus de S. Germano, *Chronicon*, ed. C. A. Garufi, Rerum Italicarum Scriptores 7.2 (Bologna, 1938), p. 57. At the current state of knowledge concerning the *Relatio* it is impossible to say which of the extant versions best transmits the text as it was actually produced in the East. I nevertheless use it since it is clear that its core was compiled in Acre.
[12] *HO*, p. 246. [13] *MP*, vol. VI, p. 348.
[14] '...en la quele yglize aourerent par dedens les sarazins a Mahomet.' *Cronaca*, p. 82.
[15] Joinville, *Vie*, pp. 154, 179, pars. 312, 364. [16] *HO*, p. 124. [17] Guglielmo, *Viaggio*, p. 246.
[18] '...nota quod sarraceni confitentur Christum natum de Maria semper virgine et de spiritu Dei, i. de flatu Dei, dicentes Deum insufflasse in beatam virginem et sic de flatu illo virginem concepisse, non intelligentes spiritum esse tertiam in trinitate personam, sed potius materialem flatum.' Paris, BnF lat. 4224, fol. 228r. Significantly, however, it seems that everything Benoit tells his readers about Islam is drawn from earlier Western authorities. The clearest example is his discussion of the Muslim paradise which, as Enrico Cerulli has shown, is wholly based on the works of Alain of Lille and William of Auvergne. E. Cerulli, *Il 'Libro della Scala' e la questione delle fonti arabo-spagnole della Divina Commedia* (Rome, 1949), p. 412. Whether Benoit used these works during his stay in the Levant seems impossible to ascertain.

[B]ear in mind that the Saracens confess that Christ was born of Mary, who remained a virgin, and of God's breath, that is God's blow, saying that God breathed into the holy virgin and that the virgin thus conceived from that blow, not understanding that the spirit is the third person in the trinity but rather [thinking that it is a] material blow.

William of Tripoli knew that the Muslims believed in one God, and was fully aware of the status of Christ and Mary in their religious system.[19] The Franciscan Fidenzio expresses awareness of the relation between the Muslim faith and the Christian one writing, in a chapter titled *De infidelitate Sarracenorum*, that the Muslims agree that there is one God, but reject the idea of the trinity.[20]

Indeed, the acquaintance with Islam in the city, as it is reflected in some of the works written in it, went far beyond such basic elements. Jacques de Vitry knew, for example, that Muslims do not eat fish which have no scales.[21] He was also familiar with the Muslim belief that instead of Christ, another, similar, man was crucified,[22] and knew that Muslims employ a particular appellation for Christians and Jews, although instead of mentioning the proper term in this context, 'people of the book', he used the term *homines legis*.[23] Fidenzio's *Liber* also reveals an acquaintance with some non-trivial elements of Islam. This is specifically evident in his discussion of the Muslim paradise in which he includes several Muslim traditions. He says, for example, that Muhammad said that superfluous elements from the food consumed by men in paradise will leave their bodies as sweat, smelling like musk, and that men in paradise will have the shape of Christ and the stature of Adam.[24] These traditions are taken from the *Masā'il 'Abd Allāh ibn-Salām*, a work attributed to a seventh-century Jew from Medina, which consists of a collection of questions put to Muhammad, along with the latter's answers, which are believed to have led the author to convert to Islam.[25] While Fidenzio obtained these traditions through Herman of Dalmatia's Latin translation of this text, known as *Doctrina Mahumet*, rather than through the Arabic original, his

---

[19] *Notitia*, pp. 222–36.

[20] Fidentius, 'Liber', pp. 20–1. Scholars who have surveyed the Western medieval literature on Islam consider his description quite accurate. J. V. Tolan, *Saracens: Islam in the Medieval European Imagination* (New York, NY, 2002), p. 211; N. Daniel, *Islam and the West*, 2nd edn. (Oxford, 1993), pp. 20–1.

[21] *HO*, p. 124.

[22] *HO*, p. 124. For this notion, see *Qur'an* 4.157. William of Tripoli's discussion of this belief is discussed later.

[23] *HO*, p. 126.   [24] Fidentius, 'Liber', p. 22.

[25] H. Daiber, '*Masa'il Wa-Adjwiba*', Encyclopedia of Islam (Leiden, 1991), vol. VI, p. 636. See also the discussion of this text in J. Kritzeck, *Peter the Venerable and Islam* (Princeton, NJ, 1964), pp. 89–96.

use of this composition reveals his effort and ability to present his readers with a rich, and at least partly accurate, picture of Islam.[26]

The *Notitia* in particular reveals an impressive level of knowledge with regard to various aspects of Islam. For example, it contains considerable accurate information with regard to its religious hierarchy, including accounts of the qadis' functions and the different levels of qadis.[27] The *Notitia* also provides its readers with an important insight concerning the non-priestly attitude of Islam, commenting that Muslims 'have neither priests nor monks, whom they should consider as mediators between God and humans,' an observation which, considered within medieval Latin discourse on Islam, reveals a rather unusual level of understanding.[28] Additionally, the *Notitia* reflects acquaintance with some of the main Muslim arguments employed in disputes with Christians, for example, the claim that the Christians took out a prophecy about Muhammad from the New Testament.[29] The description of the Muslim prayer presented in this work is also exceptionally detailed and exact.[30] Firstly, it reveals an unusual understanding of the connection between washing and entry to the mosque, while also avoiding reference to the Christian baptism.[31] Also provided are an accurate depiction of the interior of a mosque, as well as a precise description of the functions of the *qāri'* (i.e. reader of the Qur'an), the *imām* and the *khaṭīb* in the Muslim prayer. The ability of this text's author to cite a Qur'anic text which is sometimes recited as a part of the prayer (*Surat al-Ikhlāṣ*) is also unique: Lull, considered by Norman Daniel to have presented a comparatively accurate description of the Muslim prayer, was only able to cite the *Fātiḥa*.[32]

It is thus clear that there did not exist in Acre a general trend which brought all educated men to hold, and distribute, precise knowledge regarding Islam. On the other hand, it cannot be argued that the Franks of Outremer were universally ignorant about Islam. Rather, whereas some authors held and presented, with regard to some matters, high-quality information, in other cases the level of precision reflected in the

---

[26] That Fidenzio made use of Herman's translation is made clear by the similarity between the wording in both texts. Cf. Fidentius, 'Liber', p. 22; Paris, Arsenal, MS 1162, fol. 23r.

[27] *Notitia*, p. 254 and p. 398, n. 161.

[28] ' . . . non habent sacerdotes nec monachos, quos reputent inter Deum et homines mediatores,' *Notitia*, p. 258; Daniel, *Islam and the West*, p. 252.

[29] *Notitia*, pp. 236–8, 392, n. 116.

[30] *Notitia*, pp. 256–60. Engels writes that the only description he knows which is comparable to William's is Bartholomeus of Edessa's. *Notitia*, p. 399, n. 166. However, an examination of both works reveals that Barthlomeus' work could not have been William's source.

[31] Daniel, *Islam and the West*, p. 236.   [32] Daniel, *Islam and the West*, p. 237.

texts is surprisingly low. This makes it rather hard to speak of a learning process in which 'former general and imprecise impressions of the Muslims and Islam' were gradually 'replaced by more detailed, accurate descriptions'.[33] As Benjamin Z. Kedar has written, 'proximity to the Muslims evidently did not guarantee an accurate perception of their beliefs'.[34]

Menache and Kedar's comments seem, however, to look at the Frankish discourse on Islam in limited terms of knowledge and the ability to acquire it. The questions involved here are, in my opinion, wider, and involve issues such as genres, aims of writing and intended audiences.[35] In other words, the fact that an author working in Acre possessed a precise piece of knowledge concerning Islam, or was in a position to acquire it from others, does not necessarily mean that he would choose to include it in his text. Rather, such works were shaped not only by what their authors knew, or what they were in a position to learn, but also by the genre in which they were operating, their aims in writing and their intended audiences. For example, we have seen that Joinville occasionally refers to Muslims as pagans, but it is very difficult to believe that he did not know that they worshipped one god, and, in any case, he was certainly closely connected to men who would have easily corrected him with regard to this gross misunderstanding of Islam. It is more likely, then, that he knowingly used this term as a polemical, and even pejorative, appellation. Furthermore, writing a chronicle for a lay audience, the exact features of Islam were not of great importance for him. These characteristics of Joinville and his work may also explain the comment by the Templar of Tyre, whose level of acquaintance with Islamic culture must have been considerable. On the other hand, William of Tripoli, a mendicant writing for colleagues who might engage in interfaith disputes and conversion, had to be much more precise with regard to Islam's theological character. Thus, Acre's cultural situation, in which different milieus were interested in Islam for different reasons, resulted in a multi-layered discourse concerning it.

Interestingly, the complexity of discourse concerning Islam can occasionally be found within a single text. Thus, for example, we have seen that Jacques de Vitry wrote, in his *Historia orientalis*, both that Islam was

---

[33] S. Menache, 'When Jesus Met Muhammad in the Holy Land: Attitudes toward the "Other" in the Crusader Kingdom', *Medieval Encounters* 15.1 (2009), p. 73.

[34] Kedar, *Crusade and Mission*, p. 90.

[35] B. Hamilton, 'Knowing the Enemy: Western Understanding of Islam at the Time of the Crusades', *Journal of the Royal Asiatic Society*, third series 7.3 (Nov. 1997), p. 374.

monotheistic and that whenever the Muslims rule the Temple Mount they place a statue of Muhammad in al-Aqsa. It is unlikely that Jacques really thought that the Muslims kept a statue in al-Aqsa and that none of his local informants would have been able to correct this grave error. The inclusion of these two contradictory comments in a single text can perhaps be explained by the different sources Jacques found in the city on the one hand, and by the varying contexts in which he commented about Islam on the other. While Jacques' understanding of Islam as a monotheistic religion is based on a written source which circulated in the city, the so-called Gregorian Report (on which more later), his notion with regard to the Temple Mount statue may reflect a Frankish oral tradition, related, perhaps, to a comment by Fulcher of Chartres.[36] The appeal of this rumour was probably enhanced by the Muslim–Latin competition over the holy places, and perhaps also by Jacques' personal frustration at not being able to visit the holy city. It may not be accidental, then, that this imaginary observation appears in the part of the *Historia orientalis* which is devoted to holy sites, while his comment concerning Islam's monotheistic character appears in a section devoted to a detailed description of the rival religion.

SOURCES OF KNOWLEDGE CONCERNING ISLAM

1   *Latin Texts*

Given the great variation in levels of precision among different discussions of Islam composed in thirteenth-century Acre, an attempt to generally characterize Latin discourse on this subject would be of limited value. It would, however, be worthwhile to look at the sources available in Acre for Westerners interested in Islam, as these are instructive with regard to the range of possibilities open to authors working in the city.

Franks residing in Acre and interested in writing about Islam would have had a considerable number of Latin texts to rely on. This can be seen mainly through the compositions by Jacques de Vitry and William of Tripoli. As is well known, in composing his *Historia*, Jacques made extensive use of William of Tyre's work. A comparison between Jacques' and William's descriptions of the history of the Shi'ite–Sunni schism reveals that the former made use of the latter's work also with regard to the history of Islam:

---

[36] Fulcherus Carnotensis, *Historia Hierosolymitana*, ed. H. Hagenmeyer (Heidelberg, 1913), p. 290.

Jacques' *Historia orientalis*	William's *Chronicon*
A certain cousin of Muḥammad's named 'Alī ... began to be disturbed and offended since he was referred to as Muḥammad's successor, while he considered himself more worthy than Muḥammad and wished to be valued by all as an extraordinary prophet.[37]	This ... namely 'Alī, since he was ... Muḥammad's cousin, began to be greatly offended because he was referred to as his successor and not an extraordinary prophet.[38]

Jacques may have actually used William of Tyre's now-lost *Gesta orientalium principum*, since he writes that 'indeed we know this for certain about the Turks from old histories of the oriental people'.[39] As we know that working on his *Chronicon*, William cited his own Oriental history, it is possible that the phrases Jacques used appeared in both William's *Chronicon* and *Gesta*.

Perhaps more interestingly, both Jacques' *Historia orientalis* and William of Tripoli's *Notitia de Machometo* reveal that numerous short Latin texts related to Islam were accessible to authors working in Acre. Important evidence in this regard has to do with a text to which I refer as the Gregorian Report.[40] This text, or rather, compilation, appears in Matthew Paris' chronicle, under 1236, as a letter sent to Pope Gregory IX from the eastern parts by preachers (that is, Dominican friars), travelling through 'those parts'.[41] More than a decade earlier, a text very similar to that provided by Matthew – or at least the part of it including its second and third sections (on which more later) – was intensively used by Jacques de Vitry as he was producing the first chapters of his *Historia orientalis*.[42] This makes it most likely that what we have here is a compilation which circulated in the Kingdom of Jerusalem, and in all likelihood

---

[37] ' ...quidam patruelis Mahometi, nomine Haly ... commoveri cepit et indignari quod successor Mahometi vocaretur, cum se digniorem ipso Mahometo reputaret et prophetam eximium ... se vellet ab omnibus estimari'. *HO*, p. 142.

[38] 'Iste ... Hali videlicet, cum esset ... et ipsius Mehemeth patruelis, indignari cepit plurimum quod illius diceretur successor et non magis propheta eximius.' Willemus Tyrensis, *Chronicon*, vol. II, p. 891.

[39] 'De Turcis siquidem ex antiquis orientalium historiis certum habemus.' *HO*, p. 148. Another phrase was sometimes used as providing evidence regarding Jacques' sources: 'cum igitur . . .varios libros ex armariis Latinorum Graecorum et Arabum revolverem, Regum Orientalium historiae, praelia et gesta casu in manus meas devenerunt.' This phrase is, however, taken from the prologue to the *Historia orientalis*, which is now considered inauthentic. For the prologue, see Jacques de Vitry, 'Historia Hierosolymitana', pp. 1047–8. Regarding its authenticity, see *HO*, pp. 11, 14.

[40] For a critical edition and elaborate discussion of this text, see M. Vandecasteele, 'Étude compara-tive de deux versions latines médiévales d'une apologie arabo-chrétienne. Pierre le Vénérable et le Rapport Grégorien', *Academiae Analecta (Mededelingen van de Koninklijke Academie voor Wetenschappen, Letteren en Schone Kunsten van België, Klasse der Letteren)* 53 (1991), pp. 79–134.

[41] MP, vol. III, pp. 343–55.   [42] Vandecasteele, 'Étude comparative', pp. 94–7; *HO*, p. 472, n. 1.

specifically in Acre, during the first decades of the thirteenth century.[43] Furthermore, this compilation was deemed authoritative and instructive enough to be sent from the East to the pope. These circumstances make it worthwhile to examine its contents in detail.

As Vandecasteele has shown, this report is a compilation made of three units. The first is a genealogical list which begins with Abraham and ends with Muhammad I, a ninth-century emir of Cordoba. Clearly, then, this text was composed within a Mozarabic context. However, it was later commented on by someone who was ignorant enough concerning Iberian history to confuse the emir with the prophet.[44] While it is not clear whether Jacques had access to this part of the report, Matthew's testimony, according to which this text was sent from the Levant, raises the possibility that this commentator worked in Syria. The compilation's second element is a work on Muhammad which is largely based on Al-Kindī's Apology. It remains unknown where, when and under what circumstances this text was produced, but one can say that it is based on a translation of Al-Kindī's letter which is independent of that included in Peter the Venerable's collection of works on Islam.[45] The third section of the Gregorian Report is a short treatise which discusses theological matters such as Islam's monotheism and attitude to the Trinity, as well as religious practices such as marriage and divorce. As this section describes Muslims as praying facing south, it is very likely that it was composed in Latin Syria.

The examination of the Gregorian Report makes it possible to reach several conclusions with regard to the intellectual life in Outremer and specifically in Acre. Firstly, the report's third unit can probably be added to the corpus of texts composed in the Latin East (though not necessarily in Acre). Secondly, the report provides further evidence for literary continuity in Acre in the sense that texts were kept in the city in a manner that enabled authors working years apart to make use of them. Thirdly, it reveals a case in which, for unknown reasons, and under unknown circumstances, an Iberian text concerned with Islam made its way to the Latin East and was there integrated into a local compilation. This means that, at least to some degree, knowledge

---

[43] In the past this hypothesis could have been challenged by the apparent use of this compilation by Geoffrey of Viterbo in his twelfth-century *Pantheon*. However, this is not a real difficulty since, in all likelihood, the Gregorian Report was not an original part of the Pantheon but rather was inserted into it sometime in the thirteenth century. J. Donnadieu, 'La représentation de l'islam dans l'Historia orientalis. Jacques de Vitry historien', *Le Moyen Age* 114.3–4 (2008), p. 491; *Gotifredi Viterbiensis opera*, ed. G. Waitz, MGH SS 22 (Hannover, 1872), p. 280.

[44] Vandecasteele, 'Étude comparative', pp. 84–5.

[45] Vandecasteele, 'Étude comparative', pp. 85–91.

concerning Islam travelled between the two Latin territories characterized by constant contact with the rival religion: Iberia and Outremer.[46]

Sections of William's *Notitia* are possibly also based on Latin material that
circulated in the Latin East and, perhaps, specifically in Acre's Dominican
convent.[47] The presentation of such a hypothesis must be preceded by a brief
examination of the structure of this work. In the preface to his work, William
writes that this text would discuss three matters: Muhammad and the rise of
his people, the Qur'an and its compilation and the Qur'anic teachings
regarding Christian faith. However, when one examines the actual text, it
becomes clear that the third unit described by William is followed by several
sections titled: *The response of the Saracens when they are invited to Christian faith
by the above-mentioned testimony of their own book; The response of the Christians to
the above; About the lords of the Saracens; About the spiritual leaders of the Saracens
and their offices; About the Saracens' place of prayer and how they enter and remain
[there].*[48] As these sections are not mentioned in William's prologue, they are
likely additions to his work, which he, or a later editor, attached to the
composition. That these sections were not originally composed by William
but rather attached to the text he wrote can be supported by two pieces of
philological evidence. While in the parts of the *Notitia* which are described in
William's introduction the word 'caliph' is provided in Latin in the form
calipha, sections which are unaccounted for in the treatise's opening remarks
include the form *kalipha*.[49] Additionally, while in the section devoted to the
Qur'an and its compilation the *Notitia* refers to the qadi as 'their teacher'
(*doctor eorum*) and the Muslim equivalent to the Latin bishop, the passage titled
About the spiritual leaders of the Saracens and their offices mentions *Ravi* as the
person who judges in spiritual matters.[50] The easiest way to explain these
differences is that the *Notitia*'s final chapters were not composed by the same
person who wrote its core.

The presented evidence makes it very likely that William attached to the
text he was preparing short treatises which circulated in his cultural environment. One such text would have included the sections titled *The response of
the Saracens when they are invited to Christian faith by the above-mentioned testimony
of their own book* and *The response of the Christians to the above*, and would have

---

[46] Further evidence for the employment in Outremer of texts concerning Islam composed in the
Iberian context is provided by Jacques de Vitry's probable use, in his *Historia orientalis*, of the
Continuatio chronicorum beati Isidori (or a closely related text). See later in this chapter.

[47] Engels suggests that William used collections of various materials on Islam, but does not develop
this idea. *Notitia*, p. 83.

[48] *Responsio Sarracenorum quando invitantur ad fidem Christi per predicta sui libri testimonia; Christianorum
responsio ad iam dicta; De dominis Sarracenorum; De spiritualibus principibus Sarracenorum et eorum officiis;
De oratorio Sarracenorum et quomodo intrant et morantur.*

[49] Cf. *Notitia*, pp. 204, 206 (caliphe), 248, 250, 254 (kaliphe).

[50] Cf. *Notitia*, pp. 218, 254. *Ravi* is also mentioned in the depiction of the Muslim prayer, p. 258.

dealt with the manner in which Muslims were to be persuaded by the Christian faith. A second treatise probably included the chapters titled *About the lords of the Saracens* and *About the spiritual leaders of the Saracens and their offices*, and a third would have included the chapter titled *About the Saracens' place of prayer and how they enter and remain [there]*.

Additional evidence for the use, by thirteenth-century Franks, of material which was composed or collected earlier in the Latin East is provided by William of Tripoli's version of the Bahira legend, a fictional account of Muhammad's early life.[51] According to Engels, this narrative originated in the East and is particularly similar to two texts:[52] the first is a Latin text, written in, or near, Antioch, during the twelfth century, presented by its author as based on a discussion with a Greek person, acquainted with both Arabic and Latin.[53] The second is the version provided by Piloti, an Italian merchant who had spent a long time in Egypt in the early fifteenth century (1396–1438). This implies that a narrative recounting the story of Bahira, similar to the one included in the *Notitia*, circulated among Outremer's Franks as early as the twelfth century, and kept developing in the East till at least the end of the fourteenth century. It is thus probable that rather than independently inventing a legend, or hearing it from a non-Frankish resident of Outremer, William employed in this case a tradition that, by the time he was writing, had already been circulating orally, or perhaps through texts which have not reached us, among the Latins of Outremer.[54]

2 The Qur'an and Its Commentaries

The only Muslim source clearly used by Frankish authors working in Acre is the Qur'an. Most notably, at the heart of the *Notitia* the reader finds a series of translations from the Qur'anic text.[55] Chapter 7 of the work includes a precise translation of the *surat al-Fātiḥa* and the beginning of *surat al-Baqara*. The following chapter, which focuses on the Muslim paradise, ends with these comments:[56]

---

[51] *Notitia*, pp. 196–200.   [52] *Notitia*, p. 79.

[53] B. Bischoff, *Anecdota Novissima: Texte vierten bis sechzehnten Jahrhunderts* (Stuttgart, 1984), p. 113.

[54] It is noteworthy that Piloti's version is not dependent on William's and that William's is not directly dependent on the twelfth-century text. *Notitia*, pp. 79–81.

[55] For William's translations, see also Chapter 3, pp. 68–9.

[56] 'Quapropter, que liber ille continet de domino Iesu et de eius beata genitrice Maria, de sacrosancto Ewangelio et de fidelibus Christi, nolui per aliena verba narrare nec mutare sensum nec verba, et pietate vera et fide sincera transtuli de arabico in latinum et XVIIII auctoritates, quasi tot testimonia, fidei nostre rosas et lylia colligens et fasciculum faciens in unum corpusculum, hoc modicum dico opusculum, Deo iuvante peregi, redegi nec dictas auctoritates posui in ordine illius libri, ubi non est ordo, sed in ordine, quem hystoria veritatis ordinat et fidei disciplina.' *Notitia*, p. 222.

On which account, I did not want to narrate these which this book [the Qur'an] contains about Lord Christ and his holy mother Mary, about the most holy gospel, and about Christ's followers, through alien words, or to change the sense or the words, and I translated [them] in true piety and in sincere faith from Arabic into Latin. And collecting the 19 authorities, about as many pieces of testimony, roses and lilies of our faith, and making a bundle into a little collection, I accomplished, I recorded, with God's help, this modest, I say, little work. And I did not place the said authorities by the order of that book, in which there is no order, but in the order in which the narrative of truth and the doctrine of faith order [them].

Following these introductory remarks, William lists the pieces of information included in the Qur'an with regard to Christ, Mary, the Gospel and the Christians. He then presents the quotes which provide these pieces of information in a way that forms a story as close as possible to the Christian one. As Daniel has written, William's accurate use of the text is unique,[57] and Engels, who is generally critical as to the quality of William's knowledge of Islam, wrote that these translations, as well as the ones presented in chapter 7, are relatively free of errors.[58] To this should be added that, as was mentioned earlier, William, perhaps through Arabic-speaking informants, was able to appreciate the literary qualities of the Qur'an.[59]

It is noteworthy, however, that the knowledge of the Qur'an presented in the *Notitia* is far from impeccable. William writes, for example, that the Qur'an says in many places 'avoid evil and do good, and whoever would do so, will reach paradise'. This quote, however, is not found in the Qur'an, but is reminiscent of Psalms 36.27.[60] Furthermore, not all of the translations he presents are accurate. Especially noteworthy is his corruption of a verse related to Muslim attitudes towards women:

William of Tripoli	Qur'an
[Y]ou may enjoy as many women as you would like, and everyone may have two wives or three or four (and they conclude: thus then, nine!) and of others you may have as many as the hand can buy, and you may use them like a horse, a beast of burden, or bought things.[61]	[M]arry women of your choice, two, or three, or four; but if ye fear that ye shall not be able to deal justly (with them), then only one, or (a captive) that your right hands possess. That will be more suitable, to prevent you from doing injustice.[62]

---

[57] Daniel, *Islam and the West*, p. 193.   [58] *Notitia*, p. 87.   [59] See Chapter 3, p. 68.

[60] 'Declina a malo et fac bonum, et qui hoc fecerit, habebit paradysum.' *Notitia*, p. 254. Another case in which William wrongly mentions a phrase as appearing in the Qur'an appears on p. 216: 'quia sola, inquit, fides Sarracenorum facit fideles'.

[61] 'Habeatis delectationem cum mulieribus quantum vobis placeat, et habeat quisque duas uxores et tres et quatuor (et concludunt: sic ergo novem!) et de aliis habeatis, quantum potest manus emere, et utamini eis sicut equo et iumento et rebus emptis.' *Notitia*, p. 216.

[62] Qur'an 4.3. Here and elsewhere the translation used is that by Yusuf Ali.

Furthermore, a very similar, and equally corrupted, translation of this phrase appears again later in the *Notitia*.[63] It is difficult to explain the inclusion of such verses in a work that reveals so much accurate knowledge of Islam. Indeed, even the distorted phrase itself reveals, through the mention of the word 'hand', that whoever produced it actually had a very good knowledge of the Qur'anic text. Clearly, these phrases belong to the strong Latin tradition perceiving Islam as 'built upon a foundation of sexual licence which was plainly contrary to the natural and the divine law'.[64] Perhaps the power of this notion within Frankish discourse may explain why William, or an informant with whom he was working, corrupted this phrase.

These corruptions, along with other errors, brought Engels to propose that William did not himself know Arabic. Rather, Engels argues, he asked someone else to prepare for him the accurate translations used in chapters 7 and 10. The translations which appear in other parts of the work were taken, according to Engels, from collections of material on Islam which were available in William's intellectual environment.[65] That William did not work alone, and that he had access to various short treatises on Islam, settles well with the evidence presented earlier. But the important thing is that whether or not William read Arabic, the *Notitia* provides clear evidence that Acre's Frankish residents had access to precise Latin translations of at least parts of the Qur'an. Furthermore, as these translations appear to be original, one can safely assume that there were in Acre Franks who were able, perhaps with the help of native Arabic speakers, to produce accurate translations of Qur'anic sections. This is not surprising, of course, given the evidence presented earlier concerning the knowledge of Arabic among Acre's Franks.[66] On the other hand, it is noteworthy that such knowledge would have been used not only for strictly practical matters, such as the documentation of business transactions or the preparation of Frankish–Muslim peace treaties, but also for the development of a better understanding of Islam.

The accessibility of the Qur'anic text to Franks active in Acre is confirmed by several additional pieces of evidence. A comment by William shows that the Qur'anic text was rather accessible to Franks in Acre:[67]

---

[63] *Notitia*, p. 242. [64] Daniel, *Islam and the West*, p. 176. [65] *Notitia*, p. 88.
[66] See Chapters 1, pp. 32–3, 35 and Chapter 3, pp. 62–9.
[67] 'Hec ideo scripsi, ut, si forte aliqua translatio Alcorani ad manus veniat, sciat lector illam non esse huius Alcorani translationem, quam Sarraceni nunc solam tenent ubique.' *Notitia*, p. 218.

I wrote these down so that if, by any chance, some translation of the Qur'an would come to hand, the reader would know that it is not the translation of that Qur'an which alone is now held by the Saracens everywhere.

As Engels has argued, this phrase is problematic, as it does not make sense that William meant the 'quam' to refer to the word 'translatio' as the present Latin text implies. It is more likely that he meant it to refer to the word 'Qur'an'.[68] However, whatever its exact meaning may be, this phrase suggests that the *Notitia*'s readers were likely to encounter additional versions of the Qur'an, thus providing further evidence that Franks active in Acre could quite easily get hold of the Qur'anic text. The accessibility of the Qur'an to the Latins of Outremer is supported by a comment from Burchard of Mount Sion's *Descriptio terre sancte* according to which he read at least some of that book.[69] Considering his long sojourn in the Holy Land and his connections to the Dominicans of this province, this phrase should be understood as further evidence for the circulation of the Qur'anic text among the Latins, and specifically, the Dominicans, of the Holy Land.[70]

The reading of the Qur'anic Arabic text by Franks active in the Kingdom of Jerusalem is probably further corroborated by an extant Arabic manuscript: MS Paris, Bibliothèque nationale de France, arabe 384, which includes the Qur'an in Arabic and was produced in Egypt or Syria in the late twelfth or early thirteenth century. Interestingly, this manuscript contains two sets of Latin marginalia. While the identity of the author of the earlier set of comments remains a mystery, the second one should, according to Burman, be attributed to Riccoldo of Monte Croce,[71] who is known to have sailed to Acre and to have travelled through the Holy Land before going on north and then further east.[72] These circumstances make it probable that it was in Acre, or elsewhere in the Kingdom of Jerusalem, that Riccoldo obtained this copy of the Qur'an, which was already annotated by its previous Latin owner. If this was indeed the case, we have here a significant piece of evidence with regard to the study of the Qur'an in its original Arabic among the Franks of Outremer.

I have been unable to find any clear evidence for the direct use, on the part of Frankish authors working in Acre, of additional written Muslim texts. The *Notitia* does, however, provide evidence that William of Tripoli was able to obtain original knowledge of commentaries on the

---

[68] *Notitia*, p. 385, n. 65.   [69] Laurent, *Peregrinatores*, p. 53.   [70] See Chapter 1, pp. 23–4.
[71] T. E. Burman, 'How an Italian Friar Read His Arabic Qur'an', *Dante Studies* 125 (2007), pp. 93–109.
[72] R. George-Tvrtković, 'The Ambivalence of Interreligious Experience: Riccoldo da Monte Croce's Theology of Islam', *unpublished PhD thesis, University of Notre Dame* (2007), pp. 59–62.

Qur'an. Discussing the Muslim negation of the crucifixion of Christ, William writes:[73]

> Glossators say that they crucified Judas who had entered a cave where he prayed in order to seek him and when he left there appeared in him Christ's effigy and they crucified him.

For the composition of these phrases, William could not have relied solely on the Qur'anic text, since there (4.157) it is only said that Christ was not crucified but that it thus seemed to the Jews:

> That they said (in boast), 'we killed Christ Jesus the son of Mary, the apostle of God'; but they killed him not, nor crucified him, but so it was made to appear to them.

Al-Rāzī, who presented his readers with five possible interpretations for this Qur'anic text, included an explanation according to which the head of the Jews sent a man named Titayus to look for Christ in order to have him killed. When Titayus entered the house in which Christ was found, God took the latter out of it through the roof, and made the former look just like Christ. Titayus was then crucified and killed.[74] Al-Rāzī's version is not identical to William's but, as William's text cannot be understood as relying solely on the Qur'an, and as no Western source transmitting this tradition was yet found, the similarity between the two makes it probable that William was able to gain access to some exegetical Muslim tradition.[75]

Jacques de Vitry also shows an acquaintance with a piece of Muslim commentary on the Qur'an. He wrote that Muhammad called the apostles 'men dressed in white' ('viros albis indutos').[76] This refers to Qur'an 3.52 where it is said that 'When Jesus found unbelief on their part he said: "Who will be my helpers to (the work of) God?" Said the Disciples: "We are God's helpers... "' The Arabic word translated here as 'disciples' is *ḥawāriyyūn*. While this word is, according to Thomas Burman, an Ethiopic word for 'disciples', Qur'anic commentators believed that it was based on the root HWR which could mean 'to make white.' Thus Jacques

---

[73] 'Glosatores dicunt, quod crucifixerunt Iudam, qui intraverat ad ipsum querendum in spelunca, ubi oravit, et dum exiret, apparuit in eo effigies Christi et hunc crucifixerunt.' *Notitia*, p. 234.

[74] Fakhr al-Dīn al-Rāzī, *Al-Tafsir Al-Kabir* (Beirut, 1990), parts 11–12, pp. 79–80 [Arabic].

[75] That Muslims believe that it was not Christ who was crucified, but rather someone who resembled him, was known to many Western authors. This was known, for example, to Jacques de Vitry; see *HO*, p. 124. However, the idea that the man who was crucified was earlier sent to look for Christ in a certain place (be it a house or a cave), and that God in some miraculous manner brought Christ out of that place, was not identified by Engels in Catholic sources. *Notitia*, p. 390, n. 105. I have also been unable to find a parallel to this story in Latin literature.

[76] *HO*, p. 128.

reveals here an acquaintance with an element of Qur'an commentary. It is impossible to say how this piece of Muslim exegesis reached him, but since it was known to both Robert of Ketton and the anonymous commentator of MS Arsenal 1162,[77] it is likely that Jacques learned it from a Latin, rather than through direct communication with a Muslim.

3   Direct and Indirect Communication with Muslims

Acre's Latin inhabitants would have met Muslims on various occasions, such as travel, commercial exchanges and diplomatic contacts. Captivity of Franks in the hands of Muslims and vice versa would have also created a forced encounter between the followers of both faiths. Occasionally, the extant sources provide a glimpse of such encounters and reveal that indeed in some of them theological themes were discussed. Thus, for example, Joinville describes, both in his *Credo* [**1:8**] and in his *Vie de Saint Louis*, a brief interfaith discussion which had taken place when he was kept, along with numerous other Frankish combatants, as a captive following the battle of Mansurah. If we are to trust Joinville, an old Muslim approached them, telling the count of Bretagne that he understood that Christians believed in a God who had been captured, beaten and put to death for them, and had risen again on the third day. As the count confirmed this, the old man told him that the Frankish prisoners should therefore not complain as they did not yet suffer for Christ what he had suffered for them. The old Muslim then added that if Christ had had the power to rise again, he would surely liberate the Frankish captives when he wished to do so.[78] It is hard to interpret this conversation. In the *Credo* version of this anecdote Joinville wrote that he thought the man was sent by God, since not long after he had left, the captives were notified that the king negotiated their liberation. Perhaps the old Muslim meant to ridicule the captives and possibly, as is implied by the *Credo* text, he was even considered insane. But be that as it may, we do see here an exchange concerning theological matters, even if in a very rudimentary level, between Franks and Muslims.

Fidenzio also had a chance to communicate with Muslims concerning matters of faith in the context of captivity. Telling his readers that Muslims abhor images, Fidenzio recounts a conversation he had with regard to this issue when, following Frankish Tripoli's fall (1289), he went

---

[77] T. E. Burman, *Religious Polemic and the Intellectual History of the Mozarabs, c. 1050–1200* (Leiden, 1994), pp. 141–3.

[78] Jean, Sire de Joinville, *Histoire*, pp. 430–2, pars. 813–14. The same episode appears with slight variations in Joinville, *Vie*, pp. 164–6, par. 337. There are slight differences between the two accounts.

to assist Christian captives held by the Mamluk army. According to his account:[79]

[S]ome Muslims called me, and asked me 'why do you Christians worship paintings and images?' I replied saying, 'you are wrong since Christians do not worship images or paintings, but worship and venerate the saints who are in heaven and whom the images represent.'

In both Joinville's and Fidenzio's accounts the engaged Latins learned little, if anything, concerning Muslim theology. This, however, might be the result of a narrative by which the Latin authors wished to show that they revealed their truth to the Muslims, rather than that they had learned something from the Muslims they had encountered. Equally, this might genuinely reflect conditions in which it was not easy to communicate and whatever exchange did develop would have been more polemic than instructive, and would have been restricted to a very basic level of understanding.

On some occasions, however, the outcome of such brief encounters was more substantial, especially when the Latins involved could speak Arabic well and were genuinely curious about Islam, and when the Muslims they met were relatively knowledgeable about their own faith. This seems to have been the case with some encounters Yves the Breton had with Muslims.[80] Joinville tells us that Yves, a Dominican friar, who, we are informed, 'savoit le sarrazinois,' was sent by Louis IX, while he was in Acre, to Damascus. Returning to the Frankish capital, the envoy recounted that he had seen in Damascus an old woman carrying a ladle full of fire in one hand and a vial full of water in the other. Asked what she intended to do with these, she replied that she wanted to burn paradise with fire and quench hell with water so that both would cease to exist and thus people would stop acting out of hope of paradise or fear of hell. Rather, they would simply act for the love of God. Yves certainly did not meet such a woman, as this anecdote is really a version of a Muslim story told about an eighth-century woman mystic.[81] Rather, he must have heard this account from a Muslim, later reshaping it from a tale he heard to an incident he allegedly witnessed.[82] Alternatively, it was Joinville who

---

[79] 'Et cum ergo ambularem per exercitum quidam Sarraceni vocaverunt me, et fecerunt mihi questionem dicentes: "quare vos Xpistiani picturas et ymagines adoratis?" Quibus ego respondi dicens: "vos erratis, quia Xpistiani non adorant ymagines aut picturas, sed adorant et venerantur Sanctos qui sunt in celo, quos ymagines representant."' Fidentius, 'Liber', p. 21.

[80] For Yves, see Chapter 1, pp. 22–3, 35.

[81] B. Z. Kedar, 'Some New Sources on Palestinian Muslims before and during the Crusades', in H. E. Mayer (ed.), *Die Kreuzfahrerstaaten als multikulturelle Gesellschaft* (Munich, 1997), p. 139; for the story, see Joinville, *Vie*, p. 218, par. 445.

[82] This is also Kedar's suggestion. Kedar, 'Some New Sources', p. 139.

changed the story, either in order to make his narrative more appealing, or because, writing decades after his sojourn in the Levant, he simply did not remember precisely what he had heard from Yves.[83] Be that as it may, the inclusion of this anecdote in Joinville's work provides evidence for dialogues between Muslims and Franks in which the latter did have a chance to become acquainted with non-trivial elements of Islamic tradition.

This is also the case with Yves' attempts to learn about the Nizarite Isma'ilis, commonly known as the Assassins. Sent by Louis IX as an envoy to the head of the Syrian Nizaris, known as the 'Old Man of the Mountain', Yves had a chance to discuss with him theological matters.[84] During this encounter, Yves saw a book which the 'Old Man of the Mountain' was in the habit of reading and which, Hamilton argues, can probably be related to a text known as the *Kerygmata Petrou*. Joinville's depiction of this conversation also includes an echo of the Isma'ili belief in a succession of speaker-prophets each succeeded by a spiritual legatee, who interpreted the inner meaning of the revealed messages. According to this system, Jesus was a speaker-prophet and Simon-Peter, his interpreter.[85] Not surprisingly, this conversation also included a polemic element, when Yves tried to explain to the Isma'ili leader, to no avail, of course, that his beliefs were wrong. Clearly, Joinville's understanding of the Isma'ili tradition was very vague, but this was not necessarily the case with Yves. As was already noted, Joinville composed his *Vie de Saint Louis* decades after he had returned from the Holy Land, so that his memory of the news brought by Yves to Acre must have been imprecise at best. It is consequently very likely that Yves was able to gain from this discussion considerably more than is reflected in Joinville's account. At the same time, this example also reveals, as Hamilton argued, 'how very difficult it could be for Western inquirers, even those who were well-educated, who spoke Arabic, and who were prepared to discuss theology with Muslim religious leaders, to understand the information they were given'.[86]

The evidence concerning Yves the Breton is instructive also in an additional respect. It shows that people like him, who had a reasonable command of Arabic, as well as opportunities to travel in Muslim territories and communicate with Muslims knowledgeable in religious matters, played an important role in the discourse that developed in Acre concerning Islam. Such figures would have brought pieces of information

---

[83] Joinville, *Vie*, p. 378, par. 769.   [84] Joinville, *Vie*, p. 228, pars. 462–3.
[85] Hamilton, 'Knowing', p. 377; F. Daftary, *The Isma'ilis: Their History and Doctrines* (Cambridge, 1990), p. 139.
[86] Hamilton, 'Knowing', p. 377.

concerning the rival religion to the city, where these would have, at least occasionally, been shared with members of different milieus. Indeed, as we have seen, Yves, a learned Dominican, discussed Islam with lay nobles such as Joinville, though, one may assume, he probably brought still more detailed information to his colleagues in the city's Dominican convent.

While the extant sources include very limited evidence for the Latin accumulation of knowledge concerning Islam through direct communication with Muslims, this does not necessarily mean that such occurrences were in reality so rare. Possibly, the sources' relative silence in this respect derives not from the fact that such exchanges did not take place, but rather from the authors' view that such encounters were not worth documenting. Indeed, it does seem likely, that, as in Yves' case, some curious Latins, and particularly those who could communicate in Arabic — by themselves or through translators working with them — made an effort to acquire a degree of acquaintance with Islam through Muslim informants. Such exchanges would help to explain the appearance, in our texts, of pieces of knowledge concerning Islam which other sources cannot account for. Particularly relevant, in this context, are pieces of information unlikely to have been transmitted to Latins through Oriental Christians or Jews, such as the descriptions of the mosque's interior and the Muslim prayer which are included in the *Notitia*.[87]

4   The Role of Oriental Christians and Jews as Mediators

The cultural characteristics of the Latin East raise the possibility that some information concerning Islam entered Latin circles through the mediation of Oriental Christians and Jews. The potential of such transfer of knowledge was considerable, as command of Arabic would have been much more common among members of these groups than among the Franks, and, furthermore, many of their members would have been much better informed concerning Islam than their Latin neighbours.[88]

However, perhaps disappointingly, evidence for such contacts is hard to come by. Jessalynn Bird suggested that Jacques de Vitry and Oliver of Paderborn used Oriental Christian sources with regard to Islam, but did not provide any evidence in support of this claim.[89] Jean Donnadieu also argued for the strong presence of Oriental Christian elements in Jacques

---

[87] *Notitia*, pp. 256–60.

[88] Laura Minervini argued that the Oriental Christians played the role of mediators between the Muslim and Western worlds. Minervini, 'Modelli culturali', pp. 347–8.

[89] J. L. Bird, 'Crusade and Conversion after the Fourth Lateran Council (1215): Oliver of Paderborn's and James of Vitry's Missions to Muslims Reconsidered', *Essays in Medieval Studies* 21 (2004), p. 27.

de Vitry's discussion of Islam and expressed the view that Jacques' knowledge of Islam derived first and foremost from his direct contacts with Oriental Christians.[90] However, Donndieu's actual evidence for this claim is not convincing. Firstly, he sees Jacques' use of Al-Kindī's Apology as supporting his argument, but, as we have seen, Jacques did not use Al-Kindī's work, but rather a Latin compilation which included a section based on this text.[91] Donnadieu continues in his attempts to prove the existence of such contacts by arguing for the similarity between certain claims made by Jacques and those which appear in Byzantine texts. However, this too is not convincing, as in none of the cases mentioned does Donnadieu prove that the argument under discussion was never before used by Westerners. Indeed, at least in some cases, it is easy to show that what Donnadieu presents as common to Jacques and to Byzantine authors was also used in Western literature. Thus, for example, Donnadieu sees Jacques de Vitry's comment regarding Muhammad's sexual power as evidence for the connection between his arguments and those used in Byzantine polemics. But by the time Jacques was working on his *Historia*, such comments had already appeared in Western works, such as Peter Alfonsi's *Dialogo*.[92] This is also the case with Donnadieu's attempt to tie Jacques' mention of the Muslim notion of forgery of the scriptures with Byzantine discourse concerning Islam: this Muslim belief was known in the West at the time and is also referred to in the third part of the Gregorian Report which, as we argued earlier, is a Latin text, probably composed in Frankish Syria.[93] The same goes for Donnadieu's attempt to connect Jacques' depiction of Muhammad's deception of Ḥadīja concerning his illness with Bartholomew of Edessa's work, since, as Vandecasteele has shown, this narrative is closely related to that provided by the *Continuatio Chronicorum Beati Isidori*.[94] Thus it should be admitted that while it is likely that Jacques obtained some knowledge concerning Islam from Oriental Christians with whom he communicated, he was mainly working in this context within Outremer's Latin tradition, in which the Gregorian Report played a major role, and to some extent also within the more general framework of Western discourse on Islam.

That being said, some evidence, mainly indirect, can be found for contacts between Oriental Christians and Franks in the context of the

---

[90] Donnadieu, 'La representation', pp. 487–508.   [91] Donnadieu, 'La representation', pp. 490–2.

[92] Donnadieu, 'La representation', p. 499; Pedro Alfonso de Huesca, *Diálogo contra los Judíos*, eds. J. Tolan, K.-P. Mieth, E. Ducay and M. Jesús Lacarra (Huesca, 1996), p. 97.

[93] Donnadieu, 'La representation', p. 504; Petrus Venerabilis, *Schriften zum Islam*, ed. and trans. R. Glei (Altenberge, 1985), p. 58.

[94] Donnadieu, 'La representation', p. 499; Vandecasteele, 'Étude comparative', p. 96; PL 96.321.

study of Islam. Firstly, the version of Muhammad's life presented in William of Tripoli's *Notitia* is strongly related to an earlier one described by its Latin author as based on a conversation with a Greek. While it is hard to assess the trustworthiness of this attribution, it does support the hypothesis that such contacts did take place. That in his composition of the *Notitia* William was dependent on information originating in an Oriental Christian environment is further supported by the historical narrative which he provides for the beginning of Islam. The first chapter of the *Notitia* begins with a presentation of the rich Christian religious life in Egypt around 600 AD, which provides the background for the life of Bahira, the monk who, according to this narrative, educated Muhammad.[95] This is a clear clue to the involvement of Oriental Christians, probably Copts, in the production of this narrative, since without such intervention it would be difficult to explain why a portrayal of Muhammad's life should begin with praise for the Egyptian-Christian tradition. Egyptian, or Oriental Christian, fingerprints are also recognizable further along in the narrative provided by William. Having recounted how, following Bahira's death, Muhammad and his followers invaded and conquered Syria, the narrative focuses on the Muslim occupation of Egypt, which resulted, according to this version, from a conflict between Egyptian natives, on the one hand, and Greeks, on the other.[96] Another clue for such involvement in the composition of the *Notitia* appears when William directs against Islam the well-known argument that had the Qur'an really been God's book, it would have been widely read and accepted by all nations and languages. William notes in this context that there are twenty written languages, a figure which the text's editor was able to find only in Eastern Christian texts.[97] That William was able to receive pieces of knowledge from Oriental Christians in general, and specifically from Copts, is not surprising given the significant evidence for exchanges, in various contexts, between Latins and members of these groups which we have been able to trace.[98]

A significant piece of evidence with regard to the function of Oriental Christians as intermediators between Latins and Muslims in the context of attempts to understand the theological views of the rival group is provided by Joinville. He recounts how John the Armenian, King Louis IX's artilleryman, went to Damascus in order to buy materials needed for his work. In the city's market he met a very old man, and a theological debate developed between the two, which was later reported to Frankish nobles

---

[95] *Notitia*, pp. 196–8.   [96] *Notitia*, pp. 202–4.

[97] *Notitia*, pp. 240, 392–3, n. 120. The sources mentioned by Engels are: the *Chronicon Paschale*, Eutychius and an anonymous introduction to Psalms.

[98] See, in particular, Chapter 2, p. 54, Chapter 3, pp. 67–8 and Chapter 6.

in Acre.[99] Although this specific discussion did not result in a transfer of authentic information regarding Islam, it does reveal the possibility that Oriental Christians shared with Franks the contents of conversations they had had with Muslims, and which at least occasionally would have contributed to Frankish acquaintance with Islam.

The Acre corpus provides no explicit evidence for a Jewish contribution to Latin acquaintance with Islam. And yet the *Notitia* does include several clues implying that its authors were assisted by Jewish informants. Firstly, in two places in the work the term *Ravi* appears as denoting a Muslim spiritual leader.[100] Engels was unable to identify the sources for this tradition and proposed that it was connected to the Jewish term *Rabbi*. One can consequently suggest that the word *Ravi* found its way into the *Notitia* as a result of a misunderstanding between a Latin author and a Jewish informant who tried to convey to him knowledge concerning Islam while occasionally employing Hebrew terminology.

Engels identified one additional place in the *Notitia* which provides possible evidence for Jewish influence. This occurs in the section devoted to the description of a hypothetical debate between a Muslim and a Christian. Having provided evidence from the Qur'an with regard to Christ, Mary and Christ's followers, the text describes the Muslim response to such a presentation. This is followed by a recommended Christian reply which includes, inter alia, a discussion of the nature of the Qur'anic text. One of the arguments presented in this context is that while the biblical text includes precepts commanding and prohibiting various actions, the Qur'an includes no such injunctions. In the presentation of this argument, one reads the following:[101]

Also, in the doctrine of doing, these four books [the Pentateuch, Psalms, the Book of Prophets and the Gospel][102] have precepts which order and prohibit: *do this!* And *do not do that!* Hence, there are 613 precepts in the Pentateuch: 248 affirmative [precepts], as many as there are bones in the human body; the remaining are negative, as many as there are days in a year. The affirmative ones say *do!* The negative ones say *do not do!* And in this the holy gospel agrees [with the Pentateuch], saying: *do to others what you would have them do to you!*[103] And *do not do to others what you do not wish that would be done to you!*[104] But in your book, no precept of decency, that concerns good customs or faith, is given.

---

[99] Joinville, *Vie*, pp. 218–20, pars. 446–8.   [100] *Notitia*, pp. 88–9, 254, 258.

[101] 'Item in doctrina agendorum illi quatuor libri habent precepta, que iubent et prohibent: *Fac hoc!* et *Non facies illud!* Unde in lege sunt DC et XIII precepta: affirmativa CCXLVIII, quot ossa sunt in humano corpore; reliqua sunt negativa, quot sunt dies anni. Illa affirmativa dicunt *Fac!*, illa negativa dicunt *Ne facias!* Et in hoc concordat sanctum Ewangelium dicens: *Quecumque vultis, ut faciant vobis homines, hec eadem facite illis! Et quod tibi non vis fieri, aliis non feceris!* In libro autem tuo nullum preceptum honestatis ad bonos mores vel ad fidem pertinens datur.' *Notitia*, p. 242.

[102] *Notitia*, p. 214.   [103] Matthew 7.12.   [104] Tobit 4.16.

As Engels observed, the ideas presented here are taken from the Jewish tradition.[105] The enumeration of the precepts (all in all 613) and their division into two categories, i.e. precepts to do something (248) and precepts to refrain from doing something (365), are found in the Talmud, as is also the correspondence between the first figure and the number of the human body's members (not bones, as William says) and that between the second figure and the days of the year:[106]

> R. Simlai when preaching said: Six hundred and thirteen precepts were communicated to Moses, three hundred and sixty-five negative precepts, corresponding to the number of solar days [in the year], and two hundred and forty-eight positive precepts, corresponding to the number of the members of man's body.

The centrality of this enumeration, its division and the numerical analogies in medieval Jewish culture is attested to by its appearance in Maimonides' *Sefer Mitzvot* (*Book of Precepts*), as well as by the success of the early thirteenth-century *Sefer Mitzvot Gadol* (*The Big Book of Precepts*) by Moses ben Jacob of Coucy, both of which are built around these notions. Notably, a copy of a compendium based on the latter was brought to Acre by a Jewish father and son several years after the completion of the *Notitia*.[107] Obviously, this specific copy could not have been used by the Latin author of this section or by an informant of his, but the fact that two Jews brought it with them from Europe attests to the importance with which Western Jews regarded it at the time. Further evidence for the presence of this manner of enumeration and division of precepts in the East comes from Samaritan circles: it appears in a liturgical poem written by Aaron ben Manir, a Samaritan from Damascus, who had probably learnt about it in one of the Jewish communities of Syria.[108] Considering that this enumeration of precepts does not seem to have been well known to medieval Christian scholars,[109] but was indeed central in Jewish and Samaritan circles, it becomes most likely that in compiling the earlier-cited phrases, a Latin author was assisted by a Jewish informant.

Further evidence points in the same direction. The *Notitia*'s argument that Muhammad could not have been a true prophet because he was not of Jewish origin possibly also reflects Latin exchanges with Jews concerning Islam: such an argument would have been quite extraordinary in

---

[105] *Notitia*, p. 394, n. 126.   [106] Makot 23b, trans. A. E. Silverstone.

[107] Wolfson, 'The Parma Colophon', pp. 39–47.

[108] M. Haran, 'The Song of the Precepts of Aaron ben Manir', *Proceedings of the Israel Academy of Sciences and Humanities* 5 (1971–6), pp. 174–209.

[109] An examination of the very rich digital collection of Latin texts known as the CLCLT-7 does not reveal even one reference to the enumeration and division of precepts as it appears in the *Notitia*.

Christian polemic, and some Christian authorities would have even objected to it.[110] Jewish involvement in the composition of the *Notitia* may also explain the mention of the direction of Jewish prayer in the discussion of that of Muslims.[111]

These various Jewish fingerprints are interestingly all missing from the *De statu Sarracenorum*, which, according to Engels, is a Western adaptation of the *Notitia*.[112] The removal of every single one of these comments may mean that the Jewishness of at least some of them was apparent to medieval readers and was thought distasteful by some. Perhaps the ability to use them in the *Notitia*, as compiled in Acre during the early 1270s, attests to a unique cultural situation in the city at the time. Unfortunately, however, given the lack of additional evidence in this regard, one must leave this proposal as a hypothesis which cannot, at this stage, be confirmed.

CONCLUSION

Intellectual activity in thirteenth-century Acre did not bring about a major advancement in Western acquaintance with Islam, and no projects of the kind initiated by Peter the Venerable were undertaken in it. But by restricting our perspective to the question of whether Acre made a significant contribution to Western knowledge of Islam, we risk missing some important insights with regard to Outremer's cultural and intellectual histories. The first conclusion from the present chapter is that many of the Latins who resided in the city or travelled through it were curious about Islam. Since the Latins interested in this religion had diverse aims in mind and as they differed with regard to their accessibility to trustworthy sources, a multilayered discourse developed in Acre regarding Islam. Thus one finds in texts written in the city statements which reflect no real understanding of Islam but, at the same time, also observations which result from the accumulation of considerable knowledge concerning it. And yet, while authors working within a variety of traditions provided their readers with different kinds of comments and narratives concerning Islam, this does not mean that these discourses were isolated from one another. Rather, we have seen, for example, how a lay noble such as Joinville inserted into his work information coming from a Dominican friar. Furthermore, the connection and communication between different cultural groups with regard to the understanding of Islam was not

---

[110] *Notitia*, p. 244. Daniel, *Islam and the West*, pp. 89–93.
[111] *Notitia*, p. 256, and p. 400, note 174; Daniel, *Islam and the West*, p. 241.
[112] On the relation between the texts, see [**1:17**].

limited to Acre's Latin population. Indeed, we have seen that Oriental Christians and Jews facilitated, in a manner which is impossible to reconstruct in detail, Latin learning about Islam and its history. On the other hand, the evidence for direct communication with Muslims in the context of acquiring knowledge concerning their religion is rather limited.

The examination of the discourse concerning Islam in thirteenth-century Acre resulted in two additional conclusions. Firstly, we have seen that a systematic study of the texts composed in the city reveals that the number of works concerning Islam which actually circulated in Acre is considerably larger than previously thought. Secondly, this chapter also shows that at least a degree of literary continuity existed in the Kingdom of Jerusalem, and specifically in Acre. In other words, institutions in the city preserved Latin works, thereby enabling later authors to use and develop them. Thus we have seen, for example, that the compiler who produced the Gregorian Report used an earlier text on Islam, probably composed in Syria, and that William of Tripoli in all likelihood also made use of several works on Islam which circulated in the city. Such examples are significant in that they make it difficult to accept Prawer's argument according to which there existed in the Kingdom of Jerusalem no 'mechanism for the preservation and transmission of Oriental culture which might have been acquired by a previous generation'.[113]

---

[113] Prawer, *The Latin Kingdom of Jerusalem*, p. 530.

Chapter 6

THEOLOGICAL EXCHANGES WITH ORIENTAL CHRISTIANS

The Frankish presence in Outremer enabled, or at least potentially enabled, Westerners to gain a deeper acquaintance with Eastern cultural and religious groups, including numerous Oriental Christian sects.[1] But did Westerners, in fact, exploit this opportunity, acquiring information regarding these groups while in the East? Varied answers have been given to this question. While Bernard Hamilton has written that the Frankish presence in the Levant contributed much to Western acquaintance with various Oriental Christian groups, Benjamin Z. Kedar and David Jacoby argued that the Western clerics who settled in the Frankish Levant 'were not interested in, or capable of, intellectual give-and-take with Oriental Christian . . . scholars'.[2] This chapter attempts to provide an answer to this question with regard to thirteenth-century Acre. But before turning to the city and to the period following 1191, it is worthwhile to look at this problem with regard to the Kingdom of Jerusalem before the battle of Hattin.

The sources from this earlier period reveal a dual picture with regard to Latin attempts to acquire knowledge from Eastern Christian groups. On the one hand, from a very early stage, members of the Latin clergy perceived knowledge held by indigenous Christians concerning local customs and traditions as authoritative, and were therefore highly receptive concerning such information. Early evidence for this Latin attitude comes from Raymond of Aguilers' depiction of the Latin discovery of the true cross. According to his account, following the First Crusade's capture of Jerusalem, the Latins inquired into the whereabouts of the true cross. The local Christians first refused to reveal the precious relic, but were later persuaded to do so by what they perceived as God's support of the

---

[1] Some of the material presented in this chapter was published in a paper of mine: 'Benoit d'Alignan and Thomas Agni', pp. 189–200.

[2] Hamilton, *The Latin Church*, pp. 368–9; Kedar, 'The Subjected Muslims of the Frankish Levant', p. 174; Jacoby, 'Society', p. 108.

Franks.[3] Whether or not this is a faithful portrayal of the events, it does suggest that from early on the Latins valued local Christian knowledge and traditions. Twelfth-century sources provide further indirect evidence for the adoption of local customs and perceptions by the Latins. Thus, for example, the Latins enthusiastically joined the Holy Fire ceremony, and gradually became inclined to refer to the Church of the Holy Sepulchre as the Church of the Resurrection, a term based on the Greek *Anastasis*.[4] Similarly, the appearance in Frankish circles of a tradition according to which Jacob saw the heavenly ladder in the Lord's Temple is also likely to have been the result of Eastern Christian influence.[5]

On the other hand, till late in the twelfth century the Latins of the kingdom reveal a very restricted degree of interest in the characteristics of the various Eastern Christian groups they encountered. Thus, quite surprisingly, there is no text preceding the 1160s which enumerates and characterizes these groups. John of Würzburg's pilgrimage account, composed in the early 1160s, is the first text to enumerate a considerable number of such groups but it too provides no real information about them, and even the learned William of Tyre mentions no non-Chalcedonian group.[6] In other words, at that stage the Latins were interested in what members of various Eastern Christian groups had to say about local traditions but made no effort to acquire and organize knowledge with regard to the groups themselves.[7]

FROM THE 'TRACTATUS DE LOCIS ET STATU SANCTE TERRE IEROSOLIMITANE' TO JACQUES DE VITRY: EARLY STAGES IN THE ACCUMULATION OF KNOWLEDGE CONCERNING EASTERN CHRISTIANITIES

Late in the twelfth century, and probably after 1187, Frankish attitudes to Eastern Christianities seem to have undergone a significant change.

---

[3] J. H. Hill and L. L. Hill (eds.), *Le 'Liber' de Raymond d'Aguilers* (Paris, 1969), p. 154.

[4] C. MacEvitt, *The Crusades and the Christian World of the East: Rough Tolerance* (Philadelphia, PA, 2008), pp. 115–22; Kedar, 'Eastern Christians', pp. 139–40; B. Z. Kedar, 'Some New Light on the Composition Process of William of Tyre's *Historia*', in S. B. Edgington and H. J. Nicholson (eds.), *Deeds Done beyond the Sea: Essays on William of Tyre, Cyprus and the Military Orders Presented to Peter Edbury* (Farnham, 2014), pp. 7–10.

[5] B. Z. Kedar and Denys Pringle, '1099–1187: The Lord's Temple and Solomon's Palace', in O. Grabar and B. Z. Kedar (eds.), *Where Heaven and Earth Meet: Jerusalem's Sacred Esplanade* (Jerusalem, 2009), p. 136.

[6] R. B. C. Huygens (ed.), *Peregrinationes tres: Saewulf, Iohannes Wirziburgensis, Theodericus*, CCCM 139 (Turnhout, 1994), pp. 137–8; A.-D. von den Brincken, *Die 'Nationes Christianorum Orientalium' im Verständnis der lateinischen Historiographie* (Vienna, 1973), p. 425.

[7] MacEvitt, *The Crusades and the Christian World*, pp. 102–6; Von den Brincken, *Die Nationes*, pp. 424–6.

The first testimony for this comes from the *Tractatus de locis et statu sancte terre ierosolimitane* [3:32], a text which is unfortunately difficult to date. The text's editor, Benjamin Kedar, suggests that it was written in the two decades preceding 1187. More recently, however, Paolo Trovato dated the work, on philological grounds, to after 1198, and suggested it was compiled in Acre.[8] Be that as it may, this is the first Latin text composed in the Kingdom of Jerusalem which includes descriptions of a considerable number of Eastern Christian groups.[9] Furthermore, this compilation (or possibly some similar text no longer extant which preceded it) exerted considerable influence on the discourse in Acre concerning such groups, providing a model, inter alia, to Jacques de Vitry and Burchard of Mount Sion. In that, the *Tractatus* opens a new period in the Kingdom of Jerusalem with regard to interest concerning Eastern Christianities, one in which considerable work was undertaken in Acre in order to acquire and systematize knowledge concerning both the customs and theological views of their members.[10]

Unfortunately, nothing is known concerning the context in which the *Tractatus*' anonymous author worked. Kedar writes that he was not a Frankish inhabitant of the Kingdom of Jerusalem, since in his text he distinguishes between animals unique to the Holy Land and others 'common in our lands'.[11] However, this phrasing does not rule out the possibility that the anonymous author had spent several years in Outremer or even that he had held some office there. In any case, it is unlikely that a short-term visitor compiled such a work without the support of a Latin milieu knowledgeable concerning the different aspects of the Holy Land touched upon in the text. The production of the *Tractatus* thus probably reflects a novel trend among the learned Latins of Outremer which should be dated to either the first years of the Second Kingdom – and probably also to Acre – or, perhaps, to the last decades of the First Kingdom.

It is not easy to explain the shift that produced the cultural environment in which the *Tractatus* was not only composed but also came to be influential. A partial explanation may perhaps be provided by the growing papal interest in Eastern Christian groups caused in part by the new Latin

---

[8] Kedar, 'The *Tractatus*', pp. 119–20; P. Trovato, *Everything You Always Wanted to Know about Lachmann's Method* (Padua, 2014), p. 286.

[9] A. Jotischky, 'Ethnographic Attitudes in the Crusader States: Franks and Indigenous Orthodox People', in K. Ciggaar and H. Teule (eds.), *East and West in the Crusader States: Context-Contacts-Confrontations* III (Leuven, 2003), pp. 4–5.

[10] It is noteworthy, however, that in Byzantium elaborate discussions between Latins and Greeks took place already in the twelfth century. A. Cameron, *Arguing it Out: Discussion in Twelfth-Century Byzantium* (Budapest, 2016), pp. 59–99.

[11] Kedar, 'The *Tractatus*', pp. 120, 128.

rule of large Orthodox populations in Cyprus and Constantinople. These new circumstances forced the papal curia to solve a wide range of new questions which required at least some acquaintance with Eastern Christianity.[12]

Whether the *Tractatus* was compiled in Acre or not, it certainly circulated there. A manuscript now in Munich includes an interpolation, likely inserted into the text in Acre, concerning a controversy between the Teutonic and Hospitaller orders which took place in the city during the last decade of the twelfth century.[13] More significant in this context is Jacques de Vitry's employment of the *Tractatus* in his attempt to provide a complete survey of the different Christian groups he encountered in the East: not only does he include in both his 1216 letter [1:3] and his *Historia orientalis* [1:4] a survey of various Eastern Christian groups in a manner reminiscent of that which characterizes the anonymous report, but, at least in the *Historia*, one can easily find phrases dependent on the *Tractatus*.[14]

However, in his engagement with Eastern Christianities, Jacques went further than his written source. In fact, the structure of his letter reveals that, while writing it, he was actively working to accumulate additional knowledge with regard to these groups. Thus, in the account of his arrival to Acre, which he famously described as a nine-headed monster, Jacques mentions the Nestorians, but says nothing about them; later in the epistle, however, having recounted a journey to Sidon, Beirut and Tripoli, he returns to this group, now providing information concerning their beliefs.[15] Furthermore, in the *Historia orientalis*, the descriptions of the various Oriental Christian groups are much more developed than their parallels in the letter. In other words, Jacques's work provides evidence for an ongoing process of learning about various Eastern Christian communities.

How did Acre's famous bishop acquire information about Eastern Christian groups which cannot be accounted for by the *Tractatus*? For one thing, he clearly obtained knowledge concerning Eastern Christianity through Franks more familiar with the kingdom and the Levant than himself.[16] More significantly, Jacques also learned much

---

[12] Jotischky, 'Ethnographic Attitudes', pp. 16–18. [13] Kedar, 'The *Tractatus*', p. 132.

[14] See the respective descriptions of the *Suriani*: 'preliis velut mulieres inutiles', *HO*, p. 294, 'armis inutiles', Kedar, 'The *Tractatus*', p. 124; 'semper tributarii', *HO*, p. 294, 'ubique tributarii', Kedar, 'The *Tractatus*', p. 124. Also noteworthy are, in this respect, Jacques' references to the languages used by each of the groups. For these, see Chapter 3, p. 70.

[15] See, respectively, Jacques de Vitry, *Lettres*, p. 563 and p. 577.

[16] Perhaps Jacques was recalling such a discussion when he wrote: 'Quidam autem eorum [of the *Suriani*], ut audivi, in die Epiphanie singulis annis se baptizabant.' Jacques de Vitry, *Lettres*, p. 565 ('Some of them, as I heard, baptized themselves every year on the day of Epiphany'). Jacques also

about Eastern Christianities by direct discussions with their members. Thus, in the *Historia*, he explicitly refers to a conversation he had with Jacobites, in which, Jacques recounts, they rejected the notion that Christ has only one nature, and that when asked why they made the sign of the cross with one finger, they answered that the use of one finger symbolizes the existence of one divine essence, while the Trinity is symbolized by the finger's parts.[17]

That Jacques also communicated with adherents of the Orthodox Church is evident: he says that he preached to the city's *Suriani* and that they promised to be obedient to him.[18] In another occasion he describes discussions he had with both Greek- and Arabic-speaking followers of the Orthodox Church:[19]

When we diligently inquired of *Greci* and *Suriani* why they detest the Jacobites and why they had expelled them from their community, they asserted that the main cause was that they [the Jacobites] had fallen into the worst wretched heresy asserting there is only one nature, just as there is one person, in Christ.

Particularly noteworthy within the context of Jacques' exchanges with members of Eastern churches is a conversation he had with a Syrian monk. Interestingly, the part of this discussion that Jacques chose to document refers to the question of whether John the Baptist ate locusts during his stay in the desert:[20]

Because, however, it did not seem true to me that Christ's holy Baptist who refused to be fed bread [Luke 7.33] ate the flesh of locusts, I diligently asked a Syrian monk, whose monastery was in those parts, housing a great number of monks leading extremely severe lives under one abbot, of what sort were the locusts which Saint John is said to have eaten in that Jordanian desert. And he replied immediately that in his refectory a certain herb, found in large quantities around his monastery, is often served to the monks to eat which they called

---

explicitly mentions a discussion he had with a merchant who informed him about the Nestorians of the land of Prester John. Jacques de Vitry, *Lettres*, p. 577.

[17] *HO*, p. 310.   [18] Jacques de Vitry, *Lettres*, pp. 564–5.

[19] 'Cum autem a Grecis et Surianis diligenter inquireremus ob quam causam Iacobitas detestarentur et eos a suo eiecissent consortio, hanc esse causam precipuam asserebant quod in damnatam et pessimam haeresim incidissent, unam naturam tantum quemadmodum unam personam in Christo esse asserentes.' *HO*, p. 308. For the meaning of the terms *Greci* and *Suriani*, see Pahlitzsch, *Graeci und Suriani im Palästina der Kreuzfahrerzeit*, pp. 14–15.

[20] 'Quoniam autem verisimile mihi non videbatur quod beatus Christi baptista locustarum carnes manducaret, qui pane etiam vesci renuebat, quesivi diligenter a quodam Surianorum monacho cuius cenobium in partibus illis erat, habens maximam monachorum multitudinem sub uno abbate, vitam arctissimam ducentium, cuiusmodi essent locuste quas in solitudine illa Iordanica beatus Ioannes manducasse perhibetur. Qui mihi statim respondit quod frequenter in refectorio suo quedam herba monachis ad edendum apponebatur, quam languste id est locustam nominabant, cuius circa monasterium suum magna habebatur copia, adiungens quod illa esset quam edebat beatus Ioannes. Sed et de melle silvestri ex apibus in deserto illo frequenter copiose reperiebant.' *HO*, pp. 220–2.

languste, that is locust. He added that it was this herb that Saint John ate. But they also often found large quantities of wild bees' honey in that desert.

In this discussion, Jacques did not intend to learn about the 'errors' of the Syrian monk, nor did he aim to persuade him to accept the authority of the Catholic Church. Rather, he used the knowledge of the monk, to whom he ascribed a high degree of acquaintance with the territory in which John the Baptist had been active, as a source for a better understanding of the biblical verse: 'and the same John had his raiment of camel's hair, and a leathern girdle about his loins; and his meat was locusts and wild honey' (Matthew 3.4). In other words, Jacques perceived this Syrian monk as being in a better position than himself, or his Latin colleagues, to understand John the Baptist's manner of living, and thus believed that he was capable of solving an exegetical difficulty he encountered. In this Jacques appears to have continued the twelfth-century tradition.

Jacques' learning process resulted in the accumulation of considerable information regarding Eastern Christianities. That this information was not trivial at that time in the West can be inferred from the fact that Acre's bishop sent his letter to several *magistri Parisienses,* some of whom are known from other sources.[21] Had this information been common in the West, Jacques would have thought it superfluous to include it in a letter addressed to such learned men.

At this point, it is worthwhile to characterize Jacques' work with regard to Oriental Christianity. Firstly, his discussions with members of these groups seem to have been rather informal, and were not perceived as involving representatives of two parties, or as a part of some organized effort to reunite the Christian world. Furthermore, no disciplinary approach is evident here: Jacques does not threaten the Oriental Christians he meets with any temporal punishments, nor does he promise worldly benefits. Lastly, Jacques' interest in these groups is not strictly theological, and he dedicates a considerable part of his discussions to their cultural characteristics.[22]

Note that the inclination to informal discussions with members of Oriental Christian groups was not unique to Jacques. Oliver of

---

[21] Jacques de Vitry, *Lettres,* pp. 502, 558.

[22] Jacques' tendency to include in his grievances against Greeks matters of custom that have nothing to do with doctrine was identified by Andrew Jotischky, who also argued that Acre's bishop 'was not alone in such apparently loose thinking about the beliefs of other traditions.' See A. Jotischky, 'The Frankish Encounter with the Greek Orthodox in the Crusader States', in M. Gervers and J. M. Powell (eds.), *Tolerance and Intolerance: Social Conflict in the Age of the Crusades* (Syracuse, NY, 2001), pp. 100–1. Concerning Jacques' interest in the linguistic characteristics of other Christian groups, see Chapter 3, p. 70.

Paderborn mentions a discussion he had with a Maronite, and also says that while he was in Antioch he carefully examined (*examinavimus*) the Nestorians. Oliver differs from Jacques, however, in his focus on matters of faith.[23] Another Western author who dealt with Oriental Christianity is Thietmar. His description of Oriental Christianity is very brief, and in composing it he made use of the *Tractatus*,[24] but he clearly did directly communicate with members of the Orthodox clergy.[25]

During the following decades new approaches with regard to Eastern Christian groups came to dominate Acre. Exchanges with members of these groups became more formal, were characterized by a stronger emphasis on theological difference and were more firmly tied to attempts to unite the church. This, however, is not to say that the earlier kinds of discourse disappeared. Some Latins in Acre are likely to have continued to be interested in various characteristics of Eastern Christian societies and to perceive members of these groups as bearers of authentic knowledge concerning the Holy Land. Evidence for such continuity is provided by Burchard of Mount Sion, who, as we have seen, was most likely connected to Acre's Dominican circles in the 1280s. The text of his *Descriptio* reveals his interest in various aspects of Eastern Christian cultures, and one gets the impression that his exchanges with members of the Eastern churches were often friendly and informal.[26] Additionally, in a passage which appears in a manuscript of the *Descriptio* but is not included in the text published by Laurent, Burchard recounts that he acquired information concerning the Holy Land from both *Syri* and *Sarraceni*,[27] and indeed, discussing the Dead Sea, he refers to what he heard from the Greek patriarch concerning the lake's dimensions.[28] Evidence that late thirteenth-century Frankish interest in Eastern Christians was not restricted to theological matters is also provided by the *Notitia de Machometo* [**1:17**]. This account frames the story of the rise of Islam within the history of Christianity in Egypt, implying that Acre's Dominicans communicated with Oriental Christians, probably Copts, concerning their historical past.[29]

Before moving on to explore the beginnings of Dominican contacts with Oriental Christianity, it is worthwhile to present echoes of late

---

[23] Oliverus Scholasticus, *Historia Damiatina*, pp. 264–7.   [24] See Kedar, '*Tractatus*', p. 121.

[25] Laurent, *Thietmari Peregrinatio*, pp. 36, 50–1.

[26] For Burchard's connections to the Dominicans of the Holy Land, see Chapter 1, pp. 23–4. For his attitudes towards Eastern Christians, see, for example, Laurent, *Peregrinatores*, pp. 53, 91–3.

[27] 'A Syris vel a Sarracenis et aliis terre ipsius habitatoribus quos ductores et interpretes frequenter mecum habui diligentissime de omnibus investigans.' ('Most diligently inquiring of Syrians, Muslims and other inhabitants of that land, whom I often had with me as guides and translators, about everything.') Zwickau, fol. 113v.

[28] Rubin, 'Burchard', p. 179.   [29] See Chapter 5, p. 134.

twelfth or early thirteenth-century discussions between Latins and Copts, which may be connected to Acre's culture, and which survive in an Arabic text: this is a medieval paraphrase of a polemic work by Peter of Malig, a Coptic bishop living around the end of the twelfth century, which survived in Abū al-Barakāt's *Catalogue of Christian Writings*.[30] According to this paraphrase, Peter discussed in his work errors of various Christian groups, including those of the Franks. His discussion reveals considerable knowledge of Catholic theology and he is able, for example, to discuss the addition of the *filioque*, as well as the Catholic belief in the two natures of Christ. Just like Jacques, Peter included in his work not only Frankish theological errors but also cultural characteristics which he found disturbing, such as visiting baths with private parts exposed or shaving beards.

One statement in particular connects Peter's discussion of the Franks to the discourse of thirteenth-century Acre. He argues that the Franks neglect the baptism of slaves and captives they hold out of fear that this would prevent the Latins from further exploiting them.[31] The closeness of this comment to one Jacques made on the same subject is remarkable:[32]

Who could have enumerated all of the sins of the other Babel where Christians denied baptism to their Muslim slaves although the Muslims themselves asked for it earnestly and with tears? Their lords, into whose council let not my soul come [cf. Genesis 49.6], said 'if these would become Christians we will not be able to thus press them hard at will.'

The controversy concerning the baptism of Muslim slaves was so dominant within thirteenth-century Frankish society that it came to involve Pope Gregory IX, who wrote about it twice to Patriarch Gerold.[33] Clearly, Peter's comments in this regard reveal that its echoes also reached the Copts in Egypt. The Coptic bishop probably learned about this issue through co-religionists of his who were in contact with Franks, perhaps

---

[30] Almost nothing else is known about Peter. G. Graf, *Geschichte der christlichen arabischen Literatur*, 5 vols. (Vatican, 1947), vol. II, pp. 340–4. The quite detailed paraphrase by Abu l'Barakat is presented and translated to German in W. Riedel, 'Der Katalog der christlichen Schriften in arabischer Sprache von Abu 'lBarakat', *Nachrichten von der Königlichen Gesellschaft der Wissenschaften: philologisch-historische Klasse* (1902), pp. 635–706. For Peter, see also O. H. E. Burmester, 'On the Date and Authorship of the Arabic Synaxarium of the Coptic Church', *Journal of Theological Studies* 39 (1938), pp. 249–53.

[31] Riedel, 'Der Katalog', pp. 658, 693.

[32] 'Quis enumerare posset omnia alterius Babilonis flagicia, in qua Christiani servis suis Sarracenis baptismum negabant, licet ipsi Sarraceni instanter et cum lacrimis postularent? Dicebant enim domini eorum, in quorum consilio non veniat anima mea: "Si isti Christiani fuerint, non ita pro voluntate nostra eos angariare poterimus."' Jacques de Vitry, *Lettres*, p. 567.

[33] See regarding this issue also B. Z. Kedar, 'Multidirectional Conversion in the Frankish Levant', in J. Muldoon (ed.), *Varieties of Religious Conversion in the Middle Ages* (Gainesville, FL, 1997), pp. 191–2; Kedar, *Crusade and Mission*, pp. 147–9, 212–13.

in Acre itself. This text can thus be seen as providing evidence, from a Coptic source, for discussions between Latins and Oriental Christians on matters of theology and religious practice.

Given the existence of other indications for Coptic presence in Acre, as well as for their contacts with the city's Franks, this is not surprising. We have mentioned a series of Western Marian legends which, having probably been translated in the city, reached Coptic circles [3:42], and a French–Arabic glossary intended for the use of Copts coming to study with Franks in Acre.[34] The Coptic fingerprints in the historical narrative provided by the *Notitia*, as well as the reference to the arrival of flagellants to Acre in a Coptic chronicle point in the same direction.[35]

THE BEGINNINGS OF DOMINICAN CONTACTS WITH ORIENTAL CHRISTIANITY

The development of communication with Eastern Christians in Acre was strongly influenced by the establishment of the Dominican convent in the city in the late 1220s. A letter dated to 1237, sent by Philip, the Dominican prior of the Holy Land, to Pope Gregory IX, reveals a new stage in the exchanges between Latins and Eastern Christians in the Kingdom of Jerusalem, connected to a growing motivation regarding the union of the church.[36] In this letter Philip describes his contacts with the Jacobite patriarch, Ignatius II:[37]

The patriarch of the Eastern Jacobites, a man venerable in learning, conduct and age ... came to worship in Jerusalem. Expounding to him the word of the catholic faith, we have been able, with the support of divine grace ... to get him to promise and provide an oath to obey the holy Roman Church.

In the following lines, the Dominican prior adds that two archdeacons, one Jacobite and the other Nestorian, did the same as the patriarch, and that his friars were also in contact with the Jacobite patriarch of Egypt, and

---

[34] For the Marian legends, see Chapter 3, pp. 67–8. Concerning the dictionary, see Chapter 2, p. 54.

[35] Kedar, 'Latins and Oriental Christians in the Frankish Levant', p. 215.

[36] It is noteworthy that by this date members of the Latin clergy had already successfully discussed with both Maronites and Armenians their union with the Catholic Church, but, as members of the Kingdom of Jerusalem's clergy played no significant role in these earlier initiatives, one should indeed see the 1237 letter as evidence for a new trend among Acre's Latins. For the union with the Maronites, see Hamilton, *The Latin Church*, pp. 332–4. For the Armenian case, see C. A. Frazee, 'The Christian Church in Cilician Armenia: Its Relations with Rome and Constantinople to 1198', *Church History* 45.2 (June, 1976), pp. 180–3.

[37] 'Nam patriarcha Jacobitarum Orientalium, vir quidem venerabilis scientia, moribus, et aetate ... venit adorare in Jerusalem. Cui verbum catholicae fidei exponentes, ad tantum divina cooperante gratia pervenimus ut ... obedientiam sanctae Romanae ecclesiae promitteret et juraret.' MP, vol. III, p. 397. Another version of this letter appears in Scheffer-Boichorst, *Chronica Albrici*, p. 941.

had already persuaded him, inter alia, to prohibit his followers from circumcising their sons in the Muslim manner.[38] Such activities on the part of the Dominicans must have had an intellectual aspect: the negotiations Philip described could not have taken place unless the Dominicans were at least partially acquainted with the 'errors' of these various groups, and, as testified by the letter, they certainly included the exchange, and implicitly also the translation, of written texts.[39] Furthermore, at least some of the Eastern clergy with whom the Dominicans negotiated were of considerable learning: thus, for example, Ignatius' successor, Yūhannā ibn al-Ma'danī, who accompanied the latter on his pilgrimage, composed several works, while Ignatius himself wrote at least one text within the context of Jacobite–Nestorian conflicts.[40] In other words, the motivation to unite various groups under the leadership of the Catholic Church must have been a driving force for Dominicans who were active in the Kingdom of Jerusalem to learn more regarding Oriental Christian groups, and to develop argumentation suitable for negotiations and debates with their members. During the thirteenth century, much of this work must have taken place in Acre, where the largest of the Latin East's Dominican convents seems to have been located.[41]

SYSTEMATIC STUDY, DISPUTATIONS AND INTERROGATIONS:
BENOIT D'ALIGNAN AND THOMAS AGNI

The next body of evidence available from Acre with regard to theological exchanges with members of Oriental Christianity has to do with two figures who played a significant role within the city's intellectual milieu: Benoit d'Alignan and Thomas Agni. Before delving into their involvement in theological exchanges with members of Eastern Christian groups in Acre, it would be expedient to provide some general information about the activities of the two in Outremer. Thomas, who had earlier headed the Roman province of the Dominican order, arrived in the Levant in the spring of 1259 as the bishop of Bethlehem and papal legate, and held these offices there till shortly before February 1264. He reached Outremer again in October 1272, now as the patriarch of Jerusalem, the bishop of Acre and papal legate, and remained there until his death in September 1277.[42]

---

[38] MP, vol. III, pp. 397–8.

[39] Philip writes that the patriarch of the Eastern Jacobites, Ignatius II, provided the friars with his confession of faith.

[40] Graf, *Geschichte*, vol. II, pp. 267–9.　　[41] Kedar, *Crusade and Mission*, p. 145.

[42] A. L. Redigonda, 'Agni, Tommaso', *Dizionario biografico degli Italiani* (Rome, 1960), vol. I, pp. 445–6.

Benoit, who served as the bishop of Marseilles, spent two relatively brief periods in the Latin East. He arrived in the kingdom during the autumn of 1239, and was still there in December 1240, but was back in Marseilles in April 1242. In August 1260 Benoit was still in the West, but in October of that year we find him again in the Levant, and he was still there in September 1261. In March 1262 he was probably already back in Marseilles.[43] Benoit held no formal office in the East, but, if we are to trust the *De constructione castri Saphet* [2:40], wielded enough influence to initiate an extremely expensive project – the building of the castle of Safad.[44] Benoit in all likelihood also wrote significant parts of his *Tractatus super erroribus quos citra et ultra mare invenimus* [2:24] in Acre.

The two are significant for our exploration of the study of Oriental Christianities in Frankish Acre mainly because, as will soon become evident, their attitude towards these groups tended to be much more systematic, strict and disciplinary than that which characterized figures such as Jacques de Vitry. The differences in this respect between Jacques on the one hand, and Benoit and Thomas on the other, should probably be understood within the context of a growing inclination in the West to define and categorize groups holding non-Orthodox beliefs.[45] In Edward Peters' words, by the mid-thirteenth century, 'much of the ambiguity and hesitation that had characterized the attitudes toward heresy on the part of church-men, councils and popes was gone: in its place were the formal disciplines of theology and law'.[46] Indeed, as Andrew Jotischky has shown, it was during the 1230s that a coherent papal ideology towards Eastern Christians began to emerge, and in the 1240s we see Pope Innocent IV engaging with legal difficulties arising from contacts between the Franks of Outremer and members of these groups.[47] Benoit and Thomas should thus probably be seen as Western intellectuals who brought with them to Acre new trends with regard to Catholic thinking about Eastern Christianities.

---

[43] R. B. C. Huygens (ed.), *De constructione castri Saphet* (Amsterdam, 1981), p. 39; M. Segonne, *Moine, Prélat, Croisé, Benoît d'Alignan, abbé de La Grasse, Seigneur-Evêque de Marseille* (Marseille, 1960), pp. 53, 60, 70, 75; M. Grabmann, 'Der Franziskanerbischof Benediktus de Alignano OFM und seine Summa zum Caput "Firmiter" des IV Laterankonzils', in I.-M. Freudenreich (ed.), *Kirchengeschichtliche Studien P. Michael Bihl als Ehrengabe dargeboten* (Kolmar, 1941), p. 50; Golubovich, *Biblioteca*, vol. I, pp. 239–42.

[44] Huygens, *De constructione, passim.*

[45] R. I. Moore, *The Formation of a Persecuting Society* (Oxford, 1987), p. 99.

[46] E. Peters, *Inquisition* (New York, NY, 1988), pp. 60–1.

[47] A. Jotischky, 'Mendicants as Missionaries and Travellers in the Near East in the Thirteenth and Fourteenth Centuries', in R. Allen (ed.), *Eastward Bound: Travel and Travellers 1050–1550* (Manchester, 2004), pp. 97–8.

Specifically noteworthy in this context is the fact that both Benoit and Thomas were related to the inquisition. Benoit not only hailed from Languedoc, a central arena for Catholic activity against heresy,[48] but also appended to his work on heresies two short pieces directly related to the notion of inquisition. The first is titled 'Under what formula should a person who is to be investigated about heresy swear' and the second 'about what [things] should interrogations be carried out'.[49] Thomas can also be seen as connected to this institution, as he composed (probably while in the West)[50] an important *Vita* of St. Peter of Verona, who, as Bernard Hamilton has written, 'became the first saint that the Inquisition had produced'.[51]

Further evidence that the two should be studied as representing the same cultural trend is supported by a letter signed by Benoit in Acre on 21 September 1261. In that letter, Benoit dedicated his tractate to Thomas, asking him to change whatever he thought required emendation and to distribute the text in Outremer, stating that he had already sent copies of it to Pope Alexander IV as well as to various ecclesiastical institutions in the West.[52]

We now turn to a detailed examination of the work of the two in Acre with regard to Eastern Christianities, shedding light on Thomas and Benoit's attitudes to non-Catholic Christians and, at the same time, also on their position vis-à-vis local Frankish culture.

---

[48] Benoit came from Alignan du Vent, not far from Béziers.

[49] Paris, BnF, lat. 4224, fols. 446r–448r. 'Sub qua forma iuret de heresi inquirendus'; 'Super quibus fiant interrogationes.' Much of the second of these discussions is edited in P. A. Amargier, 'Benoît d'Alignan, évêque de Marseille (1229–1268). Le contexte et l'esprit d'une théologie', *Le Moyen Age* 72 (1966), pp. 460–2. I have found no indications in these texts that they were written in the East.

[50] A Dominican decision dating to 1276 with regard to this text was taken to mean that Thomas composed it while he was patriarch. But, as Stefano Orlandi wrote, the mention of Thomas as patriarch in this decision is not sufficient proof that this work was written during the time he held this office. S. Orlandi (ed.), *S. Pietro martire da Verona. Leggenda di Fra Tommaso Agni da Lentini nel volgare trecentesco con lettera di Fra Roderico de Atencia* (Firenze, 1952), p. li.

[51] B. Hamilton, *The Medieval Inquisition* (London, 1981), p. 78.

[52] E. Baluze, *Miscellaneorum liber sextus* (Paris, 1713), pp. 350–1. 'Quem tractatum misimus Domino Papae bonae memoriae Alexandro ... et postea dirivavimus ad religiones fratrum Praedicatorum et Minorum et Cisterciensium et de poenitentia Jesu Christi, et ad alias plures, et ad Archiepiscopos et Episcopos, et diversas provincias et dioceses in partibus transmarinis, et per vos in istis partibus, ubi opus incepimus, volumus dirivari. Vos autem corrigatis quae videritis corrigenda.' ('And we have sent this treatise to lord Pope Alexander of good memory ... and afterwards we have distributed [it] to the Dominican, Franciscan, and Cistercian orders as well as to the Order of the Penitence of Jesus Christ, and to many others, and to archbishops and bishops, and to different provinces and dioceses overseas, and by you we wish [the treatise] to be distributed in these parts, where we began the work. You should correct what you will perceive that needs to be corrected.')

Benoit d'Alignan and His Tractatus super erroribus quos citra et ultra mare invenimus

Benoit's treatise, which survives in numerous manuscripts and which has received very little scholarly attention,[53] is a very long work, comprising 450 folios in one of the manuscripts, and divided into three parts: the first is dedicated to faith, the second to the humanity of Christ and the third to the church and the sacraments.[54] The prologue to a later abbreviated version of the treatise provides testimony to the manner in which Benoit perceived his original tractate:[55]

In the preceding treatise we have explained the errors which are shattered by this creed, and cited the authorities and the reasons by which the heretics toil to defend their error, and how on the other hand they can be answered by authorities, reasons, *exempla* and parables, by which heretics are more openly proven mistaken and the faithful more firmly strengthened in the Catholic faith.

In other words, Benoit perceived his work to be aimed first and foremost to present errors in faith and practice, the arguments by which they are supported by heretics and infidels and the ways in which these arguments can be refuted. As can be expected, among the groups Benoit confronted one can find Greeks,[56] Nestorians,[57] Jacobites,[58] Maronites,[59] Armenians[60] and Nubians,[61] as well as more general categories of *nationes ultramarine* or *transmarine*.[62]

While it is impossible to know where and when each section of the work was composed, the dedicatory letters do offer some indication. As we have seen, Benoit's letter to Thomas was signed in Acre in September 1261. Given that Benoit was in the Holy Land from October 1260 and that this

---

[53] This text was never printed and has been almost totally neglected by scholars. It is, however, mentioned in several studies on Benoit: Amargier, 'Benoît d'Alignan'; Segonne, *Moine*; Golubovich, *Biblioteca*, vol. I, pp. 236–53; L. C. F. Petit-Radel, 'Benoit d'Alignan, Évêque de Marseille', *Histoire littéraire de la France* 19 (1838), pp. 84–91. Two studies focus on the text itself: Villads Jensen, 'War against Muslims', pp. 181–95; Grabmann, 'Der Franziskanerbischof', pp. 50–64. Benoit and his *Tractatus* are also referred to in Kedar, *Crusade and Mission*, pp. 172, 175, 189.

[54] BnF, lat. 4224; Petit-Radel, 'Benoit', p. 90.

[55] 'In precedenti tractatu declaravimus errores qui per hoc symbolum eliduntur et posuimus auctoritates et rationes quibus erronei errorem suum defendere moliuntur, et econtra qualiter eis valeat responderi per auctoritates, per rationes, per exempla et per similitudines quibus erronei apercius convincuntur et fideles in fide catholica firmius solidantur.' BnF, lat. 4224, fol. 449r.

[56] BnF, lat. 4224, fols. 102v–103v, 289r, 325r, 345v-347v, 349r, 415v.

[57] BnF, lat. 4224, fol. 238r.   [58] BnF, lat. 4224, fols. 102v, 238v, 272r, 325r, 415v.

[59] BnF, lat. 4224, fol. 272r.   [60] BnF, lat. 4224, fols. 272r, 289r, 325r, 349r, 350r, 433r.

[61] BnF, lat. 4224, fol. 399v.

[62] BnF, lat. 4224, fols. 262v, 272r, 289r, 415v. It is noteworthy that in his work, Benoit also engages with Islam. It seems, however, that everything Benoit tells his readers about Islam is drawn from earlier Western authorities.

missive is his earliest dated dedicatory letter,[63] it is safe to assume that he completed his work on the *Tractatus* in Acre. Additionally, from another dedicatory letter sent in August 1263 by Benoit from Marseilles to William II of Agen, the newly appointed patriarch of Jerusalem,[64] we learn that Benoit started working on the tractate during what he states was his first journey to the Holy Land.[65] Compiling these pieces of information, one may conclude that Benoit began working on a tractate aimed at confronting various errors during his first visit to the East, which, as already noted, took place around 1240, and almost certainly completed it during his second sojourn there.[66]

It is likely that it was no accident that Benoit started his work while he was in the Levant. As we have seen, ever since the late twelfth century the attention of Latin clergymen visiting Outremer was drawn to the great number of what they perceived as heresies found there, as well as to the presence of various kinds of unorthodox behaviour within the Frankish society of Outremer. It is therefore reasonable to suggest that it was the encounter with that kind of reality that drove Benoit to undertake such a project. It is also clear that Benoit obtained considerable knowledge concerning Oriental Christians during his sojourns in the East. This is supported, firstly, by his recurrent comment that his text discusses errors he encountered on both sides of the sea.[67] This comment would hardly make any sense had Benoit learned about these groups in the West, via books or other intermediaries. His elaborate discussions of Oriental Christianities and the level of information he provides on them lend further support to the hypothesis that he gained much material about them in the East. Where else would a man like Benoit, who, to the best of our knowledge, had not attended any of the major study centres in Europe, be able to gain detailed information about various Oriental Christian groups?[68]

---

[63] Also extant is an undated letter to Pope Alexander IV (d. 25 May 1261). This letter must have preceded the dedication to Thomas which, as we have seen, mentions that a copy of the *Tractatus* has already been sent to the pope. Baluze's edition of the letter to Pope Alexander IV is not dated and does not mention where it was signed. Baluze, *Miscellaneorum liber*, pp. 349–50. As Golubovich argued, it is most likely that this letter was also written in the Latin East. Golubovich, *Biblioteca*, vol. I, p. 243.

[64] Baluze, *Miscellaneorum liber*, pp. 351–2.

[65] Baluze, *Miscellaneorum liber*, p. 351. 'Hoc opus incepimus olim quando primo transfretavimus pro subsidio terrae sanctae' ('We have started this work once when we first crossed the sea for the aid of the Holy Land').

[66] Golubovich also argued that it was in the East that Benoit completed his treatise. Golubovich, *Biblioteca*, vol. I, p. 242.

[67] This comment is repeated several times in his dedicatory letters. Baluze, *Miscellaneorum liber*, pp. 349, 350, 351.

[68] Amargier says that Benoit was outside the University movement. Amargier, 'Benoît d'Alignan', p. 458. Max Segonne also argued that Benoit did not receive a university education, but rather studied in a parochial school and then in a monastery. Segonne, *Moine*, p. 15.

In particular, his acquaintance with actual arguments Oriental Christians employed to support their opinions and customs gives the impression that he collected information during his stays in the East. On the matter of the *filioque* controversy, for example, he mentions Theodoretus (b. ca. 386),[69] whose authority was used by Greeks in a discussion of the *filioque* clause that took place in Nicaea in January 1234.[70] Similarly, regarding the question of fermented bread, Benoit knew not only that the Greeks argued that the Last Supper preceded Passover,[71] but also that they asserted that the word *artos* refers specifically to fermented bread.[72] Furthermore, in his discussion of purgatory, Benoit shows that he was aware of the Greek objection to the belief that the fate of the deceased can be influenced by the works of others.[73] An additional example can be found in Benoit's long discussion of the Armenian custom of using pure wine in the Eucharist. He says that the Armenians:[74]

do not mix water with wine in the sacrament saying that blood and water went out of Christ's side separately. And therefore the wine which is transubstantiated to blood in the sacrament of the altar must be separate from the water [used] in baptism.

Both textual and visual evidence confirm the existence of this perception among Armenians.[75]

Of course, it would be rash to assume that such information necessarily reached Benoit directly from Oriental Christians with whom he

---

[69] BnF, lat. 4224, fol. 103r.

[70] H. Chadwick, *East and West: The Making of a Rift in the Church* (Oxford, 2003), p. 240. For the 1234 debate, see also J. Brubaker, 'Nuncii or Legati: What Makes a Papal Representative in 1234?', in K. Stewart and J. Moreton Wakeley (eds.), *Cross-Cultural Exchange in the Byzantine World, c. 300–1500 AD*, Byzantine and Neohellenic Studies 14 (Oxford, 2016), pp. 115–28.

[71] 'Item quod obiciunt Christum anticipare Pascha absursum [*sic*] videtur cum Christum transgressorem legis pronuncient si tempus Pasche noluit observare.' BnF, lat. 4224, fol. 347r ('and that they object [saying] that Christ celebrated Pascha before its time seems absurd since they would announce Christ a transgressor of the law if he refused to observe Pascha's time'). Cf. V. Laurent and J. Darrouzès, *Dossier grec de l'Union de Lyon* (Paris, 1976), pp. 492–4. Benoit probably learned this particular detail from Innocent III's *De Sacro altaris mysterio* 4.4, PL 217.854–6.

[72] BnF, lat. 4224, fol. 346v. For Greek usage of this argument (dating to the eleventh century), see *Leonis Bulgariae Archiepiscopi Epistola*, PG 120.838.

[73] BnF, lat. 4224, fols. 288v–289r. This objection was raised by Greek monks in Acre about sixteen years after Benoit completed his work, in an interrogation initiated by Thomas Agni, which is examined later.

[74] 'Et hoc contra armenos qui non miscent aquam vino in sacramento dicentes quod sanguis et aqua separata exierunt de latere Christi. Et ideo separatum debet esse vinum quod transubstantiatur in sanguinem in sacramento altaris et aqua in baptismo.' BnF, lat. 4224, fol. 350r.

[75] F. C. Conybeare, 'Dialogus de Christi die natali', *Zeitschrift für neutestamentliche Wissenschaft und die Kunde des Urchristentums* 5 (1904), p. 332. Regarding visual representation of this perception, see T. F. Mathews and A. K. Sanjian, *Armenian Gospel Iconography: The Tradition of the Glajor Gospel* (Washington, DC, 1991), p. 159.

communicated. He may have relied on material collected earlier by Frankish churchmen who resided in the East and were well acquainted with these churches, or on texts which circulated in Outremer. Thus, for example, he may have used the *Contra Graecos*, a work written by a Dominican in Constantinople in 1252, in which the main controversial issues between the Latin and Greek churches are elaborately discussed.[76] However, there is evidence that Benoit gained at least some knowledge through direct communication with Oriental Christians. In his discussion of the *filioque* controversy, Benoit writes: 'Our teachers are accustomed to saying that the controversy between us and the Greeks is vocal rather than real. We, however, learned from experience that they really disagree [with us].'[77] Evidently, Benoit took part in a direct discussion with Greek theologians on this issue which had taught him that the opinion of 'our teachers' was wrong.

As illustrated, Benoit, a prominent member of the Western clergy, visited the Latin East twice. It was during his first sojourn in Outremer, and perhaps as a result of his encounter with a great number of errors, that he began working on the *Tractatus*; it is almost certain that he completed the project during his second visit to the East. In the treatise, which is aimed at addressing as many errors as possible, Benoit made, inter alia, a systematic attempt to present various Oriental opinions and customs to his readers, along with the argumentation used to support them. For that project he clearly collected information – at least in some cases directly from members of such groups – regarding the faith and practice of Oriental Christians.

In a way, then, he could be seen as continuing the tradition of the anonymous author of the *Tractatus de locis et statu sancte terre* or Jacques de Vitry. Yet our examination of his treatise reveals that Benoit's attitude towards Oriental Christianity and his purpose in studying it differed from those of his predecessors. First, Benoit was far more systematic in his attempts to present not only the doctrines of Oriental Christians but also the argumentation they used to justify their positions. For example, whereas Jacques was satisfied with telling his readers that the Greeks used fermented bread in the Eucharist while also reiterating the Catholic opinion on the subject, Benoit devotes several folios to

---

[76] For the text, see PG 140.485–574. For a discussion of this work, see A. Dondaine, '"Contra Graecos": Premiers écrits polémiques des Dominicains d'Orient', *Archivum fratrum praedicatorum* 21 (1951), pp. 320–446. In some issues, comparing Benoit's work with the *Contra Graecos* reveals a degree of similarity. For earlier Greek-Latin polemic works, see also Cameron, *Arguing*, pp. 59–99.

[77] 'Doctores nostri consueverunt dicere quod contradictio inter nos et grecos potius vocalis est quam realis. Nos autem iam per experientiam didiscimus quod realiter contradicunt.' BnF, lat. 4224, fol. 103r.

addressing the reasoning Greeks employ to support their position on this matter.[78] Secondly, while Jacques' (as well as Thietmar's and Burchard's) interest in such groups was not restricted to the fields of religion or theology, Benoit, at least as far as we can gather, was concerned strictly with theological controversies. Furthermore, while Jacques cannot be blamed for lacking Catholic zeal, we have seen that he thought that Oriental Christians could contribute to Catholic knowledge and understanding. Benoit, on the other hand, seems to have perceived them as simply heretics, which, according to his view, it was permitted to kill.[79]

Thomas Agni and His Activity vis-à-vis Eastern Christians

As seen in the beginning of this section, Benoit sent Thomas Agni a dedicatory letter which shows that he perceived the latter as a potential partner in his project of studying and confronting heresies. Benoit was clearly correct in this respect, and Agni revealed himself as a supporter of the former's attitude towards Eastern Christians, being personally active in the field of studying and confronting Oriental Christianity in Outremer.

In 1262 Agni convened an assembly which, according to its only extant description, was attended by Geoffrey, the 'commander of the city' (*k'ałak'apetn*),[80] the masters of both the Templar and the Hospitaller orders, all of the princes of the shores of Syria except the prince of Antioch and all of the advocates (*avukat'k'*).[81] At the heart of this event was an Armenian theologian named Mxit'ar, who was to express the Armenian position on various subjects in this forum. Before the assembly began, Thomas told Mxit'ar that he thought that he – i.e. Mxit'ar – may be useful for them, that is, the legate or the Franks in general. For the Armenian party this event was not a pleasant one. Mxit'ar begins his

---

[78] *HO*, p. 302.   [79] Villads Jensen, 'War against Muslims', pp. 183–4, 191–2.

[80] This must be a reference to Geoffrey of Sergines, who was, at the time of the assembly, regent of the Kingdom of Jerusalem. For more information on Geoffrey, see J. Riley-Smith, *What Were the Crusades?* (Basingstoke, 2009), pp. 79–82.

[81] The only surviving source for this event is an Armenian text, written by the Armenian ambassador. Měkhithar de Daschir, *Relation de la conférence tenue entre le docteur Mekhitar de Daschir envoyé du Catholicos Constantin Ier et le légat du pape à Saint Jean d'Acre*, ed. Doulaurier, *RHC, Doc. Arm.*, 2 vols. (Paris, 1869), vol. I, pp. 689–98. This discussion is also mentioned in S. P. Cowe, 'The Armenians in the Era of the Crusades 1050–1350', in M. Angold (ed.), *The Cambridge History of Christianity*, 9 vols. (Cambridge, 2006), vol. V, pp. 418–19; J. D. Ryan, 'Toleration Denied', in M. Gervers and J. M. Powell (eds.), *Tolerance and Intolerance: Social Conflict in the Age of the Crusades* (Syracuse, NY, 2001), p. 59; B. Hamilton, 'The Armenian Church and the Papacy at the Time of the Crusades', *Eastern Churches Review* 10 (1978), p. 82. It is impossible to know exactly what the author meant by stating that all of the advocates attended this assembly. In any case, it is safe to assume that a considerable number of jurists were present.

description of the assembly by saying that the legate spoke much and listened little, but in the next sentence we read that having obtained permission to pose questions, the Armenian resumed the discussion. This gap suggests that the first part of the discussion, in which the legate was by far the dominant party, was omitted either by Mxit'ar or by some later editor.

Be that as it may, when the Armenian ambassador was given the right to speak, he first argued that everything must be founded on Christ. The Franks who, rather than the legate himself, were considered by Mxit'ar to be the opposing party, concurred. Mxit'ar then challenged the Roman Church's power to judge other sees while concurrently being exempt from their judgment. He also argued that the Armenians have every right to sue the Roman Church and that that church cannot avoid their inspection. These words, he says, were very displeasing to the Franks, but they did not express their discontent due to pride, though they did respond with a question: 'Who gave you this prerogative?' Having expressed his desire that his words not offend the Franks, Mxit'ar argued his point at length, which was meant to show that Peter was in fact judged by the other apostles and did not see himself as their superior. Unfortunately, the text ends abruptly before we have a chance to read the Franks' reaction to this argument (although Mxit'ar does write, in the midst of this argument, that they were attentive). We also remain ignorant as to how this discussion ended.

It is not easy to understand what Thomas meant to accomplish in this assembly, since at the time the Armenians were at union with the Catholic Church. If we are to trust Mxit'ar, Agni clearly wished to fortify the 1198 union which was not unanimously supported by the Armenian clergy,[82] but whether for this purpose he merely meant to gain a better understanding of the Armenian ambassador's opinion regarding the union with Rome, or whether he was also interested in forcibly persuading him to acknowledge the pope's primacy, remains unclear. In any case, the assembly is most likely to have exposed a considerable, and varied, Latin audience to Armenian theological positions.

More evidence for Thomas' interest in studying and confronting Oriental Christianity comes from a text that has not been utilized thus far by historians of the Frankish Levant, known as the 'Process of Nicephorus'.[83] According to this text, two Greek monks, Nicephorus and Clement, were arrested and sent to a tribunal headed by the emperor, Michael Paleologus, for not following his decision to unite with the

---

[82] Měkhithar, 'Relation', pp. 693–4.   [83] Laurent and Darrouzès, *Dossier grec*, pp. 486–507.

Catholic Church.[84] Having failed to make the two change their minds, the emperor sent them to the papal legate at Acre, Thomas Agni, so that he could either persuade them to obey the decision regarding the union or judge them.[85] The Greek text, written by Nicephorus, describes the interrogations and the trial that he and his fellow monk Clement underwent in Frankish Acre during 1277. Initially, Thomas tried to persuade the two to accept the authority of the pope in an assembly, but, having refused to do so, they were imprisoned and tortured. They then underwent a series of interrogations conducted by men sent by Thomas. Three of these are documented in our text: the first dealt with the question of fermented bread, the second with the *filioque* controversy and the third with purgatory. This last discussion is only partially recorded since one folio is missing from the manuscript. After a period of imprisonment, the two were presented before a Frankish audience where a debate unfolded regarding the authority of various councils and of the pope. The discussion ended with the Greek monks saying that the emperor intended to assemble an ecumenical council and promising to obey its outcome. Then, at the request of a certain *kyr* Nicolas Raïsès, they were sent to Cyprus to be imprisoned there until that council would convene. After they spent ten months in the Cyprus prison, Thomas died, and they were both subsequently freed by an imperial decree.[86]

Before discussing the meaning of this text for our subject of inquiry, it is necessary to consider its credibility. There are a few aspects which make it difficult to accept this text as an exact rendering of the monks' experiences in Acre. The clearest evidence for its inaccuracy is that having mentioned that he and his companion were often interrogated by one, two or three of the legate's men, the author presents us with three quite well-structured dialogues. It seems much more likely that, in reality, the two Greeks were interrogated in different opportunities regarding various issues. Consequently, it is probable that the structure of the text does not reflect the discussions in jail as they actually took place.

But not only the discussions' structure but also their tone raises some questions. If we are to accept Nicephorus' description of the harsh

---

[84] For background concerning the union promulgated in Lyon in 1274, see M. Angold, 'Byzantium and the West 1204–1453', in M. Angold (ed.), *The Cambridge History of Christianity*, 9 vols. (Cambridge, 2005–9), vol. V, pp. 53–61; K. M. Setton, *The Papacy and the Levant, 1204–1571*, 4 vols. (Philadelphia, PA, 1976–84), vol. I, pp. 106–22.

[85] This case was not the only one in which anti-unionist Greeks were sent to be tried by Latin authorities. In 1279 two monks, Meletios and Ignatius, were sent by Michael Palaeologus to Pope Nicholas III. Laurent and Darrouzès, *Dossier grec*, p. 86; D. J. Geanakoplos, *Emperor Michael Palaeologus and the West* (Cambridge, MA, 1959), pp. 319–20. Thomas' name does not appear in the Greek text, which only speaks of the legate in Acre.

[86] At the time of Agni's death (Sept. 1277), Michael Paleologus was still emperor.

treatment and threats that the two monks suffered, one would have to question whether it is probable that an imprisoned person, having been tortured, and under constant threats of further violence, and even death, would, for example, ask his interrogators if they have no shame or condemn them for being ignorant.[87] One may consequently wonder whether the monks' tone, as described in the text, is not exaggerated, or that the level of threat the two were under is overstated.[88] Indeed, if Agni had threatened them, in front of the first assembly, with death, how could it be explained that their final punishment included only imprisonment? Furthermore, if their deeds and notions were considered so harshly, why were they liberated after the legate's death? In general, then, it can be stated that this text does not grant a fully accurate description of the events.

On the other hand, as the editors of the text have argued, it does include some highly accurate information.[89] Among other elements which support the work's authenticity one may mention Agni's title – legate – and the Greek name of the city in which he held his office – Ptolemais. Even the reconstructed dialogues themselves betray elements that seem authentic. Such is the Latin interrogator's comment that his co-religionists find it hard to believe that the division between heaven and hell is unavoidable.[90] In fact, in his seminal work, Jacques Le Goff has taken this comment as reflecting Western mental dispositions.[91] Additionally, the issues chosen for discussion, i.e. fermented bread, the *filioque* controversy and the purgatory (discussed during the interrogations) and the question of papal authority (discussed in the second assembly), also support the authenticity of the text being most probably the issues that Franks would take up first in any theological discussion with Greeks. Furthermore, Nicephorus' feeling that his life was truly threatened was not ungrounded: in his text, he refers to a precedent of martyrdom in Cyprus, and indeed, Byzantine hagiography mentions thirteen Greeks who were killed by Latins in Cyprus in 1231.[92]

---

[87] Both of these expressions appear in the discussion over the kind of bread to be used in the Eucharist. Laurent and Darrouzès, *Dossier grec*, pp. 492–4.

[88] It should be stated, however, that fervent believers may gather the courage to act in the manner described by Nicephorus.

[89] Laurent and Darrouzès, *Dossier grec*, pp. 82–8; D. Stiernon, 'Nicéphore l'hésychaste', *Dictionnaire de Spiritualité* (Paris, 1982), vol. XI, p. 202.

[90] Laurent and Darrouzès, *Dossier grec*, pp. 83–4.

[91] J. Le Goff, *La naissance du Purgatoire* (Paris, 1981), pp. 384–6.

[92] Laurent and Darrouzès, *Dossier grec*, pp. 87, 505; C. Schabel, 'The Quarrel over Unleavened Bread in Western Theology, 1234–1439', in M. Hinterberger and C. Schabel (eds.), *Greeks, Latins and Intellectual History, 1204–1500*, Bibliotheca: Recherches de Théologie et Philosophie médiévales 11 (Leuven, 2011), pp. 85–6; F. Halkin, *Bibliotheca Hagiographica Graeca*, 3 vols. (Brussels, 1957), vol. II, p. 96.

Plausibly, then, while the dialogues were probably reconstructed by Nicephorus, and while their tone seems imprecise, the basic facts provided by the text, i.e. that he and Clemens were sent to be interrogated and tried by Agni, and that they spent time in Acre's prison, are apparently trustworthy.

As was stated with regard to the conference with the Armenian theologian, in this case too it is very difficult to ascertain Thomas' main purpose. However, since, according to Nicephorus, the tortures preceded the interrogations but were not an actual part of them, it is likely that having failed to persuade the monks to change their opinion, Thomas was interested in learning what they thought and why.[93] In any case, the description of the interrogations gives the reader the feeling that the aim of the Latins was to understand the Greek positions rather than to compel them to concede to Catholic views. Such knowledge was obviously important for these men as it would have been useful for them in future contacts with Greeks.

At this point it is important to suggest that further interrogations of Greeks may have taken place in Acre. In the last paragraph of his treatise Nicephorus writes that it is aimed to instruct fellow monks as to how they ought to reply should they be interrogated by 'Italians or others similar to them'.[94] This means that Nicephorus thought it was probable that more Greeks would be summoned to interrogations by Latin clergymen. As Nicephorus and Clemens were sent for this purpose to Acre, there is no reason to rule out the possibility that others were also dispatched there.

By examining both the Armenian and the Greek texts, which are absolutely independent of one another, one may conclude that Thomas, like Benoit, made an effort to acquire knowledge concerning the theology and practices of the Eastern churches, as well as the argumentation they employed. Such knowledge, obtained by means including debates, imprisonment and interrogation, seems to have been sought mainly in order to promote the supremacy of the Catholic Church. The employment of these means also provides further support to the suggestion made earlier concerning the connection between Benoit's and Thomas' attitudes and the development of the inquisition.

Having explored in detail the available evidence concerning the activities of both Thomas Agni and Benoit d'Alignan vis-à-vis Eastern

---

[93] Le Goff wrote that Agni 'eut une franche discussion avec les deux moines grecs.' As was already mentioned, the interrogations, including the one on purgatory used by Le Goff, were carried out by Agni's men, rather than by him personally. Furthermore, describing a dialogue between prisoners and men responsible for their imprisonment as 'franche' is, at the very least, problematic. Le Goff, *La naissance*, p. 384.

[94] Laurent and Darrouzès, *Dossier grec*, p. 506.

Christian groups in Acre, we can now return to the issue of the role the two played within Outremer's Latin society. As we have seen at the outset of this discussion, both were far from permanent residents of the Latin East and spent only limited periods of time there. On the other hand, both seem to have come to the Holy Land with a strong feeling of mission. Benoit initiated the complicated and extremely expensive project of the building of the Templar castle of Safad; Thomas held the highest ecclesiastical positions in the kingdom. Furthermore, their sense of mission led them to initiate the activities we have surveyed with regard to Eastern Christian groups, and, notably, to see to it that their actions in this regard would have an impact within Frankish society. Thus Benoit not only composed a lengthy text which included considerable information concerning the Eastern churches, but also made an effort that this text would become known to the pope, on the one hand, and to the kingdom's highest church officials on the other, most likely because he hoped that this would make a useful tool for confronting non-Catholic groups. This explains why it was so important for him to ask Thomas to distribute his work in Outremer and why, having returned to Marseilles, it was still important for him to provide a copy of his *summa* to William II of Agen, when the latter was appointed patriarch of Jerusalem. The same can be said with regard to Thomas. He too wished to make his attitude to Eastern Christians influential. Otherwise he would not have bothered to have large, socially varied, audiences attend his debates with both the Armenian theologian and the Greek monks.

One may also assume that, as in other medieval interreligious debates, the assemblies initiated by Thomas were intended not only to confront 'the other' – in this case, Eastern Christians – but also to fortify the belief of the Catholic audience.[95] Indeed, it is very likely that, just like Jacques de Vitry, Benoit and Thomas were unhappy with the level of Frankish religious observance and, perhaps, specifically with what they would have perceived as local influence on Outremer's Catholic society.[96] In this sense, their effort to confront Eastern Christian groups was probably strongly related to their concern with Frankish religious observance, and they may perhaps be seen as de facto Western inspectors of

---

[95] See, for example, Novikoff's argument that 'the *Aversus Iudaeos* genre was, of course, polemical in origin, but what is equally striking is the level of internal Christian pedagogy exhibited by many of the literary and public disputations of the twelfth and thirteenth centuries'. A. J. Novikoff, *The Medieval Culture of Disputation: Pedagogy, Practice and Performance* (Philadelphia, PA, 2013), p. 219.

[96] For Jacques' view of the local Franks, see Jacques de Vitry, *Lettres*, pp. 565–7. For possible Eastern Christian influence on Latin practices in the Kingdom of Jerusalem, see pp. 139–40.

Outremer's Latin society, acting as an officeholder for the papacy in Thomas' case and, perhaps, aspiring to do so in Benoit's.

Interpreted in this manner, Benoit and Thomas' activities can be seen as preparing the ground for the next stage in Catholic activities concerning heresy in Outremer: in February 1290, Nicholas of Hanapes, the last patriarch of Jerusalem in the Frankish period, was ordered by Pope Nicholas IV to nominate inquisitors for the territories under his jurisdiction.[97] This reveals that the pope was so concerned with various beliefs and ways of worship that existed in the Latin East that he decided to nominate experts, at least some of whom were Franciscans, in order to discover what heresies were found in the kingdom and to confront them. This papal initiative can also be seen as marking the final point in the process which we have been able to trace from the late twelfth century: a growing inclination to systematically acquire information on non-Catholic customs and theological views to which was gradually added a disciplinary tendency.

POSSIBLE ARTISTIC EVIDENCE FOR CATHOLIC–GREEK DISCUSSIONS IN THE 1280s

Further evidence for Catholic–Greek discussions, or, perhaps, disputes, is possibly found in MS français 433 of the Musée Condé, which, according to Jaroslav Folda, was produced in Acre in 1282.[98] In this manuscript, which provides a French translation of Cicero's *De inventione* and the anonymous *Rhetorica ad Herennium* with a preface, a methodological epilogue and a treatise on logic [1:19], we also find a remarkable miniature (figure 1).[99]

This miniature presents, clearly enough, a Frankish teacher on the left and Frankish pupils in the centre, one of whom is holding a book, perhaps responding to a question posed by the teacher. As for the bearded men on the right, Folda suggested that they are Greeks wearing 'Palaeologan hats' or at least hats inspired by such Byzantine headgear.[100] Indeed, the hats in question resemble Byzantine hats characterized by a pyramidal top and a wide brim, and usually identified with the *skiadia* mentioned in Byzantine written sources. Interestingly, hats similar to those in the

---

[97] Philippus a Limborch, *Historia Inquisitionis* (Amsterdam, 1692), pp. 62–3. Limborch is citing here Wadding's *Annales Minorum*, entry of 1290. A partial text of this letter is found in Langlois' edition of the Register of Pope Nicholas IV: 'Eidem [i.e. Venerabili fratri Nicolao, patriarche Jerosolimitano] mandat ut in terris suae legationis inquisitores haereticae pravitatis instituat. "Ad extirpandam ubilibet... – Dat. Rome... "' E. Langlois (ed.), *Les registres de Nicolas IV*, 3 vols. (Paris, 1886, 1891), vol. I, p. 370, num. 2095.

[98] Folda, *Crusader Manuscript*, p. 44. For a more recent discussion of this manuscript, see Folda, *Crusader Art*, p. 412.

[99] Chantilly, Musée Condé 433, fol. 127v.

[100] Folda, *Crusader Art*, p. 413; Folda, *Crusader Manuscript*, p. 51.

FIGURE 1 A classroom scene from a manuscript produced in Acre

Chantilly manuscript are included in a mosaic floor in Ravenna's Church of Saint John the Evangelist, illustrating a scene from the Fourth Crusade. In this scene such hats are worn by officials of the Byzantine court standing with arms crossed before a soldier in chain mail holding a sword.[101] One can thus be certain that the Chantilly miniature represents some kind of encounter between Franks and Greeks.

Folda made an attempt to understand the miniature within the context of the text it accompanies. Notably, the illustration under discussion is placed within a section of the *Rhetorica ad Herennium* in which the anonymous author contrasts his own habit of providing original examples with that of the Greeks who present their readers with examples taken from reputable orators or poets.[102] This context helps to explain why the artist chose to include in it images of contemporaneous Latins and Greeks. That the section in the *Rhetorica* to which this illustration belongs refers to the habit of citing from previous authorities also makes clear why the miniature includes a pupil referring to an actual codex.

[101] R. Macrides. J. A. Munitiz and D. Angelov, *Pseudo-Kodinos and the Constantinopolitan Court: Offices and Ceremonies*, Birmingham Byzantine and Ottoman Studies 15 (Farnham, 2013), pp. 326–8 and pl. 19. I would like to express my gratitude to Maria Parani for her kind help concerning this matter.

[102] Folda, *Crusader Manuscript*, p. 51.

The question is whether, as Folda carefully proposed, this illustration can be related to any actual activities in the city.[103] This seems plausible as the miniature does not depict a mere dispute between a Latin author and Greek authorities, as the accompanying text would suggest, but rather a Frankish class placed between a Latin teacher and two Greek elders. Furthermore, it is noteworthy in this context that, as Folda writes, while scenes of instruction are very common in thirteenth-century illumination, the appearance of elders has no counterpart in this corpus.[104] This makes it all the more likely that this unique scene does owe something to the circumstances in Frankish Acre, where Greeks formed an integral part of the cultural environment. Given the evidence for both teaching activities in Acre and theological exchanges between Franks and Eastern Christians, it seems plausible that the miniature under discussion echoes the way in which the illuminator of the Chantilly codex perceived such activities. It is noteworthy in this context that two of the Latin pupils are looking at the Greek figures rather than at their Frankish teacher, which may perhaps refer to the aforementioned attraction of some Franks to local Christian traditions. This also settles very nicely with the content of the *Rhetorica* in the section to which this illustration is attached, as the anonymous author of the work struggles with the inclination of his contemporaries to prefer the Greek stance over his own because of the antiquity of their tradition.

THE CIRCULATION OF TEXTS

When evaluating the intellectual exchanges between Latins and Eastern Christians in Acre, one should take into consideration the circulation of written texts between members of these groups. The scale of the evidence in this regard is quite limited, which is not surprising given that the violent fall of Acre must have resulted in the destruction of practically all codices found in the city in May 1291. Within this context, the restricted evidence available is significant. Under the heading of circulation of texts between Latins and Eastern Christians two phenomena should be included. Firstly, our sources provide some traces of a Latin contribution to Oriental Christian literature. Thus, Dominicans active in Acre appear to have played a central role in the translation of a collection of Marian legends [3:42], originally written in either French or Latin, into Arabic.[105] Humbert of Romans provides evidence for an additional kind

---

[103] Folda, *Crusader Manuscript*, p. 52. It should be mentioned that in his more recent book, Folda does not tie the book in the image to the Greek notion presented in *Ad Herennium*, and is more careful regarding the two elders. Folda, *Crusader Art*, p. 413.

[104] Folda, *Crusader Manuscript*, p. 52, n. 44.   [105] See Chapter 3, pp. 67–8.

of Western contribution to Oriental literature, writing that the Maronites sent books to the Dominicans of the Holy Land with the intention that these may be corrected. While he does not state where this took place, Acre would have certainly been the most likely place for such an activity:[106]

The Maronite peoples as well, long since schismatic and corrupted, are said to have presented their books for correction wholly according to the will of the friars of the Province of the Holy Land, who showed themselves anxiously careful in their correction.

But Acre's Latin residents not only contributed to the Eastern literary corpus but also received several texts from Oriental Christians. While none of these is explicitly related to Acre, it is most likely that all of them circulated in the city and were discussed in it. Among these are the two well-known prophetical texts which reached the forces of the Fifth Crusade as they campaigned in Egypt, the *Liber filii Agap* and the *Liber Clementis*. To these one may add a third text, of a more historical nature, which also reached the crusaders in Egypt, the *Relatio de Davide*.[107]

Evidence which is possibly more directly related to Acre comes from a letter purportedly sent by a patriarch of Jerusalem to the pope and attached to a book beginning with the words 'Liber execucionis Novi Testamenti ad rebellium potestatem refrenandam et humilium justiciam conservandam'.[108] According to this letter, the information regarding the prophetic work was brought to the patriarch by his envoys, who must have also brought him the book. Richard raised the possibility that this text, just like the letters about 'King David' which reached the Frankish camp in Damietta, was brought to the Latins by Oriental Christian

---

[106] 'Maronitarum etiam populi, diu schismatici et subversi, libros suos dicuntur obtulisse corrigendos omnino ad voluntatem fratrum provinciae Terrae Sanctae, qui circa eorum rectificationem solliciti extiterunt.' Humbertus de Romanis, *Opera de vita regulari*, ed. J. J. Berthier, 2 vols. (Rome, 1889), vol. II, p. 501. This is also mentioned in Mulchahey, 'First the Bow is Bent in Study. . . ', p. 347.

[107] J. Richard, 'The *Relatio de Davide* as a Source for Mongol History and the Legend of Prester John', in C. F. Beckingham and B. Hamilton (eds.), *Prester John, the Mongols and the Ten Lost Tribes* (Aldershot, 1996), pp. 139–58; P. Pelliot, 'Deux passages de "La Prophétie de Hannan, fils d'Isaac"', *Mélanges sur l'époque des Croisades, Mémoires de l'Académie des Inscriptions et Belles-Lettres* (Paris, 1951), pp. 73–97.

[108] 'Book of the accomplishment of the New Testament for the curbing of the power of rebels and the preservation of the justice of the humble.' This letter was first edited in Jean Richard, 'Une lettre concernant l'invasion mongole?' *Bibliothèque de l'École des chartes* 119.1 (1961), p. 245. More recently the letter was discussed and reedited in P. V. Claverie, 'L'apparition des Mongols sur la scène politique occidentale (1220–1223)', *Le Moyen Age* 105 (1999), pp. 601–14. For another manuscript in which this text is included, see R. Davidsohn, 'Ein Briefkodex des XIII. und ein Urkundenbuch des XV. Jhdt', *Quellen und Forschungen aus Italienischen Archiven und Bibliotheken* 19 (1927), pp. 383–4.

merchants coming from Mosul, and Claverie raised the additional possibility that it originated in Erbil.[109] The latter also suggests that this compilation was written specifically for Westerners, and that the actual Latin version was not produced in the Kingdom of Jerusalem, but by translators working for the Mongols.[110] Whether the *Liber execucionis* reached Acre is unknown. If, as Claverie argues, the patriarch's letter should be dated to 1221, it is likely that the *Liber* actually reached him in Egypt, but as this date does not seem to be completely certain, this question must remain open.

Fidenzio [3:44] similarly speaks of a prophetic text he encountered. This is a *Liber Clementis* which he received from a Syrian Christian (*Christianus Surianus*) and which may well be a different version of the aforementioned work bearing the same title. This was a prophetical text, written in Arabic, and, according to Fidenzio, perhaps translated from Greek, describing Christ speaking to Peter and Peter to Clemens.[111] Again, what we see here is a transfer of a text from the world of Oriental Christianity to that of Catholicism.

Another possible piece of evidence for the transfer of texts from Oriental Christians to Latins in Acre is related to John of Hildesheim's *Historia trium regum*. Explaining the sources for this text, John writes:[112]

Besides these, the leaders from Vaus brought there with them books from India written in Chaldaic and Hebrew ... and these were translated into French in Acre and remained, in their translated form, in these parts with some nobles. From these very books, from what we heard and saw and from the account of others, these [which follow] were composed; certain things were taken out from various other sermons, homilies and books and were added and inserted into the present work, and redacted to form this one little book.

Surely, this description cannot be fully accepted. However, it does probably reflect a fourteenth-century tradition according to which texts coming from the Christian East reached Acre and there entered Western culture. Jean Richard goes even further, suggesting that the main source

---

[109] Richard, 'La confrérie des Mosserins d'Acre', pp. 455–7; Claverie, 'L'apparition', p. 608.

[110] Claverie, 'L'apparition', p. 607.

[111] Fidentius, 'Liber', p. 26. For this *Liber Clementis*, see also Graf, *Geschichte*, vol. I, pp. 283–92, as well as U. Monneret de Villard, *Lo Studio dell'Islam in Europa nel XII e nel XIII secolo* (Rome, 1944), pp. 65–6.

[112] 'Ceterum ibidem principes de Vaus detulerunt secum de India libros chaldaice et hebraice scriptos ... qui in Accon in gallicum fuerunt translati et in ipsis partibus apud quosdam nobiles translati permanserunt. Et ex istis libris, ex auditu et visu et aliorum relatu, haec sunt conscripta, et quaedam ex diversis aliis sermonibus et homiliis et libris sunt extracta, et his addita et praesentibus sunt inserta et in unum hunc libellum redacta.' Johannes von Hildesheim, *De gestis et translationibus sanctorum trium regum*, ed. E. Köpke, Mittheilungen aus den Handschriften der Ritter-Akademie zu Brandenburg (Brandenburg, 1878), p. 11.

of the *Historia trium regum* was written in order to enhance the renown of some Oriental Christian family in the opinion of the Frankish nobility. Richard also notes that some pieces of information which appear in this text cannot have been collected anywhere but in the Latin East.[113] If he is correct, we have before us another case in which a text compiled by Oriental Christians entered Frankish culture. Given the centrality of Acre in the text, as well as in the life and culture of the Frankish nobility, it is probable that this process was strongly related to the city.

CONCLUSION

In this chapter, we have seen that with regard to the acquaintance with Eastern Christianities, Acre stood at the forefront of Latin Christendom and provided a cultural environment in which a very considerable body of information concerning such groups was collected and organized. As far as one can tell from the extant sources, the most dominant figures active in the city in this field were Westerners who spent limited periods of time in Outremer, rather than permanent residents of the kingdom. At least in some cases, such temporary inhabitants brought with them new notions which had a considerable impact on local culture. This, as we have seen, was the case with the harsh and disciplinary attitude towards Eastern Christians brought to Acre by Benoit d'Alignan and Thomas Agni. At the same time, local culture certainly had an impact on visiting intellectuals. For example, we have seen that Benoit started working on his *Tractatus* during his first sojourn in the East and suggested that it was the encounter with a new reality that led him to do so. Furthermore, it is very likely that the aid of long-term residents in Outremer was required in order to actually communicate with members of the Eastern churches and thus gain a better acquaintance with their customs and theological views. While usually absent from the extant texts, such intermediaries probably had a significant role in the shaping of the materials collected in Acre concerning Eastern Christianities.

The exploration of this field also enabled us to reveal various mechanisms which were employed in the context of Latin attempts to acquire and distribute such new knowledge. We have seen Jacques de Vitry's informal exchanges with members of Eastern Christian groups but also, several decades after the famous bishop left the city, interrogations and public debates involving a variety of social groups. The circulation and reception of texts also played an important role in this context: the

---

[113] J. Richard, 'L'extrême-orient légendaire au moyen âge: roi David et Prêtre Jean', *Annales d'Ethiopie* 2 (1957), p. 240, n. 1.

Conclusion

Tractatus de locis, probably written in Acre, was used by later authors working in the city; Benoit d'Alignan asked Thomas Agni to distribute his text in Outremer; and several works circulated between Franks and Eastern Christians in, and around, the city. All of these reveal that, with respect to the study of Oriental Christianity, a vibrant intellectual environment developed in Frankish Acre.

CONCLUSION

We have seen at the outset of this study that several prominent historians evaluated the intellectual activities undertaken in Outremer rather pessimistically.[1] This assessment is largely due to these historians' identification of the question of intellectual productivity, or liveliness, in the Levant, with that of intercultural exchanges with Oriental and, in particular, Muslim culture. Two historiographical contexts seem to lie at the foundation of this identification: the study of intercultural exchanges in Sicily and Iberia, and the study of the effect Frankish settlement in Outremer had upon Western culture. But this point of view is obviously problematic: it is Eurocentric in the sense that it seeks to find not what intellectual climate developed in the East, but rather in what ways it contributed to Western culture.[2] It is also anachronistic, focusing on what modern historians would have liked to find rather than on a careful examination of the extant source material. Following a line of thinking similar to that suggested by Benjamin Z. Kedar,[3] my attempt in the present study has been to move away from the aforementioned approach, and to explore, in a comprehensive manner, the extant evidence concerning thirteenth-century Acre's intellectual arena and the role intercultural exchanges played in it.

The starting point for this undertaking was the awareness that several significant texts were composed in thirteenth-century Acre. The study that grew out of this realization is intended to characterize the cultural environment which enabled the composition of these works. Its first part includes two structural sections, the first of which aims to characterize the

---

[1] See the introduction, pp. 10–11.

[2] The question of the contribution to the West is central in Runciman and Prawer's surveys, but is not explicit in Mayer's. For similar criticism, see B. Z. Kedar, 'La Via sancti sepulchri come tramite di cultura araba in Occidente', in R. Greci (ed.), *Itinerari medievali e identità europea*. Atti del Congresso Internazionale di Parma, 27–8 February 1998 (Bologna, 1999), p. 181.

[3] Kedar, 'La Via', p. 181.

roles different social groups played in the city's intellectual environment, and the second of which provides a sketch of the study centres which operated in the city during the studied period. The four following chapters attempt to reconstruct the discourse in the city in four central fields of knowledge (language and translation, jurisprudence, Islam and Oriental Christianity). As each of the book's chapters includes concluding remarks, it seems redundant to repeat them here. The purpose of the following paragraphs is therefore to look at the present study's conclusions from a wider perspective which runs across the book's different parts.

While at the time I began working on this project I was aware of only several texts composed in Acre, the number of works included in the 'Acre corpus' increased as the study advanced to finally reach its dimensions as presented in the appendix. This body of evidence, forming the basis for the different sections included in the present book, shows, firstly, that a considerable number of texts, in three languages (Latin, French and Hebrew), belonging to a range of genres, and discussing a wide array of questions, were composed in the city during the studied period. When one considers that the great majority of codices which would have been found in Acre in May 1291 must have been lost, the body of extant literature from the city becomes truly impressive. Among the fields represented, most prominent are theology, 'Muslim and Oriental studies', jurisprudence, history, poetry and geography; perhaps the only major field absent from the Acre corpus is that of science. The corpus is significant not only in terms of its size and range, but also in that it includes several texts which, placed within the context of thirteenth-century Western culture, display a high degree of innovation and originality. Thus, for example, William of Rubruck's *Itinerarium* provides a great deal of information on Asia, and, in particular, on the Mongol empire, which was previously unavailable in the West; William of Tripoli's *Notitia de Machometo* reflects an unusual level of acquaintance with and understanding of Islam; and the volume prepared by John of Antioch in the city includes not only the first French translations of complete Latin works on rhetoric, but also one of the earliest vernacular treatises on logic. As for the Jewish intellectual products from the city, my survey has shown that they are much more limited, and, to a considerable degree, are the works of one major figure: Nahmanides. This includes, most notably, a body of *addenda* Nahmanides prepared to his exegesis on the Pentateuch. An interesting finding that links Latin and Jewish activities in the city is that the distribution of the texts included in the corpus over the studied period is not even: rather, most of the clearly dated products of the intellectual activity in the city, and the most original among them, date to after 1250. In other words, at least as far as one can tell from the extant material, the last decades of the kingdom, in which the military and political conditions that enabled its existence quickly deteriorated, were the most productive in terms of intellectual activity.

The different discussions presented earlier reveal a considerable number of agents who were involved, in different ways, in intellectual activities in the city. Some of these participated in processes of accumulation, development and distribution of knowledge, while others can be described as consumers of products resulting from such activities. Among these, we have seen that clergymen, mendicant friars, jurists and envoys were particularly important, and that members of other groups, such as physicians as well as notaries and scribes, who have left little traces of intellectual pursuits, also likely participated in such activities. As far as Jewish society is concerned, we have presented evidence showing that several leading scholars resided in Acre, and that the city enabled a quite unusual meeting of Jews originating in different regions which, at least occasionally, resulted in exchanges of knowledge and opinions. Many of the active participants in intellectual pursuits in Acre were not permanent residents in Outremer, but rather Westerners who spent brief or at least limited periods of time there, sometimes as a part of their career advancement. This is significant inter alia because it means that there was a constant flow of knowledge and ideas from the West to Acre's port, preventing the city from becoming a detached cultural world. On the contrary, the city's culture was characterized by continuous exchanges between permanent, or long-term, Latin residents of the Frankish East and newcomers, or short-term visitors, from the West (we return to this point in the discussion of intercultural exchanges in the city). Furthermore, to the flow of knowledge and intellectual trends from the West, one should add the weaker, but still noticeable, current of information concerning Eastern cultures, brought into the city by Westerners such as Yves le Breton or William of Rubruck who had the chance to learn directly about such cultures.

In Chapter 2 we presented evidence for teaching activities in the city. Most notably, we have seen that the mendicant orders provided teaching, as did also, in all likelihood, the cathedral. Some of the teaching provided in the city would have been innovative: by the late 1230s the Dominicans in the city had a programme for the study of Eastern languages, and in the 1250s William of Rubruck, who possessed information concerning Asia which was at the time unique, taught in the Franciscan convent. We have also provided evidence for Jewish schooling in the city which reflected various scholarly traditions, and, in contrast to the Latin centres in the city, at least occasionally attracted Jewish students from distant regions. But the distribution of knowledge in the city occurred in numerous other, less formal, ways as well. For example, we have seen that jurist-knights occasionally discussed legal matters when these were not, at that specific moment, debated in court, thus engaging in a process of informal learning. The assemblies initiated by Thomas Agni should probably also be understood within the same context, as they would have provided members of various social milieus with an opportunity to learn about both the positions of Oriental Christians and the manner in which the Latin Church opposed them. Finally, the fact that, as Prawer wrote, no university was ever created in the Kingdom of Jerusalem (and thus, obviously none existed in Acre) cannot, in itself, be seen as indicative of the city's cultural position.[4] By 1291 only a small number of universities existed in the West, and important cities such as Avignon or Pisa did not yet have such institutions.[5] Thus it would be rash to perceive every city that was short of a university at the time as lacking an intellectual centre.

An important issue is that of the preservation and development of texts in the city. For Joshua Prawer, the alleged lack of advanced teaching institutions in Outremer was related to the 'absence of any mechanism for the preservation and transmission of oriental culture which might have been acquired by a previous generation'.[6] But the documentation presented earlier reveals considerable evidence for the existence of such mechanisms. We have seen, for instance, that evidence related to *Tractatus de locis et statu sancte terre ierosolimitane* and to the *Notitia de Machometo* shows that Frankish authors were able to make use of a significant body of earlier Frankish literature circulating in Acre, thus contributing to the elaboration and development of the body of knowledge available in the city. In that sense, a learned tradition indeed evolved in the city, probably facilitated by libraries in institutions such as the mendicant houses, and in some cases also by teaching activities, such as the organized learning of Eastern languages in the Dominican convent.

A central theme in the present study, as well as in any other attempt to explore the culture of the Latin East, is that of the extent and role of intercultural exchanges in Outremer. The kind of intercultural exchange which usually receives most of the scholarly attention is that between

---

[4] Prawer, *The Latin Kingdom of Jerusalem*, p. 529.

[5] Jacques Verger lists eighteen universities as positively founded before 1291. Jacques Verger, 'Patterns', in H. de Ridder-Symoens (ed.), *A History of the University in Europe*, vol. 1: *Universities in the Middle Ages* (Cambridge, 1992), pp. 62–3.

[6] Prawer, *The Latin Kingdom of Jerusalem*, p. 530.

Latins and Muslims. As far as the extant evidence is concerned, however, this channel of communication was quite limited. Indeed, the existing explicit evidence with regard to direct communication between Acre's Latins and Muslims suggests that it took place outside the city, when Latin envoys, such as Yves the Breton, had a chance to communicate with Muslims, for example concerning their beliefs, later sharing what they had learned with interested milieus in Acre. But one should add some restrictions to these conclusions. Firstly, in many cases we do not know how information originating in Arabic or Muslim circles found its way to the Latins of the city. For example, we mentioned earlier an Arabic medical manuscript which seems to have been used by a Latin active in Acre, but there is currently no way of telling how this manuscript reached the city or whether the Frankish reader was assisted by a Muslim in his study of this text. The same is true for the considerable knowledge about Islam which accumulated in the city: as mentioned, some of it was obtained far away from the city, and it seems likely that much of it reached the Latins through Eastern Christian mediation, but it may still be the case that some of it entered Frankish circles as a result of direct contacts with Muslims in the city or in its close vicinity. Secondly, further research may reveal that in fields of knowledge less abstract than those on which the present study focuses, such as geography, the exchange of information was somewhat more intensive.[7] To this should be added that a high degree of exchange certainly took place between Muslims going through the process of conversion in the city and their Frankish instructors.

More considerable evidence was presented for exchanges between Acre's Franks and Eastern Christians. Such contacts often focused on theological matters as seen, for example, in Jacques de Vitry's discussions with members of a variety of Christian communities, and, in a very different manner, in Agni's interrogations of Nicephorus and Clement. Another aspect of the theological contacts between Latins and Eastern Christians in Acre is demonstrated by the translation of Marian legends produced there by what seems to have been a cooperation between Copts and Latins. Indeed, one may safely state that Acre was a place in which interested Westerners considerably improved their acquaintance with Eastern Christianity. But the scope of such exchanges was not limited

---

[7] An extraordinary world map, probably based on an Arabic model, is found in Oxford, Bodleian, Douce 319, a manuscript of Bruentto Latini's *Tresor*, which may have been produced in Acre. B. Roux, *Monde en Miniatures: L'Iconographie du Livre du Trésor de Brunetto Latini* (Paris, 2009), p. 381; A.-D. Von den Brincken, 'Die stumme Weltkarte im Bodleian Douce 319 – ein arabisches Dokument in einer abendländischen Handschrift', in A. Speer and L. Wegener (eds.), *Wissen über Grenzen: Arabisches Wissen und lateinisches Mittelalter* (Berlin, 2006), pp. 791–804.

to matters of Christian theology. Evidence was presented, for example, for the teaching of Copts in the city by French speakers, for Eastern Christian involvement in the shaping of the *Notitia* and for Jacques de Vitry's interest in the linguistic systems used by members of Oriental Christian groups. We have also suggested that the originality of thinking about the vernacular in the city was related to different kinds of communication between Latins and Eastern Christians which characterized Acre. As we have seen, it is likewise probable that Latins and Oriental Christians active in the city exchanged medical knowledge. In this respect the findings of this study settle very well with those of studies on other aspects of the Frankish culture.[8]

A very common theme in this book has been the aforementioned interaction between permanent Frankish residents of the Latin East and newcomers, often for short periods, from the West. John of Ancona, a learned jurist from Italy, brought with him a different way of thinking on law, but was also informed by Franks concerning local problems and customs. We have also seen that Benoit d'Alignan and Thomas Agni carried with them to the city updated Western attitudes towards non-Orthodox beliefs, but also gained much information about such groups in the city, in all likelihood assisted by local Frankish clergymen. Another noteworthy case of such interaction has to do with the writing of the *Notitia*. This text was the result of a request of a senior member of the clergy, coming to the Holy Land on pilgrimage, from a local friar. In a somewhat similar manner, Acre also enabled contacts and exchanges between Jews originating in Europe and Jews of Oriental descent. Thus, for example, we have seen how Jews from Iraq assisted Nahmanides in solving a particular difficulty he encountered in the Pentateuch.

To these major channels of intercultural exchanges, one may add several more limited ones. For example, we have presented possible evidence for the contribution of a Jewish informant to William of Tripoli's acquaintance with Islam. We have also seen that Acre facilitated communication between people originating in different parts of Latin Christendom. Thus, we have seen that during his stay in Acre, John of Ancona learned not only about the local customary law but also about the customs of other Latin territories. Similarly, it was in Acre that Nahmanides became exposed to various opinions held by French Jewish scholars.

These different types of exchanges had a profound impact on Frankish cultural life in Acre. We have seen, for example, that the Dominicans

---

[8] I. Shagrir, *Naming Patterns in the Latin Kingdom of Jerusalem* (Oxford, 2003), pp. 95–6; R. Ellenblum, *Frankish Rural Settlement in the Latin Kingdom of Jerusalem* (Cambridge, 1998), pp. 282–5.

began teaching Eastern languages in the context of theological exchanges with Oriental Christians and suggested that the innovative attitude towards the vernacular in the city resulted, at least in part, from different kinds of exchanges, such as the daily communication with non-native French speakers, or the teaching of native Arabic speakers. This demonstrates why focusing on the restricted evidence concerning direct communication between Franks and Muslims in the Latin East is not useful: without studying the different kinds of intercultural exchanges which took place in this region, it is impossible to provide a rich picture of the culture that developed in it.

The study of thirteenth-century Acre provides an opportunity to explore the notions of centre and periphery. On the one hand, Acre was clearly a peripheral city – located thousands of kilometres from the important centres of the Latin world. But this, of course, is true only looking from the West. Furthermore, as we have seen, new ideas were constantly arriving in the city, so that the impact of the geographical distance in this respect should not be overstated. Additionally, it is exactly its location that resulted in the accumulation, within Acre's walls, of considerable, sometimes highly original and innovative, knowledge concerning other cultures, languages and geographical regions. To this one should add that Acre's distance from the cores of learned activities in the West may have actually been an advantage also in the sense that it freed people working in it from some Western norms. We have suggested, for example, that the readiness to experiment with vernacular writing in fields such as logic may have resulted from the limited presence and standing in Acre of learned persons strongly committed to Latin learning. It is likely that in other fields as well, the distance from dominant centres of learning presented not only limitations but also opportunities.

Another important question is that of patronage in the city. Although the composition of several works was initiated by patrons, Acre lacked dominant figures such as Alfonso X who would have surrounded themselves with scholars and initiated learned projects. This led, in my opinion, to complex consequences: on the one hand, disappointingly for some, no major intellectual projects were initiated in the city, but, on the other, it was perhaps the absence of a towering patron which enabled Acre's authors to leave behind a great variety of texts written from different, and, as we have seen with regard to Islam, sometimes contradictory, points of view.

Finally, returning to the question of evaluation of the intellectual activity in thirteenth-century Acre, one can conclude that within this unique climate of intercultural exchanges, quite often in times of great political and military challenges, and with limited encouragement or support from dominant patrons, numerous works, dealing with a variety of fields and representing different perspectives, were written, considerable original knowledge was accumulated, diverse subjects were debated and novel ideas developed. Thus, while thirteenth-century Acre was no Toledo or Paris, it did house a vibrant and creative intellectual arena which came to its end on 18 May 1291.

APPENDIX: THE RELATION OF THE USED TEXTS TO ACRE[1]

1   A Hospitaller Prayer

MSS Paris, Bibliothèque nationale de France, fr. 6049 and 1978 include the text of a prayer recited in the Acre hospital. Most of this prayer must have been composed around 1197, while certain phrases were added to it between 1257 and 1270.[2] Taking into consideration its dating and the fact that it was to be read in the Acre hospital, one can be certain that in its extant form this prayer was written in the city.

2   The Relatio tripartita

The *Relatio tripartita* is a report by Raoul de Mérecourt, Patriarch of Jerusalem (elected in November 1215) and the masters of the Hospitaller and Templar knights, written at the request of Pope Innocent III (d. July 1216).[3] Given that all of these figures held their offices in Acre at the time, it is clear that this text was composed in the city. At this stage, since various versions of the text end at different points, it is impossible to state with any certainty what the original scope of the work was and what units it included.[4] In particular, it is questionable whether a description of Egypt which appears in some of the textual witnesses of the *Relatio* was originally a part of the report sent to the pope.[5]

---

[1] All the texts included in the appendix were used earlier except those marked with an asterisk. Their presentation here will hopefully facilitate future research.

[2] Le Grand, 'La prière', pp. 325–38.

[3] Richard, 'Pouvoir', pp. 111–12. That this work and the *Tractatus de locis et statu sancte terre* are two separate texts was shown in Kedar, 'The *Tractatus*', pp. 113–14, 119.

[4] Richard, 'Pouvoir', p. 110.

[5] J. Rubin and P. Roth, 'A Medieval Hebrew Adaptation of Two Crusading Texts: Presentation, Analysis and Edition', *Medieval Encounters* 23 (2017), pp. 514–16.

Appendix

3 Jacques de Vitry's Second Letter

As is well known, several letters written in the East by Acre's famous bishop are extant. As can be easily inferred from its content, the second of these was written in Acre during the years 1216–17.[6]

4 Jacques de Vitry's Historia orientalis

The *Historia* must have been completed after Jacques arrived to the Holy Land but before 1224. Since Jacques is known to have left the Kingdom of Jerusalem in 1225, it is clear that it was written in the East. As Jacques was Acre's bishop, it is certain that he spent much of his time in the city and thus must have written at least considerable parts of this work there. To these considerations should be added that the hypothesis that the work was written in Damietta can now safely be rejected, as it was based on a prologue to the *Historia* which in fact is not an authentic part of it.[7]

5 The Acre Section of Freidank's Bescheidenheit

That this section of Freidank's ethical compendium was at least partially written in Acre is made clear by the text itself:[8]

I have heard many a man express the wish: 'If I might get to Acre, and just see the Holy Land, I would not care if I died there on the spot.' Now I see these folk glad to be alive and anxious to get back to their homeland. I advise those who intend to come here after us to be well-equipped.

Reading the text, it is also clear that it was written during Frederick's crusade.[9]

6 A Decision by the Heads of Acre's Jewish Community

This text includes a Halakhic decision regarding excommunication, written by 'members of Acre's community'.[10]

---

[6] Jacques de Vitry, *Lettres*, pp. 558–78.   [7] *HO*, pp. 7–12.

[8] J. R. Ashcroft (trans.), 'The Crusade of Emperor Frederick II in Freidank's Bescheidenheit', in A. V. Murray (ed.), *The Crusades: An Encyclopedia*, 4 vols. (Santa Barbara, CA, 2006), vol. IV, p. 1310. For the German text, see U. Müller (ed.), *Kreuzzugsdichtung* (Tübingen, 1979), p. 102.

[9] Ashcroft, 'The Crusade', pp. 1310–11.

[10] Freimann and Goitein, *Abraham Maimuni's Responsa*, pp. 25–6.

Appendix

7 Marsilio Zorzi's Memorandum

Marsilio Zorzi, the Venetian *bailo* in Acre, wrote, between 1242 and 1244, a memorandum basically intended to enable the Venetians to maintain what they held and to obtain what was wrongly, in their opinion, taken from them.[11] Given Zorzi's office and the information he needed for the composition of this text, it is certain that at least some of the work on this report was carried out in Acre.

8 Jean de Joinville's Credo

That Jean began his work on this text in Acre is stated by him explicitly.[12] His comments also enable us to date his initial work on the *Credo* to the period between the summer of 1250 and March 1251. Note, however, that the extant text of the work dates to 1287, and was probably produced in the West.[13] Consequently, various scholars have raised different proposals as to what parts of the text are additions to, or modifications of, the 1250–1 text.[14] Be that as it may, much of Jean's work on the *Credo* was clearly undertaken in Acre.

9 A Constitutio by Eudes of Châteauroux

During his stay in Acre, Eudes sent a series of statutes, which were composed with the counsel and consent of the prelates of Syria, to the archbishop of Nicosia. The document comprising these statutes was signed in Acre in 1254.[15]

10 The Pardouns d'Acre

This short text describes forty sites in the city, along with the periods of remission of divine temporal punishment granted at each of them. Such a text must have originated in Acre. David Jacoby dated it to between

---

[11] Jacoby, 'The Venetian Privileges', pp. 155, 166–7. For Zorzi's aim in writing the work, see Berggötz, *Der Bericht des Marsilio Zorzi*, p. 101.

[12] Cited in Chapter 1, p. 21.   [13] Folda, *Crusader Manuscript*, p. 103.

[14] Friedman, *Text and Iconography for Joinville's Credo*, pp. 1–3.

[15] The text appears in Mansi, *Concilia* 26.343–47 and has been reprinted and translated in C. Schabel (ed.), *The Synodicum Nicosiense and Other Documents of the Latin Church of Cyprus, 1196–1373* (Nicosia, 2001), pp. 174–85. These statutes are discussed by B. Z. Kedar, 'Ecclesiastical Legislation in the Kingdom of Jerusalem: The Statutes of Jaffa (1253) and Acre (1254)', in P. Edbury (ed.), *Crusade and Settlement* (Cardiff, 1985), pp. 225–30.

1258 and 1264, and more recently Pringle narrowed this down to between 1258 and 1263.[16]

11   A Report by the Executors of the Will of Eudes de Nevers

As Eudes died in Acre in August 1266, this text was clearly produced in the city.[17]

12   John of Ancona's Summa iuris canonici

MS Brugge, Stadtbibliotheek 377 includes a *Summa iuris canonici* written by John of Ancona between 1265 and 1268.[18] The *summa*'s connection to Acre is attested to by a considerable number of details it provides: John was led into writing his *summa* by William, Patriarch of Jerusalem and papal legate, and by William of Lautario, archdeacon of Acre;[19] he dedicated the work to the patriarch (as well as to John Bonus, bishop of Ancona); according to his preface, at the time he began working on the *summa*, John was in charge of Templar juridical matters (*patronus in causis*); he writes that from time to time he also took care of such matters for virtually all prelates and nobles of 'this kingdom' (*alias causas quasi omnium praelatorum et nobilium regni huius per diversa tempora procurarem*).[20] This combination of social connections and professional occupations makes clear that John was active in Acre during the time in which he wrote his canonistic *summa*.

13   Nahmanides' Addenda to His Torah Exegesis

Several manuscripts include *addenda* that Nahmanides sent from the Holy Land to Iberia and that he meant to be inserted into his Torah exegesis. It is clear, inter alia through statements made in manuscripts which include these *addenda*, that they were compiled in Acre.[21]

---

[16] D. Pringle, *Pilgrimage to Jerusalem and the Holy Land, 1187–1291* (Aldershot, 2012), p. 45; Jacoby, 'Pilgrimage in Crusader Acre', pp. 105–17. For a fully annotated recent edition of the text, see Romanini and Saletti, *The* Pelrinages communes.

[17] Chazaud, 'Inventaire', pp. 164–206. Concerning this remarkable source, see also Folda, *Crusader Art*, pp. 356–8.

[18] Bertram, 'Johannes de Ancona', pp. 52, 59.

[19] Brugge, fol. 342v; Bertram, 'Johannes de Ancona', p. 61.

[20] Brugge, fol. 1r; Bertram, 'Johannes de Ancona', p. 59. For John of Ancona's work and its connection to the Kingdom of Jerusalem, see also Rubin, 'John of Ancona's *Summae*', pp. 183–218.

[21] These *addenda* have recently been the subject of a detailed examination: Ofer and Jacobs, *Nahmanides' Torah*. For the connection of these texts to Acre, see, in particular, pp. 16, 678–9.

14 Nahmanides' Letter to His Son Nahman*

This letter, usually referred to as 'Iggeret Hamussar' ('The Moral Epistle') was traditionally thought to have been written by Nahmanides during his stay in the East. Charles B. Chavel, the editor of Nahmanides' works, argued, however, that the letter itself includes no evidence for that, adding that it is unlikely that it was composed during this period in Nahmanides' life, since by then his son would have been too old for the educational tone which characterizes this text.[22] However, three manuscripts of this letter, which were not utilized by Chavel, cast a new light on this question. In them we read the following:[23]

And this is the letter that Rabbi R. Moshe, son of R. Nahman, sent from Acre across the sea, to his son. Nahman, my faithful son, always remember my deeds, that you saw standing with me and the miracles and marvels of the Lord that he did unto me and his great name sanctified by me in several things that your eyes have seen.

Several considerations reveal that this version is closer to Nahmanides' original than the two versions published by Chavel.[24] Firstly, it includes two details that a scribe would not easily be able to make up: the name of Nahmanides' son, and the location in which the famous rabbi spent most of his sojourn in the Levant. Secondly, the opening phrase is more personal and less schematic than the one found in Chavel's texts.[25] Thirdly, the ending of this version is not only much more elaborate than those which appear in Chavel's versions, but also includes a unique expression, which appears in another letter Nahmanides sent his son, and which is lacking in Chavel's texts: 'worrying and forgetting, seeing and happy'.[26] Given the evidence concerning this version's authenticity,

---

[22] Moshe ben Nahman, *Writings*, ed. Charles B. Chavel, 2 vols. (Jerusalem, 1963–4), vol. I, p. 373 [Hebrew].

[23] 'וזה הכתב שלח הרב ר' משה בר' נחמן מעכו לעבר הים לבנו. בני נחמן הנאמן לי זכור תמיד מעשי אשר ראית בעמדך אתי ונסי אל ונפלאותיו אשר עשה עמדי ושמו הגדול אשר קדש על ידי בכמה דברים אשר ראו עיניך . . .' Oxford, Bodleian Library, MS Opp. Add. Qu. 140, fol. 6a. Parma, Biblioteca Palatina, Cod. Parm. 2461, fol. 38b provides almost exactly the same text. A very similar text appears in Vatican, MS ebr. 460, fol. 107b. The text in this manuscript is somewhat unclear and the word Acre seems to have been erased. Another very early manuscript (dated to 1287), which provides a very similar text – while lacking the end of the letter and including several substantial errors – says the letter was sent from the land of Israel: Parma, Biblioteca Palatina, Cod. Parm. 2784, fol. 137b.

[24] Moshe ben Nahman, *Writings*, vol. I, pp. 374–7.

[25] In the texts published by Chavel we read as an opening the very well-known biblical verse Proverbs 1.8.

[26] 'הדואג ושוכח רואה ושמח'. This expression also appears in the Lisbon print of the letter Nahmanides sent his son from Jerusalem. In a better version of this letter, published by Benjamin Z. Kedar and

one can safely assume that Nahmanides' Moral Epistle was composed in Acre.

15 A Blessing Nahmanides Sent from Acre

Several manuscripts include a blessing to be said before going out on a journey preceded by a comment according to which it was sent by Nahmanides from Acre to Barcelona:[27]

Here is a blessing for a journey that Nahmanides, blessed be his memory, found in Acre, in a commentary to Sefer Yetzira, interpreted by R. Shmuel, son of Hofni, blessed be his memory ... and these are the ten verses Nahmanides, blessed be his memory, found in Acre and sent to Barcelona.

As the work in which Nahmanides found this blessing is unknown to us, it is impossible to know how accurate its attribution is and how far he intervened in it, but, be that as it may, the text provided in the afore-mentioned manuscripts is, in its extant form, a product of the famous rabbi's activity in Acre.

16 Document relatif au service militaire

This text, which is extant in MS Venice, Marciana app. 20, and which was published by Beugnot,[28] includes the arguments of King Hugh and James of Ibelin with regard to the question of whether the knights of Cyprus owed service outside the island.[29] These arguments, we read in the beginning of the text, were presented before Edward when he was in Acre in 1271. The text begins with the king's arguments, which are followed by those of James. In its extant form, it does not include Edward's decision. It is safe to conclude that this text, which describes a discussion that took place in Acre,

based on two Munich MSS, the expression is: 'worrying and sighing, seeing and happy' (הדואג ואונה רואה ושמח), which seems to make more sense and can be understood as a *lectio difficilior*. For the different versions of the Jerusalem letter, see Kedar, 'The Jews of Jerusalem', pp. 134–6.

[27] 'ואלו . . . . . . ל"ז הנה שמירת הדרך אשר מצא הרמב"ן ז"ל בעכו בפירוש ספר יצירה אשר פירש ר' שמואל בן חפני ז"ל . . . . . . ואלו'. 'הם העשר [כך] פסוקים אשר מצא הרמב"ן ז"ל בעכו ושלחם בברצלונה'. Vatican, Biblioteca Apostolica, MS ebr. 224, fol. 64b. For other manuscripts with this text, see Vatican, Rossiani, MS 356, fols. 83b–84b; Moscow, Ginzburg, MS 644, fols. 177b–178a; Moscow, Ginzburg, MS 1208, fols. 147a–147b.

[28] *Document relatif au service militaire*, in *RHC, Lois*, vol. II, pp. 427–34.

[29] John of Ibelin, *Le Livre des assises*, pp. 6–7; P. W. Edbury, 'The *Livre des Assises* by John of Jaffa: The Development and Transmission of the Text', in J. France and W. G. Zajac (eds.), *The Crusades and Their Sources: Essays Presented to Bernard Hamilton* (Aldershot, 1998), pp. 172–3.

and which is included in a manuscript produced in the city, originated there.[30]

17   *William of Tripoli's* Notitia de Machometo

A text titled *De statu Sarracenorum* and attributed to William of Tripoli has been known to scholars since as early as the sixteenth century,[31] and was published in 1883 within Hans Prutz's *Kulturgeschichte*.[32] In 1992 Peter Engels presented a new study of this work, in which, through his examination of the manuscripts of the *De statu*, he revealed the existence of two related – but distinct – thirteenth-century texts.[33] Engels' conclusions regarding the two texts are that the *Notitia de Machometo* was written by William of Tripoli, a member of the Dominican convent of Acre, between May and October 1271 for Theobald Visconti who was then staying in the city,[34] and that the *De statu Sarracenorum* was possibly (*möglicherweise*) written in the West, following Gregory X's death, by an author whose identity remains unknown.[35]

That the *Notitia* originated in Acre can be inferred directly from its dedication, which mentions its author as a friar in Acre's convent and its recipient as a pilgrim in the Holy Land.[36] Furthermore, several texts provide evidence concerning Theobald's stay in Acre.[37] Specifically noteworthy in this context are Marco Polo's testimony that Theobald was in Acre when elected pope,[38] the so-called *Memoria* which mentions a sermon he gave in it,[39] and the *Annales de Terre Sainte* which provides the date on which Theobald left Acre.[40] It is therefore certain that the *Notitia* was written by a resident of the city for a prominent figure who visited it.

18   *Hospitaller Statutes*

Hospitaller statutes were promulgated in Acre in September 1262, September 1263, September 1264, September 1265, June 1270 and October 1288.[41] Additionally, it is probable that the statutes promulgated

---

[30] Edbury and Folda, 'Two Thirteenth-Century Manuscripts', pp. 244, 250–1.   [31] *Notitia*, p. 32.
[32] Prutz, *Kulturgeschichte*, pp. 573–98.   [33] *Notitia*, pp. 45–74.   [34] *Notitia*, pp. 66, 71.
[35] *Notitia*, p. 66.   [36] *Notitia*, p. 194.
[37] A. Potthast, *Regesta pontificum romanorum*, 2 vols. (Graz, 1957), vol. II, pp. 1651–2.
[38] Marco Polo, *Le devisement du monde*, vol. I, p. 126.
[39] Paviot, *Projets*, pp. 237–8. For the *Memoria*, see also [3:43].
[40] P. W. Edbury, 'A New Text of the *Annales de Terre Sainte*', in I. Shagrir, R. Ellenblum and J. Riley-Smith (eds.), *In Laudem Hierosolymitani: Studies in Crusades and Medieval Culture in Honour of Benjamin Z. Kedar* (Aldershot, 2007), p. 160: 'Et a x jors de Novembre s'en parti d'Accre Theobalde qui fu esleus a pape de Rome.'
[41] *Cartulaire* 3039, 3075, 3104, 3180, 3396, 4022.

in September 1283 resulted from a chapter that took place in the city, as some of them suggest that they were produced for the Latin East.[42] Possibly, at least some other undated statutes were also promulgated in Acre.[43]

19 *John of Antioch's French translation of Cicero's* De inventione *and the anonymous* Rhetorica ad Herennium *with a Preface, a Methodological Epilogue and a Treatise on Logic*

These four texts are included in MS français 433 of the Musée Condé, first studied by Léopold Delisle and recently edited by Elisa Guadagnini.[44] That the translations of both of the Latin texts were produced in Acre is made clear by an explicit comment in the introduction that precedes them.[45] This comment also includes a date for the preparation of the translations, 1272, but one should probably prefer 1282, which appears in a different place in the manuscript and fits better our knowledge of William's biography.[46] Given that the methodological epilogue is written in the same hand, it can also be safely attributed to Acre and dated to 1282.

More problematic, in this respect, are the introduction and the treatise on logic, since both were written by another scribe.[47] Note, however, that both were included, along with the translations and the epilogue, in the project dedicated to William.[48] It is thus most likely that the introduction was composed in Acre in 1282 or around that time. The treatise on logic, which consists mostly of excerpts from the two first books of Boethius' *De topicis differentiis* translated into French, cannot be attributed to John with certainty, as he may have only incorporated it into the volume he was preparing for William. But even if that is the case, it is still clear that this treatise

---

[42] *Cartulaire* 3844. See in particular nums. 9–12, 16.

[43] *Cartulaire* 2213. It is noteworthy that these statutes are included in Vatican, Biblioteca Apostolica Vaticana, MS lat. 4852, which is referred to later.

[44] L. Delisle, 'Notice sur la Rhétorique de Cicéron traduite par Maître Jean d'Antioche', *Notices et extraits des manuscrits de la Bibliothèque Nationale et autres bibliothèques* 36 (1899), pp. 207–65; Guadagnini, *La Rectorique*.

[45] Guadagnini, *La Rectorique*, p. 79.

[46] Guadagnini, *La Rectorique*, p. 80; Folda, *Crusader Art*, p. 412; Folda, *Crusader Manuscript*, p. 45.

[47] In an elaborate review of Folda's *Crusader Manuscript Illumination* Harvey Stahl argued that the parts of the manuscript consisting of the introduction and the treatise on logic were written by a slightly later hand than the rest of the manuscript. H. Stahl, 'A Review of: *Manuscript Illumination in Saint Jean d'Acre – 1275–1291*, by Jaroslav Folda', *Zeitschrift für Kunstgeschichte* 43.4 (1980), p. 418. In his *Crusader Art in the Holy Land*, Folda answered Stahl. He does not reject Stahl's attribution of the aforementioned parts to another scribe, but sees no reason to maintain that this is a later hand. Folda, *Crusader Art*, p. 658, n. 404.

[48] Guadagnini, *La Rectorique*, pp. 2–3.

circulated in Acre and, given the absence of evidence concerning it elsewhere, it is very likely that it also originated in the city. Guadagnini suggests that John found Boethius' text, perhaps already in the form of excerpts, in the Latin manuscript from which he translated the classical works on rhetoric, and then translated it into French, producing this treatise. If this was indeed the case, the treatise indeed originated in Acre.[49]

TEXTS ALMOST CERTAINLY WRITTEN IN ACRE

20   A Responsum *by R. Samson of Sens*

One extant *responsum* of R. Samson was signed by him with the words 'Samson, son of R. Abraham, who went to the land of the living [=land of Israel]'.[50] As we know that Samson sojourned in Acre and was buried near Mount Carmel, as was usually the case with Acre's Jews,[51] it is almost certain that this answer was written in the city.

21   *The* Livre des assises de la cour des bourgeois

There seems to be an agreement among the scholars who studied this text that it was written in Acre.[52] Maurice Grandclaude argued that the *Livre* was written for Acre's court and suggested that it was composed by an inhabitant of the city.[53] Joshua Prawer claimed that this text was written in Acre between 1229 and 1244,[54] and probably between 1240 and 1244, by an anonymous middle-class burgess, who had a long career in the judicial administration of Acre.[55] According to Marwan Nader, although the *Livre* includes laws originating in various stages in the history of the Kingdom of Jerusalem and relevant to several courts, given its date, it 'must have been compiled in Acre'.[56] In other words, when one takes into consideration the legal and political circumstances characterizing the thirteenth-century

---

[49] For the treatise on logic, see Chapter 3, pp. 73–4.

[50] 'שמשון בר' אברהם אשר הלך בארצות החיים'. Oxford, Bodleian Library, MS Opp. 300, fol. 63a. Cited in E. E. Urbach, *The Tosaphists: Their History, Writings and Methods*, 2 vols. (Jerusalem, 1980), vol. I, p. 278 [Hebrew]. The answer appears in the margin of the folio, and must have been added to it after the main text was copied. While the expression 'land of the living' could also mean 'land of the dead', the context here, being a signature on a *responsum*, makes it more likely that in this case it refers to the land of Israel. For a medieval example of the use of this term referring to the land of Israel, see Rashi's commentary on Psalms 116.9.

[51] See Chapter 1, pp. 38–9.   [52] For the text, see *RHC, Lois*, vol. II, pp. 5–226.

[53] Grandclaude, *Étude*, p. 69.   [54] For this dating of the text, see Grandclaude, *Étude*, pp. 66–70.

[55] Prawer, *Crusader Institutions*, pp. 366–7.

[56] Nader, *Burgesses*, p. 55. As to the dating of the work, Nader is inclined to date the composition of its main parts to 1229–44, while he adds that the book includes laws that belong to later decades. Nader, *Burgesses*, pp. 50, 53.

kingdom and the dominance of material directly relevant to Acre within this collection, it becomes almost certain that it was compiled in the city.

22   An Anonymous Chanson

An anonymous author wrote a chanson in Outremer during 1250.[57] As this chanson was written in order to persuade Louis IX to stay in the Holy Land, and as we know that at that time, that is during the months following the defeat at Mansurah, the king was in Acre, it is almost certain that this chanson was written in the city.[58]

23   William of Rubruck's Itinerarium

The circumstances in which William of Rubruck wrote his work are made evident by comments he makes in the epilogue.[59] According to these, the provincial minister whom William met in Nicosia ordered him to remain in Acre and teach there rather than to travel to Paris as he originally intended to do. William confirms that he obeyed. We also know that the two travelled together to Antioch, and from there to Tripoli, where a Franciscan conference was held on 15 August 1255.[60] Given the length of the *Itinerarium* and the time its composition must have demanded, it is safe to assume that William wrote it after he had arrived in Acre.

24   Benoit d'Alignan's Tractatus super erroribus quos citra et ultra mare invenimus

We have seen that Benoit d'Alignan, the bishop of Marseilles, began his work on the *Tractatus* during a visit to Outremer and is very likely to have completed it during a later visit there.[61] That Benoit was active in Acre is suggested by the fact that his dedication letter to Thomas Agni was signed in the city, as well as by his involvement in decision-making in the kingdom which would have required him to be in contact with institutions and individuals based in Acre.[62] To these considerations one may add that Acre would have also been an ideal place for Benoit to acquire

---

[57] For the text of the poem, as well as for its analysis, see G. Paris, 'La Chanson composée à Acre en juin 1250', *Romania* 22 (1893), pp. 541–7; Bédier and Aubry, *Les Chansons de Croisade*, pp. 259–67.

[58] As can be seen in the title of his paper concerning this chanson, Gaston Paris had no doubt about this.

[59] For the citation, see Chapter 2, p. 51.

[60] Jackson and Morgan, *The Mission*, pp. 41, 47, 275–6.   [61] See Chapter 6, pp. 151–2.

[62] On the letter to Thomas, see Chapter 6, p. 150; for his involvement in decision-making, see Huygens, *De constructione*, pp. 36–8.

knowledge about various Eastern Christian groups. One can thus safely conclude that at least parts of Benoit's *Tractatus* were composed in the city.

25 *The* Summa super usibus feudorum

John of Ancona, author of the *Summa iuris canonici*, was also the author of a feudal *summa* written in Outremer.[63] That the feudal *summa* was written in the Latin Kingdom of Jerusalem is made clear first and foremost by the mention of figures active in it. The most important piece of evidence in this context appears in a discussion of the question of whether vassals can transfer service owed by them to others. Stephan of Savegny and James Vidal, who are mentioned here as experts in the 'customs of this kingdom', are known from a range of sources as nobles who were active in Acre and whose legal expertise was appreciated.[64] As we know that this text was written in the Kingdom of Jerusalem by a jurist who certainly spent considerable time in Acre, who, within a few years, wrote another text in the city, and who was socially connected to leading men active there, it is almost certain that this work too originated in Acre.

26 *Nahmanides' Rosh Hashana (New Year's Eve) Sermon*

On the eve of the Jewish new-year equivalent to 1269 Nahmanides presented a sermon,[65] which, as its contents make clear, was intended for an audience residing in one of the Holy Land's cities.[66] Considering the circumstances of the period, and other pieces of evidence that we have about Nahmanides' stay in the Levant, it is almost certain that this city was

---

[63] Rubin, 'John of Ancona's *Summae*', pp. 186–8.

[64] For this discussion as well as for references to sources mentioning James and Stephan, see Chapter 1, pp. 29–30.

[65] Prawer, *Jews*, p. 155. Reiner writes that the sermon was most probably preached in 1269: Reiner, 'Pilgrims', p. 81. The sermon is printed in Moshe ben Nahman, *Writings*, vol. I, pp. 211–52. For an English introduction and translation: Ramban, *Writings and Discourses*, trans. C. B. Chavel, 2 vols. (New York, NY, 1978), vol. I, pp. 235–353. For a later edition of this sermon, see M.L. Katzenelbogen (ed.), *Hidushey Ha-Ramban* (Jerusalem, 1987), vol. IV, pp. 92–190 [Hebrew]. For an attempt to contextualize this sermon with regard to the Jewish culture of the time, see Yahalom, 'Historical Background to Nahmanides' Acre *Sermon for Rosh ha-Shana*', pp. 315–42.

[66] That the sermon took place in the Land of Israel is made clear by the emphasis given in it to the special commitment of those residing in the Holy Land towards God. That it was given within a city – which, in fact, housed rare books – is indicated by Nahmanides' comment that 'in this city' he has seen 'the long Tosafoth of Rabbi Elchanan.' ('ועכשיו בעיר הזאת ראיתי התוספת הארוכות של הרב' ר' אלחנן ......'), Moshe Ben Nahman, *Writings*, vol. I, p. 229. For the English translation, see Ramban, *Writings and Discourses*, vol. I, p. 286.

indeed Acre.[67] This is also stated explicitly in a sixteenth-century manuscript which provides extracts from several works by Nahmanides.[68]

27   *Nahmanides' Letter to his Son Shlomo*★

During his stay in Acre Nahmanides most probably wrote a letter to his
son Shlomo. The letter, which bears an educational message, is titled:[69]

And this is the epistle the mentioned rabbi sent, while in the Land of Israel, to
Castile, as his son was standing before the king.

Since Nahmanides resided in Acre during most of his stay in the Levant, it
can safely be assumed that this letter was written in the city.

28   *A Collection of Materials on the Regency Disputes of 1264/6 and 1268*

Peter Edbury suggests that this collection of texts was probably produced
between Hugh III's coronation in 1269 and his departure from Acre in
1276. He also proposes that Hugh's procurators compiled it in order to
present the latter's case in the papal curia.[70] As Hugh resided in Acre
during this period, it is almost certain that this collection was prepared in
the city. Furthermore, the described discussions, presented to the *Haute
Cour*, must have taken place in Acre.

29   *Master Richard's French Translation of Vegetius'* De re militari

An Anglo-Norman translation of Vegetius' work is included in
Add. Ms. 1 of the Marlay Collection of the Fitzwilliam Museum.
At the back of the volume we read the following words:[71]

Master Richard, your clerk, who wrote your book in the city of Acre with no
opposition. . .

Using information from the rest of this dedication as well as from one of
the miniatures which appear in this manuscript, Lewis Thorpe concluded
that Master Richard prepared this manuscript in Acre between 1271 and
1272 for Eleanor of Castile as a present for Edward.[72] While this claim has

---

[67] For Nahmanides' activity in Acre, see Chapter 1, pp. 40–45.
[68] Vatican, Biblioteca Apostolica, MS ebr. 185, fol. 190a.
[69] Moshe Ben 'וזאת האגרת ששלח הרב הנזכר בהיותו בארץ ישראל לקאשטילייא בהיות בנו עומד לפני המלך'
      Nahman, *Writings*, vol. I, pp. 369–71.
[70] Edbury, 'The Disputed Regency', p. 3.
[71] 'Mastre Richard, vostre clerc, que vostre livere escrit/En la vile d'Acre sans nul contredit . . . '.
[72] L. Thorpe, 'Mastre Richard: A Thirteenth Century Translator of Vegetius', *Scriptorium* 6 (1952),
      pp. 39–50.

generally been accepted,[73] the question of whether Richard prepared, in Acre, an original translation of the work, or merely produced a copy of a translation made elsewhere remained open. This question becomes all the more intriguing as this manuscript includes the earliest extant French translation of Vegetius' popular work.

Generally, the scholars who dealt with this text either expressed no clear opinion with regard to this question, or provided no support for their convictions.[74] Extraordinary in this respect is a valuable and yet completely forgotten 1962 Nottingham dissertation by Lionel K. Carely, which offers a critical edition of the Fitzwilliam translation. According to Carely, the translation included in the Fitzwilliam manuscript is partly original and partly a copy of an earlier one. In his view, the scribe may have intended to produce an independent, new, translation, but when he encountered difficulties in his source text, he used an earlier translation to which he had access. In any case, in Carely's opinion, this translation should be associated with Acre.[75]

30   Vatican, Biblioteca Apostolica Vaticana, MS lat. 4852

As is made clear by a colophon provided by the manuscript,[76] this codex, which includes various documents that have to do with the Hospitaller order,[77] was prepared for William of Santo Stefano, who,

---

[73] Folda, *Crusader Art*, p. 408; M. D. Reeve, 'The Transmission of Vegetius's *Epitoma rei militaris*', *Aevum* 74 (Jan.–Apr. 2000), p. 316; Hamilton, 'Eleanor of Castile', p. 101; Minervini, 'Tradizioni', p. 167; Folda, *Crusader Manuscript*, pp. 129–30. Some scholars, however, reject Thorpe's interpretation. In M. Dominica Legge's opinion, it is unlikely that this work was presented to Edward when he was in the Latin East, aged thirty-two and experienced in war. See M. Dominica Legge, 'The Lord Edward's Vegetius', *Scriptorium* 7 (1953), pp. 262–5. Mary and Richard Rouse mentioned another, in my opinion more substantial, difficulty in Thorpe's interpretation: according to the text of the dedication, its author was still in the East while his lady patron was already back in France. See M. Rouse and R. Rouse, 'Context and Reception: A Crusading Collection for Charles IV of France', in K. Busby and C. Kleinhenz (eds.), *Courtly Arts and the Arts of Courtliness* (Cambridge, 2006), p. 113.

[74] Reeve, 'The Transmission', p. 316; Minervini, 'Tradizioni', p. 167; L. Thorpe, 'Mastre Richard at the Skirmish of Kenilworth?', *Scriptorium* 7 (1953), p. 120. Jaroslav Folda wrote that 'whichever the case may be, it is almost sure that the translation was done in Acre by an Englishman', but did not provide any support for this conviction. Folda, *Crusader Manuscript*, p. 17. In his *Crusader Art in the Holy Land*, Folda does not refer to this issue. Bernard Hamilton argued that Richard was the translator of the work, but did not explain why this was his opinion. See Hamilton, 'Eleanor of Castile', p. 101.

[75] Carely, 'The Anglo–Norman', pp. 52–8.

[76] Vatican, Biblioteca Apostolica Vaticana, MS lat. 4852, fol. 140v. This is cited in K. Klement, *Von Krankenspeisen und Ärzten... Die unbekannte Hospitalordnung Roger des Moulins in Vat. Lat. 4852* [forthcoming], p. 56.

[77] For a detailed description of the various texts included in the manuscript, see Klement, 'Alcune osservazioni', pp. 231–4. This is summarized in Luttrell, 'The Hospitallers', pp. 140–1. It is

as we have seen with regard to the Chantilly manuscript, was active in Acre. According to Katja Klement, this manuscript was probably produced between 1278 and 1283, and the first hand working on it and that of the Chantilly manuscript are probably identical.[78] Put together with Klement's contention that the documents' translator must have worked with the originals – which at that stage would have been in the order's archive in Acre – it becomes almost certain that this compilation was produced in the city.[79]

31 Annales de Terre Sainte★

Three versions of this text are known to scholars. Two of them, published by Reinhold Röhricht and Gaston Raynaud, conclude with the events of 1291, and thus could not have been written, in their present form, at Acre.[80] A third one, however, which was published by Peter W. Edbury,[81] appears in a manuscript which, according to Jaroslav Folda, was copied in Acre in 1290 or 1291, and ends with the events of 1277.[82] Edbury argued that the information included in this manuscript is quite similar to that found in the other two versions, especially in the part that precedes the late 1250s. Folda's identification means that this third version circulated in Acre, and it seems probable that it was at least partly written in the city. This hypothesis is significantly supported by the elaborate information provided by this text regarding events which took place in the city, such as arrivals of prominent figures to it.[83]

---

noteworthy that this manuscript is related to Paris, BnF, fr. 6049, which preserves a compilation of texts prepared following the fall of Acre. Concerning this manuscript, see also Delisle, 'Maître Jean d'Antioche', pp. 25–40.

[78] Klement, 'Alcune osservazioni', pp. 230, 240. The second section of the manuscript was, according to her analysis, probably prepared later and by a different hand: *ibid.*, pp. 238–41; Klement, *Von Krankenspeisen*, pp. 140–2.

[79] Klement, ,'Alcune osservazioni', pp. 239–41. Anthony Luttrell generally follows Klement's arguments with regard to this manuscript: Luttrell, 'The Hospitallers', pp. 139–41.

[80] Röhricht and Raynaud, 'Annales de Terre Sainte', pp. 427–61.

[81] Edbury, 'A New Text', pp. 145–61.

[82] The manuscript discussed is: Florence, Biblioteca Medicea-Laurenziana, MS Pluteus LXI.10. Folda, *Crusader Manuscript*, pp. 111–16, 192–6.

[83] Here are several examples cited from Edbury's text: 'Et a viiii jors de mai Odoart fiz dou roi d'Engleterre ariva en Accre, et Johan fiz le conte de Bertaigne, et Guillaume de Valence, oncle de Odoart, et Thomas de Clarre. Et en setembre vint en Accre Eymont le frere Odoart' (p. 160); 'Et a viii jors de octovre ariva en Accre frere Thomas de l'ordre des Preeschors patriarche de Jherusalem . . . ' (p. 161); 'A mil et cclxxvii anz a viii jors de mai vint en Accre le conte Rogier de Saint Severin . . . ' (p. 161).

TEXTS PROBABLY WRITTEN IN ACRE

32   Tractatus de locis et statu sancte terre ierosolimitane

This text, the latest edition of which was published by Kedar, was dated by him to the two last decades of the First Kingdom of Jerusalem.[84] This dating has, however, been persuasively challenged on philological grounds by Paolo Trovato, who suggests that the *Tractatus* was composed after 1198 and that it was compiled in Acre.[85] The text's connection to the city seems likely given Acre's centrality in the period following 1191, and is supported by the fact that early on this text was used by Jacques de Vitry, the city's bishop. Furthermore, one of the *Tractatus*' manuscripts includes at least one interpolation most likely to have been added to the work in Acre.[86]

33   *The* Livre au Roi

Because of its 'pro-monarchic' character the recent editor of this text argued that it must have been written in the king of Jerusalem's entourage. Given the date of its writing (1197–1205),[87] this means that the *Livre* was probably composed in Acre.

34   *A Short Latin Chronicle*

Within MS Barletta, Arch. Della Chiesa del Santo Sepolcro, ms. s.n., among various liturgical texts, is found a short chronicle which describes various events in the history of the First Crusade and the Kingdom of Jerusalem.[88] That this text was composed in Acre is probable as there is a wide agreement among scholars that the Barletta compilation in which it is included is very likely to have been produced there.[89] As the last date included in the chronicle is 1202, it is highly probable that it was composed shortly later.

---

[84] Kedar, 'The *Tractatus*', pp. 119–20.
[85] Trovato, *Everything You Always Wanted to Know about Lachmann's Method*, p. 286.
[86] Kedar, 'The *Tractatus*', pp. 121, 132.
[87] Greilsammer, *Le livre au roi*, pp. 83–6, 109–10; Grandclaude, *Étude*, pp. 46–50.
[88] Kohler, 'Un Rituel', pp. 399–401.
[89] Folda, *Crusader Art*, p. 210; Dondi, *The Liturgy*, p. 78; Salvadó, 'The Liturgy', pp. 53–4.

Appendix

35 The Carmelite Rule

The first rule of the Carmelites, confirmed by Honorius III in 1226,[90] and subsequently modified and reaffirmed by Innocent IV in 1247,[91] was probably formulated by Albert, Patriarch of Jerusalem, in the early years of the thirteenth century.[92] The unfortunate fact that no copy of the original rule reached us makes it impossible to be certain as to the precise circumstances of its writing, but as Albert was active in Acre at the time, it is probable that this text was formulated in the city.

36 A Chanson by Thibaut of Champagne

Thibaut of Champagne wrote a *chanson d'amour* in Outremer in 1239 or 1240.[93] As Thibaut must have spent a considerable part of his sojourn in the East at Acre and as it was probably there, rather than elsewhere, that he would have been able to find leisure for literary activity, it is likely that this work was composed in the city.[94]

37 The Continuations of William of Tyre's Chronicon[95]

The French continuations of William of Tyre's *Chronicon* make up a considerable corpus of texts, the classification of which is a highly complicated matter. It seems that at the current state of research it is quite impossible to state with any certainty which of the texts were

---

[90] P. Pressuti (ed.), *Regesta Honorii Papae III*, 2 vols. (Hildesheim, 1978), vol. II, p. 400.

[91] B. Zimmerman (ed.), *Monumenta Historica Carmelitana* (Lérins, 1907), vol. I, pp. 12–18.

[92] A. Jotischky, *The Perfection of Solitude* (University Park, PA, 1995), p. 124. The preferable edition of the text is: *La règle de l'Ordre de la Bienheureuse Vierge Marie du Mont Carmel*, ed. and trans. M. Battmann (Paris, 1982). This work was, however, unavailable to me during the time of writing. See also Jotischky, *The Perfection*, p. 125.

[93] Bédier and Aubry, *Les Chansons*, pp. 199–206; A. Wallensköld (ed.), *Les chansons de Thibaut de Champagne, Roi de Navarre* (Paris, 1925), pp. 61–4.

[94] Jacoby, 'Knightly Values', p. 164.

[95] Before discussing the continuations, it is worthwhile to say something about the *Chronicon*'s French translation. This translation does not seem to be strongly related to Acre. Rather, it seems to have been produced by a Western cleric who had been on a pilgrimage or crusade to the Holy Land sometime after around 1180. See J. H. Pryor, 'The *Eracles* and William of Tyre: An Interim Report', in B. Z. Kedar (ed.), *The Horns of Hattin* (Jerusalem, 1992), p. 293. Hamilton supports the view that the translation was made in the West. See B. Hamilton, 'The Old French Translation of William of Tyre as an Historical Source', in P. W. Edbury and J. P. Phillips (eds.), *The Experience of Crusading 2: Defining the Crusader Kingdom* (Cambridge, 2003), pp. 93–4, 112. More recently, Peter Edbury expressed a similar opinion: P. Edbury, 'The French Translation of William of Tyre's *Historia*: The Manuscript Tradition', *Crusades* 6 (2007), p. 94.

written in Acre.[96] We do know, however, that various versions of the continuations are included in manuscripts produced in the city,[97] meaning that at least some of the work on the continuations took place there. Peter Edbury goes further arguing that 'all of the continuations appear to have been written in the East'.[98] More specifically, he suggests that the Colbert-Fontainebleau Continuation (found in Paris, Bibliothèque nationale de France, MS fr. 2628) appeared in the Latin East in the 1240s, and that the texts found in MSS Lyon Bibliothèque de la Ville 828 and Florence, Bibliotheca Medicea Laurenziana, Pluteus LXI, 10, are the result of revisions and expansions that probably took place in Acre later in the same decade.[99]

38   Two of Eudes of Châteauroux's Sermons

Two sermons on the dead of Mansurah (8.2.1250) by Eudes are extant.[100] The sharpness of the memory of the battle, as transmitted in the sermons, implies that they were given before Eudes left for the West on 17 September 1254, and it has been argued that the most probable single date for their presentation is the first anniversary of the battle, which Louis IX appears to have spent in Acre. The first of the two is thought to have been preached in the royal chapel, while the second seems to have been presented in one of the city's religious houses.[101]

39   A Hebrew Redemption Midrash*

Oxford, Bodleian Library, Opp. Add. Qu. 128, includes a Hebrew Midrash which seems to refer to several events that took place in thirteenth-century Outremer. Among them are the capture of Acre

---

[96] Excluded from this discussion is the *Chronique d'Ernoul et de Bernard le Trésorier*, since neither of these authors seems to have been strongly connected to Acre. Ernoul was thought by Morgan to have been connected to Cyprus rather than to the Kingdom of Jerusalem, and Bernard was attached to the abbey of Corbie. See M. R. Morgan, *The Chronicle of Ernoul and the Continuations of William of Tyre* (London, 1973), pp. 41–50. It is noteworthy, however, that Bernard Hamilton argues that this text was written in the Holy Land: Hamilton, 'Knowing', pp. 382–3. In this he seems to follow Jean Richard, who wrote that Ernoul was a *poulain* and did not incline to accept Morgan's hypothesis about him: J. Richard, 'L'arrière-plan historique des deux cycles de la croisade', *Zeitschrift für französische Sprache und Literatur*, Beiheft 11 (Stuttgart, 1987), p. 12.

[97] Folda, *Crusader Manuscript, passim.*   [98] Edbury, 'The French Translation', p. 94.

[99] P. Edbury, 'New Perspectives on the Old French Continuations of William of Tyre', *Crusades* 9 (2010), p. 111.

[100] They are found in a collection of Eudes' sermons, which survives in Arras, Bibliothèque municipal, MS 137. P. J. Cole, *The Preaching of the Crusades to the Holy Land, 1095–1270* (Cambridge, MA, 1991), p. 179. The sermons are published in that volume on pp. 235–43.

[101] Cole, D'Avray and Riley-Smith, 'Application of Theology to Current Affairs', pp. 230–1.

by the Franks in 1191, Louis IX's Egyptian campaign, the end of the Ayyubid dynasty and the rise of the Mamluks.[102] As the situation described by the author is one in which Christians, rather than Muslims, hold the Holy Land, and as Acre takes a central place in his work, it is probable that this text was written in the city. This is further supported by the considerable extant evidence for the existence of a significant Jewish community in thirteenth-century Acre.

40   De constructione castri Saphet

This text, which describes the construction of the Castle of Safad, was written by an anonymous author closely related to Benoit d'Alignan. Not much else can be said about the author of this work save that he seems to have been associated in some manner with the Templar order. It is also clear that this author spent some time in the Latin East, although Huygens' claim that the author was in this region during the events he describes seems rash. Possibly he was in the East only during Benoit's second visit, and had heard about previous events from people who witnessed them. The text must have been written between 1260 and 1266.[103] As Acre takes a prominent place within this work,[104] and as Benoit himself seems to have spent much time in the city,[105] it is likely that this text was written there.

41   *A Manual of Commercial Practice*

According to David Jacoby, the manual of commercial practice which appears in MS Venice, Bibl. Marciana, Mss. Italiani, Cl. XI, n. 87, fols. 1r–7r, was written between 1262 and the early 1270s by a Venetian living in Acre. The suggestion that its author lived in the city is based on the decisive emphasis given to Acre throughout the text. It is also noteworthy that to this manual is attached a nautical guide, which, in its extant form, also seems to have been written from the perspective of a resident of the city.[106]

---

[102] E. E. Urbach, 'A Midrash of Redemption from Late Crusader Times', *Eretz Israel* 10 (Jerusalem, 1971), pp. 58–63 [Hebrew].
[103] Huygens, *De constructione*, pp. 10–11.   [104] Huygens, *De constructione*, pp. 36–8, 43.
[105] See [2:24].
[106] Jacoby, 'A Venetian Manual', pp. 403–28, and specifically pp. 417–18. For the portulan, see P. Gautier Dalché, *Carte marine et portulan au XIIe siècle* (Rome, 1995), pp. 40–1, 181–2 (where a transcription of the text appears). Gautier Dalché argues that rather than a partial portulan, this is a 'memory aid' written by the same merchant who composed the commercial guide. David Jacoby thinks that this is a low-quality copy of an existing portulan (I thank Professor David Jacoby for sending me unpublished material regarding this manuscript).

42   *A Translation of a Set of Marian Legends from French or Latin into Arabic*

Enrico Cerulli, who wrote a groundbreaking work on this collection, suggested that this translation project, which led to the adoption of the legends by the Coptic Church,[107] occurred between 1237 and 1289 in Dominican circles in the East, probably in Acre. Cerulli also argued that the legends were probably translated from French.[108] His *terminus post quem* is based on the mention, in one of the legends, of Jordan of Saxony, Master of the Dominicans (d. 1237), while his *terminus ante quem* is the date of the earliest manuscript. Daniel Baraz suggests that the collection was produced between about 1250 and 1289,[109] and claims that at least some of the legends may have been translated from Latin.[110] With regard to the connection of the translation to the Dominicans, Baraz's work supports Cerulli's suggestion.[111]

But what can one say about the connection of this translation project to Acre? Cerulli's suggestion that the legends were translated in the city is based on the mention, in one of the stories, of the Monastery of Saint John in Acre.[112] Baraz is more sceptical, saying that the mention of this institution in the translation does not necessarily mean that it was produced in or near it. It does probably mean, however, that the translator was somehow connected to it.[113] While Baraz's criticism of Cerulli's argument is justified, the possibility that this translation project took place in Acre is supported by evidence concerning Coptic presence in the city as well as by the fact that Acre housed the most important Dominican centre in the kingdom.[114]

---

[107] Kedar, 'Latins and Oriental Christians in the Frankish Levant', p. 217; K. N. Ciggaar, 'Manuscripts as Intermediaries: The Crusader States and Literary Cross-Fertilization', in K. N. Ciggaar, A. Davids and H. G. B. Teule (eds.), *East and West in the Crusader States* (Louvain, 1996), p. 145; Baraz, 'Coptic-Arabic', pp. 23–4. Regarding the story about the icon of Saydanya, see also L. Minervini, 'Leggende dei cristiani orientali nelle letterature romanze del medioevo', *Romance Philology* 49.1 (Aug. 1995), pp. 6–10.

[108] E. Cerulli, *Il libro etiopico dei Miracoli di Maria* (Rome, 1943), pp. 531–5; E. Cerulli, '"Il suicidio della peccatrice" nelle versioni araba ed etiopica del Libro dei Miracoli di Maria', *Annali dell'Istituto Orientale di Napoli*, n.s. 19 (1969:2), pp. 151, 179 [I have not yet been able to reach this paper]. These conclusions are cited in Baraz, 'Bartolomeo da Trento', p. 71.

[109] Baraz, 'Bartolomeo da Trento', p. 76.

[110] For Cerulli's opinion cited by Baraz, and for the latter's opinion, see Baraz, 'Bartolomeo da Trento', pp. 71, 76–7.

[111] Baraz, 'Bartolomeo da Trento', pp. 75–6.

[112] Baraz cites this in his unpublished MA thesis: D. Baraz, 'Collections of Marian Legends in the East: An Example of Intercultural Contacts between West and East in the Late Middle Ages', unpublished MA Thesis, Hebrew University of Jerusalem (1991), p. 84 [Hebrew]. Benjamin Kedar supports Cerulli's suggestion that the legends were translated in Dominican circles in Acre. See Kedar, 'Latins and Oriental Christians in the Frankish Levant', p. 217.

[113] Baraz, 'Collections', p. 84.

[114] Concerning Coptic presence in the city, see Chapter 2, p. 54, Chapter 5, p. 134 and Chapter 6, pp. 145–7; regarding the Dominican centre, see Chapter 2, pp. 49–50.

43 A Geographical Treatise Aimed to Guide Future Western Armies Coming to Outremer

Two texts, the *Via ad Terram Sanctam* and the *Memoria*, both written, in their present form, following the fall of Acre, are based on a common source written before the fall of Tripoli (26 April 1289). This text included the elements that the *Via ad Terram Sanctam* and the *Memoria* share (albeit with some variations): the discussion of the Western ports most suitable for departing on a crusade; the best ports for disembarking in the Levant; a plan for a campaign advancing from Armenia through Antioch towards Hama, Damascus and finally Jerusalem; and an itinerary from Gaza to Cairo.[115] That this original treatise was written in the East is easy to prove: the author speaks about armies coming from the West as 'ceaus d'outre mer'.[116] It is impossible to prove that this text was written in Acre, but this is highly probable given the large amount of information presented here which is likely to have been available only in the kingdom's central institutions.

44 *Fidenzio of Padua's* Liber recuperationis terre sancte[117]

It is unclear when and where Fidenzio wrote his treatise, but we do know that it was dedicated to Pope Nicholas IV just a few months before the fall of Acre.[118] It is also clear that Fidenzio spent at least two periods of time in Outremer: the first before the Council of Lyon and the second following it, probably up to 1290. During at least some of the period he spent in Outremer, Fidenzio served as the *vicarius provincialis* of the Franciscan order in the Holy Land, an office whose holder must have spent considerable time in Acre.[119] Furthermore, Fidenzio explicitly states that some of the information presented in the treatise reflects first-hand knowledge,[120] and includes in it references to the city.[121] Thus, while one cannot be certain which parts of the work were actually written in Acre, it is clear that much of the material included in it was collected while Fidenzio resided in the city.

---

[115] Paviot, *Projets*, pp. 19–20, 32–3, 173–81, 260–78.   [116] Paviot, *Projets*, pp. 19, 173.

[117] Fidentius, 'Liber', pp. 1–60.   [118] Fidentius, 'Liber', pp. 6–7, 9.

[119] F. Simonelli, 'Fidenzio da Padova', in *Dizionario Biografico degli Italiani* (Rome, 1997), vol. XLVII, pp. 412–14.

[120] Fidentius, 'Liber', p. 9.

[121] For example: 'I once had a discussion with certain Christians from Egypt who came to Acre.' ('Ego aliquando tractatum habui cum aliquibus Christianis de Egipto qui veniebant in Accon.') Fidentius, 'Liber', p. 49.

BIBLIOGRAPHY

SOURCES

Manuscripts

Latin Manuscripts

Benoit of Alignan, *Tractatus super erroribus quas citra et ultra mare invenimus*:
Paris, Bibliothèque nationale de France, lat. 4224.

Burchard of Mount Sion, *Descriptio Terrae Sanctae*:
Florence, Biblioteca Medicea Laurenziana, MS Plut. 76.56.
Zwickau, Ratsschulbibliothek, 1.12.5.

Herman of Dalmatia, *Doctrina Mahumet*:
Paris, Arsenal, MS 1162.

John of Ancona, *Summa iuris canonici*:
Brugge, Stadtbibliotheek 377.

John of Ancona, *Summa super usibus feudorum*:
Bamberg, Staatsbibliothek, Can. 48.
Nürnberg, Stadtbibliothek, Cent. II 90.
Paris, Bibliothèque nationale de France, lat. 16008.

French Manuscripts

Jean d'Antioche, French translations of Cicero's *De inventione* and the anonymous *Rhetorica ad Herennium* with a preface, a methodological epilogue and a treatise on logic:
Chantilly, Musée Condé, fr. 433.

Bibliography

Hebrew Manuscripts

Isaac from Acre, *Otzar Ha-Hayim*:
Moscow, Ginzburg 775.

Nahmanides, *Letters*:
Oxford, Bodleian Library, Opp. Add. Qu. 140.
Parma, Biblioteca Palatina, Cod. Parm. 2461.
Parma, Biblioteca Palatina, Cod. Parm. 2784.
Vatican, Biblioteca Apostolica, ebr. 460.

Nahmanides, *Shmira Laderekh* (a blessing sent from Acre):
Moscow, Ginzburg 644.
Moscow, Ginzburg 1208.
Vatican, Biblioteca Apostolica, ebr. 224.
Vatican, Rossiana, ebr. 356.

Printed Sources

Abraham Abul'afia, *Otzar Eden Ganuz*, ed. A. Gross, Jerusalem, 2000 [Hebrew].
Abraham Maimuni, *Wars of the Lord*, ed. R. M. Margalioth, Jerusalem, year not stated [Hebrew].
Abraham Zacuto, *The Book of Lineage*, ed. Z. Filippowski, London, 1857, reprint. Jerusalem, 1963 [Hebrew].
Alvarus of Cordova, *Indiculus luminosus*, PL 121.514–55.
Ashcroft, J. R. (trans.), 'The Crusade of Emperor Frederick II in Freidank's Bescheidenheit', in A. V. Murray (ed.), *The Crusades: An Encyclopedia*, 4 vols., Santa Barbara, CA, 2006, vol. IV, pp. 1310–11.
Baluze, E., *Miscellaneorum liber sextus*, Paris, 1713.
Bédier, J. and P. Aubry (eds.), *Les Chansons de Croisade*, Paris, 1909, reprint. New York, 1971.
Berger, E. (ed.), *Les registres d'Innocent IV*, Paris, 1911.
Berggötz, O. (ed.), *Der Bericht des Marsilio Zorzi. Codex Querini-Stampalia IV3 (1064)*, Kieler Werkstücke, Reihe C: Beiträge zur europäischen Geschichte des frühen und hohen Mittelalters 2, Frankfurt a/M, 1990.
Broadhurst, R. J. C. (trans.), *The Travels of Ibn Jubayr*, London, 1952.
Cicero, *Rhetorici libri duo qui vocantur de inventione*, ed. E. Stroebel, Stuttgart, 1965.
Crawford, P. F. (trans.), *The 'Templar of Tyre'*, Farnham, 2003.
Cronica di Giovanni Villani [ed. not mentioned], 7 vols., Florence, 1823.
Daunou P. and J. Naudet (eds.), *Vie de Saint Louis par le confesseur de la reine Marguerite*, RHGF 20, Paris, 1840.
De Wailly, N., L. Delisle and Ch. Jourdain (eds.), *Chronique de Primat*, RHGF 23, Paris, 1894.
Delaville le Roulx, J., *Les archives, la bibliothèque et le trésor de l'ordre de Saint-Jean de Jérusalem a Malte*, Paris, 1883.
Denifle, H. and A. Chatelain (eds.), *Chartularium Universitatis Parisiensis*, 4 vols., Paris, 1899, reprint., Brussels, 1964.

Bibliography

Fakhr al-Dīn al-Rāzī, *Al-Tafsir Al-Kabir*, Beirut, 1990 [Arabic].

Fidentius de Padua, 'Liber recuperationis terre sancte', in Girolamo Golubovich, *Biblioteca Bio-Bibliografica della Terra Santa e dell'Oriente francescano*, 5 vols., Florence, 1913, vol. II, pp. 1–60.

Filippo Da Novara, *Guerra di Federico II in Oriente*, ed. S. Melani, Naples, 1994.

Fitting, H. (ed.), *Lo Codi in der lateinischen Übersetzung des Ricardus Pisanus*, Halle, 1906.

Freimann, Abraham H. and S. D. Goitein (eds.), *Abraham Maimuni's Responsa*, Jerusalem, 1937 [Hebrew].

Fulcherus Carnotensis, *Historia Hierosolymitana*, ed. H. Hagenmeyer, Heidelberg, 1913.

Gaufridus de Belloloco, *Vita Sancti Ludovici*, eds. P. Daunou and J. Naudet, RHGF 20, Paris, 1840.

Gerardus de Fracheto, *Vitae fratrum ordinis praedicatorum*, ed. B. M. Reichert, Leuven, 1896.

Glick, S. (with Y. Schwartz, A. Levin and A. Grossman), *Seride Teshuvot of the Ottoman Empire Sages: From the Cairo Genizah in the Elkan Nathan Adler Collection of the Library of the Jewish Theological Seminary of America*, 2 vols., Ramat Gan, 2016 [Hebrew].

Gotifredi Viterbiensis opera, ed. G. Waitz, MGH SS 22, Hannover, 1872.

Gottofredo Da Trani, *Summa super titulis decretalium*, Lyon, 1519, reprint. Darmstadt, 1992.

Greilsammer, M. (ed.), *Le livre au roi*, Paris, 1995.

Guadagnini, E. (ed.), *La Rectorique de Cyceron tradotta da Jean d'Antioche, Edizione e glossario*, Pisa, 2009.

Guglielmo di Rubruk, *Viaggio in Mongolia*, ed. and Italian trans. P. Chiesa, Milan, 2011.

Guiraud, J. (ed.), *Les registres d'Urbain IV*, Paris, 1901, 1906.

Halkin, F., *Bibliotheca Hagiographica Graeca*, 3 vols., Brussels, 1957.

Havlin, S. Z. (ed.), *Rashba's Responsa*, Rome, ca. 1470, reprint. Jerusalem, 1977 [Hebrew].

Hieronymus, *Epistularum pars I*, ed. I. Hilberg, CSEL 54, Vienna, 1996.

Hill, J. H. and L. L. Hill (eds.), *Le 'Liber' de Raymond d'Aguilers*, Paris, 1969.

Horace, *Epistles Book II and Epistle to the Pisones ('Ars Poetica')*, ed. N. Rudd, Cambridge, 1989.

Humbertus de Romanis, *Opera de vita regulari*, ed. J. J. Berthier, 2 vols., Rome, 1889.

Huygens, R. B. C. (ed.), *De constructione castri Saphet*, Amsterdam, 1981.

Huygens, R. B. C. (ed.), *Peregrinationes tres: Saewulf, Iohannes Wirziburgensis, Theodericus*, CCCM 139, Turnhout, 1994.

Isaac of Acre, '*Meirat Einayim*', ed. A. Goldreich, unpublished PhD thesis, Hebrew University (1981) [Hebrew].

Jacques de Vitry, 'Historia Hierosolymitana', in *Gesta Dei per Francos*, ed. J. Bongars, Hanau, 1611.

Jean, Sire de Joinville, *Histoire de Saint Louis, Credo et Lettre à Louis X*, ed. and trans. N. De Wailly, Paris, 1874.

Johannes von Hildesheim, *De gestis et translationibus sanctorum trium regum*, ed. E. Köpke, Mittheilungen aus den Handschriften der Ritter-Akademie zu Brandenburg, Brandenburg, 1878.

John of Ibelin, *Le livre des assises*, ed. P. W. Edbury, Leiden and Boston, MA, 2003.

Judah Alharizi, *Taḥkemoni or the Tales of Heman the Ezraḥite*, ed. J. Yahalom and N. Katsumata, Jerusalem, 2010 [Hebrew].

Katzenelbogen, M. L. (ed.), *Hidushey Ha-Ramban*, Jerusalem, 1987 [Hebrew].

Kausler, E. H. (ed.), *Livre des assises de Jérusalem*, Stuttgart, 1839.

Keil, H. (ed.), *Grammatici Latini*, 8 vols., Leipzig, 1855–80, reprinted Hildesheim, 1961.

Langlois, E. (ed.), *Les registres de Nicolas IV*, Paris, 1886, 1891.

Laurent, J. C. M. (ed.), *Thietmari Peregrinatio*, Hamburg, 1857.

Laurent, J. C. M. (ed.), *Peregrinatores medii aevi quatuor*, Leipzig, 1873.

Lehmann, K. (ed.), *Consuetudines Feudorum*, Göttingen, 1896.

Lichtenberg, A. (ed.), *The Collection of Maimonides' Responsa and Letters*, Leipzig, 1859 [Hebrew].

Madre, A. (ed.), *Raimundi Lulli opera Latina*, CCCM 35, Turnhout, 1981.

Marco Polo, *Le devisement du monde*, ed. P. Ménard, 6 vols., Geneva, 2001.

Marx, F. (ed.), *Ad C. Herennium de ratione dicendi*, Leipzig, 1964.

Mayer, H. E., *Die Urkunden der Lateinischen Könige von Jerusalem*, MGH, 4 vols., Hanover, 2010.

Mĕkhithar de Daschir, 'Relation de la conférence tenue entre le docteur Mekhitar de Daschir envoyé du Catholicos Constantin Ier et le légat du pape à Saint Jean d'Acre', ed. Doulaurier, *RHC, Doc. Arm.*, 2 vols., Paris, 1869, vol. I, pp. 689–98.

Muhammad Ibn Abd al-Aziz al-Hamawi, *Al-Tarikh al-Mansuri*, ed. A. Dudu, Damascus, 1981.

Müller, G. (ed.), *Documenti sulle relazioni delle città toscane coll'Oriente cristiano e coi Turchi*, Florence, 1879, reprint. Rome, 1966.

Müller, U. (ed.), *Krezzugsdichtung*, Tübingen, 1979.

[Nahmanides] Moshe ben Nahman, *Exegesis on the Torah*, ed. C. B. Chavel, 2 vols., Jerusalem, 1972 [Hebrew].

[Nahmanides] Moshe ben Nahman, *Writings*, ed. C. B. Chavel, 2 vols., Jerusalem, 1963–4 [Hebrew].

[Nahmanides] Ramban, *Commentary on the Torah*, trans. C. B. Chavel, 5 vols., New York, 1971–6.

[Nahmanides] Ramban, *Writings and Discourses*, trans. C. B. Chavel, 2 vols., New York, 1978.

Nobel, P. (ed.), *La Bible d'Acre: Genèse et Exode*, Besançon, 2006.

Oliverus Scholasticus, *Historia Damiatina*, ed. H. Hoogeweg, Bibliothek des Litterarischen Vereins 202, Tübingen, 1894.

Orlandi, S. (ed.), *S. Pietro martire da Verona. Leggenda di Fra Tommaso Agni da Lentini nel volgare trecentesco con lettera di Fra Roderico de Atencia*, Florence, 1952.

Pauli, S. (ed.), *Codice diplomatico del sacro militare ordine Gerosolimitano*, 2 vols., Lucca, 1733–7.

Paviot, J. (ed.), *Projets de croisade*, Paris, 2008.

Pedro Alfonso de Huesca, *Diálogo contra los Judíos*, ed. J. Tolan, K.-P. Mieth, E. Ducay and M. Jesús Lacarra, Huesca, 1996.

Pertz, G. H. and K. Rodenberg (eds.), *Epistolae saeculi XIII e regestis Pontificum Romanorum*, MGH 1, Berlin, 1883.

Petrus Venerabilis, *Schriften zum Islam*, ed. and trans. into German R. Glei, Altenberge, 1985.

Bibliography

Philip of Novara, *Le Livre de Forme de Plait*, ed. and trans. P. W. Edbury, Nicosia, 2009.

Philippe de Navarre, *Les quatre ages de l'homme*, ed. M. De Fréville, Paris, 1888.

Philippus a Limborch, *Historia Inquisitionis, Amsterdam, 1692*.

Pignatelli, C. and D. Gerner (eds.), *Les traductions françaises des Otia Imperialia de Gervais de Tilbury par Jean d'Antioche et Jean de Vignay, edition de la troisième partie*, Geneva, 2006.

Pitra, J.-B. (ed.), *Analecta novissima Spicilegii Solesmensis, altera continuatio*, 2 vols., Tusculum, 1888.

Potthast, A., *Regesta pontificum romanorum*, 2 vols., Graz, 1957.

Pressuti, P., *Regesta Honorii Papae III*, 2 vols., Hildesheim, 1978.

Prior, O. H. (ed.), *L'image du monde de maître Gossouin. Rédaction en prose: Texte du manuscrit de la Bibliothèque nationale fonds français no. 574, avec corrections d'après d'autres mss., notes et introduction*, Lausanne, 1913.

Reichert, B. M. (ed.), *Acta capitulorum generalium*, Rome, 1898.

Reiffenberg, Le Baron de (ed.), *Chronique rimée de Philippe Mouskes, Évêque de Tournay au treizième siècle*, vol. ii, Brussels, 1838.

Roger Bacon, *Opus Majus*, ed. J. H. Bridges, 3 vols., London, 1897–1900, reprint. Frankfurt, 1964.

Roger Bacon, *Opera quaedam hactenus inedita*, ed. J. S. Brewer, London, 1859.

Röhricht, R., 'Lettres de Ricoldo de Monte-Croce', *Archives de l'Orient latin* 2 (1884), pp. 258–96.

Röhricht, R. and G. Raynaud (eds.), 'Annales de Terre Sainte', *Archives de l'Orient Latin* 2 (1884), pp. 427–61.

Romanini, F. and B. Saletti, *The Pelrinages Communes, the Pardouns de Acre and the Crisis in the Crusader Kingdom, History and Texts*, Padova, 2012.

Ryccardus de S. Germano, *Chronicon*, ed. C. A. Garufi, Rerum Italicarum Scriptores 7.2, Bologna, 1938.

Rymer, T. (ed.), *Foedera, conventiones, litterae*, 3 vols., London, 1816.

Salimbene de Adam, *Cronica*, ed. G. Scalia, CCCM 125-125A, 2 vols., Turnhout, 1998.

Schabel, C. (ed.), *The Synodicum Nicosiense and Other Documents of the Latin Church of Cyprus, 1193–1373*, Nicosia, 2001.

Scheffer-Boichorst, P. (ed.), *Chronica Albrici monachi Trium Fontium a monacho novi monasterii Hoiensis interpolata*, MGH SS 23, Hanover, 1874, reprint. Stuttgart, 1963.

Shailat, I. (ed.), *The Letters and Essays of Moses Maimonides*, 2 vols., Jerusalem, 1995 [Hebrew].

Shirman, H. (ed.), 'Elegies on Persecutions in Eretz Israel, Africa, Spain, Germany and France', in *Kovetz 'al Yad*, new series, book iii (13.1), Jerusalem, 1940, pp. 25–74 [Hebrew].

Solomon ben Adereth [Rashba], *Responsa*, ed. A. Zeleznick, 5 vols., Jerusalem, 1997–2005 [Hebrew].

Strehlke, E. (ed.), *Tabulae ordinis Theutonici*, Berlin, 1869, reprint. Toronto, 1975.

Thomas Aquinas, *Opuscula omnia*, ed. R. P. P. Mandonnet, 5 vols., Paris, 1927.

Van Adrichem, C., *Theatrum Terrae Sanctae*, Cologne, 1682.

Wallensköld, A. (ed.), *Les chansons de Thibaut de Champagne, Roi de Navarre*, Paris, 1925.

Bibliography

Weiland, L. (ed.), *Emonis et Mekonis Werumensium Chronica*, MGH SS 23, Hannover, 1874, reprint. Stuttgart, 1963.

Willelmus Tyrensis, *Chronicon*, ed. R. B. C. Huygens, CCCM 63-63a, 2 vols., Turnhout, 1986.

Zimmerman, B. (ed.), *Monumenta Historica Carmelitana*, Lérins, 1907.

SECONDARY LITERATURE

Abel, F.-M., 'Le Couvent des Frères Prêcheurs à Saint-Jean d'Acre', *Revue biblique* 43 (1934), pp. 265–84.

Abulafia, David, 'Trade and Crusade, 1050–1250', in M. Goodich, S. Menache and S. Schein (eds.), *Cross Cultural Convergences in the Crusader Period*, New York, NY, 1995, pp. 1–20.

Aharonov, A. E., 'Seder Ha-yahas Bi-shene Nusahim', *Ets Hayyim* 27 (2017), pp. 349–87 [Hebrew].

Allmand, C., *The De re militari of Vegetius: The Reception, Transmission and Legacy of a Roman Text in the Middle Ages*, Cambridge, 2012.

Aloni, N., 'Twelve Writers and Dozens of Books in the Middle Ages', *Aresheth: An Annual of Hebrew Folklore* 6 (1980), pp. 9–39 [Hebrew].

Amargier, P. A., 'Benoît d'Alignan, évêque de Marseille (1229–1268). Le contexte et l'esprit d'une théologie', *Le Moyen Age* 72 (1966), pp. 443–62.

Angold, M., 'Byzantium and the West 1204–1453', in M. Angold (ed.), *The Cambridge History of Christianity*, 9 vols., Cambridge, 2005–9, vol. V, pp. 53–78.

Ashtor (Strauss), E., *The History of the Jews in Egypt and Syria under Mamluk Rule*, 3 vols., Jerusalem, 1944–70 [Hebrew].

Aslanov, C., *Evidence of Francophony in Mediaeval Levant*, Jerusalem, 2006.

Aslanov, C., 'L'ancien français, sociolecte d'une caste au pouvoir: Royaume de Jérusalem, Morée, Chypre', in B. Fagard, S. Prévost, B. Combettes and O. Bertrand (eds.), *Évolutions en français. Études de linguistique diachronique*, Berne, 2008, pp. 3–19.

Assaf, S., *Sources and Studies in Jewish History*, Jerusalem, 1946 [Hebrew].

Attiya, H. M., 'Knowledge of Arabic in the Crusader States in the Twelfth and Thirteenth Centuries', *Journal of Medieval History* 25.3 (1999), pp. 203–13.

Balme, F., 'La Province dominicaine de Terre-Sainte, de janvier 1277 à octobre 1280', *Revue de l'Orient Latin* 1 (1893), pp. 526–36.

Baraz, D., 'Collections of Marian Legends in the East: An Example of Intercultural Contacts between West and East in the Late Middle Ages', unpublished MA thesis, Hebrew University (1991) [Hebrew].

Baraz, D., 'Coptic-Arabic Collections of Western Marian Legends: The Reception of a Western Text in the East: A Case of Intercultural Relations in the Late Middle Ages', *Acts of the Fifth International Congress of Coptic Studies*, II, Rome, 1993, pp. 23–32.

Baraz, D., 'Bartolomeo da Trento's Book of Marian Miracles', *Orientalia Christiana Periodica* 60 (1994), pp. 69–85.

Barone, G., 'Les couvents des mendiants, des collèges déguisés?', in O. Weijers (ed.), *Vocabulaire des collèges universitaires (XIIIe–XVIe siècles)*, Turnhout, 1993, pp. 149–57.

Barzon, A., *Codici miniati della Biblioteca Capitolare di Padova*, Padua, 1950.

Bibliography

Baumgärtner, I., 'Burchard of Mount Sion and the Holy Land', *Peregrinations: Journal of Medieval Art and Architecture* 4.1 (Spring, 2013), pp. 5–41.

Beddie, J. S., 'Some Notices of Books in the East in the Period of the Crusades', *Speculum* 8.2 (Apr. 1933), pp. 240–2.

Ben-Sasson, M., 'Tradition and Change in the Patterns of Controversy of the Descendants of Maimonides', in J. Blau and D. Doron (eds.), *Heritage and Innovation in Judaeo-Arabic Culture*, Jerusalem, 2000, pp. 71–94 [Hebrew].

Bertram, M., 'Johannes de Ancona: Ein Jurist des 13. Jahrhunderts in den Kreuzfahrerstaaten', *Bulletin of Medieval Canon Law* 7 (1977), pp. 49–64.

Bird, J. L., 'Crusade and Conversion after the Fourth Lateran Council (1215): Oliver of Paderborn's and James of Vitry's Missions to Muslims Reconsidered', *Essays in Medieval Studies* 21 (2004), pp. 23–47.

Bischoff, B., 'The Study of Foreign Languages in the Middle Ages', *Speculum* 36.2 (1961), pp. 209–24.

Bischoff, B., *Anecdota Novissima: Texte vierten bis sechzehnten Jahrhunderts*, Stuttgart, 1984.

Bishop, A., 'Adaptations of the Roman *Lex Aquilia* in the Burgess Assizes of Jerusalem', *Proceedings of the Third International Symposium on Crusade Studies* [forthcoming].

Borst, A., *Der Turmbau von Babel*, 4 vols., Stuttgart, 1957–63.

Boureau, A., 'Intellectuals in the Middle Ages, 1957–95', in M. Rubin (ed.), *The Work of Jacques Le Goff and the Challenges of Medieval History*, Woodbridge, 1997, pp. 145–55.

Brubaker, J., 'Nuncii or Legati: What Makes a Papal Representative in 1234?', in K. Stewart and J. Moreton Wakeley (eds.), *Cross-Cultural Exchange in the Byzantine World, c. 300–1500 AD*, Byzantine and Neohellenic Studies 14, Oxford, 2016, pp. 115–28.

Brun, L., 'Primat', in G. Dunphy (general editor), *Encyclopedia of the Medieval Chronicle*, 2 vols., Leiden, 2010, vol. II, p. 1235.

Brundage, J. A., 'Latin Jurists in the Levant: The Legal Elite of the Crusader States', in M. Shatzmiller (ed.), *Crusaders and Muslims in Twelfth Century Syria*, Leiden, 1993, pp. 18–42.

Brunel, C., 'David d'Ashby, auteur méconnu des *Faits des Tartares*', *Romania* 79 (1958), pp. 39–46.

Buchthal, H., *Miniature Painting in the Latin Kingdom of Jerusalem*, Oxford, 1957, reprint. London, 1986.

Burman, T. E., *Religious Polemic and the Intellectual History of the Mozarabs, c. 1050–1200*, Leiden, 1994.

Burman, T. E., 'How an Italian Friar Read His Arabic Qur'an', *Dante Studies* 125 (2007), pp. 93–109.

Burman, T. E., *Reading the Qur'an in Latin Christendom 1140–1560*, Philadelphia, PA, 2007.

Burmester, O. H. E., 'On the Date and Authorship of the Arabic Synaxarium of the Coptic Church', *The Journal of Theological Studies* 39 (1938), pp. 249–53.

Burnett, C., 'Antioch as a Link between Arabic and Latin Culture', in I. Draelants, A. Tihon and B. van den Abeele (eds.), *Occident et Proche-Orient: Contacts scientifiques au temps des Croisades*, Turnhout, 2000, pp. 1–78 [reprint. in: idem, *Arabic into Latin in the Middle Ages*, Farnham, 2009].

Bibliography

Burnett, C. 'The Coherence of the Arabic-Latin Translation Program in Toledo in the Twelfth Century', *Science in Context* 14 (2001), pp. 249–88 [reprint. in: idem, *Arabic into Latin in the Middle Ages*, Farnham, 2009].

Cameron, A., *Arguing it Out: Discussion in Twelfth-Century Byzantium*, Budapest, 2016.

Carely, L. K., 'The Anglo-Norman Vegetius: A Thirteenth Century Translation of the *De re militari*', unpublished PhD thesis, University of Nottingham (1962).

Cerulli, E., *Il libro etiopico dei Miracoli di Maria*, Rome, 1943.

Cerulli, E., *Il 'Libro della Scala' e la questione delle fonti arabo-spagnole della Divina Commedia*, Rome, 1949.

Cerulli, E., 'Il suicidio della peccatrice nelle versione araba ed etiopica del Libro dei Miracoli di Maria', *Annali dell'Istituto Orientale di Napoli*, n.s. 19 (1969.2), pp. 147–79.

Chadwick, H., *East and West: The Making of a Rift in the Church*, Oxford, 2003.

Charpentier, J., 'William of Rubruck and Roger Bacon', *Geografisca Annaler* 17, Supplement: Hyllningsskrift Tillagnad Sven Hedin (1935), pp. 255–67.

Chazaud, A.-M., 'Inventaire et comptes de la succession d'Eudes, comte de Nevers (Acre, 1266)', *Mémoires de la société des antiquaires de France,* sér. 4, 2 (1871), pp. 176–80.

Ciggaar, K. N., 'Manuscripts as Intermediaries: The Crusader States and Literary Cross-Fertilization', in K. N. Ciggaar, A. Davids and H. G. B. Teule (eds.), *East and West in the Crusader States*, Louvain, 1996, pp. 131–51.

Ciggaar, K. N., 'An Illuminated Aristotelian Manuscript from the Crusader States. Some Preliminary Remarks', *Eastern Christian Art* 3 (2006), pp. 25–35.

Claverie P. V., 'L'apparition des Mongols sur la scène politique occidentale (1220–1223)', *Le Moyen Age* 105 (1999), pp. 601–14.

Cole, P. J., *The Preaching of the Crusades to the Holy Land, 1095–1270*, Cambridge, MA, 1991.

Cole, P., D. L. d'Avray and J. Riley-Smith, 'Application of Theology to Current Affairs: Memorial Sermons for the Dead of Mansurah and on Innocent IV', *Historical Research* 63 (1990), pp. 227–47.

Conybeare, F. C., 'Dialogus de Christi die natali', *Zeitschrift für neutestamentliche Wissenschaft und die Kunde des Urchristentums* 5 (1904), pp. 327–34.

Copeland, R., *Rhetoric, Hermeneutics and Translation in the Middle Ages*, Cambridge, 1991.

Copeland, R., *Pedagogy, Intellectuals, and Dissent in the Later Middle Ages: Lollardy and Ideas of Learning*, Cambridge, 2001.

Copeland, R., with I. Sluiter (eds.), *Medieval Grammar and Rhetoric: Language Arts and Literary Theory, AD 300–1475*, Oxford, 2009.

Cornish, A., *Vernacular Translation in Dante's Italy*, Cambridge, 2011.

Cowe, S. P., 'The Armenians in the Era of the Crusades 1050–1350', in M. Angold (ed.), *The Cambridge History of Christianity*, 9 vols., Cambridge, 2006, vol. V, pp. 404–29.

Cox, V., 'Ciceronian Rhetoric in Italy, 1260–1350', *Rhetorica* 17.3 (Summer, 1999), pp. 239–88.

Cuffel, A., 'Call and Response: European Jewish Emigration to Egypt and Palestine in the Middle Ages', *The Jewish Quarterly Review*, N.S. 90.1.2 (Jul.–Oct., 1999), pp. 61–101.

Bibliography

Daftary, F., *The Isma'ilis: Their History and Doctrines*, Cambridge, 1990.

Daiber, H., 'Masa'il Wa-Adjwiba', *Encyclopedia of Islam*, 2nd edn., Leiden, 1991, vol. VI, pp. 636–9.

D'Alverny, M.-T., 'Deux traductions latines du Coran au moyen âge', *Archives d'histoire doctrinale et littéraire du moyen âge* 22–3 (1946–8), pp. 69–131.

Daniel, N., *Islam and the West*, 2nd edn., Oxford, 1993.

Daunou, P., 'Urbain IV, Pape', *Histoire littéraire de la France* 19 (1838), pp. 49–66.

Davidsohn, R., 'Ein Briefkodex des XIII. und ein Urkundenbuch des XV. Jhdt', *Quellen und Forschungen aus Italienischen Archiven und Bibliotheken* 19 (1927), pp. 373–88.

De Bastard, A., 'La colère et la douleur d'un templier en Terre Sainte', *Revue des langues romanes* 81 (1974), pp. 333–73.

De la Cruz Vergari, E., 'Édition critique d'une traduction française anonyme en prose du XIII$_e$ siècle de l'*Epitoma rei militaris* de Végèce', unpublished PhD thesis, University of Barcelona (2016).

De Libera, A., *Penser au moyen âge*, Paris, 1991.

Delisle, L., 'Notice sur la Rhétorique de Cicéron traduite par Maître Jean d'Antioche', *Notices et extraits des manuscrits de la Bibliothèque Nationale et autres bibliothèques* 36 (1899), pp. 207–65.

Delisle, L., 'Maître Jean d'Antioche, traducteur et Frère Guillaume de Saint-Ettienne, hospitalier', *Histoire Littéraire de la France* 33 (1906), pp. 1–40.

Derbes, A. and M. Sandona, 'Amazons and Crusaders: The *Histoire Universelle* in Flanders and the Holy Land', in D. H. Weiss and L. Mahoney (eds.), *France and the Holy Land*, Baltimore, MD, 2004, pp. 187–229.

Dodu, G., *Histoire des institutions monarchiques dans la Royaume latin de Jérusalem 1099–1291*, Paris, 1894.

Dominica Legge, M., 'The Lord Edward's Vegetius', *Scriptorium* 7 (1953), pp. 262–5.

Dondaine, A., '"Contra Graecos": Premiers écrits polémiques des Dominicains d'Orient', *Archivum fratrum praedicatorum* 21 (1951), pp. 320–446.

Dondi, C. *The Liturgy of the Canons Regular of the Holy Sepulchre of Jerusalem: A Study and a Catalogue of the Manuscript Sources*, Bibliotheca Victorina XVI, Turnhout, 2004.

Donnadieu, J., 'La représentation de l'islam dans l'Historia orientalis. Jacques de Vitry historien', *Le Moyen Age* 114.3–4 (2008), pp. 487–508.

Edbury, P., 'Feudal Obligations in the Latin East', *Byzantion* 47 (1977), pp. 328–56.

Edbury, P., 'The Disputed Regency of the Kingdom of Jerusalem, 1264/6 and 1268', *Camden Miscellany* 27, Camden 4th series 22 (1979), pp. 1–47 [reprint. in: idem, *Kingdoms of the Crusaders*, Aldershot, 1999].

Edbury, P., 'Law and Custom in the Latin East: Les Letres dou Sepulcre', in B. Arbel (ed.), *Intercultural Contacts in the Medieval Mediterranean: Studies in Honour of David Jacoby*, London, 1996, pp. 71–9.

Edbury, P., *John of Ibelin and the Kingdom of Jerusalem*, Woodbridge, 1997.

Edbury, P., 'The *Livre des Assises* by John of Jaffa: The Development and Transmission of the Text', in J. France and W. G. Zajac (eds.), *The Crusades and Their Sources: Essays Presented to Bernard Hamilton*, Aldershot, 1998, pp. 169–79.

Edbury, P., 'The French Translation of William of Tyre's *Historia*: The Manuscript Tradition', *Crusades* 6 (2007), pp. 69–105.

Edbury, P., 'A New Text of the *Annales de Terre Sainte*', in I. Shagrir, R. Ellenblum and J. Riley-Smith (eds.), *In Laudem Hierosolymitani: Studies in Crusades and Medieval Culture in Honour of Benjamin Z. Kedar*, Aldershot, 2007, pp. 145–61.

Edbury, P., 'New Perspectives on the Old French Continuations of William of Tyre', *Crusades* 9 (2010), pp. 107–13.

Edbury, P., with J. G. Rowe, *William of Tyre*, Cambridge, 1988.

Edgington, S., 'Medicine and Surgery in the *Livre des Assises de la Cour des Bourgeois de Jérusalem*', *Al-Masāq* 17.1 (2005), pp. 87–97.

Edgington, S., 'Antioch, Medieval City of Culture', in K. Ciggaar and M. Metcalf (eds.), *East and West in the Medieval Eastern Mediterranean*, vol. I, Orientalia Lovaniensa Analecta 147 (2006), pp. 247–59.

Eifler, G., 'Freidank', *Lexikon des Mittelalters*, München, 1989, vol. IV, pp. 894–5.

Ellenblum, R., *Frankish Rural Settlement in the Latin Kingdom of Jerusalem*, Cambridge, 1998.

Emanuel, S., 'R. Yehiel of Paris: His Biography and Affinity to Eretz-Yisrael', *Shalem* 8 (2008), pp. 86–99 [Hebrew].

Emanuel, S., 'Pages from the Halakhic Notebook of a Thirteenth-Century Pilgrim', *Ginzei Qedem* 7 (2011), pp. 145–65 [Hebrew].

Emanuel, S., '"From Where the Sun Rises to Where it Sets": The Responsa by *Rashba* to the Sages of Acre', *Tarbiz: Quarterly for Jewish Studies* 83.3 (September 2015), pp. 465–89 [Hebrew].

Fishbane, E. P., *As Light before Dawn: The Inner World of a Medieval Kabbalist*, Stanford, CA, 2009.

Folda, J., *Crusader Manuscript Illumination at Saint-Jean d'Acre 1275–1291*, Princeton, NJ, 1976.

Folda, J., *Crusader Art in the Holy Land, from the Third Crusade to the Fall of Acre, 1187–1291*, Cambridge, MA, 2005.

Folda, J., with P. Edbury, 'Two Thirteenth-Century Manuscripts of Legal Texts from Saint-Jean d'Acre', *Journal of the Warburg and Courtauld Institutes* 57 (1994), pp. 243–54.

Fraser, C. M., 'Bek, Antony (I) (*c.*1245–1311)', *Oxford Dictionary of National Biography* (Oxford, 2004), online edition. [www.oxforddnb.com/view/article/1970, accessed 4 Nov. 2009.]

Frazee, C. A., 'The Christian Church in Cilician Armenia: Its Relations with Rome and Constantinople to 1198', *Church History* 45.2 (June 1976), pp. 166–84.

Friedman, L. J., *Text and Iconography for Joinville's Credo*, Cambridge, MA, 1958.

Friedman, M. A., 'The Nagid, the Nasi and the French Rabbis: A Threat to Abraham Maimonides' Leadership', *Zion: A Quarterly for Research in Jewish History* 82.2–3 (2017), pp. 193–266 [Hebrew].

Friedman, Y., 'Pages from a Halachic Notebook of R. Eliyahu from Acre', *Emunat Itekha* 93 (Dec. 2011), pp. 8–23 [Hebrew].

Gautier Dalché, P., *Carte marine et portulan au XIIe siècle*, Rome, 1995.

Geanakoplos, D. J., *Emperor Michael Palaeologus and the West*, Cambridge, MA, 1959.

George-Tvrtković, R., 'The Ambivalence of Interreligious Experience: Riccoldo da Monte Croce's Theology of Islam', unpublished PhD thesis, University of Notre Dame (2007).

Bibliography

Gil, M., *A History of Palestine, 634–1099*, trans. E. Broido, Cambridge, 1992.

Giordanengo, G., 'Les Feudistes', in *El Dret Comú i Catalunya: Actes del II Simposi Internacional*, Barcelona, 1992, pp. 67–139.

Goitein, S. D., *Jewish Education in Muslim Countries*, Jerusalem, 1962 [Hebrew].

Goitein, S. D., *Palestinian Jewry in Early Islamic and Crusader Times*, Jerusalem, 1980 [Hebrew].

Golubovich, Girolamo, *Biblioteca Bio-Bibliografica della Terra Santa e dell'Oriente francescano*, 5 vols., Florence, 1906–1927.

Grabmann, M. Der Franziskanerbischof Benediktus de Alignano OFM und seine Summa zum Caput "Firmiter" des IV Laterankonzils', in I.-M. Freudenreich (ed.), *Kirchengeschichtliche Studien P. Michael Bihl als Ehrengabe dargeboten*, Kolmar, 1941, pp. 50–64.

Graf, G., *Geschichte der christlichen arabischen Literatur*, 5 vols., Vatican, 1947.

Grandclaude, M., *Étude critique sur les Livres des assises de Jérusalem*, Paris, 1923.

Grivaud, G., 'Littérature', in A. Nicolaou-Konnari and C. Schabel (eds.), *Cyprus: Society and Culture 1191–1374*, Leiden and Boston, MA, 2005, pp. 219–84.

Guadagnini, E., 'Cicéron et Boèce en Orient: quelques réflexions sur la *Rectorique* de Jean d'Antioche', in A. Petrina (ed.), *The Medieval Translator* 15, Turnhout, 2013, pp. 37–46.

Halkin, F., *Bibliotheca Hagiographica Graeca*, 3 vols., Brussels, 1957.

Hamilton, B., 'The Armenian Church and the Papacy at the Time of the Crusades', *Eastern Churches Review* 10 (1978), pp. 61–87.

Hamilton, B., *The Latin Church in the Crusader States*, London, 1980.

Hamilton, B., *The Medieval Inquisition*, London, 1981.

Hamilton, B., 'Eleanor of Castile and the Crusading Movement', *Mediterranean Historical Review* 10 (1995), pp. 92–103.

Hamilton, B., 'The Latin Church in the Crusader States', in K. Ciggaar, A. Davids and H. Teule (eds.), *East and West in the Crusader States*, 3 vols., Leuven, 1996, vol. I, pp. 1–20.

Hamilton, B., 'Knowing the Enemy: Western Understanding of Islam at the Time of the Crusades', *Journal of the Royal Asiatic Society*, third series 7.3 (Nov. 1997), pp. 373–87.

Hamilton, B., 'The Old French Translation of William of Tyre as an Historical Source', in P. W. Edbury and J. P. Phillips (eds.), *The Experience of Crusading 2: Defining the Crusader Kingdom*, Cambridge, 2003, pp. 93–112.

Haran, M., 'The Song of the Precepts of Aaron ben Manir', *Proceedings of the Israel Academy of Sciences and Humanities* 5 (1971–6), pp. 174–209.

Henshke, D., 'Maimonides as His Own Commentator', *Sefunot* 23 (2003), pp. 117–63 [Hebrew].

Henshke, D., 'Two Maimonidean Comments', *Hama'ayan* 50.2 (2009), pp. 90–3 [Hebrew].

Hiestand, R., 'Un centre intellectuel en Syrie du nord?' *Le Moyen Age* 100 (1994), pp. 7–36.

Holt, P. M., 'Qalāwūn's Treaty with Acre in 1283', *English Historical Review* 91 (October, 1976), pp. 802–12.

Holt, P. M., *Early Mamluk Diplomacy (1260–1290). Treaties of Baybars and Qalāwūn with Christian Rulers*, Leiden, 1995.

Idel, M., 'Eretz-Israel and Prophetic Kabbalah', *Shalem* 3 (1981), pp. 119–26 [Hebrew].

Ineichen, G., 'Il glossario arabo-francese di messer Guglielmo e maestro Giacomo', *Atti dell'Instituto Veneto di Scienze, Lettere ed Arti* 130 (1971–2), pp. 353–407.

Jackson, P., 'The Crisis in the Holy Land in 1260', *The English Historical Review* 95 (July, 1980), pp. 481–513.

Jackson, P., *The Mongols and the West*, Harlow, 2005.

Jackson, P., 'Ashby, David of (*fl.* 1260–1275)', *Oxford Dictionary of National Biography* (Oxford, 2008), online edition. [www.oxforddnb.com/view/article/92435, accessed 1 Oct. 2014.]

Jackson, P. with D. Morgan, *The Mission of Friar William of Rubruck*, London, 1990.

Jacobs, J., 'Books Encountered by Ramban after He Arrived in the Land of Israel', *Jerusalem Studies, an Internet Journal* 11 (2012), pp. 1–14 [Hebrew].

Jacoby, D., 'Crusader Acre in the Thirteenth Century: Urban Layout and Topography', *Studi medievali*, 3rd series 20 (1979), pp. 1–45.

Jacoby, D., 'Montmusard, Suburb of Crusader Acre: The First Stage of Its Development', in B. Z. Kedar, H. E. Mayer and R. C. Smail (eds.), *Outremer: Studies in the History of the Crusader Kingdom of Jerusalem Presented to Joshua Prawer*, Jerusalem, 1982, pp. 205–17.

Jacoby, D., 'La littérature française dans les états latins de la Méditerranée orientale à l'époque des croisades: diffusion et création', in *Essor et fortune de la chanson de geste dans l'Europe et l'Orient latin: Actes du XIe Congrès international de la Société Rencesvals pour l'étude des épopées romanes*, Padoue-Venise, 1982; Modena, 1984, pp. 617–46 [reprint. in: idem, *Studies on the Crusader States and on Venetian Expansion*, Northampton, 1989].

Jacoby, D., 'Knightly Values and Class Consciousness in the Crusader States of the Eastern Mediterranean', *Mediterranean Historical Review* 1 (1986), pp. 158–86 [reprint. in: idem, *Studies on the Crusader States and on Venetian Expansion*, Northampton, 1989].

Jacoby, D., 'Pèlerinage médiéval et sanctuaires de Terre Sainte: La perspective vénitienne', *Ateneo veneto*, Anno CLXXIII, 24 (1986), pp. 27–58 [reprint. in: idem, *Studies on the Crusader States and on Venetian Expansion*, Northampton, 1989].

Jacoby, D., 'A Venetian Manual of Commercial Practice from Crusader Acre', in G. Airaldi and B. Z. Kedar (eds.), *I comuni italiani nel regno crociato di Gerusalemme*, Collana storica de Fonti e Studi 48, Genoa, 1986, pp. 403–28 [reprint. in: idem, *Studies on the Crusader States and on Venetian Expansion*, Northampton, 1989].

Jacoby, D., 'Three Notes on Crusader Acre', *ZDPV* 109 (1993), pp. 83–96.

Jacoby, D., 'The Venetian Privileges in the Latin Kingdom of Jerusalem: Twelfth and Thirteenth-Century Interpretation and Implementation', in B. Z. Kedar, J. Riley-Smith and R. Hiestand (eds.), *Montjoie: Studies in Crusade History in Honour of Hans Eberhard Mayer*, Aldershot, 1997, pp. 155–75 [reprint. in: idem, *Commercial Exchange across the Mediterranean: Byzantium, the Crusader Levant, Egypt and Italy*, Aldershot, 2005].

Jacoby, D., 'Pilgrimage in Crusader Acre: The Pardouns d'Acre', in Y. Hen (ed.), *De Sion exibit lex et verbum domini de Hierusalem: Essays on Medieval Law, Liturgy, and*

Literature in Honour of Amnon Linder, Cultural Encounters in Late Antiquity and the Middle Ages 1, Turnhout, 2001, pp. 105–17.

Jacoby, D., 'Society, Culture, and the Arts in Crusader Acre', in D. H. Weiss and L. Mahoney (eds.), *France and the Holy Land*, Baltimore, MD, 2004, pp. 97–137.

Jacoby, D., 'Aspects of Everyday Life in Frankish Acre', *Crusades* 4 (2005), pp. 73–105.

Jacoby, D., 'Refugees from Acre in Famagusta around 1300', in M. J. K. Walsh, T. Kiss and N. Coureas (eds.), *The Harbour of all This Sea and Realm: Crusader to Venetian Famagusta*, Budapest, 2014, pp. 53–67.

Jotischky, A., *The Perfection of Solitude*, University Park, PA, 1995.

Jotischky, A., 'The Frankish Encounter with the Greek Orthodox in the Crusader States', in M. Gervers and J. M. Powell (eds.), *Tolerance and Intolerance: Social Conflict in the Age of the Crusades*, Syracuse, NY, 2001, pp. 100–16.

Jotischky, A., 'Ethnographic Attitudes in the Crusader States: Franks and Indigenous Orthodox People', in K. Ciggaar and H. Teule (eds.), *East and West in the Crusader States: Context-Contacts-Confrontations III*, Leuven, 2003, pp. 1–19.

Jotischky, A., 'Mendicants as Missionaries and Travelers in the Near East in the Thirteenth and Fourteenth Centuries', in R. Allen (ed.), *Eastward Bound: Travel and Travellers 1050–1550*, Manchester, 2004, pp. 88–106.

Kanarfogel, E., 'The *'Aliyah* of "Three Hundred Rabbis" in 1211: Tosafist Attitudes toward Settling in the Land of Israel', *Jewish Quarterly Review* 76 (1986), pp. 191–215.

Kanarfogel, E., *Jewish Education and Society in the High Middle Ages*, Detroit, MI, 1992.

Kedar, B. Z., 'The Jews of Jerusalem, 1187–1267, and the Role of Nahmanides in the Re-Establishment of Their Community', in B. Z. Kedar (ed.), *Jerusalem in the Middle Ages, Selected Papers*, Jerusalem, 1979, pp. 122–36 [Hebrew].

Kedar, B. Z., *Crusade and Mission*, Princeton, NJ, 1984.

Kedar, B. Z., 'Ecclesiastical Legislation in the Kingdom of Jerusalem: The Statutes of Jaffa (1253) and Acre (1254)', in P. W. Edbury (ed.), *Crusade and Settlement*, Cardiff, 1985, pp. 225–30 [reprint. in: idem, *The Franks in the Levant, 11th to 14th Centuries*, Aldershot, 1993].

Kedar, B. Z., 'The Subjected Muslims of the Frankish Levant', in J. M. Powell (ed.), *Muslims under Latin Rule, 1100–1300*, Princeton, NJ, 1990, pp. 135–74 [reprint. in: idem, *The Franks in the Levant, 11th to 14th Centuries*, Aldershot, 1993].

Kedar, B. Z., 'A Symposium', in B. Z. Kedar (ed.), *The Horns of Hattin*, Jerusalem, 1992, pp. 341–66.

Kedar, B. Z., 'Multidirectional Conversion in the Frankish Levant', in J. Muldoon (ed.), *Varieties of Religious Conversion in the Middle Ages*, Gainesville, FL, 1997, pp. 190–9 [reprint. in: idem, *Franks, Muslims and Oriental Christians in the Latin Levant*, Aldershot, 2006].

Kedar, B. Z., 'Some New Sources on Palestinian Muslims before and during the Crusades', in H. E. Mayer (ed.), *Die Kreuzfahrerstaaten als multikulturelle Gesellschaft*, Munich, 1997, pp. 129–40 [reprint. in: idem, *Franks, Muslims and Oriental Christians in the Latin Levant*, Aldershot, 2006].

Kedar, B. Z., 'The Outer Walls of Frankish Acre', *Atiqot* 31 (1997), pp. 157–80 [reprint. in: idem, *Franks, Muslims and Oriental Christians in the Latin Levant*, Aldershot, 2006].

Kedar, B. Z., 'The *Tractatus de locis et statu sancte terre ierosolimitane*', in J. France and W. G. Zajac (eds.), *The Crusades and Their Sources: Essays Presented to Bernard Hamilton*, Aldershot, 1998, pp. 111–33 [reprint. in: idem, *Franks, Muslims and Oriental Christians in the Latin Levant*, Aldershot, 2006].

Kedar, B. Z., 'Intellectual Activities in a Holy City: Jerusalem in the Twelfth Century', in B. Z. Kedar and R. J. Z. Werblowsky (eds.), *Sacred Space: Shrine, City, Land. Proceedings of the International Conference in Memory of Joshua Prawer*, London, 1998, pp. 127–39 [reprint. in: idem, *Franks, Muslims and Oriental Christians in the Latin Levant*, Aldershot, 2006].

Kedar, B. Z., 'Latins and Oriental Christians in the Frankish Levant, 1099–1291', in A. Kofsky and G. G. Stroumsa (eds.), *Sharing the Sacred: Religious Contacts and Conflicts in the Holy Land*, Jerusalem, 1998, pp. 209–22 [reprint. in: idem, *Franks, Muslims and Oriental Christians in the Latin Levant*, Aldershot, 2006].

Kedar, B. Z., 'On the Origins of the Earliest Laws of Frankish Jerusalem: The Canons of the Council of Nablus, 1220', *Speculum* 74 (1999), pp. 310–35 [reprint. in: idem, *Franks, Muslims and Oriental Christians in the Latin Levant*, Aldershot, 2006].

Kedar, B. Z., 'La Via sancti sepulchri come tramite di cultura araba in Occidente', in R. Greci (ed.), *Itinerari medievali e identità europea. Atti del Congresso Internazionale di Parma, 27–28 febbraio 1998*, Bologna, 1999, pp. 181–201 [reprint. in: idem, *Franks, Muslims and Oriental Christians in the Latin Levant*, Aldershot, 2006].

Kedar, B. Z., 'Religion in Catholic–Muslim Correspondence and Treaties', in A. D. Beihammer, M. G. Parani and C. D. Schabel (eds.), *Diplomatics in the Eastern Mediterranean 1000–1500*, Leiden, 2008, pp. 407–21.

Kedar, B. Z., 'A Review of: Denys Pringle, The Churches of the Crusader Kingdom of Jerusalem, A Corpus, III', *Israel Exploration Journal* 60.1 (2010), pp. 122–4.

Kedar, B. Z., 'The Eastern Christians in the Frankish Kingdom of Jerusalem: An Overview', in M. Gálik and M. Slobodník (eds.), *Eastern Christianity, Judaism and Islam between the Death of Muhammad and Tamerlane (632–1405), Proceedings of the Humboldt-Kolleg, June 25–28, 2008, Dolná Krupá, Slovakia*, Bratislava, 2011, pp. 137–47.

Kedar, B. Z., 'Some New Light on the Composition Process of William of Tyre's *Historia*', in S. B. Edgington and H. J. Nicholson (eds.), *Deeds Done beyond the Sea: Essays on William of Tyre, Cyprus and the Military Orders Presented to Peter Edbury*, Farnham, 2014, pp. 3–11.

Kedar, B. Z. with D. Pringle, '1099–1187: The Lord's Temple and Solomon's Palace', in O. Grabar and B. Z. Kedar (eds.), *Where Heaven and Earth Meet: Jerusalem's Sacred Esplanade*, Jerusalem, 2009, pp. 132–49.

Kirstein, K.-P., *Die Lateinischen Patriarchen von Jerusalem*, Berlin, 2002.

Klement, K., 'Alcune osservazioni sul Vat. Lat. 4852', *Studi Melitensi* 3 (1995), pp. 229–43.

Klement, K., *Von Krankenspeisen und Ärzten . . . Die unbekannte Hospitalordnung Roger des Moulins in Vat. Lat. 4852* [Forthcoming].

Kohler, C., 'Un Rituel et un Bréviere du Saint-Sépulcre de Jérusalem (XIIe–XIIIe siècle)', *Revue de l'Orient Latin* 8 (1900–1), pp. 383–500.

Kritzeck, J., *Peter the Venerable and Islam*, Princeton, NJ, 1964.

Kuk, S. H., 'R. Yehiel of Paris and the Land of Israel', *Me'assef Zion* 5 (1933), pp. 97–102 [Hebrew].

La Monte, J. L., *Feudal Monarchy in the Latin Kingdom of Jerusalem, 1100–1291*, Cambridge, MA, 1932.

Laurent, V. and J. Darrouzes, *Dossier grec de l'Union de Lyon*, Paris, 1976.

Le Goff, J., *La naissance du Purgatoire*, Paris, 1981.

Le Goff, J., *Intellectuals in the Middle Ages*, trans. Teresa L. Fagan, Oxford, 1993.

LeClerc, V., 'Nicholas de Hanapes, Patriarche de Jérusalem', *Histoire Littéraire de la France* 20 (1842), pp. 51–78.

Le Grand, L., 'La prière des malades dans les hospitaux de l'ordre de Saint-Jean de Jérusalem', *Bibliothèque de l'École des chartes* 57 (1896), pp. 325–38.

Levy, R., *Chronologie approximative de la littérature française du moyen âge*, Beihefte zur Zeitschrift für Romanische Philologie 98 (1957).

Lock, P., *Routledge Companion to the Crusades*, New York, NY, 2006.

Lucas, R. H., 'Mediaeval French Translations of the Latin Classics to 1500', *Speculum* 45 (1970), pp. 225–53.

Lusignan, S., *Parler vulgairement: Les intellectuels et la langue française aux XIIIᵉ et XIVᵉ siècles*, Paris, 1987.

Luttrell, A., 'The Hospitallers' Early Written Records', in J. France and W. G. Zajac (eds.), *The Crusades and Their Sources. Essays Presented to Bernard Hamilton*, Aldershot, 1998, pp. 135–54.

Macrides, R., J. A. Munitiz and D. Angelov, *Pseudo-Kodinos and the Constantinopolitan Court: Offices and Ceremonies*, Birmingham Byzantine and Ottoman Studies 15, Farnham, 2013.

MacEvitt, C., *The Crusades and the Christian World of the East: Rough Tolerance*, Philadelphia, PA, 2008.

Mann, H. K., *The Lives of the Popes in the Middle Ages, vol. 15: Alexander IV to Gregory X*, London, 1929.

Mann, J., *The Jews in Egypt and in Palestine under the Fatimid Caliphs*, 2 vols., New York, 1970.

Maspero, G., 'Le vocabulaire français d'un Copte du XIIIᵉ siècle', *Romania* 17 (1888), pp. 481–512.

Mathews, T. F. and A. K. Sanjian, *Armenian Gospel Iconography: The Tradition of the Glajor Gospel*, Washington DC, 1991.

Mayer, H. E., *The Crusades*, trans. John Gillingham, Oxford, 1988.

Mayer, H. E., *Die Kanzlei der lateinischen Könige von Jerusalem*, MGH Schrften, 40, 2 vols., Hanover, 1996.

Mayer, H. E., 'Einwanderer in der Kanzlei und am Hof der Kreuzfahrerkönige von Jerusalem', in H. E. Mayer (ed.), *Die Kreuzfahrerstaaten als multikulturelle Gesellschaft*, München, 1997.

Meijers, E. M., *Études d'histoire du droit*, eds. R. Feenstra and H. F. W. D. Fischer, 3 vols., Leiden, 1959.

Melamed, A., 'The Hebrew Versions of the Story on Aristotle and Alexander's Wife', *Daat: A Journal of Jewish Philosophy and Kabbalah* 74/75 (2013), pp. 325–56 [Hebrew].

Menache, S., 'When Jesus Met Muhammed in the Holy Land: Attitudes toward the "Other" in the Crusader Kingdom', *Medieval Encounters* 15.1 (2009), pp. 66–85.

Mews, C. J. and J. N. Crossley (eds.), *Communities of Learning: Networks and the Shaping of Intellectual Identity in Europe, 1100–1500*, Turnhout, 2011.

Micheau, F., 'Médecins orientaux au service des princes latins', in I. Draelants, A. Tihon and B. van den Abeele (eds.), *Occident et Proche Orient: Contacts scientifiques au temps des Croisades*, Bruxelles, 2000, pp. 95–115.

Minervini, L., 'Leggende dei cristiani orientali nelle letterature romanze del medioevo', *Romance Philology* 49.1 (August, 1995), pp. 1–12.

Minervini, L., 'Tradizioni linguistiche e culturali negli Stati Latini d'Oriente', in A. Pioletti and F. Rizzo-Nervo (eds.), *Medioevo Romanzo e Orientale. Oralità, scrittura, modelli narrativi*, Messina, 1995, pp. 155–72.

Minervini, L., 'La lingua franca mediterranea. Plurilinguismo, mistilinguismo, pidginizzazione sulle coste del Mediterraneo tra tardo medioevo e prima età moderna', *Medioevo romanzo* 20 (1996), pp. 231–301.

Minervini, L., 'Produzione e circolazione di manoscritti negli Stati Crociati: biblioteche e scriptoria latini', in A. Pioletti and F. Rizzo-Nervo (eds.), *Medioevo Romanzo e Orientale. Il viaggio dei testi. III Colloquio Internazionale, Venezia, 10–13 ottobre 1996*, Soveria Mannelli, 1999, pp. 79–96.

Minervini, L., 'Outremer', in P. Boitani, M. Mancini and A. Vàrvaro (eds.), *Lo spazio letterario del medioevo, 2. Il medioevo volgare*, vol. I, *La produzione del testo*, Rome, 2001, pp. 611–48.

Minervini, L., 'Modelli culturali e attività letteraria nell'Oriente latino', *Studi medievali* 43 (2002), pp. 337–48.

Minervini, L., 'La français dans l'orient Latin (XIIIe–XIVe siècles). Éléments pour la caractérisation d'une *scripta* du Levant', *Revue de Linguistique Romane* 74 (2010), pp. 119–98.

Minervini, L., 'Les emprunts arabes et grecs dans le lexique français d'Orient (XIIIe–XIVe siècle)', *Revue de Linguistique Romane* 76 (2012), pp. 99–197.

Mitchell, P. D., *Medicine in the Crusades*, Cambridge, 2004.

Monfrin, J., 'Humanisme et traductions au Moyen Age', *Journal des savants* (Jan.–Mar. 1963), pp. 161–90.

Monfrin, J., 'Humanisme et traductions au Moyen Age', in A. Fourrier (ed.), *L'humanisme médiéval dans les littératures romanes du XIIe au XIVe siècle*, Paris, 1964, pp. 217–46.

Monneret de Villard, U., *Lo Studio dell'Islam in Europa nel XII e nel XIII secolo*, Rome, 1944.

Montner, S., 'R. Shem Tov Ben Isaac of Tortosa about the Life of the European Jewish Physician and His Ethics', in Y. L. Hacohen-Maimon (ed.), *Sinai, A Jubilee Volume*, Jerusalem, 1958, pp. 321–37 [Hebrew].

Moore, R. I., *The Formation of a Persecuting Society*, Oxford, 1987.

Morgan, M. R., *The Chronicle of Ernoul and the Continuations of William of Tyre*, London, 1973.

Mulchahey, M., *'First the Bow is Bent in Study . . .' Dominican Education before 1350*, Toronto, 1997.

Mulchahey, M., 'Dominican Educational Vocabulary and the Order's Conceptualization of Studies before 1300. Borrowed Terminology, New Connotations', in M. C. Pacheco (ed.), *Le vocabulaire des écoles des Mendiants au moyen âge*, Turnhout, 1999, pp. 89–118.

Bibliography

Nader, M., *Burgesses and Burgess Law in the Latin Kingdoms of Jerusalem and Cyprus 1099–1325*, Aldershot, 2006.

Novikoff, A. J., *The Medieval Culture of Disputation: Pedagogy, Practice and Performance*, Philadelphia, PA, 2013.

Ofer, Y., with J. Jacobs, *Nahmanides' Torah Commentary Addenda Written in the Land of Israel*, Jerusalem, 2013 [Hebrew].

Olszowy-Schlanger, J., 'Learning to Read and Write in Medieval Egypt: Children's Exercise Books from the Cairo Geniza', *Journal of Semitic Studies* 48.1 (Spring 2003), pp. 47–69.

Pahlitzsch, J., *Graeci und Suriani im Palästina der Kreuzfahrerzeit*, Berliner Historische Studien 33, Berlin, 2001.

Painter, S., 'The Crusade of Theobald of Champagne and Richard of Cornwall, 1239–1241', in K. M. Setton (ed.), *A History of the Crusades*, 6 vols., Philadelphia, PA, 1955–89, vol. II, pp. 463–86.

Paris, G., *La Littérature française au Moyen Age (XIe–XIVe siècle)*, Paris, n.d.

Paris, G., 'La Chanson composée à Acre en juin 1250', *Romania* 22 (1893), pp. 541–7.

Pelliot, P., 'Les Mongols et la papauté II', *Revue de l'Orient Chrétien* 28 (1931–2), pp. 3–84.

Pelliot, P., 'Deux passages de "La Prophétie de Hannan, fils d'Isaac"', *Mélanges sur l'époque des Croisades, Mémoires de l'Académie des Inscriptions et Belles-Lettres*, Paris, 1951, pp. 73–97.

Peters, E., *Inquisition*, New York, NY, 1988.

Petit-Radel, L. C. F., 'Benoit d'Alignan, Évêque de Marseille', *Histoire littéraire de la France* 19 (1838), pp. 84–91.

Pignatelli, C., 'Un traducteur qui affiche ses croyances: l'ajout d'exempla au corpus des otia imperialia de Gervais de Tilbury dans la traduction attribuée à Jean d'Antioche', in M. Colombo Timelli and C. Galderisi (eds.), *'Pour acquerir honneur et pris'. Mélanges de moyen français offerts à Giuseppe Di Stefano*, Montréal, 2004, pp. 47–58.

Pignatelli, C., 'Italianismes, provençalismes et autres régionalismes chez Jean d'Antioche traducteur des *Otia imperialia*', in C. Galderisi and J. Maurice (eds.), *'Qui tant savoit d'engin et d'art'. Mélanges de philologie médiévale offerts à Gabriel Bianciotto*, Poitiers, 2006, pp. 367–77.

Power, A., *Roger Bacon and the Defence of Christendom*, Cambridge, 2013.

Poznanski, S., *Babylonische Geonim im nachgaonäischen Zeitalter*, Berlin, 1924.

Prawer, J., *Histoire du royaume latin de Jérusalem*, 2 vols., Paris, 1970.

Prawer, J., *The Latin Kingdom of Jerusalem: European Colonialism in the Middle Ages*, London, 1972.

Prawer, J., *Crusader Institutions*, New York, 1980.

Prawer, J., *The History of the Jews in the Latin Kingdom of Jerusalem*, Oxford, 1988.

Prawer, J., *The History of the Jews in the Latin Kingdom of Jerusalem*, Jerusalem, 2000 [Hebrew].

Pringle, D., 'Notes on Some Inscriptions from Crusader Acre', in I. Shagrir, R. Ellenblum and J. Riley-Smith (eds.), *In Laudem Hierosolymitani: Studies in Crusades and Medieval Culture in Honour of Benjamin Z. Kedar*, Aldershot, 2007, pp. 191–209.

Pringle, D., *The Churches of the Crusader Kingdom of Jerusalem. A Corpus*, IV. Acre and Tyre, Cambridge, 2009.

Pringle, D., *Pilgrimage to Jerusalem and the Holy Land, 1187–1291*, Aldershot, 2012.

Prutz, H., *Kulturgeschichte der Kreuzzüge*, Berlin, 1883.

Pryor, J. H., 'The *Eracles* and William of Tyre: An Interim Report', in B. Z. Kedar (ed.), *The Horns of Hattin*, Jerusalem, 1992, pp. 270–93.

Redigonda, A. L., 'Agni, Tommaso', *Dizionario biografico degli Italiani*, Rome, 1960, vol. I, pp. 445–7.

Reeve, M. D., 'The Transmission of Vegetius's *Epitoma rei militaris*', *Aevum* 74 (Jan.–Apr. 2000), pp. 243–354.

Reiner, E., 'Pilgrims and Pilgrimage to Eretz Yisrael 1099–1517', unpublished PhD thesis, Hebrew University (1988) [Hebrew].

Reiner, E., '"Oral Versus Written": The Shaping of Traditions of Holy Places in the Middle Ages', in Y. Ben-Arieh and E. Reiner (eds.), *Studies in the History of Eretz Israel, Presented to Yehuda Ben Porat*, Jerusalem, 2003, pp. 308–45 [Hebrew].

Richard, J., 'Le début des relations entre la papauté et les Mongols de Perse', *Journal Asiatique* 237 (1949), pp. 291–7.

Richard, J., 'L'extrême-orient légendaire au Moyen Âge: roi David et Prêtre Jean', *Annales d'Ethiopie* 2 (1957), pp. 225–44.

Richard, J., 'Une lettre concernant l'invasion mongole?' *Bibliothèque de l'École des chartes* 119.1 (1961), pp. 243–5.

Richard, J., 'La confrérie des Mosserins d'Acre et les marchands de Mossoul au XIIIe siècle', *L'Orient Syrien* 11 (1966), pp. 451–60.

Richard, J., *La papauté et les missions d'Orient au moyen âge*, Rome, 1977.

Richard, J., 'Le comté de Tripoli dans les chartes du fonds des Porcellet', *Bibliothèque de l'École des chartes* 130.2 (1972), pp. 339–82.

Richard, J., 'L'arrière-plan des deux cycles de la croisade', *Zeitschrift für französische und Literatur*, Beiheft 11, Stuttgart, 1987, pp. 6–16 [reprint. in: idem, *Croisades et États latins d'Orient*, Aldershot, 1992].

Richard, J., 'The *Relatio de Davide* as a Source for Mongol History and the Legend of Prester John', in C. F. Beckingham and B. Hamilton (eds.), *Prester John, the Mongols and the Ten Lost Tribes*, Aldershot, 1996, pp. 139–58.

Richard, J., 'Pouvoir royal et patriarcat au temps de la Cinquième Croisade, à propos du rapport du patriarche Raoul', *Crusades* 2 (2003), pp. 109–19.

Riedel, W., 'Der Katalog der christlichen Schriften in arabischer Sprache von Abu 'l Barakat', *Nachrichten von der Königlischen Gesellschaft der Wissenschaften: philologisch-historische Klasse* (1902), pp. 635–706.

Riley-Smith, J., *The Knights of St. John in Jerusalem and Cyprus c. 1050–1310*, London, 1967.

Riley-Smith, J., *The Feudal Nobility and the Kingdom of Jerusalem 1174–1277*, London, 1973.

Riley-Smith, J. (ed.), *The Oxford History of the Crusades*, Oxford, 1999.

Riley-Smith, J., 'The Death and Burial of Latin Christian Pilgrims to Jerusalem and Acre, 1099–1291', *Crusades* 7 (2008), pp. 165–80.

Riley-Smith, J., *What Were the Crusades?*, Basingstoke, 2009.

Robinson, I. S., 'Reform and the Church, 1073–1122', in D. Luscombe and J. Riley-Smith (eds.), *The New Cambridge Medieval History IV, c. 1024–1198, Part I*, Cambridge, 2004, pp. 268–334.

Bibliography

Roest, B., *A History of Franciscan Education*, Leiden, 2000.

Roest, B., *Franciscan Learning, Preaching and Mission, c. 1220–1650*, Leiden, 2015.

Röhricht, R., 'Syria sacra', *ZDPV* 10 (1887), pp. 1–48.

Roth, P., 'Later Provençal Sages – Jewish Law (Halakhah) and Rabbis in Southern France, 1215–1348', unpublished PhD thesis, Hebrew University (2012) [Hebrew].

Rotter, E., 'Windrose statt Landkarte. Die geografische Systematisierung des Heiligen Landes und ihre Visualisierung durch Burchardus de Monte Sion um 1285', *Deutsches Archiv für Erforschung des Mittelalters* 69 (2013), pp. 45–106.

Rouse, M. and R. Rouse, 'Context and Reception: A Crusading Collection for Charles IV of France', in K. Busby and C. Kleinhenz (eds.), *Courtly Arts and the Arts of Courtliness*, Cambridge, 2006, pp. 105–80.

Roux, B., *Monde en Miniatures: L'Iconographie du Livre du Trésor de Brunetto Latini*, Paris, 2009.

Rubin, J., 'John of Ancona's *Summae*: A Neglected Source for the Juridical History of the Latin Kingdom of Jerusalem', *Bulletin of Medieval Canon Law* 29 (2012), pp. 183–218.

Rubin, J., 'Benoit d'Alignan and Thomas Agni: Two Western Intellectuals and the Study of Oriental Christianity in the 13th-Century Kingdom of Jerusalem', *Viator* 44.1 (Spring 2013), pp. 189–99.

Rubin, J., 'Burchard of Mount Sion's *Descriptio Terrae Sanctae*: A Newly Discovered Extended Version', *Crusades* 13 (2014), pp. 173–90.

Rubin, J., 'A Missing Link in European Travel Literature: Burchard of Mount Sion's Description of Egypt', *Mediterranea: International Journal on the Transfer of Knowledge* 3 (2018), pp. 55–90.

Rubin, J., 'The Beginnings of the Study of Foreign Languages in the Dominican Order: Regulation, Implementation and Impact', in C. Linde (ed.), *Making and Breaking the Rules. Discussions, Implementation, and Consequences of Dominican Legislation* [forthcoming].

Rubin, J. and P. Roth, 'A Medieval Hebrew Adaptation of Two Crusading Texts: Presentation, Analysis and Edition', *Medieval Encounters* 23 (2017), pp. 508–30.

Runciman, S., *A History of the Crusades*, 3 vols., Cambridge, 1951–4.

Russ-Fishbane, E. R., 'Between Politics and Piety: Abraham Maimonides and His Times', unpublished PhD thesis, Harvard University (2009).

Ryan, J. D., 'Toleration Denied', in M. Gervers and J. M. Powell (eds.), *Tolerance and Intolerance: Social Conflict in the Age of the Crusades*, Syracuse, NY, 2001, pp. 55–64.

Salvadó, S. E., 'The Liturgy of the Holy Sepulchre and the Templar Rite: Edition and Analysis of the Jerusalem Ordinal (Rome, Bib. Vat. Barb. Lat. 659) with a Comparative Study of the Acre Breviary (Paris, Bib. Nat., Ms. Latin 10478)', unpublished PhD thesis, Stanford University (2011).

Savage-Smith, E., 'New Evidence for the Frankish Study of Arabic Medical Texts in the Crusader Period', *Crusades* 5 (2006), pp. 99–112.

Schabel, C., 'The Quarrel over Unleavened Bread in Western Theology, 1234–1439', in M. Hinterberger and C. Schabel (eds.), *Greeks, Latins and Intellectual History, 1204–1500*, Bibliotheca: Recherches de Théologie et Philosophie médievales 11, Leuven, 2011, pp. 85–127.

Schaller, M. H., *Stauferzeit: Ausgewählte Aufsätze*, Hannover, 1993.

Scholem, G., 'On the Study of "Torat Ha-Gilgul" in 13th-Century Kabbalah', *Tarbiz* 16 (1945), pp. 135–50 [Hebrew].

Segonne, M., *Moine, Prélat, Croisé: Benoît d'Alignan, abbé de La Grasse, Seigneur-Evêque de Marseille*, Marseille, 1960.

Setton, K. M., *The Papacy and the Levant, 1204–1571*, 4 vols., Philadelphia, PA, 1976–84.

Shagrir, I., *Naming Patterns in the Latin Kingdom of Jerusalem*, Oxford, 2003.

Shweka, R., '"And every day they make quarrels": A Chapter from the History of the Jewish Community in Jerusalem in the 13th Century according to Letters of R. Yehiel the Frenchman', *Sefunot: Studies and Sources on the History of Jewish Communities in the East*, n.s. 10 (2017), pp. 13–55 [Hebrew].

Simonelli, F., 'Fidenzio da Padova', in *Dizionario Biografico degli Italiani*, Rome, 1997, vol. XLVII, pp. 412–14.

Stahl, H., 'A Review of "Crusader Manuscript Illumination at Saint Jean d'Acre, 1275–1291" by Jaroslav Folda', *Zeitschrift für Kunstgeschichte* 43.4 (1980), pp. 416–23.

Städtler, T., *Zu den Anfängen der französischen Grammatiksprache*, Beihefte zur Zeitschrift für romanische Philologie 223, Tübingen, 1988.

Städtler, T., 'Témoins précoces de la terminologie grammaticale française', *Travaux de linguistique et de philologie* 37 (1999), pp. 123–9.

Stern, E., 'Acre during the Crusader Period and Its Maritime Aspects in the Light of Archaeological and Recent Historical Research', unpublished PhD thesis, University of Haifa (2015) [Hebrew].

Stiernon, D., 'Nicéphore l'hésychaste', *Dictionnaire de Spiritualité*, Paris, 1982, vol. XI, pp. 198–203.

Stump, E., *Boethius's De topicis differentiis*, London, 1978.

Ta-Shema, I., 'Tosafot', *Encyclopedia Judaica*, Jerusalem, 1971, vol. XV, pp. 1278–83.

Ta-Shema, I., 'A New Chronography on the 13th Century Tosaphists', *Shalem* 3 (1981), pp. 319–24 [Hebrew].

Ta-Shema, I., *Studies in Medieval Rabbinic Literature* 4, Jerusalem, 2010 [Hebrew].

Thomson, S. H., 'The Texts of Michael Scot's *Ars Alchemie*', *Osiris* 5 (1938), pp. 523–59.

Thorpe, L., 'Mastre Richard: A Thirteenth Century Translator of Vegetius', *Scriptorium* 6 (1952), pp. 39–50.

Thorpe, L. 'Mastre Richard at the Skirmish of Kenilworth?' *Scriptorium* 7 (1953), pp. 120–1.

Tibble, S., *Monarchy and Lordships in the Latin Kingdom of Jerusalem, 1099–1291*, Oxford, 1989.

Tolan, J. V., *Saracens: Islam in the Medieval European Imagination*, New York, NY, 2002.

Townend, M., 'Contacts and Conflicts: Latin, Norse and French', in L. Mugglestone (ed.), *The Oxford History of English, Updated Version*, Oxford, 2006.

Trovato, P., *Everything You Always Wanted to Know about Lachmann's Method*, Padua, 2014.

Two Maimonidean Comments', *Hama'yan* 50.2 (2009), pp. 90–3 [Hebrew].

Tyler, E. M. (ed.), *Conceptualizing Multilingualism in England, c.800–c.1250*, Turnhout, 2011.

Urbach, E. E., 'A Midrash of Redemption from Late Crusader Times', *Eretz Israel* 10, Jerusalem, 1971, pp. 58–63 [Hebrew].

Bibliography

Urbach, E. E., *The Tosaphists: Their History, Writings and Methods*, 2 vols., Jerusalem, 1980 [Hebrew].

Van den Wyngaert, A., 'Frère Guillaume de Cordelle, O.F.M.', *La France Franciscaine* 4 (1921), pp. 52–71.

Vandecasteele, M., 'Étude comparative de deux versions latines médiévales d'une apologie arabo-chrétienne. Pierre le Vénérable et le Rapport Grégorien', *Academiae Analecta (Mededelingen van de Koninklijke Academie voor Wetenschappen, Letteren en Schone Kunsten van België, Klasse der Letteren)* 53 (1991), pp. 79–134.

Vecchio, S., 'Elia d'Assisi', *Dizionario biografico degli italiani*, Rome, 1993, vol. XLII, pp. 450–8.

Verger, J., 'Patterns', in H. de Ridder-Symoens (ed.), *A History of the University in Europe*, 3 vols., Cambridge, 1992–2004, vol. I, pp. 35–74.

Villads Jensen, K., 'War against Muslims According to Benedict of Alignano OFM', *Archivum Franciscanum Historicum* 89.1–2 (1996), pp. 181–95.

Von den Brincken, A.-D., *Die 'Nationes Christianorum Orientalium' im Verständnis der lateinischen Historiographie*, Vienna, 1973.

von den Brincken, A.-D., 'Die stumme Weltkarte im Bodleian Douce 319 – ein arabisches Dokument in einer abendländischen Handschrift', in A. Speer and L. Wegener (eds.), *Wissen über Grenzen: Arabisches Wissen und lateinisches Mittelalter*, Berlin, 2006, pp. 791–804.

Welter, J. T., *L'Exemplum dans la littérature religieuse et didactique du Moyen Âge*, Paris-Toulouse, 1927, reprint. Geneva, 1973.

Williams, S. J., 'Philip of Tripoli's Translation of the Pseudo-Aristotelian *Secretum secretorum* Viewed within the Context of Intellectual Activity in the Crusader Levant', in I. Draelants, A. Tihon and B. van den Abeele (eds.), *Occident et Proche-Orient: Contacts scientifiques au temps des Croisades*, Turnhout, 2000, pp. 79–94.

Williams, S. J., *The Secret of Secrets: The Scholarly Career of a Pseudo-Aristotelian Text in the Latin Middle Ages*, Ann Arbor, MI, 2003.

Wogan-Browne, J. (ed.), *Language and Culture in Medieval Britain: The French of England* c.1100–c.1500, Woodbridge, 2009.

Wolfson, I. S. J., 'The Parma Colophon of Abraham ben Ephraim's Book of Precepts', *Journal of Jewish Studies* 21 (1970), pp. 39–47.

Yahalom, S., 'The Historical Background to Nahmanides' Sermon for Rosh-Ha-Shana in Acre', *Shalem* 8 (2008), pp. 100–25 [Hebrew].

Yahalom, S., 'Historical Background to Nahmanides' Acre *Sermon for Rosh ha-Shana*: The Strengthening of the Catalonian Center', *Sefarad* 68.2 (Jul.–Dec., 2008), pp. 315–42.

Yeshaya, J. J. M. S., 'A Hebrew Elegy by Yosef ben Tanhum Yerushalmi on the Death of His Father and the Mamluk Conquest of Acre', *Frankfurt Jewish Studies Bulletin* 39 (2014), pp. 33–52.

INDEX

Index